The Escape from Balance Sheet Recession and the QE Trap

The Escape from Balance Sheet Recession and the QE Trap

A Hazardous Road for the World Economy

RICHARD C. KOO

WILEY

Other Wiley Editorial Offices

John Wiley & Sons, 111 River Street, Hoboken, NJ 07030, USA

John Wiley & Sons, The Atrium, Southern Gate, Chichester, West Sussex, P019 8SQ, United Kingdom

John Wiley & Sons (Canada) Ltd., 5353 Dundas Street West, Suite 400, Toronto, Ontario, M9B 6HB, Canada

John Wiley & Sons Australia Ltd., 42 McDougall Street, Milton, Queensland 4064, Australia

Wiley-VCH, Boschstrasse 12, D-69469 Weinheim, Germany

ISBN 978-1-119-02812-3 (Hardcover)
ISBN 978-1-119-02816-1 (ePDF)
ISBN 978-1-119-02817-8 (ePub)

Set in 10/12pt Garamond by Aptara Inc., New Delhi, India

10 9 8 7 6 5 4 3 2 1

To my dearest wife, Chyen-Mei

Contents

Foreword

The global economy underwent a major ordeal after the housing bubbles in Europe and the United States burst in 2007. Almost six years have passed since the Federal Reserve followed the Bank of Japan's lead a decade earlier and took U.S. interest rates down to zero, yet the unemployment remains elevated and industrial output has only recently recovered to the levels of 2008. In Europe, the unemployment rate is running near the euro-era high of 12 percent even though the European Central Bank (ECB) also cut interest rates to zero. The picture for output is even bleaker: Although German industrial production has recovered to the levels of 2007, output in France and Spain is no greater than it was in 1994, and in Italy production has fallen back to 1987 levels. United Kingdom industrial production is no higher than it was in 1992. In Japan, which was geographically far removed from the Western bubbles, the mood has improved since "Abenomics" was launched at the end of 2012, but industrial output remains stuck at the levels of 2003. Some have dubbed this situation "secular stagnation."

Amid these economic difficulties, national policy discussions have been characterized by a severe lack of consensus. Even today, nearly seven years after the bubbles burst, the debate remains as tangled as ever. In the United States, the two main political parties are at loggerheads with each other over the fiscal deficit and the debt ceiling, and in Europe the fiscal consolidation thought to be essential to economic and credit market recovery has enfeebled the economy, with some observers warning of social unrest and a crisis of democracy itself.

National debates have also been characterized by an absence of consensus on monetary policy, with those arguing in favor of further monetary accommodation to counter deflationary pressures facing off against those who insist additional easing will lead to renewed financial imbalances or worse. Some say more structural reform is needed, while others argue that now is not the time because reforms could exacerbate already high levels of unemployment.

A similar rift in opinion can be observed on the question of nonperforming loan disposals in the banking sector. While some recommend pushing ahead with bad loan write-offs, others say that would only compound the problem by prompting a further fall in asset prices. On the subject of the rating agencies, some believe these firms deserve a harsh lashing with the regulatory whip because they not only issued questionable ratings on subprime securities but also exacerbated the sovereign debt crisis. Others, meanwhile, insist that killing the messenger will not solve the underlying problems.

There is something to be said for all of these views. But the sharp division in expert opinion makes it difficult for even the most capable political leaders to make informed decisions. The media in many countries insist the current turmoil and economic slump are attributable to a lack of leadership, yet each offers a different policy prescription. This wide discrepancy in the views of purported experts suggests we are experiencing not only an economic crisis but also a crisis in economics. Most economists failed to predict the current crisis, and the economics profession itself has fallen into a state of complete disarray in its attempt to answer the question of what should be done.

Fortunately, the nations of the West have one thing in their favor: All of these issues—monetary accommodation, fiscal stimulus, the rating agencies, banking problems, and structural reform—were debated in Japan 15 years earlier. The debates in Japan were no less contentious than the ones currently now under way in the West, but in the end those of us in Japan (or at least I) learned that the post-bubble recession was no ordinary economic downturn but rather an entirely different kind of recession that has been overlooked by traditional economic theory.

It was overlooked because traditional theories never considered recessions brought about by a private sector that was minimizing debt instead of maximizing profits. But the private sectors in most countries in the West today are minimizing debt or maximizing savings in spite of zero interest rates, behavior that is at total odds with traditional theory. The private sector is minimizing debt because liabilities incurred during the bubble remain, while the value of assets bought with borrowed funds collapsed when the bubble burst, leaving balance sheets deeply underwater. With everyone saving or paying down debt and no one borrowing, even at zero interest rates, the economy started shrinking.

Such recessions are not new and have occurred on a number of occasions in the past, most notably the Great Depression, but orthodox economics has no name for recessions triggered by a private sector that chooses to minimize debt. So I called it a balance sheet recession. Over the past two years this term has finally gained currency in the West because there are too many recent economic phenomena that cannot be explained by orthodox economic theory but *can* be explained using balance sheet recession theory.

Nevertheless, many continue to oppose the argument that Western countries are facing the same kind of recession that Japan experienced

15 years ago. There are at least two reasons for this. One is that policy-makers fear their economies will also undergo a "lost decade" like Japan's; the other is the conceit that they would never make the same mistakes that Japan did. But in many respects they are faithfully repeating Japan's policy missteps because they have not tried to learn from its experience.

The first reason stems from fear. But almost seven years after the bubbles collapsed, there are no signs Western economies are returning to a more normal footing. Conditions in Europe are still severe. Even in the United States, which opted for bolder monetary and fiscal accommodation, conditions are nowhere near where they should be according to traditional economics after keeping interest rates at zero for over six years. With the Fed pledging to keep interest rates at exceptionally low levels for years to come, the U.S. central bank is effectively saying it will take at least that long for the U.S. economy to return to normal. This state of affairs is a far cry from the situation 15 years ago, when senior officials at the Fed routinely criticized the Bank of Japan for not easing aggressively enough, insisting the Japanese economy would pick up immediately if only the central bank took a more active role.

The belief among Western officials that they would never repeat Japan's mistakes is attributable in part to substandard foreign journalists in Japan who have helped create major misconceptions overseas. Intelligent, insightful foreign correspondents are never in shortage when a nation has a strong economy and is in the global spotlight, but few seek assignments in a country with a weak economy and, it is presumed, little to teach the world. In the late 1980s, when Japan was a global economic leader, the quality of foreign correspondents was extremely high. Their knowledge of Japan was so extensive that I learned a great deal from them each time they interviewed me.

Once Japan started to lose momentum in the 1990s, however, these individuals departed for the rapidly growing economies of Southeast Asia and China. The sole job requirement for their replacements seemed to be the ability to come up with likely sounding reasons for Japan's economic slump, with many just asking foreign financial firms in Tokyo—because they spoke English—for a quick sound bite. Many of those firms, however, were in Japan to buy assets on the cheap, and anything that prevented them from accomplishing their bargain hunting was labeled an "impediment to Japanese recovery," including delays in structural reforms and bad loan disposals. Even fiscal stimulus by the government was given a bad rap because it kept the economy from collapsing and prevented the fire sale of assets.

It is said that people will believe any story that is repeated often enough, and those outside Japan, who could not see for themselves that Japan was actually suffering from balance sheet problems rather than structural problems, ended up believing that Japan's slump was attributable solely to poor policy choices resulting from a lack of political will to implement structural reforms.

That mindset made it difficult for policymakers in the West to accept warnings and policy recommendations issued by senior Japanese officials and myself before the Lehman failure and the global financial crisis (GFC). In *Balance Sheet Recession—Japan's Struggle with Uncharted Economics and Its Global Implications* (John Wiley & Sons, Singapore, March 2003), I warned that a housing-bubble-dependent U.S. economy could eventually fall into a severe balance sheet recession. And about six months before the collapse of Lehman Brothers, then–Japanese finance minister Fukushiro Nukaga recommended to Treasury secretary Hank Paulson that the United States quickly inject capital into distressed financial institutions. Both warnings, unfortunately, went unheeded. Had the U.S. authorities listened to my warning and implemented Mr. Nukaga's proposal, the severity of both the balance sheet recession triggered by the housing bubble collapse and the financial crisis sparked by the Lehman bankruptcy could have been lessened substantially.

In the same book I also warned that in the event of a balance sheet recession, Europe—where governments' hands are tied by the Maastricht Treaty, which makes no allowance for the possibility of such a recession—would be hit much harder than either Japan or the United States. Unfortunately, this projection also turned out to be prescient. Making matters worse, many European officials misdiagnosed balance sheet problems for structural problems, first in post–IT bubble Germany, then in post–global financial crisis (GFC) peripheral countries, prolonging recessions in both cases.

In this book I will begin by discussing the similarities between Japan in the past and the West today. I will then present the basic mechanics of balance sheet recessions with a focus on theoretical aspects before returning to recent developments in the global economy. The book will also cover quantitative easing or QE, which is one of the problematic policy byproducts of a balance sheet recession and its aftermath, the QE trap.

It is said that there is no Democratic or Republican way of collecting garbage. Once the disease is correctly identified and its treatment is made known, the extreme social and political polarization that has characterized the United States and other countries over the past seven years should subside. Once a patient is diagnosed as having pneumonia, for example, the treatment is basically the same anywhere in the world. Although it may be years before the general public is made fully aware of this economic malady, I am encouraged that more and more people and organizations—including the International Monetary Fund (IMF) and the Bank for International Settlements (BIS)—are coming to appreciate the concept of balance sheet recessions. It is my hope that readers will leave with a deeper understanding of the problems faced by Western economies today and a better idea of how to overcome this predicament in light of Japan's experience over the past 20 years.

Notes on the Data Used in This Book

- The data used in this book are current as of June 30, 2014.
- Within the text, there are many references to the data as they were released originally. Many if not most of these data were subsequently revised repeatedly, but revised data typically have far less impact on the markets or the policy debate. Since it was the initial releases that drove changes in both asset prices and subsequent policy, the text refers to the statistics that changed history, not the revised numbers that may be in the database now. However, when revised numbers shed light on what was earlier seen as a puzzle, the revisions are mentioned as well.
- The United States is the only developed economy to provide seasonally adjusted flow-of-funds data. For other countries, I used four-quarter moving averages to capture the trend in the case of national data. For sectoral data in individual countries, the X-12-ARIMA package was used to obtain seasonally adjusted values for gross financial asset and liability flows. The additive seasonal adjustment mode was used since these flows are sometimes negative.

About the Author

Richard C. Koo (Tokyo, Japan) is the Chief Economist of Nomura Research Institute, with responsibilities to provide independent economic and market analysis to Nomura Securities, the leading securities house in Japan, and its clients. Before joining Nomura in 1984, Mr. Koo, a U.S. citizen, was an economist with the Federal Reserve Bank of New York (1981–1984). Prior to that, he was a Doctoral Fellow of the Board of Governors of the Federal Reserve System (1979–1981). Best known for developing the concept of balance sheet recession, he has also advised several Japanese prime ministers on how best to deal with Japan's economic and banking problems. In addition to being one of the first non-Japanese to participate in the making of Japan's five-year economic plan, he was also the only non-Japanese member of the Defense Strategy Study Conference of the Japan Ministry of Defense for 1999 to 2011. Currently he is serving as a Senior Advisor to the Center for Strategic and International Studies (Washington, D.C.). He is also an Advisory Board Member of the Institute for New Economic Thinking (New York City), and a charter member of the World Economic Association.

Author of many books on Japanese economy, his last book, *The Holy Grail of Macroeconomics: Lessons from Japan's Great Recession* (John Wiley & Sons, 2008), has been translated into and sold in five different languages. Mr. Koo holds BAs in Political Science and Economics from the University of California at Berkeley (1976), and an MA in Economics from the Johns Hopkins University (1979). From 1998 to 2010, he was a visiting professor at Waseda University in Tokyo. In financial circles, Mr. Koo was ranked first among over 100 economists covering Japan in the Nikkei Financial Ranking for 1995, 1996, and 1997, and by the *Institutional Investor* magazine for 1998. He was also ranked first by Nikkei Newsletter on Bond and Money for 1998, 1999, and 2000. He was awarded the Abramson Award by the National Association for Business Economics (Washington, D.C.) for the year 2001. Mr. Koo, a native of Kobe, Japan, is married with two children.

The Escape from Balance Sheet Recession and the QE Trap

CHAPTER 1

Balance Sheet Recession Theory—Basic Concepts

The greatest similarity between the Western economies today and the Japanese economy of 20 years ago is that both experienced the collapse of a massive, debt-financed bubble. Balance sheet recessions occur only when a nationwide asset bubble financed by debt bursts. Since nationwide debt-financed bubbles occur only rarely, balance sheet recessions are few and far between.

Figure 1.1 compares conditions in the U.S. housing market with those in Japan 15 years earlier. As the graph shows, the two markets trod identical paths in terms of the magnitude of the increase in prices, the duration of that increase, the magnitude of the subsequent decline in prices, and the duration of that decline. In other words, the United States can now expect to face the same set of conditions that Japan once did. The situation in Europe is similar (Figure 1.2).

Europe's housing bubbles and the subsequent collapse were even larger in scale. In Ireland, for instance, house prices rebased to 100 in 1995 rose to 514 by 2007 before falling back to 273 today. Similar price spikes occurred in Greece, Spain, and other Eurozone countries. Germany was the sole exception. Although the Germans operated under the same monetary policy and low interest rates as other members of the Eurozone, they did not experience an asset price bubble—in fact, house prices fell significantly, as the bottom line in Figure 1.2 demonstrates. When prices are rebased to 100 in 1995, German house prices had slipped to 90 in 2006. This lack of synchronicity between Germany and other Eurozone economies was a major contributor to the recent euro crisis, something that will be discussed in detail in Chapter 5.

Central banks responded to these burst bubbles and the economic weakness that followed by lowering interest rates dramatically. In the United States, the Fed cut rates at the fastest pace in its history, taking short-term

1

FIGURE 1.1 The U.S. Housing Bubble Comparable to the Japanese Housing Bubble 15 Years Earlier

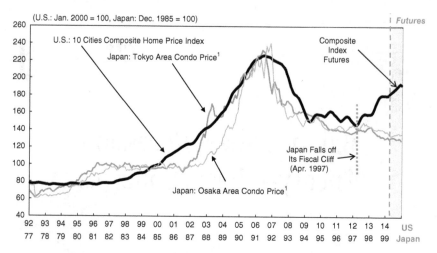

Note: Per m², five-month moving average

Sources: Bloomberg; Real Estate Economic Institute, Japan; S&P, S&P/Case-Shiller® Home Price Indices, as of June 6, 2014.

FIGURE 1.2 Europe's Experiences with House Price Bubbles

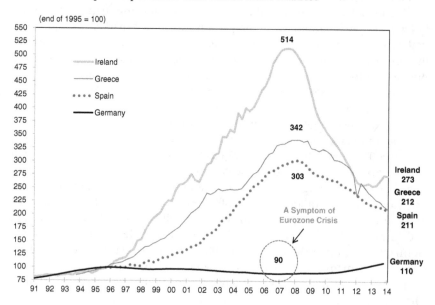

Notes: Ireland's figures before 2005 are existing house prices only. Greece's figures are flats' prices in Athens and Thessaloniki.

Source: Nomura Research Institute (NRI), calculated from Bank for International Settlements (BIS) data.

FIGURE 1.3 Drastic Interest Rate Cuts Had Little Effect on Economies

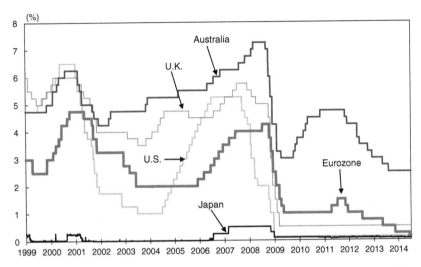

Sources: Bank of Japan (BOJ), Federal Reserve Board (FRB), European Central Bank (ECB), Bank of England (BOE), and Reserve Bank of Australia (RBA) (as of June 4, 2014).

rates down to zero by late 2008. The Bank of England (BOE), the European Central Bank (ECB), and the Reserve Bank of Australia also slashed rates (Figure 1.3).

However, the reaction of these economies to the rate cuts has been muted at best—and this despite the fact that the United States, United Kingdom, and European interest rates have been at all-time lows for more than five years.

Figure 1.4 shows U.S. industrial output and the unemployment rate. In spite of zero interest rates and the Fed's massive quantitative easing (QE) program, industrial production has only recently recovered to the levels of the 2007 peak. The unemployment rate, meanwhile, remains at an elevated level, reflecting stubbornly weak labor market conditions.

The U.S. labor market has traditionally held a reputation for flexibility. The ease with which companies could shed employees during economic downturns was responsible for the economy's relatively high sensitivity to interest rates—a measure of the speed with which it reacts to changes in interest rates—since businesses could respond swiftly to changes in rates and other external factors. An unemployment rate of over 6 percent after five years of zero interest rates is unprecedented.

Similar conditions can be observed in the Eurozone. Industrial output there has only just recovered to the levels of 2004, while the unemployment rate remains in double-digit territory at 11.6 percent (Figure 1.5). Although

FIGURE 1.4 The United States Regains Bubble-Peak Industrial Production after a Six-Year Period

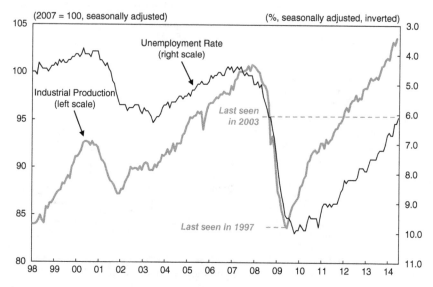

Sources: U.S. Department of Labor; FRB.

FIGURE 1.5 Bursting of the Housing Bubble Weakens Eurozone Economies

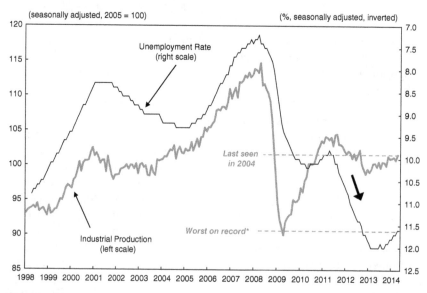

*No data before 1998.

Source: Eurostat.

FIGURE 1.6 Industrial Production in Europe

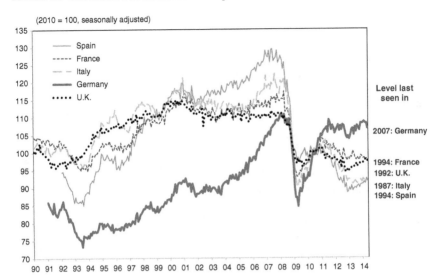

Sources: Eurostat; Office for National Statistics U.K. (ONS).

the ECB has taken interest rates down to an all-time low of 0.15 percent, Europe's unemployment rate is at a post-1998 high. And in certain countries conditions are even worse. As Figure 1.6 shows, industrial production in France and Spain remains stuck at the levels of 1994, and in Italy output is no higher than it was in 1987. Spain has an unemployment rate of 25.1 percent, similar to the levels seen in the United States during the Great Depression. And with unemployment running at 10.1 percent in France and 12.6 percent in Italy, a recovery is still far off. Germany, which is responsible for about one third of Eurozone gross domestic product (GDP), is the exception, with industrial output having recovered to the levels of 2007 and approaching an all-time high. The unemployment rate there is also running at 5.1 percent, the lowest level since comparable statistics began in 1991.

GDP and Inflation Fueled by Growth in Money Supply, Not Monetary Base

Industrial output and employment are not the only key indicators that have yet to recover. The money supply and private credit in these countries have hardly grown at all in spite of sharply lower interest rates and quantitative easing (QE). Figures 1.7 to 1.10 show three key monetary indicators: the

FIGURE 1.7 Drastic Liquidity Injections Resulting in Minimal Increases in Money Supply and Credit: United States

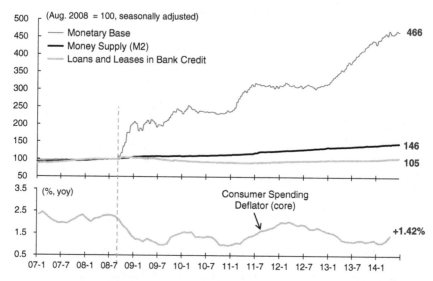

Note: Commercial bank loans and leases, adjustments for discontinuities made by NRI.

Sources: FRB; U.S. Department of Commerce.

monetary base, or base money, which tells us how much liquidity the central bank has supplied; the money supply, which indicates how much money is actually available for use by the private sector; and private credit, which shows how much the private sector has borrowed (in the United States, this is defined as total outstanding commercial bank loans and leases). It is important to look at all three because central banks can always supply liquidity (base money) by buying government or corporate bonds from private financial institutions. But for those funds to leave the financial sector, banks must lend them to someone in the real economy (private credit). In other words, liquidity (base money) provided by the central bank will stay in the banking system unless private financial institutions extend more credit to private borrowers.

The money supply, an indicator of how much money is available for the private sector to use, is mostly made up of bank deposits. Economists watch the money supply closely because it tends to be closely correlated with the inflation rate and nominal GDP. There are numerous definitions of the money supply ranging from M1 to M4, and their usefulness as indicators varies from one economy to the next. Figures 1.7 to 1.10 use the money supply definition considered most useful by the central bank in each country.

FIGURE 1.8 Drastic Liquidity Injections Resulting in Minimal Increases in Money Supply and Credit: Eurozone

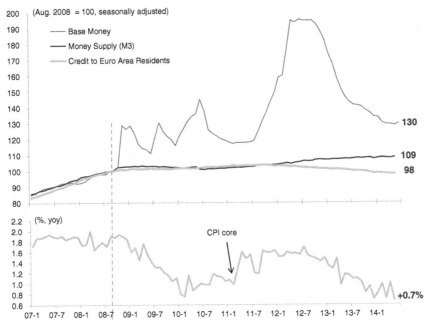

Note: Base money's figures are seasonally adjusted by NRI.

Sources: ECB; Eurostat.

Traditional economics teaches that these three indicators should move together. In other words, a 10 percent increase in the monetary base should ultimately lead to a 10 percent increase in the money supply and a 10 percent increase in private credit. That rule was largely valid in the pre-Lehman textbook world, when the three lines moved more or less together.

But this correlation between the three indicators has broken down completely in the post-Lehman world. The level of liquidity in the system, rebased to 100 at the time of the Lehman failure, rose to 466 as the Fed supplied liquidity under QE. Under ordinary circumstances this would cause both the money supply and private credit to increase from 100 to 466. Yet as Figure 1.7 shows, the money supply has grown to only 146, and private credit has barely recovered to pre-Lehman levels at 105. In other words, these indicators have completely decoupled. Some academics and pundits argue that the economy would improve if only the central bank would turn up the dials on the printing press, but the only aggregate the printing press can influence directly is the monetary base. It is the money supply and

FIGURE 1.9 Drastic Liquidity Injections Resulting in Minimal Increases in Money Supply and Credit: U.K.

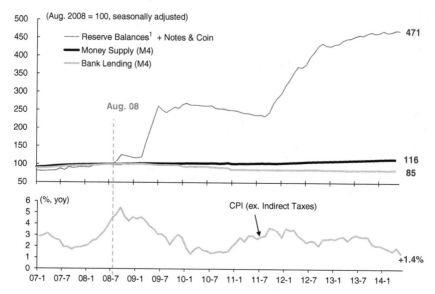

Notes: 1. Reserve Balances data are seasonally unadjusted. 2. Money supply and bank lending data exclude intermediate financial institutions.

Sources: BOE; ONS.

private credit, indicators of money available for private-sector use, that have a direct impact on GDP and inflation.

Monetary policy is effective if central bank accommodation increases money and credit for the private sector to use. In the United States, however, there has been little growth in either private credit or the money supply. As a result, U.S. inflation has slowed even after three rounds of quantitative easing by the Fed, as shown by the bottom line in Figure 1.7. That we have not seen a more pronounced economic recovery and an acceleration of inflation is attributable to the absence of growth in private credit and the money supply.

The same phenomenon can be observed in Europe. Figure 1.8 shows that these three indicators moved largely in line with each other until Lehman went bankrupt. Subsequently, growth in both private credit and the money supply has been modest at best in spite of massive base money expansion and repeated ECB rate cuts.

Figure 1.9 shows that in the United Kingdom as well, the three indicators moved largely in tandem prior to the collapse of Lehman and the Bank

FIGURE 1.10 Drastic Liquidity Injections Resulting in Minimal Increases in Money Supply and Credit: Japan

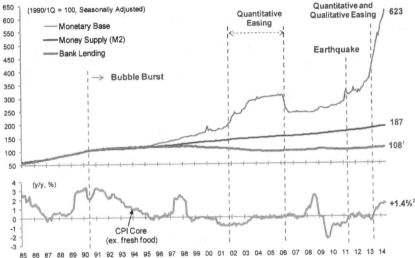

Notes: 1. Figures for bank lending are seasonally adjusted by NRI. 2. Excluding the impact of consumption tax.

Source: BOJ.

of England's massive QE program. Readers may remember the boast by Paul Fisher, BOE's executive director for markets, that the Bank would not repeat Japan's mistakes and would engage in bold quantitative easing to boost the money supply and drive an economic recovery. Those of us in Japan sat back and waited to see if the BOE could do what Bank of Japan (BOJ) could not do, but in the end the U.K. money supply did not grow at all. Bank lending—that is, private credit—actually shrank, and continued shrinking. The monetary base may have expanded sharply, but the U.K. economy fell into a severe double-dip recession in 2011, and it was only in mid-2013 that the economy finally began to exhibit signs of recovery. The unusual movements in these three indicators observed in the West since 2008 mirrored those seen in Japan after its asset price bubble collapsed in 1990 (Figure 1.10).

In Japan, too, the three indicators began to decouple after the bubble burst in 1990. Amid a deepening economic slump, domestic politicians and academics strongly urged the Bank of Japan to stimulate the economy by increasing the supply of base money, and eventually the Bank did just that. When rebased to 100 in 1990 Q1, the monetary base stood at 376 when the term of the last BOJ governor, Masaaki Shirakawa, expired in March

2013. Yet the money supply—the amount of money available for the private sector to spend—expanded only 80 percent over the 23-year period, and private credit hardly grew at all. Without significant growth in these two indicators there is no reason why the economy should recover, and in fact it has not.

Under the "quantitative and qualitative easing" (QQE) policy of current governor Haruhiko Kuroda, base money had grown to 623 as of June 2014. His action, a key component of Abenomics, prompted an enthusiastic response from foreign investors who pushed Japanese stock prices 80 percent higher and the yen 20 percent lower. The weaker yen then pushed up Japanese prices somewhat. Although the foreign investor-led market movements changed the Japanese economic landscape in no small way, it remains to be seen whether the Japanese themselves will come to share the foreign enthusiasm. This point is discussed in detail in Chapter 4.

Japan Fell into Balance Sheet Recession in 1990s

So why did both Japan and the Western economies experience this unusual decoupling? To answer this question properly, we need to consider a special economic phenomenon not found in any economics textbook or business book (and that is no exaggeration). Businesses and households in all of these countries have been paying down debt in spite of near-zero interest rates, yet there is no university economics department or business school that teaches that the private sector should pay down debt at a time when money can be borrowed for free.

The view of orthodox economics is that when private businesses are paying down debt at a time of zero interest rates, it means managers cannot find a good use for money that is essentially free. Any company run by such incompetent managers should either fire them or cease operation and return its capital to shareholders, who should be able to find better places to invest their money—after all, companies exist because they are better than individuals at making money. Individuals, either directly or indirectly, invest their savings in businesses capable of generating profits, in return for which they hope to receive interest or dividend payments. Economists operating within this intellectual framework cannot envision a situation in which companies not only stop borrowing but actually start paying down existing debt in spite of zero interest rates. That is why such a case does not feature in any business school or economics text. Yet the private sectors in Japan, the United States, and Europe have all been increasing savings and paying down debt since their bubbles burst, deeply undermining the effectiveness of monetary policy.

FIGURE 1.11 Japan's Corporate Deleveraging with Zero Interest Rates Lasted for over 10 Years

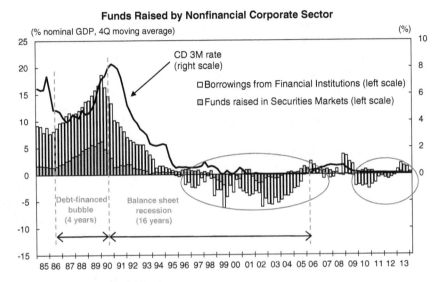

Funds Raised by Nonfinancial Corporate Sector

Sources: BOJ; Cabinet Office, Japan.

Japanese companies, for instance, stopped taking out new loans and began paying down existing debt around 1995 in spite of short-term interest rates near zero. Figure 1.11 shows funds procured by Japanese firms from banks and the capital markets together with short-term interest rates. Interest rates had already fallen to near zero in 1995, but companies were not borrowing—in fact, they were stepping up the pace of their debt pay-downs. This decline in fundraising activity began soon after the bubble burst, at a time when inflation rates were still in positive territory, and by 2002/2003 debt was being retired at the unprecedented rate of ¥30 trillion a year, or 6 percent of Japan's GDP.

The same phenomenon was observed in Europe and the United States starting in 2008, with businesses and households rushing to save more and pay down existing debt in spite of positive inflation rates and significantly negative real interest rates.

When the companies that ordinarily borrow money to expand their businesses stop doing so as a group and begin paying down debt, the economy loses two key sources of demand. First, companies themselves stop investing cash flows. Second, the corporate sector stops borrowing and spending the savings of the household sector. The resulting drop in aggregate demand then tips the affected countries into severe recessions.

Plunging Asset Prices Create Balance Sheet Problems for Businesses

Why would private companies that would ordinarily be induced by low interest rates to borrow money choose instead to pay down existing loans at a time when rates have fallen to zero or near-zero levels? The answer is that the prices of assets they bought with borrowed money experienced catastrophic declines after the bubbles collapsed, severely impairing their balance sheets. Figure 1.12 shows commercial real estate prices in Japan's six largest cities along with the TOPIX and the price of golf club memberships. As the graph shows, commercial real estate prices plunged 87 percent from their peak in a country whose economy was famously said to operate on the "land standard," and golf club memberships fell even further in value.

While asset prices sank, the money borrowed by households and businesses to acquire those assets remained intact. In other words, the value of assets purchased with borrowed money fell to a fraction of its original level, while the value of outstanding debt held steady. For a company that bought a ¥10 billion property with, say, ¥1 billion of its own money and ¥9 billion of debt, the bubble's collapse took the value of the land down to ¥2 billion, yet the company still had ¥9 billion in debt. In effect, there

FIGURE 1.12 Collapse in Asset Prices Prompted Private Sector Deleveraging

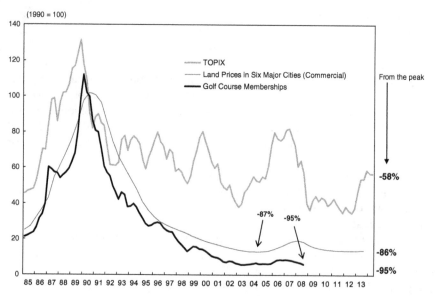

Sources: Tokyo Stock Exchange; Japan Real Estate Institute; *Nikkei Sangyo Shimbun.*

was an unrealized loss of ¥7 billion on the property and a corresponding impairment of the corporate balance sheet.

Japanese Firms Rushed to Repair Balance Sheets by Paying Down Debt

A company is effectively bankrupt when its liabilities exceed its assets. But there are two types of bankruptcy. In an ordinary bankruptcy, customers stop buying a firm's products—be they automobiles or cameras—and eventually the business loses enough money that it becomes insolvent. In this case, bankruptcy is a natural result of the market's rejection of the firm's products.

But what happened in Japan starting in 1990 was different. Japan boasted the world's largest trade surplus throughout most of this period, which implies that global consumers liked Japanese products and that Japanese companies had both outstanding technology and the ability to develop appealing products. The recurring trade frictions with the United States during the 1990s were evidence of both the quality of Japanese products and the demand for those products.

In other words, the fundamentals of Japanese businesses—their ability to develop technologies and sell products—were still healthy. Cash flows were strong and profits were reported year after year. But the collapse of the bubble and the resulting plunge in domestic asset prices opened a large hole in corporate balance sheets. Many companies saw their net worth plunge into negative territory. Tens of thousands—perhaps hundreds of thousands—of Japanese businesses found themselves in this situation after the bubble burst.

When a business still has healthy cash flows but faces severe balance sheet problems, its response will be the same whether it is a Japanese, U.S., German, or Taiwanese firm. It uses cash flow from the core business to retire debt as quickly as possible. Loans can be paid down as long as the main business continues to generate cash flow. And since asset prices will never turn negative, the balance sheet will eventually be repaired if the firm keeps paying down debt. At that point in time the company will return to the profit-maximization mode envisioned in economics texts. Until then, however, the chief priority for businesses that have healthy cash flows but are technically insolvent is not the maximization of profit but the minimization of debt.

During this process, these companies will present a happy face to journalists and analysts and discuss their optimistic earnings forecasts while quietly if not secretly doing everything in their power to pay down the debt. Discovery of the balance sheet problems by someone outside the company could have severe repercussions for the firm's creditworthiness and credit rating. Media reports that a company was effectively insolvent, for example, would result in major turmoil starting the next day. Banks would cut off its access to credit, and suppliers would start requiring cash settlements instead of allowing the firm to pay on installments or by drafts. The firm would face a struggle to survive. That is why companies with impaired balance sheets but healthy cash flows place first priority on (quietly) paying down their debt so that they can get out of this embarrassing and dangerous situation as soon as possible.

Adding urgency to this task was the fact that Japanese firms had been using substantially more leverage than their U.S. or European counterparts through the end of the 1980s. They borrowed heavily because they enjoyed high growth rates and the price of the assets they acquired using borrowed funds rose continually up to the point of the bubble's collapse. Any businessperson employing high leverage would be sensitive to the attendant risks and, upon seeing the slightest sign of a recession or a drop in asset prices, would quickly move to pay down debt, as that constitutes the most effective form of self-defense.

The act of deleveraging is not only the right thing but also the responsible thing to do (if we ignore the decision not to divulge balance sheet problems to outsiders). A company that has a healthy core business will eventually be able to pull itself out of the red using cash flows. It is only a matter of time. And the alternative—a declaration of bankruptcy—would have huge repercussions for all involved.

Shareholders do not want to hear that their shares have become worthless, and creditors do not want to hear that their assets have gone bad. Nor do company employees want to hear that their services are no longer needed. The correct and preferable course of action from the perspective of all corporate stakeholders, therefore, is to pay down debt with cash flow. As long as cash flow remains healthy, time will solve the issue of technical insolvency. That is why so many Japanese firms began paying down debt in the 1990s.

"Correct" Private Sector Behavior Tipped Japan into Contractionary Equilibrium

The private sector began paying down debt after the debt-financed asset bubble collapsed, leaving only debt in its wake. This was both responsible and correct behavior for individual businesses and households, but as a result of their actions the economy as a whole experienced what are known as fallacy-of-composition problems. A fallacy of composition refers to a situation in which behavior that is correct for individuals or companies has undesirable consequences when everyone engages in it. Japan has confronted many such problems over the past 20 years, and the West has confronted the same problem for the past seven years.

A fallacy of composition problem arises because a nation's economy will stall if people stop borrowing and spending the funds that are returned to the financial system as others save or pay down debt. If everyone joins the latter group, leaving no one to borrow and spend, aggregate demand will contract by the amount of unborrowed savings.

In an ordinary economy, banks and securities firms (i.e., the capital markets) act as intermediaries and channel funds saved by households or repaid by businesses into the hands of other borrowers. For example, assume that a household with income of ¥1,000 spends ¥900 and saves the remaining ¥100. The ¥900 that was consumed becomes income for someone else and resumes circulating in the economy. The ¥100 that was saved is lent out via banks or securities firms to companies that borrow and spend (invest) it. Hence the initial ¥1,000 in income generates a total of ¥1,000 (¥900 + ¥100) in expenditures, keeping the income stream flowing.

To continue with this analogy, if there are not enough companies to borrow the ¥100 in household savings, or if they only want to borrow ¥80, banks will offer reduced loan rates in an attempt to attract more borrowers. If this is a nationwide problem, the central bank will also lower interest rates, since a shortage of borrowers implies that money is not circulating and that the economy is weak. Lower interest rates will encourage companies that were hesitant to borrow at high interest rates to borrow and spend. That, in turn, will ensure the full ¥1,000 (¥900 + ¥100) passes into the hands of others, keeping the economy's engine going. On the other hand, if there are too many borrowers and companies are competing for funds, market principles will see that interest rates rise, so that only those willing to borrow at the higher rates will borrow and spend the ¥100. That is how an economy normally functions.

During the past 20 years in Japan, however, no borrowers stepped up to the plate even after interest rates fell to zero (Figure 1.11). That is hardly surprising, since companies struggling with insolvency had no interest in borrowing more money just because it had become cheaper. In fact, companies paid down tens of trillions of yen in debt each year in spite of near-zero interest rates. And banks were not allowed to lend money to companies they knew were technically insolvent, particularly when the banks themselves had balance sheet problems. Under these circumstances, there was no one willing to borrow and spend the hypothetical ¥100 in household savings even with interest rates at zero. Instead, the money stayed with the bank as unborrowed savings, representing a leakage from the economy's income stream. Hence only ¥900 of the original ¥1,000 was spent to become income for other people or businesses.

The household that received that ¥900 as income may also want to consume 90 percent of that amount (¥810) and save the remaining 10 percent (¥90). Here as well the ¥810 would become someone else's income, but with no borrowers the remaining ¥90 would remain in the banking system as unborrowed savings. In Japan, the absence of borrowers at a time of zero interest rates persisted for more than 10 years starting in 1995, as shown in Figure 1.11, because the fall in asset prices was so large. As this process is repeated, the initial income of ¥1,000 is reduced to ¥900, ¥810, ¥729, and so on, sending the economy into a deflationary spiral. And all this is happening at a time of zero interest rates. Since there was no name in the economics literature for a recession triggered by private-sector debt minimization, I dubbed it a balance sheet recession.

The resulting economic weakness not only depresses asset prices further but also squeezes the corporate profits funding the debt paydowns, adding to the pressures on companies striving to deleverage. While paying down debt to restore solvency is the right and responsible thing to do for individual companies, it can lead to disastrous fallacy-of-composition problems when companies do so as a group. This is precisely what happens during a balance sheet recession, when a burst asset bubble prompts the private sector to turn from maximizing profits to minimizing debt.

And when the private sector stops borrowing money even at zero interest rates, any funds supplied to financial institutions by the central bank remain stuck within the financial system because there are no borrowers. That is why growth in private credit and the money supply has been so sluggish post-Lehman despite dramatic expansion of the monetary base by central banks. The key implication here is that the effectiveness of monetary policy diminishes dramatically as the private sector switches from maximizing profit to minimizing debt. This point will be discussed in detail in Chapter 2.

Incidentally, the ¥1,000 example discussed above looks only at household savings. The actual decline in aggregate demand would also have to include net debt paydowns by the corporate sector. Without any borrowers, the sum of these two amounts would remain within the banking system and thereby constitute a leakage from the economy's income stream.

Collapse of Japan's Bubble Destroyed ¥1,500 Trillion in Wealth

The fact that so many Japanese companies began paying down debt at once highlights the severity of the balance sheet damage incurred when the asset bubble collapsed. Figure 1.13 illustrates the wealth destroyed by falling land and share prices from 1990 onward. In these two asset categories alone, ¥1,570 trillion in wealth, equal to the entire stock of personal financial assets

FIGURE 1.13 Cumulative Capital Losses on Shares and Land since End-1989 Reach 1,570 Trillion Yen

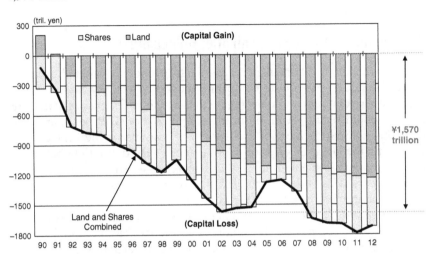

Source: Cabinet Office, Japan National Accounts.

in Japan, evaporated after the bubble burst. In other words, the plunge in asset prices eliminated national wealth equal to three years of 1989 gross domestic product. To the best of my knowledge, no other nation in history has experienced such a large economic loss during peacetime.

Yet Japan was not the first nation to experience a massive peacetime loss of national wealth. In the Great Depression, which began in 1929, the U.S. private sector rushed to pay down debt in response to a plunge in the price of stocks and other assets. Americans had been going into debt to buy everything from shares to consumer durables as the bubble economy pushed asset prices ever higher. But the stock market crash that began in New York in October 1929 sent asset prices tumbling and left behind only the associated debt. People then tried to reduce their liabilities by using personal and corporate income to pay down debt, and as a result there were no borrowers no matter how far the Fed cut rates.

The United States entered the kind of deflationary spiral described above, with income falling from $1,000 to $900 to $810 and so on, and after just four years U.S. GNP had plunged 46 percent from its 1929 peak. The unemployment rate was 25 percent nationwide and exceeded 50 percent in major cities. Share prices fell to one eighth their peak levels. Still, national wealth lost in the crash amounted to only one year (1929) of GNP, approximately a third of the damage incurred by Japan. This underscores the severity of the damage caused when the Japanese bubble burst in 1990.

This also explains why it took so long for Japanese companies to repair their balance sheets.

Why Japanese GDP Did Not Fall after Bubble Burst

More than ¥1,500 trillion in national wealth evaporated after the bubble burst (Figure 1.13) as private companies moved collectively to deleverage. With the corporate sector deleveraging to the tune of 6 percent of GDP and the household sector saving on average 4 percent of GDP per year, Japan could have lost 10 percent of its GDP every year, just as the United States did during the Great Depression. Yet Japanese GDP did not fall below the bubble-era peak—in either nominal or real terms—even once over the next 20-plus years. This is despite the fact that commercial land prices plunged 87 percent and fell back to the levels of 1973 (Figure 1.14).

This brings us to the biggest difference between Japan's recession and the Great Depression. Like the United States, Japan fell into a deflationary spiral and could easily have seen its GDP drop to a fraction of the peak, but that did not happen.

So who has been saving and who has been borrowing in Japan over the past 20 years? Figure 1.15a summarizes flow-of-funds data, which tell us which sectors of the economy are saving and which are borrowing. The area above the zero centerline in this graph indicates a financial surplus,

FIGURE 1.14 Japan's GDP Grows Despite Major Loss of Wealth and Private Sector Deleveraging

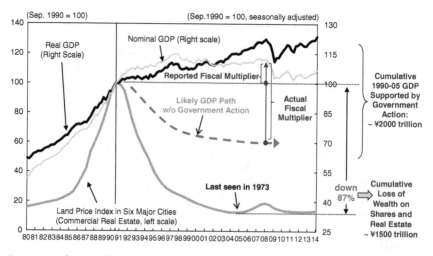

Sources: Cabinet Office; Japan Real Estate Institute.

FIGURE 1.15a Japan's Recession Driven by Dramatic Change in Corporate Behavior

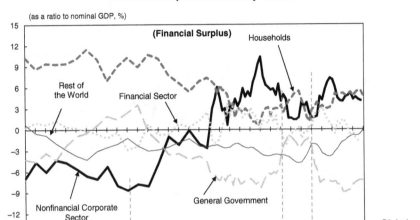

Financial Surplus or Deficit by Sector

Note: All entries are four-quarter moving averages. For the latest figures, four-quarter averages ending in 2014 Q1 are used.

Sources: BOJ, Flow of Funds Accounts; and Government of Japan, Cabinet Office, National Accounts.

which means sectors above that line were supplying funds to the broader economy (i.e., they were net savers). Sectors below that line were running a financial deficit, which means they were borrowing funds (and hence were net investors).

These data typically divide the economy into five sectors—household, nonfinancial corporate, financial, government, and the rest of the world—and are compiled in such a way that at any point in time the five should sum to zero. The graph therefore shows which sectors in the Japanese economy are saving and which are borrowing and spending those savings. Heavy volatility in some sectors makes the graph in Figure 1.15a difficult to read, so Figure 1.15b takes the figures for financial firms and nonfinancial corporations and adds them together (since both experienced major balance sheet problems) to produce four instead of five sectors. A four-quarter moving average is also used to compensate for seasonal fluctuations. Moving averages are often used to help identify the underlying trend in flow-of-funds data.

To understand what this graph is telling us, consider what it would look like in an ideal world. In such a world, the household sector would sit at

FIGURE 1.15b Identifying the Underlying Trend in Japan's Recession

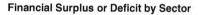

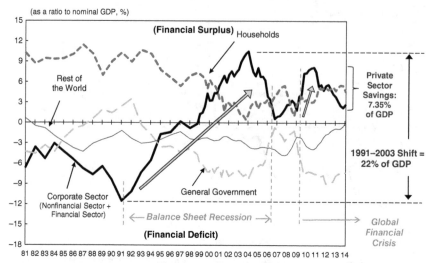

Note: All entries are four-quarter moving averages. For the latest figures, four-quarter averages ending in 2014 Q1 are used.

Sources: BOJ, Flow of Funds Accounts; and Government of Japan, Cabinet Office, National Accounts.

the top (net saver) and the corporate sector at the bottom (net investor), with the remaining two sectors—government and the rest of the world—located near the centerline. A household sector near the top of the graph indicates a high household savings rate, while a corporate sector near the bottom means that businesses are actively borrowing and investing, which translates to a high rate of investment. For the government and the rest of the world to fall near the centerline indicates the nation's fiscal and external balances are in equilibrium. This is the ideal situation for an economy.

Did conditions in Japan ever approach this ideal? The answer is yes: at the peak of the bubble, in 1990. At the time, Japan's household sector was located at the top of the graph, the corporate sector was at the bottom, the rest of the world had a modest deficit (below the zero line), and the government had a modest surplus (above the zero line). The deficit for the rest of the world implies that other countries were borrowing money from Japan—that is, that Japan was running a current account surplus. The surplus for the government sector signifies a fiscal surplus. In short, Japan's economy in 1990 was characterized by the perfect combination of a high savings rate, a high investment rate, and fiscal and current account surpluses. Just over a decade earlier, in 1979, Harvard professor Ezra Vogel had published *Japan as Number One: Lessons for America,* which became a bestseller in Japan. In a sense, the book's title was an accurate reflection of conditions at the time. From the perspective of flow-of-funds data, Japan's economy in 1990 was in an ideal position, and it is hardly surprising that Japan was seen as being unchallenged on the global economic stage.

Unfortunately, Japanese investment was in a bubble in 1990, and everything changed when the bubble burst. The plunge in asset prices that began in 1990 opened a large hole in the corporate sector's balance sheet, prompting businesses to begin deleveraging, and funds raised by the sector declined steadily starting in 1990.

The number of companies paying down debt continued to rise, and by 1998 the corporate sector as a whole had become a net saver, lifting it above the centerline in the graph. This implies that businesses not only stopped borrowing the household sector's savings but also began using their own cash flows to pay down debt. From that point onward the corporate sector continued to run a financial surplus—starting in 2000 it actually saved more than households. Businesses, ordinarily the largest borrowers in an economy, became the biggest savers, and instead of borrowing from financial institutions they paid loans back to them, which is a dangerous set of circumstances for any economy. In Japan these conditions persist even today. These conditions have also been seen in Germany since 2003 and in many Western countries since 2008.

Because businesses not only stopped borrowing money to invest but also began using their own cash flows to pay down debt, corporate-sector demand equal to 22 percent of GDP was lost between 1990 and 2003 (Figure 1.15b). In other words, the plunge in asset prices eliminated corporate-sector demand equivalent to more than 20 percent of GDP. Such a drastic loss of demand will trigger a recession no matter how strong the economy. Thus Japan found itself heading toward another Great Depression.

Fiscal Stimulus Saved Japan's Economy

If so, why did Japan's GDP never fall below its bubble-era peak? The short answer is that the government decided to borrow and spend the ¥100 in the preceding example.

The government continued to run a fiscal surplus in 1990 and 1991, immediately after the bubble burst, because tax revenues remained high. But as the economy weakened sharply starting in 1992, policymakers decided that the economy had entered a cyclical (i.e., ordinary) downturn and that a year or two of fiscal stimulus would suffice to prime the pump and get the economy rolling again. This was precisely the same view espoused in 2008 by Lawrence Summers, the Obama administration's first NEC chairman, who believed a large jolt of fiscal stimulus would be enough to put the economy back on track (see Chapter 3). It is therefore hardly surprising that the pork-loving politicians of the ruling Liberal Democratic Party (LDP) recommended the government stimulate the economy by repairing and building infrastructure such as roads and bridges.

Fiscal stimulus is essentially debt-financed spending by the government. In the context of the example above, the government steps in to borrow and spend the ¥100 that the household sector saved but the corporate sector did not borrow and is therefore lying fallow in the banking system. By doing so, it ensures that the original ¥1,000 in income generates ¥1,000 (¥900 + ¥100) in expenditures, preventing a contraction in GDP. That is why Japan's GDP did not decline.

Initially the fiscal stimulus appeared to stabilize the economy as expected, and everyone was reassured to see the government's economic policies had worked. But the economy weakened again as the impact of that spending faded in the next year. Why did the stimulus, instead of priming the pump, have only a temporary effect on the economy? The answer is simple. When commercial real estate prices fall 87 percent from their peak and destroy some ¥1,500 trillion in national wealth in a country, it is impossible for businesses to repair their balance sheets in a year or two. Ordinarily it takes at least several years. And for those unlucky companies that bought at the peak of the real estate market, it might take 20 years to do so. They will continue to pay down debt as long as their businesses continue to generate cash. And in the meantime they will no longer borrow the household sector's savings, forcing the government to administer an annual dose of fiscal stimulus to fill the resulting gap.

Japan's fiscal deficits therefore rose sharply, as shown in Figure 1.16, and the public debt climbed to the levels we see today. But it was precisely because the government spent this money that GDP remained above the bubble-era peak in spite of a dramatic shift in corporate behavior and the loss of national wealth amounting to three full years of GDP. In other words, this annual dose of fiscal stimulus enabled the government to prevent a deflationary gap.[1]

---

[1] In orthodox economics, a deflationary gap refers to the difference between potential and actual GDP. One shortcoming of this definition is that the size of the gap varies greatly depending on how potential GDP is estimated. For the purposes of this book a deflationary gap is defined as the amount of unborrowed private savings—that is, the sum of household savings and net debt repayments by the corporate sector— left sitting in the banking system because of an absence of borrowers. This sum is equivalent to leakages from the economy's income stream and does not suffer from the numerous problems involved in estimating potential GDP.

FIGURE 1.16 Japanese Government Borrows and Spends Unborrowed Savings of Private Sector to Sustain GDP

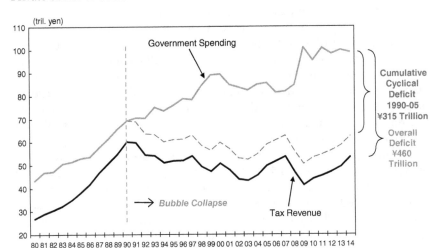

Note: FY2014 is initial budget and FY2013 includes supplementary budget.

Source: Ministry of Finance, Japan.

"Good" Fiscal Deficits Were Not Perceived as Such

This policy left Japan with a huge public debt. But if the government had not stimulated the economy in this way, GDP would probably have fallen to half or less than half of its peak level—and that is in an optimistic scenario. When the crash in U.S. asset prices during the Great Depression destroyed wealth equivalent to a year of 1929 GNP, output plunged 46 percent. As Japan lost wealth equal to more than *three years* of 1989 GDP, the resulting hit to the economy would almost certainly have been substantially greater. This disastrous outcome was averted only because the government administered fiscal stimulus early on and continued to do so over an extended period of time. Its actions ultimately prevented the economy from falling over the precipice.

The fallacy-of-composition problems noted above occurred because businesses and households did what they thought was right and paid down debt. And it was because the government did exactly the opposite—in effect taking the other side of the bet—that an economic tragedy was averted. By correctly administering fiscal stimulus, the government prevented the economic crisis from causing a devastating drop in living standards. By 2005, corporate balance sheets in Japan were fully repaired, leaving only the government balance sheets to be repaired. In that sense, Japan's fiscal stimulus was one of the most successful economic policies in human history.

Unfortunately, many policymakers, academics, and members of the press both in Japan and overseas were unable to see things in this light and they made it difficult for the government to apply fiscal stimulus in a predictive way. After all, the entire edifice of traditional economics is built on the assumption that the private sector always allocates resources better than the public sector. But this assumption is valid only when private-sector balance sheets are healthy and it is maximizing profits, a condition that has not been satisfied in Japan for the past 20 years or in many Western economies for the past six.

It took people so long to understand and overcome this recession because no university teaches that technically insolvent companies will choose to minimize debt instead of maximize profit. Even today, one would be hard-pressed to find a university-level economics textbook that teaches that companies will sometimes decide to pay down debt at a time of zero interest rates. And governments seldom explain that fiscal stimulus is necessary because the private sector is paying down debt or because living standards cannot be sustained without it.

Even the Japanese government's success in averting an economic crisis with fiscal stimulus elicited misguided criticism of its economic policy. In particular, most of those taking a superficial view of Japan's economy—including the International Monetary Fund (IMF) up to 1997—insisted that Japan remained in an economic slump because the government was spending money inappropriately. They argued that the hundreds of trillions of yen in fiscal stimulus administered since the bubble must have been wasted because the economy was only treading water.

They assumed, in other words, that Japan's economy would have been able to achieve zero growth without any fiscal stimulus. They argued that the modest growth in output after trillions of yen in government expenditures implied an extremely low fiscal multiplier, which in turn meant the money had been wasted on useless public works programs. Those journalists who had nothing better to do combed Japan for examples of wasteful public works projects and cited them as evidence the government had wasted taxpayer money. They said GDP growth was low or nonexistent and the economy had failed to enter a self-sustaining recovery because the government's massive fiscal stimulus in the form of public works investment had been wasted on unnecessary projects. In short, they bashed the stimulus based on the totally unfounded assumption that Japan would have been able to maintain zero growth without any help from the government.

In reality, it was only because the government boosted fiscal expenditures to the extent it did that the economy was able to tread water, avoiding a devastating drop in living standards. It is nothing short of a miracle that

Japanese GDP remained above the bubble-era peak in spite of an 87 percent fall in commercial real estate prices and the corporate sector's rush to pay down debt worth 6 percent of GDP a year. And it was a miracle made possible by government spending.

Japan's cumulative fiscal deficit increased by ¥460 trillion in the 16 years from 1990 until the corporate sector stopped paying down debt in 2005. While certainly large, it was a *good* fiscal deficit because Japan's GDP might well have collapsed along with the bubble had the government not incurred it.

The dotted line in Figure 1.14 shows a scenario in which the government did nothing and Japan's GDP fell back to 1985 levels one year before the bubble began. When the Roaring Twenties in the United States ended with the stock market crash of 1929 and the country lost national wealth equal to a year of GNP, the resulting deflationary spiral prompted a 46 percent decline in GNP. Given that precedent, it would hardly be surprising if Japan, which lost wealth equivalent to three years of GDP, had seen output drop by more than half. However, the dotted line in the figure conservatively assumes that GDP fell back only to the level of 1985. As GDP was ¥330 trillion in 1985, the gap between this line and actual GDP would be at least ¥120 trillion to ¥180 trillion, although the exact figure would depend on whether GDP fell suddenly or gradually. If we assume this state of affairs continued for 15 years, the cumulative loss of output would be ¥150 trillion × 15 = ¥2,250 trillion.

This implies that Japan was able to "buy" ¥2,250 trillion of GDP with fiscal stimulus of ¥460 trillion, which is a bargain by any standard. Amid an 87 percent decline in land prices and the evaporation of ¥1,500 trillion in national wealth, this ¥460 trillion in government spending prevented Japan's GDP from falling even as the private sector began collectively paying down debt. While mistakes were made—the policy failures of 1997 and 2001 will be discussed later—it would be no overstatement to say this was one of the most successful fiscal stimulus programs in human history.

Nevertheless, the media, the IMF, and orthodox academic economists were unable to understand this. They repeatedly criticized government spending on public works projects based on the misguided assumption that GDP could have been sustained at around the bubble-peak level of ¥450 trillion without any action from the government.

Balance Sheet Recessions and the Limitations of Econometric Models

When using econometric models to estimate multipliers, economists start with an implicit assumption that the economy is in a stable equilibrium that requires no external support. That is because these models measure the fiscal multiplier by calculating the extent to which fiscal stimulus boosted the economy *from a given stable equilibrium*. In other words, those arguing that Japan's fiscal stimulus had a low multiplier using these models are implicitly assuming that the economy has been at or near equilibrium for the past 20 years.

In reality, however, the Japanese economy has been far from equilibrium for the past 20 years. Just keeping output from shrinking has required fiscal stimulus in excess of 8 percent of GDP. Without the support of government demand, Japan's economy could easily have fallen into a deflationary spiral in which income shrank from ¥1,000 to ¥900, from ¥900 to ¥810, and so on.

An accurate measurement of the fiscal multiplier requires that we make a presumption about where GDP would have been in the absence of fiscal support and then compare that with the actually measured level. But without fiscal stimulus, Japan would either be in the midst of a massive deflationary spiral or would already have entered the final stage of that process, better known as a depression.

The correct fiscal multiplier would therefore be based on the difference between actual GDP and depression-level GDP. That gap is massive and produces a multiplier far larger than the commonly reported figure of 1.1 or 1.2. For instance, if we assume that GDP would have followed the dotted line in Figure 1.14 in the absence of the ¥460 trillion fiscal stimulus, the cumulative ¥2,000 trillion gap between that and actual GDP suggests the actual multiplier was more than 4.

Unfortunately, most of the econometric models in use today are built around the assumption that the economy is at or near equilibrium. Such models are basically useless when the economy is far from equilibrium, as it is today. Yet many economists in Japan and elsewhere are unaware of this basic limitation and use the meaningless estimates of fiscal multipliers from these models to criticize fiscal stimulus as being an ineffective waste of money.

In 1997, for example, the IMF and the Organisation for Economic Co-operation and Development (OECD) recommended that Japan reduce its fiscal deficits based on the view that a reduction in "ineffective" government expenditures would not have a substantial adverse economic impact. Before compiling their recommendations both organizations dispatched teams to Japan to conduct interviews, and I happened to be among those interviewed. Although I strongly warned against spending cuts or tax hikes, my views were not incorporated in the final recommendations presented to the Japanese government. Then-prime minister Ryutaro Hashimoto accepted their suggestions and pushed through spending cuts and tax hikes in an attempt to reduce the deficit.

FIGURE 1.17 Japan's Fall from Its Fiscal Cliff in 1997 and 2001: Weakened Economy, Reduced Tax Revenue, and Increased Deficit

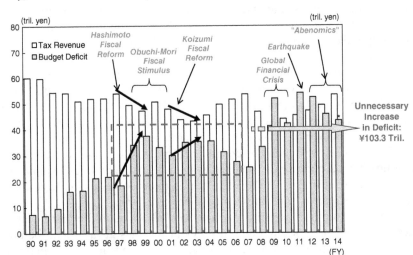

Note: Latest figures (*) are estimated by MOF. From FY2011, figures include reconstruction taxes and bonds.

Source: Ministry of Finance, Japan.

As a result of his actions, Japan's economy shrank for an unprecedented five consecutive quarters (as reported at that time), which also triggered a massive banking crisis. That is the natural outcome when the government scales back spending at a time when households are saving but companies are not borrowing. Tax revenues declined in spite of higher tax rates as the economy collapsed, and the fiscal deficit, instead of falling by ¥15 trillion as initially forecast, actually increased by ¥16 trillion (Figure 1.17). It took 10 years for the deficit, which rose by 72 percent as a result of these actions, to fall back to its original level.

The economic collapse that began in 1997 demonstrated the extent to which economic activity was being supported by fiscal expenditures during the balance sheet recession—in other words, it showed that the fiscal multiplier was actually very large. The next year the IMF team returned to my office and apologized for their mistake by saying, "We are sorry for the Japanese people." However, the IMF made exactly the same mistake during the Asian currency crisis in 1997 and again in Europe starting in 2008. Apparently, those covering Japan at the IMF in 1997 were not covering Europe in 2008. It was only in the autumn of 2012 that the IMF acknowledged its errors in Europe by admitting that fiscal multipliers were much larger than it had assumed.

Fiscal Stimulus Works in Two Stages

A closer examination suggests that fiscal stimulus administered during a balance sheet recession works in two stages. There is the marginal impact of fiscal expenditures until the deflationary gap is closed, and the marginal impact after it is closed. In other words, the marginal impact of a ¥1 trillion increase in fiscal stimulus from ¥35 trillion to ¥36 trillion when the deflationary gap is ¥40 trillion could be meaningfully different from that of a ¥1 trillion increase from ¥40 trillion to ¥41 trillion. In the former case, the spending occurs against the headwind of a deflationary gap that is trying to push the broader economy into a contractionary equilibrium, and the knock-on effects will naturally be limited. In the latter case, there are no such headwinds because the deflationary gap has already been eliminated, and the marginal impact of the ¥1 trillion is likely to be just as large as in an ordinary economy with no balance sheet recession.

Only the former type of impact has been observed in the past because fiscal stimulus has typically been insufficient and has always been behind the curve, especially in peacetime. Moreover, it is technically difficult to distinguish the marginal impact of spending in excess of the deflationary gap from that of spending to neutralize the deflationary gap. What is measured is the average knock-on effect of the *total* fiscal deficit. But since most of the government expenditures are being used to counteract the headwinds noted above, the estimated multiplier—although as noted above this figure itself is meaningless when an economy is not in equilibrium—is bound to be small.

FDR Made Same Mistake in 1937

Interestingly, President Roosevelt made exactly the same mistake in the United States as the Hashimoto administration did 60 years later in Japan. Roosevelt became president in 1932 after Herbert Hoover's balanced budget policy failed. He set about rebuilding the U.S. economy in 1933 with a shift to an activist fiscal policy called the New Deal. Although his policy was largely ad hoc and inconsistent, Roosevelt still succeeded in nearly doubling federal government spending between 1933 and 1936, and by 1937 some economic indicators had recovered to the levels of 1929.

Roosevelt was fundamentally opposed to deficit spending and mistakenly took this recovery as a sign that it was time to start reducing the deficit. When he did so in 1937, the U.S. economy collapsed almost instantly: share prices plunged by 50 percent, industrial production dropped by 30 percent, and the unemployment rate surged higher. This was a natural outcome of the fact that the government was effectively the only borrower between 1933 and 1937. The private sector did not increase borrowing at all during this period.

Roosevelt quickly reversed course and restored the government's fiscal stimulus, but it took a great deal of time and money to close the wound that was reopened in 1937. In the end, a full-fledged U.S. economic recovery would have to wait for the attack on Pearl Harbor in December 1941 and the massive expansion of fiscal expenditures unleashed by the war.

In February 1997, just two months before the Hashimoto administration embarked on its fiscal consolidation program, Shigeru Fujita and I jointly published an essay in the weekly magazine *Shukan Toyo Keizai* in which we examined America's experience in 1937 and pointed out the dangers of premature deficit-reduction efforts. Although this article failed to stop the tax hikes and spending cuts that were implemented in April 1997, the fact that the Japanese economy collapsed as a result of those measures—just as we had predicted—drew a great deal of attention from figures in the media and government. As a result, I was given the opportunity to make a variety of proposals for fiscal and banking policy.

The Ministry of Finance bureaucrats who pushed for austerity refused to acknowledge their mistakes in 1997. They continued to argue that although the poor economic performance in 1997 Q2, just after the Hashimoto administration raised the consumption tax, could not be helped, consumption in Q3 that year actually rose in year-over-year terms. They insisted the subsequent weakness in the economy was the result of other factors such as banking sector problems and the Asian currency crisis. But as University of Tokyo professor Tatsuo Hatta has pointed out, a closer examination of consumption data for 1997 Q3 shows that the only item showing a marked increase was food—and this was in reaction to sharply reduced demand in the year-before quarter due to an *E. coli* outbreak. Sales of consumer durables fell as predicted in response to the consumption tax hike, offering proof that the government's fiscal retrenchment was responsible for the economy's decline.

In the America of the 1930s as well, fiscal deficits as a percentage of federal spending actually peaked not during the Roosevelt administration's New Deal but rather in 1932, when Hebert Hoover was president and the economy was still in the doldrums. Hoover adopted an activist fiscal policy that year, but tax revenues fell to just 40 percent of federal spending. Revenues declined because Hoover held an unflinching belief in the importance of balanced budgets and had been reluctant to administer fiscal stimulus until 1931. The experiences of both Japan in 1997 and the United States in 1932 offer proof that during a balance sheet recession, when the private sector is looking backwards, the government should be wary of cutting off fiscal support for the economy. Trying to rein in the deficit at such times risks producing not only a sharp deterioration in the economy but also an increase in the fiscal deficit as tax revenues plunge.

The Koizumi administration (2001–2006) made the same mistake. Prime minister Junichiro Koizumi declared the need for fiscal reform and capped new government bond issuance at ¥30 trillion, or about 6 percent of GDP, in 2001. But this attempt to rein in expenditures during a balance sheet recession prompted a further slump in the economy, and the revenue shortfall resulting from the decline in tax receipts caused the fiscal deficit to widen significantly (Figure 1.17). The deficit rose in spite of painful cutbacks in spending on public works projects because the private sector was not borrowing money, and the economy weakened as a result.

For fiscal consolidation to succeed, the private sector must be willing and able to borrow and spend the money that the government is no longer borrowing because of the tax hikes and spending cuts. If this condition is satisfied, there is no reason why fiscal retrenchment should cause GDP to fall, and if GDP does not fall fiscal retrenchment should be successful.

This condition is fulfilled under ordinary economic conditions—in other words, when the private sector is maximizing profits and there is no balance sheet problem. The determining factor in the success of fiscal consolidation then becomes the government's commitment. But during a balance sheet recession this condition—the private sector's willingness to borrow—is not satisfied. That means there is no reason why fiscal consolidation should succeed regardless of how committed the government is. In fact, there is a danger that the fiscal deficit will *increase*, as it did in Japan in 1997.

Reactive Fiscal Stimulus Is Far Less Efficient

During a balance sheet recession, undertaking fiscal stimulus early and sufficiently will minimize the ultimate (cumulative) deficit. If fiscal stimulus succeeds in stabilizing the economy, private incomes will be sustained, and the private sector can use that income to pay down debt and complete its balance sheet repairs.

But a delay in fiscal stimulus will cause the recession to grow that much deeper, depressing asset prices further and reducing the income available for the private sector to pay down debt, both of which prolong balance sheet adjustments. If fiscal stimulus comes only after the economy weakens and asset prices fall, further expenditures will be required at a time when the wound is already wide open. When the economy is about to contract from ¥1,000 to ¥900 and then to ¥810, economic activity will stabilize at ¥1,000 if the government injects ¥100 in fiscal stimulus at the outset. Two years of such stimulus would result in total economic activity of ¥2,000 and ¥200 in fiscal deficits.

But if the government waits a year before taking action, the economy will already have contracted to ¥900. At that point it will take ¥190 in stimulus to restore the economy to its original state, and total economic activity over the two-year period will amount to ¥1,900. In other words, ¥100 will be lost forever. The sum of the fiscal deficit and this lost economic activity is ¥290. This is ¥90, or 45 percent, more than if the government had injected fiscal stimulus from the start as a preventive measure. While some may argue that the fiscal deficit was ¥10 less in the second case, a real-world contraction of the economy to ¥900 will not only cause asset prices to fall but will also lower tax revenues, thereby producing a larger fiscal deficit. In addition, the weak economy reduces the amount of income available for people to repair their balance sheets, thereby prolonging the recession.

Japan's fiscal stimulus helped businesses repair their balance sheets while successfully sustaining economic activity. Japan's unemployment rate never went beyond 5.5 percent. However, fiscal stimulus was never carried out proactively. Successive Japanese governments administered stimulus only after the economy had stalled—in other words, they were always behind the curve. Hence they ran unnecessarily large fiscal deficits, and economic activity and jobs that might have been saved were lost permanently while the government wasted time vacillating between fiscal stimulus and consolidation. During a balance sheet recession the economy will fall into a vicious cycle as soon as unborrowed savings accumulate in the private sector. Consequently, applying fiscal stimulus after the symptoms emerge will always be less efficient than doing so proactively. During such a recession, proactive fiscal stimulus is essential to sustaining economic activity and minimizing the ultimate cost of treatment, which is measured by the cumulative fiscal deficit.

Fiscal Deficits Are Easily Financed during Balance Sheet Recessions

One issue that is always raised when making a case for fiscal stimulus during a balance sheet recession is the question of how to finance the spending. This sort of argument is especially common in countries already running large fiscal deficits and in the Eurozone periphery, where countries are unable to sell government bonds on the market and are said to have no "fiscal space."

The question of how to finance fiscal deficits during balance sheet recessions and the lack of "fiscal space" in the Eurozone periphery are two completely different issues. The latter issue is something unique to the Eurozone and will be discussed in detail in Chapter 5. The former question—how to finance a fiscal deficit in this type of recession—can be ignored in practice unless the country is a member of the Eurozone. That may surprise many readers, but it is easy to see once the driving mechanisms of balance sheet recessions are understood.

A balance sheet recession occurs when the private sector collectively becomes a net saver (where saving includes paying down debt) in spite of ultra-low interest rates. The unborrowed private savings created by the lack of private borrowers then leaks out of the economy's income stream. In the example discussed above, the absence of borrowers for the ¥100 saved by the private sector means this money stays within the financial system, becoming unborrowed savings and leaking from the income stream. Consequently, economic activity of ¥1,000 shrinks to ¥900, and as the cycle repeats it contracts to ¥810, ¥729, and so on as the economy's decline accelerates. The unborrowed savings that were saved but not borrowed by the private sector then pile up at private financial institutions.

Many if not most of the loan officers and fund managers charged with investing these funds at financial institutions are prevented by government regulation from taking on too much principal risk or currency risk. Fund managers at pension funds or life insurance companies operate under particularly tight regulatory constraints that have been enacted to protect pensioners and so on. Restrictions on principal risk mean fund managers cannot invest the entire sum in equities, the value of which could potentially fall to zero. Instead, they must invest a significant portion of their funds in loans or bonds that have a low probability of becoming worthless. Although they are not prohibited entirely from taking on principal or currency risk, they *are* prevented from assuming excessive risk. There is a huge amount of managed money subject to such restrictions in any country.

Fund managers face an extremely difficult situation in a balance sheet recession. They face huge inflows of funds because the private sector is saving and paying down debt, yet there are few attractive destinations for this money because the private sector as a whole is no longer borrowing.

The only remaining borrower that issues debt and carries no foreign exchange risk is the government with its fiscal deficits. As a result, fund managers responsible for investing the unborrowed savings have no alternative but to purchase government bonds. Most of this money therefore flows into the government bond market, sending bond prices sharply higher while yields plunge in spite of large and continuing deficits.

This phenomenon was first observed in Japan 20 years ago. At the time, orthodox proponents of fiscal consolidation insisted the Japanese government bond (JGB) market would crash in no time if the government continued to run such large fiscal deficits. Twenty-four years have passed since then and we are still nowhere close to that sort of situation. In fact, JGB prices rose and yields fell in spite of continued increases in the deficit and the public debt. Western hedge funds also engaged in targeted short-selling of JGBs on numerous occasions because they saw the JGB market as a bubble ready to burst, but each time they failed spectacularly, incurring heavy losses in the process. The steep decline in JGB yields was not a bubble but rather a natural result of the balance sheet recession. Sweden also saw its 10-year government bond yield fall below 2 percent in 2011.

The same thing has happened in the United States and the United Kingdom since 2008. Yields on 10-year government debt fell below 2 percent at one point even though both countries were running massive fiscal and trade deficits. Although the central banks of these two countries were also buying, the key reason, as will be discussed in detail below, was that businesses and households in the United States and the United Kingdom had not only stopped borrowing money but were actually saving money despite near-zero interest rates.

Self-Corrective Mechanism for Economies in Balance Sheet Recessions

This phenomenon of government bond yields falling during a balance sheet recession is an essential component of the self-corrective mechanism that all economies possess. During such a recession the unborrowed savings of the private sector flow into the government bond market, pushing down bond yields. That makes it possible for the government to administer fiscal stimulus, thereby maintaining GDP and by extension private-sector incomes, which enables businesses and households to repair their balance sheets that much sooner. Once balance sheet repairs have been completed, the private sector can resume borrowing money, at which time interest rates will rise. That will be the signal for the government to proceed with its own balance sheet repairs via fiscal consolidation.

This self-corrective mechanism will function in any country outside the Eurozone. Unfortunately, Japan in 1997 and the United Kingdom in 2010 completely ignored the message being sent by the market in the form of ultra-low government bond yields. Instead they focused solely on the size of the deficit and chose to pursue fiscal consolidation. In 1997, Japan's government chose to engage in deficit-reduction efforts because so much attention had focused on the fact that the national debt was about to exceed Italy's as a percentage of GDP. But the policy debate at the time completely overlooked the fact that at the peak of Italy's fiscal deficits its government bonds were yielding 14 percent, whereas the yield on 10-year JGBs in 1997 was just 2.3 percent. The messages being sent by the two bond markets were telling us that the two countries suffered from entirely different problems. When Japan ignored that message and followed Italy down the path of deficit reduction, it fell into a devastating double-dip recession.

Many advocates of free-market economics have a tendency to suddenly turn communist when confronted with a fiscal deficit. In other words, they tend to focus solely on the size of the deficit and ignore its price—that is, the yield on government debt. But the reason why market economies function more effectively than the communist alternative is that they allow people to make decisions on the basis of both quantity and price. If quantity were the only criterion, we would experience the same kinds of problems as a planned economy that ignores the price mechanism.

Japan has also ignored the need for fiscal stimulus being signaled by ultra-low government bond yields on many occasions over the past 20 years, as have the United States and the United Kingdom since 2008 (Chapter 2 will discuss how this important signal has been lost under QE). However, there is nothing so dangerous as a government that tries to manage the economy while ignoring the market's most important message: government bond yields.

Balance sheet recession theory tells us that the deflationary gap in an economy facing such a recession is equal to the amount of private unborrowed savings. In other words, private financial institutions hold unborrowed savings equal to the amount of fiscal stimulus needed to stabilize the economy. Financing the fiscal deficits needed during a balance sheet recession will not be a problem as long as those savings flow into government debt.

These unborrowed savings (at a time of zero interest rates) are responsible for the weakness in the economy, and it is because the economy is so weak that fiscal stimulus is necessary. The savings go unborrowed because businesses and households respond to the burst bubble and resulting damage to their balance sheets by shifting priority from maximizing profit to minimizing debt. Hence there should be no difficulty financing fiscal deficits incurred for this reason—with the exception of countries in the Eurozone, as will be explained in a later chapter.

Two Types of Fiscal Deficits Require Different Responses

The discussion above suggests that there are two kinds of fiscal deficit: the ordinary variety, which leads to inflation, rising interest rates, and a misallocation of resources, and the kind that occurs during a balance sheet recession and does not cause interest rates to rise. These two types of fiscal deficit also have completely different characteristics. The first occurs as a result of government mismanagement, the second as a result of private sector mismanagement. But only the former is typically discussed in university economics classes. Here, the government runs a deficit for political reasons—sometimes to ensure its reelection—at a time when the private sector is a willing borrower. The government ends up competing with the private sector for a limited supply of private savings, crowding out private investment and pushing inflation and interest rates higher. And if the government happens to use money less efficiently than the private sector, the allocation of limited resources will be distorted in proportion to the size of the fiscal deficit, with funds flowing to inefficient sectors. If the deficit is of this type, the government and voters should do everything they can to reduce it. By doing so they will improve the allocation of resources, keep inflation and interest rates in check, and enable more efficient economic growth led by the private sector.

Every few decades, however, the private sector loses all sense of discipline and becomes caught up in a bubble. Blinded by the prospect of quick profits, businesses and households borrow heavily and become increasingly leveraged in the belief that investments in certain assets are a sure thing. Once the bubble collapses and the dream ends, people come to their senses and realize they had been chasing a bubble and had bid asset prices up to unwarranted levels. As soon as they realize the prices they paid will not be coming back anytime soon, they begin the process of repairing their damaged balance sheets by deleveraging. The balance sheet recession starts the moment that businesses and households wake up to their mistake.

When the fiscal deficit increases because of economic weakness caused by this change in private behavior, the cause is not policy failures or greedy politicians but rather the private sector's willing participation in the bubble. It is a byproduct of the fact that once the bubble burst and they returned to their senses, they moved collectively to repair their balance sheets, as they should have.

In this type of recession, there is no reason for deficit-reduction efforts to succeed until the cause of those deficits—the damage to private balance sheets—is removed. If the government pursues fiscal consolidation during this period, the unborrowed savings of the private sector will increase, leading to further economic weakness. In that case the fiscal deficit may actually *increase*, as happened in Japan in 1997.

When the deficit is of this type, it is not particularly meaningful to talk about a misallocation of resources because if the government did not utilize those resources, they would simply go unemployed. And unemployment is the worst form of resource allocation.

How does one distinguish between the two varieties of fiscal deficit? The most convenient indicator outside the Eurozone is government bond yields. Other conditions being equal, a fiscal deficit that arises because of government mismanagement will send bond yields higher, while a deficit resulting from mismanagement in the private sector will push yields lower. The fact that—with the exception of a few countries in the Eurozone—government bond yields have fallen to historic lows following the bubble's collapse demonstrates that the fiscal deficits in these countries were caused by errors in the private sector.

Fiscal Deficits Must Be Viewed Relative to Private Savings

The fact that businesses and households allowed the bubble to form and expand also demonstrates that the private sector is not always a more efficient allocator of resources than the government. In some cases, in fact, it may behave far more irresponsibly than any government. But economists—pointed exceptions including Hyman Minsky and Japan's Seki Obata[2]—have not seriously addressed the problem of asset bubbles. They continue to assume that the private sector always behaves correctly and that all fiscal deficits are bad.

As a result of this predisposition, most of the debate surrounding fiscal deficits has consisted of asking (1) how to minimize the deficit and (2) if it is in fact a necessary evil, whether the private sector has adequate savings to finance it. In other words, the policy debate always begins with the *size* of the deficit and how to reduce or finance what is by definition undesirable borrowing.

National policy debates regarding fiscal deficits have almost never asked how large a deficit must be to return unborrowed private savings to the economy's income stream. Because the vast majority of economists today assume the private sector always allocates resources efficiently and seeks to borrow money to maximize profits, they cannot conceive of a situation in which the private sector wants to minimize debt at a time of zero interest rates. Nor can they envision a fiscal deficit resulting from private sector mismanagement during a bubble.

It is this mindset that has created a world in which many people know the size of their nation's fiscal deficit or public debt, but only a fraction of a percent know how much the private sector is saving. Most have never seen that number nor even heard someone else mention it.

Many Spaniards and most people outside Spain with an interest in the nation's economy know the Spanish government is running a fiscal deficit worth 7.1 percent of GDP, but few are aware that Spain's private sector is saving 8.6 percent of GDP.

This ignorance of private sector savings is not a problem when the economy is not in a balance sheet recession and the private sector is investing its savings in textbook fashion. But it becomes a major problem in a balance sheet recession when the private sector as a group starts saving heavily

---

[2] Seki Obata, *Subete no Keizai wa Baburu ni Tsujiru* (Kobunsha: Tokyo, 2008).

in spite of zero interest rates. However, economists who never envisioned such a scenario continue to ignore the size and ramifications of excessive private savings, focusing instead on the size of fiscal deficits and arguing for deficit-reduction efforts.

The question of whether a fiscal deficit is too large can only be answered in the context of private savings. Clamoring about the size of a deficit without knowing how much the private sector is saving makes no sense. If a government is running a fiscal deficit of 6 percent of GDP at a time when the private sector is saving 12 percent of GDP, the economy will fall into a deflationary spiral in which GDP contracts by 6 percent a year unless the difference can be made up with exports (that is, foreign borrowings). In that case, a fiscal deficit of 6 percent of GDP is actually too small to stabilize the economy, yet it would typically prompt economists and the media to call for deficit reduction—as happened in Japan in so many occasions. But if the private sector is saving more than 6 percent of GDP a year, the economy will not stabilize unless the government runs an even larger deficit.

This problem is particularly acute in the Eurozone where the Maastricht Treaty makes no allowance for balance sheet recessions. Chapter 5 will discuss this issue in greater detail, but the Treaty prohibits member countries from running fiscal deficits in excess of 3 percent of GDP, and the "fiscal compact" adopted in 2011 mandates various penalties in an attempt to strengthen enforcement of that cap. The problem is that private sectors in many Eurozone nations have been saving far in excess of 3 percent of GDP since 2008. Figure 1.18 shows what has been happening to the financial balance of private sector as a whole (households + nonfinancial corporations + financial institutions) in four Eurozone countries and the United Kingdom. It indicates that except for the United Kingdom recently, the private sectors of the other four Eurozone countries have been saving far more than the size of their budget deficits, even at near-zero interest rates. And all have fallen into destructive balance sheet recessions because the Treaty prevented the Eurozone governments from administering the only medicine that works in this kind of recession—fiscal stimulus. In the United Kingdom, it was the deliberate choice of the Cameron government not to put in the fiscal stimulus that led to its double-dip recession in 2011.

Consequences of Leaving Things Up to the Market in a Balance Sheet Recession

Many argue that instead of trying to support the economy with fiscal stimulus, the government should allow it to fall as far as it wants to fall. Wiping out distressed and zombie businesses, banks, and households, they say, will clean up the economy and hasten the eventual recovery.

FIGURE 1.18 Europe in Balance Sheet Recession: Eurozone Private Sector Savings Are Greater Than Their Governments' Fiscal Deficits

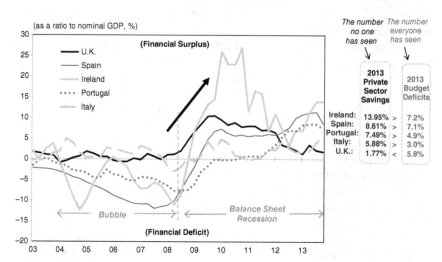

*Private Sector = Household Sector + Nonfinancial Corporate Sector + Financial Sector. *Note:* All entries are four-quarter moving averages. For the latest figures, four-quarter averages ending in 2013 Q4 are used. Budget deficits in Euro area in 2013 are from Apr. 23, 2014, release by Eurostat.

Sources: Eurostat; Office for National Statistics UK; Banco de España, National Statistics Institute, Spain; The Central Bank of Ireland, Central Statistics Office Ireland; Banco de Portugal; Banca d'Italia and Italian National Institute of Statistics.

In economics this is often referred to as the Austrian school, and it was espoused by many in Europe and the United States in the wake of the bankruptcy of Lehman Brothers and the global financial crisis (GFC). Most of its proponents were either university academics with ironclad job security or managers of so-called vulture funds seeking to acquire distressed assets for a song. In other words, they would either be unaffected by or would actually benefit from the policies they were advocating. But implementing such policies during a balance sheet recession would cause tremendous damage to the economy.

That was proved beyond the shadow of a doubt by Herbert Hoover's Treasury secretary, Andrew Mellon, who endorsed such policies with the famous words, "Liquidate labor, liquidate stocks, liquidate the farmers, liquidate real estate ... it will purge the rottenness out of the system.... Values will be adjusted, and enterprising people will pick up the wrecks...." His approach caused U.S. GNP to plunge 46 percent from the 1929 peak and pushed urban unemployment up to 50 percent by 1933. Not even

Roosevelt's New Deal was sufficient to drag the U.S. economy out of the resulting morass; it took the astronomical fiscal stimulus necessitated by World War II to do that.

Even with these two massive doses of fiscal stimulus and additional military spending for the Korean conflict, it was not until 1959, nearly 30 years after the New York stock market crash, that U.S. interest rates returned to normal—that is, to the average level of the 1920s. In other words, it took that long for the private sector to regain its willingness to borrow.

Mellon's approach will not work during a balance sheet recession because the problem is far too big. If those whose balance sheets were impaired as a result of mistakes made during the bubble represent only a small portion of the broader economy, the Austrian approach is not only possible but may be preferable in certain cases—preferable in the sense that if those who participated in the bubble are punished, they are less likely to repeat their mistakes in the future.

For this approach to work, however, it is essential that only a small fraction of the economy be involved in the bubble. This group must be small enough that if they all went under, the economy would be capable of absorbing the loss and moving forward. If 5 percent are in trouble and the remaining 95 percent are healthy, the latter group should survive and return to health even if the 5 percent are removed in a surgical strike.

But if the ratios are reversed, with 95 percent in the distressed category and just 5 percent in the healthy group, this sort of approach would be entirely counterproductive.

The reason, once again, is fallacy-of-composition problems. If only one person liquidates his bad assets, the sale of those assets on the market is unlikely to create any problems. But if everyone does so at the same time, there will be no buyers. Asset prices will plunge, reducing the value of both the assets they had planned to sell and the assets that are still in their possession, further undermining their balance sheets. A nationwide drop in asset prices would also affect the balance sheets of potential buyers, drastically reducing their number.

Thus we can see the Austrian approach is valid only in cases where the distressed portion of the economy is quite small or in which the country itself is small and surrounded by foreign investors able and willing to buy its assets. If the economy is small enough that a sharp devaluation of the currency would not invite severe criticism from neighboring nations, temporary economic weakness caused by the surgical removal of bubble participants could probably be addressed to some extent by a devaluation and a corresponding rise in exports.

The financial crisis that occurred in the early 1990s in Nordic countries was quickly dealt with by national authorities. But that was possible only because a steep decline in the value of local currencies boosted external demand enough to offset the decline in domestic demand. Riksbank governor Stefan Ingves said the sharp currency devaluation made things much easier for policymakers in the region.[3]

But when a significant portion of the domestic economy is caught up in the problems, or when the nation itself is fairly large, the use of Austrian methods can trigger a national or even a global depression as it did in the 1930s.

GFC Triggered by Insistence on Market Principles

Further proof of this was recently provided by the collapse of Lehman Brothers and the GFC that followed. In September 2008, in a meeting held at the New York Fed just before Lehman Brothers went under, U.S. Treasury secretary Hank Paulson declared that the government would not use taxpayer money to bail out the firm and that its fate would be left up to the market. Within 24 hours of that announcement the GFC had begun. Paulson, having insisted on the application of market principles in this case, was forced to come up with a plan to rescue insurer AIG on the very afternoon of the day that Lehman failed, and a month later he had to persuade taxpayers' representatives in Congress to provide $700 billion in aid for the financial industry under the Troubled Assets Relief Program (TARP).

The decision to allow Lehman to fail had such massive consequences because so many other Western financial institutions were suffering from identical problems.

Most financial institutions at that time owned large amounts of collateralized debt obligations (CDOs) containing subprime mortgages, whose value had plunged. Fearing more failures, institutions became increasingly unwilling to lend to each other, which almost caused the interbank market to freeze up. Lehman's collapse also forced other firms with similar problems to rush en masse to protect themselves by building up cash reserves. Consequently, they stopped lending money to nonfinancial corporations and individuals. The resulting shutdown of the financial system was what triggered the synchronous GFC.

If Lehman had been the only firm holding toxic CDOs—that is, if 5 percent of the economy was distressed and 95 percent was sound—applying market principles and allowing the investment bank to fail would probably not have sparked a global crisis. But in September 2008 those ratios were

---

[3] "Kensho Kiki wa Sattaka: Ri-man shokku 5 nen (14) Oshu ni Seiji no Fusakui, Ginko Kyusai, Kokka Shizumeru" *Nihon Keizai Shimbun,* December 1, 2013, p. 11.

reversed, with most Western financial institutions facing the same problems. Allowing one firm to go under caused the rest to rush to protect themselves, and the broader financial system experienced massive fallacy-of-composition problems.

Volcker Understood Systemic Crises

One man who understood this difference between the 5 percent and the 95 percent from the start and who used that understanding to rescue the global economy and financial system was former Federal Reserve chairman Paul Volcker. The U.S. financial system stood at the brink of complete collapse in August 1982, which may come as news to some readers.

The trigger was the Latin American debt crisis, which began when Mexico defaulted on its international obligations that month. Once bankers realized Mexico was in trouble, the contagion spread almost instantly throughout Latin America, affecting such countries as Argentina, Brazil, Chile, and Venezuela. Most leading U.S. banks that had lent heavily to the region suddenly found themselves facing technical insolvency.

Fortunately for both the United States and the world, Mr. Volcker understood from the outset that this was a problem affecting the 95 percent and not the 5 percent. Starting the Friday that Mexico defaulted, he announced a series of measures that successfully prevented the crisis from spreading to the United States or the global economy.

I remember the events of August 1982 well because I was in the thick of it as an economist at the New York Fed in charge of eurodollar syndicated loans, the principle vehicle by which American banks lent to Latin American countries. What I remember most clearly is how the Fed's attitude toward U.S. banks changed overnight. Until that Friday we had admonished U.S. lenders to reduce their exposure to these countries with their shaky economic fundamentals and military dictatorships. The New York Fed had been issuing these warnings for more than three years starting in 1979, but they had been completely ignored by U.S. banks.

But the day that Mexico validated our fears by defaulting, Mr. Volcker, who was at the Board in Washington, D.C., placed a call to the New York Fed and told us to make sure that not a single U.S. bank with exposure of more than one million dollars to Mexico pulled out of the country.

This marked a complete reversal of policy from a day earlier, when we were demanding that U.S. lenders reduce their exposure to Mexico. The Fed chairman, who had discovered that morning that Mexico was bankrupt, was effectively telling us to ask U.S. banks to continue lending to it. At first we were shocked by this directive, but we quickly realized this was a problem affecting the 95 percent and not the 5 percent, and we began asking banks to keep lending to Mexico. It was only because of Volcker's sudden change of course that the Latin American debt crisis never caused any major problems and was eventually resolved without having to ask Congress for a taxpayer bailout.

Although the resolution process took more than 10 years, there was no credit crunch, and the vast majority of Americans were completely unaware that they were in the midst of a massive financial crisis that had left most of the large U.S. banks technically insolvent. Because neither Congress nor the media knew of nor made a big fuss over the problems, even many financial "experts," including academics, know very little about this crisis, which occurred in 1982. That only underscores the speed and validity of Mr. Volcker's response to the crisis and reminds us that there is one kind of approach for problems affecting the 5 percent and another for problems affecting the 95 percent.

Little to Be Gained from Bashing Those Who Have Already Come to Their Senses

The dichotomy between a 5 percent problem and a 95 percent problem is also the dichotomy between a mistake made by a handful of people and one made by the vast majority of people. If only a small group acted in error, they can rightfully be blamed for choosing the wrong path despite having other alternatives. But when 95 percent have made the same mistake, punishing them can shake society to its very foundations. All we can do is say the public made a collective error, hope it learns from the experience, and try to make sure the 5 percent who foresaw what was coming become leaders of society.

The very fact the economy is in a balance sheet recession is proof that people have come to their senses and acknowledged that they were chasing unsustainable asset prices. They would not be deleveraging if they thought bubble-peak prices were coming back soon. There is little to be gained from taking to task people who are aware of their mistakes and are trying to correct their behavior. And if the government stands by and does nothing as the economy falls into a deflationary spiral, even those who did not participate in the bubble will suffer tremendously.

The only people with the right to make the Austrian "liquidate!" argument are those who publicly warned in advance that the economy was in a dangerous bubble. Those who did not—and this includes well-known economists and pundits—did not have a correct understanding of the economy and to that extent are part of the problem and not part of the solution. Such individuals have no right to proclaim smugly that the economy should be allowed to fall until it can fall no further. If anything, these individuals should be "liquidated" from their teaching positions until they have the correct model of the economy in their heads.

Recovery from Balance Sheet Recession Takes Time

Rescuing everyone takes time. In the Latin American debt crisis, it took more than 10 years before U.S. banks were truly healthy again. When the problem affects the majority of society, the burden cannot be shifted to another group—the only option is to wait for the entire society to get better. If the government decides to waive all debt for insolvent businesses and households, for example, the problem merely shifts to the entities that lent them the money, that is, banks and depositors.

In a balance sheet recession, the only option is to use fresh *flows* of savings to slowly repair balance sheets burdened by the *stock* of excessive debt. The greater the damage to balance sheets, the more time it takes to clean them up. If a company has a ¥10 billion hole in its balance sheet and can generate ¥2 billion a year in cash flow that can be used to pay down debt, for example, the repair process will take five years.

But as more firms embark on this process and start using a majority of their free cash flows to pay down debt, the recession worsens, squeezing cash flow and leading to further declines in the asset prices that triggered the recession in the first place. That is why the government—which is outside the fallacy-of-composition problems—has to proactively take the other side of the bet, so to speak, from the private sector and prevent a vicious cycle.

If the government makes the mistake of opting for fiscal consolidation, a recession that people expected would end in two to three years—like Japan's in 1997—may persist for seven years, or 10. And if the Austrian approach is adopted under such conditions, the balance sheets of borrowers and lenders alike will collapse. Recovery will then require either astronomical fiscal stimulus or capital inflows from the sale of assets to foreigners.

Forward Guidance Important for Fiscal as Well as Monetary Policy

Much attention has focused on the importance of forward guidance in the monetary policy arena over the past few years. By announcing in advance that it will not raise interest rates for a specified period of time, the central bank reassures households and businesses and tries to persuade them to engage in the consumption or investment they had given up on because of concerns about an eventual rise in interest rates. This also represents the final hope for monetary policymakers when interest rates have already been lowered to zero and the limitations of quantitative easing are quickly becoming apparent. As the Fed starts to wind down its QE program, policymakers hope that presenting a worried bond market with forward guidance—that is, pledging not to raise interest rates until some point in the future—will help to prevent turmoil.

Forward guidance for monetary policy will be discussed in detail in Chapter 2, but for now let it be said that this concept also applies to fiscal policy. After all, the question of how long a government will continue to support the economy with fiscal policy has a major bearing on the behavior of businesses and households being forced to undertake balance sheet adjustments.

Assume, for example, that the government announces it will continue to support the economy with fiscal policy this year and next but will embark on a program of fiscal consolidation after two years in an attempt to halve the fiscal deficit four years from now. People expecting their own balance sheet repairs to take another five years must find ways to protect themselves given the likely hit to the economy after the first two.

They might lose their jobs when the economy starts to weaken in the third year, or asset prices could fall further, making more balance sheet repairs necessary. The proper response for businesses and households would then be to scale back consumption or investment and boost savings during the first two years, which will undermine the effectiveness of the government's fiscal stimulus.

And if the economy actually does weaken three years from now, incomes will fall, asset prices will slide, and the originally anticipated five-year adjustment period will be stretched out to seven years, or perhaps 10. Not only will the recession be prolonged, but the cumulative fiscal deficit will increase. This is why inappropriate forward guidance on fiscal policy has significant adverse implications for both the government and the private sector during balance sheet recessions.

People will be much more confident about the future if the government pledges to support the economy with fiscal stimulus for five years, 10 years, or however many years it takes, urges the private sector to focus on cleaning up its balance sheet, and promises that repairs to the public balance sheet will be undertaken only after the private sector finishes its adjustments. That reduces the likelihood of further deterioration in the economy, which in turn lowers the possibility of a sharp fall in asset prices. People are also less likely to worry about losing their jobs.

In this case, the balance sheet adjustments initially expected to take five years might actually be completed on schedule. In that case, people can start thinking about what they should do five years from now today, which removes a large source of uncertainty from their lives and has positive implications for the economy.

In short, forward guidance on fiscal policy can have a tremendous impact during a balance sheet recession. Unfortunately, few policymakers—including those who recognize the risks posed by a balance sheet recession—understand this and put it into practice.

Even Fed chairman Ben Bernanke, who is well aware of the risks entailed by a balance sheet recession and issued strong warnings against premature fiscal consolidation in the phrase "fiscal cliff," continues to say that fiscal consolidation will be required over the longer run. This may seem like the right thing and the responsible thing to say, but it can adversely affect the economy if the "short term" envisioned by Mr. Bernanke is shorter than the time people think it will take them to address their balance sheet problems.

The pledge to halve the deficit in four years was actually made by President Obama when he unveiled his first economic package soon after being inaugurated in 2009. While this $787 billion fiscal stimulus was the right response to the circumstances in which the United States found itself following the Lehman collapse and the GFC, pledging to halve the deficit in four years was entirely counterproductive, since the U.S. economic recovery took far longer than anticipated by the White House. When fighting for re-election in 2012, President Obama was criticized repeatedly by his Republican opponent, Mitt Romney, for having failed to carry through on this pledge. As a result the contest was much closer than it might have been otherwise.

Fiscal Consolidation: Better Too Late Than Too Early

That begs the question of how long the government should support the economy with fiscal stimulus. Here we encounter a major technical problem. Because balance sheet recessions are so rare, there is little statistical data showing how much time an economy needs to recover from a balance sheet recession of a given severity. If there were numerous past instances of balance sheet recessions and statistical analysis showed a certain amount of time was generally required to repair the damage from the loss of a certain amount of national wealth following a burst bubble, the government would have a basis for saying when it would commence deficit-reduction efforts. But as yet there are no such data.

With no past data to rely on, governments are likely to take an overly optimistic view of the situation, partly for political reasons, which causes people facing balance sheet problems to suspect the government does not understand their problems. That, in turn, may prompt them to become even more cautious and pessimistic about the future.

How should the government deal with the uncertainty surrounding the time needed for balance sheet repairs? Simply put, it needs to err in the direction that will minimize costs in the event it is wrong.

In other words, the losses resulting from ending fiscal stimulus too soon should be compared with those resulting from ending it too late, and the government should choose the option resulting in the smaller loss. In practice, this means comparing the impact of discontinuing fiscal stimulus while the economy is still in a balance sheet recession with that of continuing it even after the recession is over.

In the first case, the economy will fall into a deflationary spiral, with income contracting from ¥1,000 to ¥900, from ¥900 to ¥810, and so on as the economy slips into a double-dip recession. The number of unemployed will rise sharply, asset prices will drop further, and ultimately the balance sheet recession will last far longer than initially anticipated. This is the sort of tragic outcome that followed premature attempts to reduce the deficit by Japan in 1997 and by the United States in 1937.

In the second instance, where fiscal stimulus is continued ever after the recession ends, the government continues to run large fiscal deficits in spite of the fact that the private sector is now trying to borrow money. The result in this case is inflation, higher interest rates, the crowding out of private investment, and the inefficient allocation of resources.

The damage in the former scenario is clearly far greater than in the latter. In the first case, the economy is plunged into a severe deflationary spiral accompanied by a sharp rise in unemployment. In the second instance, the worst-case scenario entails stagflation and less-than-ideal GDP growth rates, but no mass unemployment or poverty.

In practice, people forced to pay down debt because of balance sheet problems tend to experience a kind of debt-related trauma that acts as a psychological block to borrowing even after they have cleaned up their balance sheets. This aversion to debt, which is discussed in more detail in Chapter 4, is one of the problems that appears when an economy emerges from a balance sheet recession. And because of it the post-recession recovery in private loan demand is likely to be modest at best. The flip side to this is that the negative impact of any fiscal stimulus administered by the government in the recession's aftermath is also likely to be limited.

The above should make it clear that the damage from premature fiscal consolidation during a balance sheet recession is far more severe than the damage due to fiscal consolidation that comes too late. If the authorities are to be wrong, they should err on the side of ending fiscal consolidation too late rather than too early.

It was in 2011 that Ben Bernanke realized the risk of a delayed recovery and first mentioned forward guidance in the context of monetary policy. Initially he pledged not to raise rates until 2013. As he came to a better understanding of the severity of the balance sheet problem, that threshold was moved back to 2014, and then to 2015.

These changes in the Fed's forward guidance for monetary policy are evidence of the authorities' lack of confidence in their estimates of the time needed for the private sector to repair its balance sheet. If they are unsure, fiscal stimulus should also be continued until 2015 at the earliest.

By pledging to begin raising rates in 2015, the Fed is saying it will have taken eight years for the U.S. economy to return to a normal footing from the peak of the housing bubble in 2007. In effect, it is acknowledging that a long time will be needed for the United States to pull out of its balance sheet recession. This is in sharp contrast to 2008, when U.S. policymakers and private opinion leaders alike were boasting the economy would be back to normal in two to three years because the United States would not repeat Japan's mistakes. Now they understand there are no policy shortcuts in a world of balance sheet recessions.

Three Points to Consider Regarding Costs for Future Generations

Another question that always comes up concerns Japan's large public debt—which currently stands at some 240 percent of GDP—and the burden it will place on future generations. Even those who understand the effectiveness of fiscal stimulus in treating a balance sheet recession hesitate to support it when told it may entail large costs for future generations. But that sort of hesitation is precisely why Japan's balance sheet recession lasted for more than 20 years.

While this concern about the cost to future generations is understandable, three things need to be kept in mind. First, there is no threshold for predicting at what point fiscal deficits will result in critical damage to an economy. Kenneth Rogoff and Carmen Reinhart (2011) argued that problems start to emerge when public debt exceeds 90 percent of GDP, but their analysis draws no distinction between balance sheet recessions, which are a borrower-side problem, and financial crises, which are a lender-side problem. Questions have also emerged about their methodology.

The United Kingdom had public debt equal to 250 percent of GDP in 1945, but that did not cause the nation to vanish from the global economic landscape. Had the British people refused to build more Spitfire fighters and Avro Lancaster bombers because of deficit concerns, Britain itself would have disappeared from the map and become part of Hitler's Third Reich. The public debt grew as large as it did because the nation had committed itself to defeating Hitler, and that was clearly the right decision.

A balance sheet recession represents the aftermath of major blunders made by the private sector during an asset price bubble, and the price for treating the resulting injury is never small. But at the same time, it will take decades—or longer—for the next balance sheet recession of this magnitude to appear because people who have been caught up in one bubble will not make the same mistake again. The next balance sheet recession will not occur until people who experienced the last one have left this world, which gives the government plenty of time to put its fiscal house in order. Ten or 20 years may not be sufficient for Japan to reduce its debt to sustainable levels, but three or four decades should be enough if the deficit reduction policies are accompanied by proper growth enhancing measures. This point is discussed further in the section on Abenomics in Chapter 4.

Following a recovery from a balance sheet recession, any cyclical swings in the economy should be addressed using monetary policy, which regains its effectiveness once the private sector resumes borrowing.

A second point to keep in mind is that the legacy of fiscal stimulus for future generations includes positive elements—such as a sound economy— as well as negative ones like a higher public debt. It would be far preferable for a future generation to inherit an economy that is recovering because adequate treatment had been provided—even if that meant a large increase in the public debt—than to receive one that had no added debt but was on the verge of collapse because it was still bleeding from an open wound.

To better understand this point, consider the Great Depression in the United States. We will call people born before 1933 Generation A (the current generation) and those born subsequently Generation B (future generations). When Generation A confronted a severe balance sheet recession, Herbert Hoover rejected the use of fiscal stimulus to support economic activity. Because the government refused to increase fiscal expenditures, it did not leave a heavy debt burden for the next generation (the budget deficit actually increased in 1932, Hoover's last year in office, because of higher government expenditures, but for the purposes of this argument it will be assumed that no debt was left behind). In return, Generation A bequeathed to Generation B an economy that was in the midst of the Great Depression. The nationwide unemployment rate was more than 25 percent—and easily exceeded 50 percent in urban areas—and GNP had fallen to half of the 1929 peak.

To treat this gaping wound Generation B was forced to engage in massive public works spending that started with the New Deal. The fiscal deficit eventually grew to more than 30 percent of GNP in 1944. During the Great Depression, poverty prevented millions of young people from going to school and forced them to look for work instead. The life plans of these young people—the "next generation"—were effectively destroyed by the policy decisions of the Hoover administration with its insistence on balanced budgets. Without World War II and the massive fiscal expenditures it entailed, the Great Depression might have dragged on even longer, destroying educational and vocational opportunities for subsequent generations. The ultimate burden borne by Generation B would almost certainly have been smaller and less painful if Generation A had prevented the wound from widening by using fiscal stimulus to sustain economic activity at around 1929 levels, just as Japan did 60 years later. Having to redeem government bonds issued by Generation A would have been a far better outcome if those fiscal outlays had prevented an economic collapse.

Japan Had a Shot at Full Recovery in 1996 . . .

A third point to keep in mind is that attempts to reduce the fiscal deficit in a balance sheet recession are unlikely to succeed. Fiscal expenditures are the only thing preventing such an economy from falling into a deflationary spiral, and once the government abandons that role the risk is that the economy will suddenly collapse, as it did in the United States in 1937 and in Japan in 1997. Tax revenues will then plummet, which may push the deficit higher in spite of the government's intentions.

In 1996, the year before the Hashimoto government embarked on its ill-fated deficit-reduction program, Japan posted G7-leading GDP growth of 4.4 percent in real terms. Asset strippers from New York and overseas Chinese investors from Hong Kong and elsewhere were visiting Tokyo late that year in search of commercial real estate deals. They were drawn by the fact that Japanese real estate prices had plunged while rents had remained fairly stable, resulting in yields that were attractive on a global basis. Had the government not embarked on fiscal consolidation in 1997, the previous year's GDP momentum might well have continued while domestic asset prices bottomed on buying by foreign investors.

In the event, however, the Hashimoto government's tax hikes and spending cuts caused the economy to buckle. Output shrank for five straight quarters, preventing foreign investors from doing due diligence on the investment properties they were considering. In this process, the potential buyer carefully estimates a property's future revenues and costs in a bid to determine whether the investment is worth making. The economic meltdown made it impossible for investors to project future revenue streams, effectively preventing them from doing their due diligence. The flight of these foreign investors from Japan coincided with the disastrous economic slump to spur a renewed decline in asset prices. In the end, commercial real estate fell another 53 percent from the levels of 1997, striking a huge blow to private sector balance sheets across the country.

A look at the land price graph in Figure 1.12 shows a clear change in the trend around 1997. Real estate prices in 1997 were down sharply from the peak, but as Figure 1.12 illustrates they were still at the level of 1985, a year before the bubble began. This means businesses and households that had not participated in the bubble were largely unaffected. Had land prices stabilized there, most Japanese businesses would have been able to absorb the associated losses and still engage in forward-looking activity. In effect, they would simply have given back the paper gains accumulated during the bubble years.

But the 53 percent fall in land prices from 1997 levels took property prices back to where they had been in 1973. The vast majority of Japan's private sector—the only exception being debt-free businesses and households—now faced major balance sheet problems.

If Japan's "Generation A" had not opted for fiscal consolidation in 1997, Generation B would have enjoyed a higher standard of living with smaller fiscal deficits. Japan's fiscal deficits could well have remained around the 1996 level of ¥22 trillion, in which case the cumulative debt taken on by the government starting in 1997 would have been at least ¥100 trillion less than it is today as shown in Figure 1.17. Moreover, the economy might have been far healthier and stronger than it is today. Were it not for this policy misstep in 1997, the Japanese economy might have fully emerged from the balance sheet recession around 2000. In that sense, the problems Japan faced after 1997 were—like those of the United States after its premature attempt at deficit reduction in 1937—entirely unnecessary.

Proponents of fiscal consolidation always warn against leaving loans for our children to repay, but the example above demonstrates that attempts to reduce the fiscal deficit during a balance sheet recession are only likely to enfeeble the economy and may actually increase the deficit.

Economists have had many debates on fiscal deficits, but few of these debates have considered the health of the economy left to the next generation. Not surprisingly, their conclusion is almost always biased in favor of reducing deficits. The glaring absence of balance sheet recessions from orthodox economics has also made economists reluctant to recommend the one medicine that can treat this kind of recession—fiscal stimulus.

Conflation of Balance Sheet and Structural Problems Extends Recession

When an economy does not respond to standard monetary accommodation and fiscal stimulus is unable to prime the pump, many pundits will blame structural problems and argue that structural reforms are needed. Balance sheet recessions are often confused with structural problems because neither responds to traditional macroeconomic policies. As a result, economists and the media tend to attribute what are actually balance sheet recessions to structural problems. They do so because there has been so much discussion of structural problems since the Reagan and Thatcher era of the 1980s, while until recently only a handful of economists outside Japan had ever heard of balance sheet problems. There is consequently a tendency for orthodox economists to blame "structural problems" when standard monetary or fiscal policy fails to produce the expected recovery.

Structural problems were in fact at the root of many of the issues that confronted Reagan and Thatcher in the 1980s: a labor market plagued by frequent strikes, a steady decline in the quality of manufactured products, inflation, trade deficits, and high interest rates. The supply-side reforms they championed were the right response to those conditions.

Their mistake, however, was to view microeconomic structural reforms as being part of macroeconomic policy. The Reagan reforms were initially rolled out as part of an economic package intended to give an immediate jolt to the economy. Reagan famously used the Laffer curve, which illustrates the relationship between tax rates and tax revenues, to argue that if people were given $50 they would quickly spend it and boost the economy in the process. However, the Reagan administration did not realize that microeconomic structural reforms take a decade or even longer to produce results.

It was not until the Clinton era that Reagan's supply-side reforms began to bear fruit. The economy muddled through Reagan's eight years in office and George H.W. Bush's four, and despite major diplomatic triumphs like the end of the Cold War the Republicans were eventually pushed out of the White House by a young Bill Clinton who proclaimed, "It's the economy, stupid!" Clearly, the Republicans' supply-side reforms did not have the anticipated effect on the economy in the short to medium term.

The impact of the Reagan reforms began to be felt during the eight years of the Clinton administration, when the economy picked up along with startup activity, particularly in the IT sector, and long years of budget deficits gave way to fiscal surpluses.

Ryutaro Hashimoto in 1997 repeated Reagan's mistake of treating supply-side reforms as macroeconomic policy, and what is worse, he did so during a balance sheet recession. While he knew fiscal consolidation would take a toll on the economy, he thought the adverse impact could be neutralized by the accompanying structural reforms. The government even released estimates showing how many jobs would be created by the six proposed reforms.

Treasury secretary Lawrence Summers in the United States and I[4] strongly opposed the Hashimoto government's proposals because both of us

---

[4] Richard Koo and Shigeru Fujita, "Zaisei-saiken no Jiki wa Shijo ni Kike: Zaisei-saiken ka Keiki-kaifuku ka" *Shukan Toyo Keizai,* February 8, 1997, pp. 52–59.

remembered the bitter experience of the Reagan administration, which had also argued that supply-side reforms would lift the economy quickly. But in the end we were ignored. The Japanese economy shrank for five straight quarters, tax revenues fell, and Japan's budget deficit actually increased by 72 percent.

The experiences of Japan and the United States should make it clear that structural reforms cannot serve as a substitute for macroeconomic policy. Unfortunately, few understand this or are trying to warn against it. In fact, "structural reforms" sound so appealing to most policymakers and pundits that in the Eurozone, which is suffering from a serious balance sheet recession, the policy debate has focused almost entirely on such reforms while ignoring macroeconomic policy, much like Japan during the Hashimoto and Koizumi administrations.

The Koizumi government completely ignored the fact that Japan was in a balance sheet recession and pushed ahead with the slogan that there could be "no economic recovery without structural reform." But there was to be no recovery *with* structural reform, either. The only thing that increased during the Koizumi era, in the words of one newspaper, were the fees paid to directors at the now-privatized Japan Highway Public Corporation.

The structural reforms championed by German Prime Minister Gerhard Schroeder in the first half of the 2000s under the moniker Agenda 2010 also mistook balance sheet problems for structural problems. The German economy was actually suffering from a serious balance sheet recession following the collapse of the IT bubble in 2000, as will be discussed in Chapter 5. But it was diagnosed as having structural problems because it did not respond to the ECB's monetary easing. Numerous structural reforms failed to lift the economy out of its slump, to the extent that Germany came to be known as the "sick man of Europe." The Japanese authorities in 1997, the German authorities in 2005, and the Eurozone authorities today were unaware that the distressed private sector had become a huge net saver in spite of record low interest rates, and they did not understand the dangers that posed.

Structural problems are of an entirely different nature from balance sheet problems. The former must be addressed with microeconomic reforms in the labor market and elsewhere, while the latter require the continuous application of fiscal stimulus. The problems in an economy suffering balance sheet problems will snowball unless the government quickly and effectively borrows and spends the unborrowed savings of the private sector with fiscal stimulus. Structural problems, in contrast, gradually sap the economy's vitality over an extended period of time.

Many countries today face both kinds of problems. In such cases it is necessary to treat the balance sheet problems first and then move on to the structural issues because the former can destroy the economy very quickly.

Reversing this order can have devastating consequences. Yet few nations, including the European countries, seem to realize they are in a balance sheet recession, and as a result they continue to administer the wrong kind of treatment.

The difference between structural problems and balance sheet problems is like the difference between diabetes and pneumonia. Structural reforms are essentially a means of treating the diabetes. The patient must be kept from getting too much nourishment and must exercise more to achieve long-term improvements in his physical condition. A balance sheet recession, on the other hand, is like pneumonia. Left untreated, it can cause a sudden and dangerous deterioration in the patient's condition. The patient can actually die unless properly looked after in the first three days.

Not only do these two diseases sometimes occur simultaneously, but their treatments are incompatible. A diabetic needs to eat less, while a patient with pneumonia needs sufficient nutrition to fight off the disease. Since the treatments are not only different but also contradictory, the attending physician must decide which to deal with first. The obvious answer is pneumonia, which requires immediate treatment. There will be plenty of time afterwards to attend to the diabetes.

Distinguishing Balance Sheet Recessions from Structural Problems and Financial Crises

How do we distinguish between balance sheet problems and structural problems? Outside of the Eurozone the quickest indicator is interest rates, and particularly the yields on government debt. Interest rates fall sharply in a balance sheet recession, which is triggered by a shortage of borrowers. The lack of borrowers also means slow growth in the money supply and even slower growth in credit. That, together with the shortfall in aggregate demand, means the inflation rate is likely to be much lower in economies suffering from balance sheet recessions than in those suffering from structural problems.

In the Eurozone, however, government bond yields may not always respond correctly for the reasons described in Chapter 5, so they must be employed in combination with the ECB's policy rate and the flow-of-funds data used in this book. When a private sector is running a financial surplus in spite of very low policy or deposit rates, that is a strong indication the economy is in a balance sheet recession.

There will be times, however, when the private sector ends up in financial surplus because bad loan problems have left banks unable to lend. This is a financial crisis, which stems from problems at lenders, as opposed to a balance sheet recession, which is caused by problems on

FIGURE 1.19 Except for Three Occasions, Post-1990 Japanese Banks Prove to Be Willing Lenders

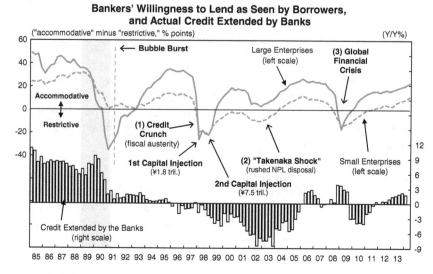

Bankers' Willingness to Lend as Seen by Borrowers, and Actual Credit Extended by Banks

Note: Shaded areas indicate periods of BOJ monetary tightening.

Source: BOJ, Tankan, "Loans and Discounts Outstanding by Sector."

the borrower side. The distinction between these two problems is easy to draw because loan rates (as opposed to policy rates) rise sharply during a financial crisis.

In the case of Japan, the question of whether the main cause of the recession is insufficient demand for funds or insufficient supply is easy to answer, as the Bank of Japan collects information about bank lending attitudes from 10,000 corporate borrowers, including small businesses, in its quarterly *Tankan* survey.

A comparison of these data with bank borrowing by Japanese enterprises (Figure 1.19) shows that banks have been willing lenders except for the brief credit crunch in 1997 and 1998, but businesses chose not to borrow because of balance sheet problems. Other central banks should take this opportunity to launch their own surveys similar to the "lending attitude of financial institutions" question in the BOJ's *Tankan*. These data are extremely useful in determining whether the problem is at the lenders or the borrowers.

Countries that do not periodically carry out a comprehensive survey of borrowers like the *Tankan* need to look at the divergence between the policy rate and bank lending rates, whether foreign banks are entering or leaving the market, corporate bond market trends (since bond issuance can serve as a substitute for bank financing), and surveys of market participants to determine whether the problems are at the borrowers or the lenders.

If the spread between the policy rate and bank lending rate is widening, if foreign banks are expanding their operations, and if bond issuance is increasing, chances are high that the economy is suffering from lender-side problems. But if the spread is narrowing, foreign banks are leaving, and bond issuance is falling, chances are high that the economy is suffering from borrower-side problems, that is, a balance sheet recession.

Democracies Are Ill-Equipped for Dealing with Balance Sheet Recessions

Exacerbating this characteristic of balance sheet recessions—the long time required for recovery—is the fact that democracies are ill-prepared for dealing with such recessions. People must act based on a strong sense of personal responsibility and self-reliance for a democracy to function properly. But this principle runs counter to the use of fiscal stimulus, which involves depending on "big government" and waiting for a recovery. During a balance sheet recession, people with sound balance sheets will vociferously object to fiscal stimulus and with it the implications of big government, especially once they learn that the stimulus will help rescue people and institutions that participated in the bubble.

Moreover, traditional university economics courses do not even discuss the possibility of a balance sheet recession. As a result, most people are not aware that this kind of recession is triggered by fallacy-of-composition problems that occur when individuals begin doing the right and responsible thing by repairing their balance sheets. When the government tries to administer fiscal stimulus under these conditions, the media, pundits, and ordinary citizens who do not understand balance sheet recessions are quick to argue that politicians are wasting taxpayer money on useless projects to win reelection.

For the past 20 years the Japanese media have self-righteously and almost reflexively equated fiscal stimulus with pork-barrel politics. In the United States, members of the Tea Party, the Republican Party splinter group that has become so influential, have effectively staked their political careers on preventing the federal government from undertaking fiscal stimulus. German Chancellor Angela Merkel's decision to ram through a fiscal compact calling on all Eurozone countries to follow Germany's example and pursue fiscal consolidation was based on a similar philosophy.

These responses are rooted in false diagnoses of an economic sickness by doctors who think there is only one kind of recession and only one kind of deficit and who have never heard of balance sheet recessions. Since this type of recession is not covered by economic courses offered at universities, it is difficult to convince these people of the need for fiscal stimulus.

Keynes Also Overlooked Private-Sector Debt Minimization

In 2009 I was invited to Cambridge University to give a speech in an auditorium called Keynes Hall where Keynes himself had taught. I said during the address that "it is almost impossible to maintain fiscal stimulus in a democracy during peacetime." Afterwards an older gentleman who was a professor at the university approached the lectern and said, "In 1940, Keynes stood exactly where you are standing right now and said exactly what you just said." In other words, Keynes faced the same problem we do today when he urged the use of fiscal stimulus during the Great Depression.

After the massive fiscal stimulus associated with World War II led to quick recoveries in the world's economies, Keynes' theories came to be featured in every economics textbook. Unfortunately, as I pointed out in *The Holy Grail of Macroeconomics: Lessons from Japan's Great Recession*, Keynes himself did not realize that the Great Depression had been triggered by the private sector's decision to minimize debt. Keynes was unable to free himself from the traditional assumption that the private sector always seeks to maximize profit, and because he tried to explain the Great Depression within that framework by invoking concepts such as the marginal efficiency of capital, he completely overlooked the possibility that a private sector burdened with balance sheet problems would choose instead to minimize debt. Consequently, his *General Theory*, published in 1936, did not note that the fiscal stimulus Keynes himself was proposing should be implemented only when the private sector was seeking to minimize debt (what I called the "Yin" phase in *The Holy Grail*).

Because this critical condition for fiscal stimulus was omitted, postwar economists assumed that Keynes' fiscal stimulus would be effective in treating all recessions, and from the 1940s to the early 1970s, the United States and other governments used fiscal stimulus to fine-tune their economies. However, their expectations were ultimately betrayed as the 1970s brought inflation, high interest rates, and a misallocation of resources under big government. Keynes' star fell as a result.

This outcome can be explained as follows. The United States and the United Kingdom spent astronomical sums of money to procure armaments during World War II, which quickly enabled the private sector to clean up its balance sheet. During wartime the government placed large orders with firms with technical know-how to supply needed equipment regardless of the state of their balance sheets. A company asked by the government to build 3,000 fighter planes as quickly as possible would need to borrow money and invest in facilities no matter what its balance sheet looked like. Presented with such a large order from the government, however, banks would suddenly be willing to lend, sparking a virtuous cycle. And the cash flow generated by that order would enable the business to clean up its balance sheet. By late 1950, the private sector had also begun to borrow money (what I called the textbook or "Yang" phase).

But while the private sector soon completed its balance sheet repairs, governments maintained an activist fiscal policy long after the war ended, eventually bringing about the undesirable side effects noted above.

I used the word "peacetime" in my speech at Cambridge because during war, when a nation's survival is at stake, no one complains about government spending on armaments or air-raid shelters. There is no danger of getting bogged down in endless debates over how to spend the money either, because the answer to the question during wartime is clear to all involved.

I used the word "democracy" because in an autocratic state, only one person, the dictator, needs to be persuaded in order to both administer and maintain fiscal stimulus. But in a democracy such policies cannot be implemented and maintained during peacetime unless tens of millions of people understand the need for fiscal stimulus.

Adolf Hitler and Franklin Roosevelt were both elected in 1933 when Germany and the United States were in severe balance sheet recessions. The German unemployment rate reached 28 percent that year and U.S. rate was not that far behind at 25 percent. Although both began to address the problem with fiscal stimulus, Roosevelt, worried about the criticisms from deficit hawks, reversed course in 1937, resulting in a serious double-dip recession and unemployment rate increasing to nearly 20 percent again. Hitler, on the other hand, stayed the course and by 1938, German unemployment had fallen to 2 percent. And nothing is worse than a dictator with a wrong agenda having the right economic policy, especially when the democracies around him are held hostage to orthodox policies and remain unable to implement correct policies.

More recently, the Chinese government implemented a 4 trillion RMB fiscal stimulus in November 2008 when it was facing a sharp fall in both domestic asset prices and exports. As a percentage of GDP, the stimulus was more than double the size of President Barak Obama's $787 billion package unleashed three months later. At that time, Western observers were laughing when the Chinese government announced that it was going to maintain 8 percent growth. China's growth soon reached 12 percent in 1Q 2010, and nobody was laughing.

The U.S. government, on the other hand, was extremely cautious with its fiscal stimulus because of the fear that the stimulus package might be criticized for wasting money. As a result, it could not offer the kind of positive jolt its designers had hoped for. The Obama Administration's inability to renew and sustain the fiscal stimulus package due to Republican opposition slowed down the subsequent U.S. recovery in no small way.

I used the word "maintaining" in my speech in Keynes Hall because expectations for (temporary) fiscal stimulus arise whenever a country experiences a major shock (like the Lehman failure and the GFC). At the emergency G20 meeting held in Washington two months after Lehman Brothers collapsed, all 20 nations agreed to administer a dose of fiscal stimulus—a decision attributable in no small part to the efforts of Japanese prime minister Taro Aso. Formerly a corporate executive, Aso was one of the few Japanese politicians who understood from the beginning that Japan was in a balance sheet recession. He knew that fiscal stimulus was the key to maintaining Japanese GDP when the private sector was saving 8 percent of GDP at zero interest rates. And at the G20 meeting he used the graph in Figure 1.14 to tell the leaders of the other 19 countries that Japan was able to maintain its GDP at above the bubble peak for the entire post-bubble period with fiscal stimulus in spite of commercial real estate prices falling 87 percent from the peak to the level of 1973. He argued that the global economic slump triggered by the Lehman failure could be reversed with the application of fiscal stimulus by the entire G20.

The G20 ultimately agreed to and administered fiscal stimulus in 2009, and the global economy staged a V-shaped recovery instead of falling into a depression, as had been feared. In that sense, Japan's experience contributed to the global economic rebound. But as soon as the economy started to show signs of life, deficit hawks took over the G20 policy debate. When a country faces a balance sheet recession in peacetime, expectations for fiscal stimulus pick up when the economy weakens, but as soon as the economy starts to show signs of life there are calls to reduce the deficit. If the government tries to trim the deficit when the private sector is minimizing debt, the economy will weaken again, prompting renewed demands for fiscal stimulus. As a result, fiscal stimulus during a balance sheet recession in peacetime tends to be an on-again, off-again affair that greatly delays the recovery.

Those Who Prevent Crises Never Become Heroes

That Japan was able to maintain GDP at the bubble-era peak for so long in spite of the loss of so much national wealth and a private sector that was collectively paying down debt offers an important lesson. Japan demonstrated that no matter how large the bubble and how extensive the damage to private balance sheets, the continuous administration of fiscal stimulus from the beginning in sufficient quantities can sustain incomes, enabling people to press ahead with balance sheet repairs. This represents a huge improvement over previous bubble collapses, which almost without exception triggered a depression or depression-like conditions that lasted for many years.

The Japanese media, however, did not understand the significance of Aso's contribution in preventing a global depression. Instead, they tried to portray his administration as a caretaker government before the general election scheduled for 2009 and devoted a great deal of coverage to the prime minister's misreading of a single Chinese character in one speech. Partly as a result of such publicity, the LDP was defeated in the election held in August 2009. British prime minister Gordon Brown, another leader who understood what a balance sheet recession was and used fiscal stimulus to address it, was also defeated in his quest for re-election.

It is often said that people who prevent crises never become heroes, and the experience of Aso and Brown bears that out. Hollywood teaches us that for there to be a hero there must first be a crisis. When Aso and Brown, both of whom *prevented* crises, were removed from office, the G20 lost the only people able to explain the need for fiscal stimulus during a balance sheet recession.

Democracy Plus Balance Sheet Recession Equals "Secular Stagnation"

The global fiscal stimulus carried out in 2009 helped stabilize the world's economy. But that very success elicited calls in Japan and elsewhere for orthodox deficit-reduction efforts. And at the Toronto summit in 2010, with Aso and Brown now out of the picture, the G20 leaders agreed on a plan to halve their fiscal deficits in three years—this in spite of the fact that the private sectors in these countries continued to save massively in order to repair their severely damaged balance sheets.

The resulting fiscal retrenchment sent the developed economies into reverse, with the United Kingdom and many parts of Eurozone falling into double-dip recessions. Japan under the new Democratic Party of Japan (DPJ) government, which understood nothing of balance sheet recessions, stagnated as well.

In the United States, however, Fed chairman Ben Bernanke and others soon realized that this agreement had been a mistake. Bernanke kept the United States from pursuing premature fiscal consolidation by coining the expression "fiscal cliff," thereby making it the first country to renege on the agreement. Consequently, the United States—alone among the developed economies—continued to post modest economic growth, while

Japan, the United Kingdom, and continental Europe faced severe economic weakness.

Partly because of subsequent reflection on this error, the pendulum had swung back toward a recognition of the importance of fiscal stimulus by the time the St. Petersburg G20 summit was held in 2013, exactly three years after the Toronto meeting. Even the *Nikkei* ran a front-page story noting that "the official statement expressed the view that the global economy recovery was too weak, and the major economies agreed unanimously to focus on restoring growth instead of reducing fiscal deficits." Although the three years following the Toronto summit were completely wasted from a global economic perspective, at least these countries are now heading in the right direction. The risk remains, however, that this will turn out to be just another phase in an on-again, off-again cycle of fiscal stimulus in a democracy during peacetime.

The above examples show that there is no need to suffer stagnation even if the private sector is minimizing debt if proper policies are put in place, but that democracies are very bad at implementing such policies during peacetime. This predicament will stay with democracies until the general public (the tens of millions) is made aware of the fallacy-of-composition problem called balance sheet recession and how to remedy it. Until then, the far-from-ideal on-again, off-again cycle of fiscal stimulus and the resultant delayed recovery will make people feel as though they are in "secular stagnation."

Appendix to Chapter 1: Summary of Yin and Yang Phases of Economy

The fact that the private sector could be minimizing debt when faced with daunting balance sheet problems suggests that there are at least two phases to an economy, a normal phase where the private sector has a healthy balance sheet and is maximizing profits, and a balance sheet recession phase where it is minimizing debt. I called the former the "Yang" phase and the latter the "Yin" phase in my previous book, *The Holy Grail of Macroeconomics*.[5] I argued there that the Yin phase is the long-overlooked other half of macroeconomics. Readers interested in that discussion are invited to take a look at Chapter 5 of that book. For convenience, charts summarizing that chapter are reproduced here as Figures 1.20 and 1.21.

---

[5] This Yin and Yang cycle is basically similar to what Bank for International Settlements (BIS) calls "financial cycle" in the 2014 Annual Report.

FIGURE 1.20 Contrast between Textbook Economy and Balance Sheet Recession

	Textbook Economy "Yang"	Balance Sheet Recession "Yin"
1) Fundamental driver	Adam Smith's "invisible hand"	Fallacy of composition
2) Private financial condition	Assets > Liabilities	Assets < Liabilities
3) Behavioral principle	Profit maximization	Debt minimization
4) Outcome	Greatest good for greatest number	Depression if left unattended
5) Monetary policy	Effective	Ineffective (liquidity trap)
6) Fiscal policy	Counterproductive (crowding-out)	Effective
7) Prices	Inflationary	Deflationary
8) Interest rates	Normal	Very low
9) Savings	Virtue	Vice (paradox of thrift)
10) Remedy for Banking Crisis a) Localized	Quick NPL disposal Pursue accountability	Normal NPL disposal Pursue accountability
b) Systemic	Slow NPL disposal Fat spread	Slow NPL disposal Gov. capital injection

Source: Richard Koo, *The Holy Grail of Macroeconomics: Lessons from Japan's Great Recession* (Singapore: John Wiley & Sons, 2008, p. 176).

FIGURE 1.21 Yin-Yang Cycle of Bubbles and Balance Sheet Recessions

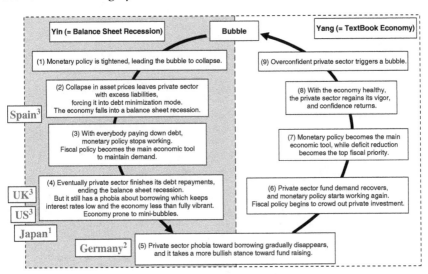

Notes: 1. Recovering from 1990 Heisei bubble. 2. Recovering from 2000 IT bubble. 3. Recovering from 2008 housing bubble.

Source: Richard Koo, *The Holy Grail of Macroeconomics: Lessons from Japan's Great Recession* (Singapore: John Wiley & Sons, 2008, p. 160).

CHAPTER 2

Monetary Policy and the Quantitative Easing Trap

The discussion thus far has focused on fiscal policy during a balance sheet recession, but the authorities have another tool at their disposal: monetary policy. Economics textbooks tell us the government can manage the economy with a combination of monetary and fiscal policy.

High expectations have been placed on monetary accommodation in the wake of the global financial crisis (GFC) in 2008 and again as the first "arrow" of Abenomics, the colloquial term for the Abe administration's economic policy unveiled in Japan in late 2012. Moreover, many economists seriously believe Japan's recession has lasted as long as it has because of bad policy decisions by the Bank of Japan (BOJ). Their emphasis on monetary policy is due to the fact that for the past 30 years the economics profession has emphasized the primacy of monetary policy over fiscal policy, and since the 1970s most of the policies enacted in response to economic fluctuations in nearly all developed economies have been monetary in nature. This led to high expectations for central banks in Japan and the West during the recent GFC.

The world's central banks responded to those expectations in the wake of the Lehman collapse by taking interest rates to zero or near-zero levels in a record amount of time. They also introduced aggressive quantitative easing (QE) programs. Yet their economies remained depressed. In the United States, the money supply and private credit registered only modest growth in spite of negative real interest rates (Figure 1.7). There are also no signs of a pick-up in inflation—U.S. inflation rates actually resumed falling in 2013 even as the Fed supplied massive amounts of liquidity.

More disappointingly, the Fed chairman's mention of the possibility of winding down QE in mid-2013 sparked an "unwarranted" surge in long-term interest rates, to use Bernanke's term. That, in turn, weakened both the U.S. housing market and emerging markets and underlined the danger that winding down QE could create major problems for the economy as it heads toward recovery. This came as a shock to the central banks that had expanded these programs so aggressively over time. The surge in long-term interest rates indicated that while implementing QE only produced minimal benefits, the process of winding down QE could entail serious risks not only for the country in question but also for the global economy, including the emerging markets. I called this risk the "QE Trap."

Monetary Policy Impotent without Demand for Funds

The unprecedented decline in the effectiveness of monetary policy in the Western economies echoes Japan's experience from 1990 onward. From 1995 until Abenomics was unveiled in 2013, monetary policy had virtually no impact in Japan in spite of near-zero interest rates and QE. There was no recovery in the stock market, the real estate market, or the real economy. Japan's asset price bubble during the latter half of the 1980s occurred at a time when the BOJ's official discount rate was 2.5 percent. Yet only a few years later, in February 1993, a policy rate of 2.5 percent did nothing to stimulate the economy or lift asset prices. The BOJ subsequently took interest rates down to zero, but even that had no effect.

What was responsible for the dramatic change in the Japanese economy's response to monetary stimulus after the bubble? In a word, it was the precipitous decline in the number of borrowers as private balance sheets were impaired by the bubble's collapse. Although no economics textbook has ever explicitly said so, the existence of private sector borrowers is a necessary condition for monetary policy to work. Monetary policy loses its effectiveness if this condition is not satisfied.

Ordinarily, if the central bank responds to an overheated economy by raising interest rates, some borrowers will stop borrowing and spending, causing demand to fall. And if the economy turns down, cutting interest rates will increase the number of borrowers, boosting demand when they spend the money they have borrowed.

Since Japan's bubble burst, however, not only did the number of borrowers drop dramatically, but existing borrowers began paying down debt in spite of zero interest rates. They had to pay down debt because the nationwide plunge in asset prices left many of them technically insolvent. And businesses and households struggling to reduce their debt overhang had no interest in borrowing more money no matter how many times the central bank cut rates. There would not be many lenders either, especially when the lenders knew that borrowers were technically insolvent. Monetary policy loses its effectiveness under these conditions.

However, many economists both in Japan and elsewhere did not understand this because orthodox economics had never addressed the shift in private sector behavior from profit maximization to debt minimization due to balance sheet problems. Hence they argued the economy would recover if the BOJ would boost the money supply by providing more liquidity and push for negative real interest rates by adopting high-enough inflation targets. They then put a great deal of pressure on the Bank to do so.

Mechanisms for Money Supply Growth

To understand the proposition that monetary policy stops working when there are no borrowers, it is first necessary to understand the relationship between base money, which is supplied by the central bank, and aggregates such as private credit or the money supply, which indicate how much money is actually available for the private sector to spend. The monetary base consists of the amount of deposits the commercial banks have with the central bank, together with notes and coins in circulation. It is almost entirely under the control of the central bank in the sense that, by selling or buying assets, the bank can control the amount of monetary base in the banking system. Monetary base is also referred as liquidity.

The money supply, which consists mostly of bank deposits, also includes notes and coins in circulation. It is closely monitored by economists because growth in the money supply signifies an increase in the amount of money available for the private sector to spend and therefore provides a boost to the economy and inflation. The private credit is important because when the central bank supplies liquidity, the commercial banks that receive it cannot give away money: they have to lend money for those funds to come out of the banking system and enter the real economy.

Economics textbooks describe the process of money supply growth as follows. It begins with a decision by the central bank—like the Bank of Japan—to supply liquidity to commercial banks. Typically this is done by purchasing government bonds or highly rated corporate debt from those banks. The purchases are paid for when the central bank credits the amount to the accounts of the commercial banks. This increases the monetary base but not money supply, because funds deposited with the central bank are not yet available for businesses and households to spend.

The commercial bank (which we will call Bank A) then tries to lend these funds out to earn interest income. In doing so, it sets aside a portion of the new deposit from the central bank to meet reserve requirements and lends out the remainder. The statutory reserve ratio for commercial banks is set by the authorities and forces banks to keep in reserve a portion of the money entrusted to them as deposits, effectively preventing them from lending out the entire amount. This is done to ensure the bank has enough funds on hand to pay off depositors who want to make withdrawals. When a loan is made, the commercial bank increases the borrower's bank deposit by the amount of the loan and also increases the asset side of its balance sheet by the amount of the new loan. At this point, the money supply and bank lending have both increased. The borrower is then able to use the borrowed funds as she sees fit.

Once the money is spent, the person receiving it deposits the funds in his own bank (which we will call Bank B). When this happens, Bank A withdraws the amount from its deposit with the central bank and transfers it to Bank B's account with the central bank. Bank B then tries to lend out the new deposit after setting aside required reserves.

Money lent out in this fashion is spent by the borrower and deposited in yet another bank by the recipient, and that bank sets aside the necessary reserves and lends out the remainder. Both deposits (= money supply) and loans (= credit) in the banking system continue to increase as this process is repeated, and the process is repeated until the entire amount of liquidity supplied by the central bank has been set aside as reserves.

The amount placed in reserve depends on two factors: the statutory reserve rate, which is set by the banking authorities, and the amount of excess reserves added by the bank itself. If the bank sets aside only the portion required by law, the total increase in deposits will equal the reciprocal of the statutory reserve rate. If the statutory reserve rate is 10 percent, for example, deposits will increase by an amount equal to 10 times (1 divided by 10 percent) the liquidity supplied by the central bank.

The ratio of the money supply to the base money (liquidity) originally injected by the central bank is called the money multiplier. In the previous example, if the entire amount of the initial liquidity injection ended up as required reserves, the money multiplier would be 10.

It should now be clear that at a time of no borrowers, liquidity supplied by the central bank will not increase the money supply because commercial banks will be unable to lend the funds supplied by the central bank. When there are no borrowers, in other words, the money multiplier becomes zero at the margin. And if the private sector collectively starts paying down debt, the money multiplier can actually turn negative.

Businesses and households paying down debt typically withdraw money from their bank accounts and use it to repay the lender. Under ordinary circumstances, that bank would then proceed to lend the money to some other borrower, increasing the new borrower's deposits. Hence there is no net change in the money supply or private credit. But when the private sector as a group begins paying down debt, commercial banks cannot find new borrowers for the money returned by existing borrowers, causing both bank deposits and the money supply to shrink. When there are no borrowers, therefore, debt paydowns cause the money supply to shrink by a nearly equal amount. During the Great Depression, American businesses and households withdrew money from their bank accounts and used it to pay down debt, causing the U.S. money supply to plunge by 33 percent. That tipped the economy into deflation and exacerbated the recession.[1]

When the private sector as a group begins paying down debt, in other words, the money multiplier will turn negative at the margin and the money supply will not grow no matter how much liquidity the central bank injects.

Government Borrowing Drove Money Supply Growth in Japan

Japanese businesses paid down debt for more than a decade starting in the mid-1990s (Figure 1.11). Yet Japan's money supply (M2 + CDs) did not decrease during this period, but actually grew at a rate of 2 percent to 4 percent a year (Figure 1.10). This seemingly contradictory phenomenon is explained by Figure 2.1, which shows the bank borrowers that were responsible for the money supply growth. The graph illustrates changes in Japanese bank balance sheets between 1998, when Japanese companies became net re-payers of debt, and 2007,[2] when their deleveraging stopped. During this period there is a steady increase in bank deposits, which are the chief component of the money supply and represent a liability for banks. An increase in bank liabilities requires a corresponding increase in bank assets. But a look at assets shows that private credit fell heavily as companies began minimizing debt, while lending to the government in the form of government bond ownership increased sharply. In other words, the money supply did not contract even though the private sector was paying down debt because the government was running large fiscal deficits and was borrowing money from the banks to fund those deficits.

Money returns to the banking sector as the private sector pays down debt. Banks try to lend this money out, but when the private sector as a group is paying down debt there are no borrowers. The government, however, is running a deficit that must be financed by issuing debt. Since there are no willing borrowers in the private sector, banks that want to earn interest are forced to buy bonds issued by the government, the sole remaining borrower.

The proceeds of the bond sales are used to fund the construction of roads and bridges, and those expenditures become income for construction

---

[1] The detail of how this happened is explained in Richard Koo, *The Holy Grail of Macroeconomics: Lessons from Japan's Great Recession* (Singapore: John Wiley & Sons, 2008), Chapter 3.

[2] When the ¥200 trillion Japan Post Bank was included in the banking statistics starting in 2003, the BOJ continued to publish the old series alongside the new series but only until 2007.

FIGURE 2.1 Japan's Money Supply Has Been Kept Up by Government Borrowings

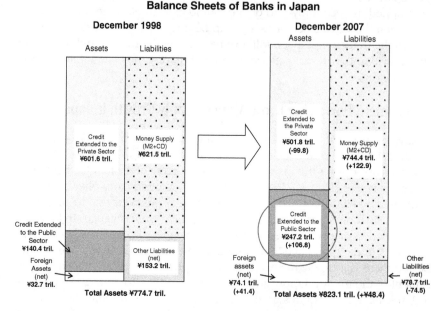

Balance Sheets of Banks in Japan

Source: BOJ, Monetary Survey.

firms and their workers and suppliers. When they deposit the payment from the government in a bank, deposits in the banking system increase. Banks try to lend these deposits out but fail again because the private sector as a whole is still focused on paying down debt, and eventually they are forced to buy bonds issued by the sole remaining borrower, the government. Japan's money supply grew as this process was repeated at banks across Japan.

Economics Dogged by Incorrect Analysis of Great Depression

In that case, why was the BOJ criticized so sharply for saying monetary policy has lost its effectiveness by academics inside and outside Japan starting over a decade ago, leading eventually to the appointment of reflationists like Haruhiko Kuroda and Kikuo Iwata to the Bank's top posts? The answer is that the discipline of economics has been in the clutches of an incorrect theory for the past 20 years.

I was born in 1954, and when I studied economics at the undergraduate and graduate level in the United States in the 1970s, the standard view was that Roosevelt's New Deal policies had rescued the U.S. economy from the Great Depression of the 1930s. Although this was rejected by Milton Friedman and others, the generally accepted view—at least until the mid-1970s—was that fiscal stimulus, symbolized by the New Deal policies, was the main reason for the eventual recovery.

In the 1980s, however, a group led by Christina Romer, professor at UC Berkeley and the first chair of the Council of Economic Advisers during the Obama administration's first term, argued that this interpretation was wrong and that it was actually a change in monetary policy that had pulled the U.S. economy out of the Great Depression. They cited the fact that as the U.S. economy headed toward recovery from 1933 to 1936, the fiscal deficit did not increase substantially as a percentage of gross domestic product (GDP), while the money supply surged sharply higher.[3] Thus began a rewriting of history by a group that eventually counted among its members such academic heavyweights as Ben Bernanke, Paul Krugman, and Jeffrey Sachs.

According to their arguments, some of which had previously been put forth by Milton Friedman, the money supply contracted so sharply between 1929 and 1933 because of Fed policy errors, and that, in turn, was why the Great Depression had been so severe. Furthermore, they said, it was the Fed's change of course in 1933 that prompted a sharp expansion of the money supply and sparked a U.S. recovery. Bernanke, who viewed himself as a disciple of Friedman, sent the older scholar a congratulatory message on his 90th birthday saying, in essence, "You're right, it was the Federal Reserve that was responsible."

In the latter half of the 1990s, just as this view came to dominate U.S. academic circles, the Bank of Japan started arguing that Japan's problems—like the Great Depression—could not be resolved with monetary policy. That sparked a round of BOJ bashing from this group of economists, who insisted the Japanese economy would recover quickly if only the BOJ undertook bold monetary accommodation like the Fed had in 1933. From their perspective, Japan's predicament seemed a perfect opportunity to demonstrate the validity of their arguments.

But their theory, which held that recessions could be overcome with monetary policy alone, contained a major error. The money supply is a bank liability, and for it to grow bank assets must also grow. These academics focused only on trends in the money supply and forgot to analyze the growth on the asset side of banks' balance sheets during the 1930s.

As a result, they overlooked the fact that the only driver of U.S. money supply growth in 1933 and beyond was government borrowing; private credit did not increase at all. In other words, the money supply could not have grown without government borrowing to fund the New Deal.

---

[3] Christina D. Romer, "What Ended the Great Depression," NBER Working Paper 3829, 1991.

Figure 2.2 shows U.S. bank balance sheets at the time. It is clear that lending to the private sector plunged from 1929 to 1933 as the private sector responded to the stock market crash of 1929 by paying down debt, which led directly to a decrease in both bank assets (i.e., lending) and bank liabilities (i.e., deposits).

A look at the period from 1933 to 1936 shows that bank deposits expanded sharply, as noted by Romer, but lending to the private sector with its balance sheet problems did not increase at all. It is lending to the *government* that grew, and that was because the government had to borrow from the private sector to finance the New Deal policies of President Roosevelt.

This was first revealed in Chapter 3 of my previous book, *The Holy Grail of Macroeconomics: Lesson from Japan's Great Recession* (John Wiley & Sons, 2008; original Japanese version published in 2006). This discovery focused attention on balance sheet recession theory in Western academic circles.

Scholars like Bernanke, Krugman, Romer, and Temin who had previously insisted monetary policy had pulled the United States out of the Great Depression began to argue in favor of fiscal stimulus after the above revelation. A paper coauthored by Krugman with Gauti Eggertsson and published in the *The Quarterly Journal of Economics* in 2012 was titled, "Debt, Deleveraging, and the Liquidity Trap: A Fisher-Minsky-Koo Approach." In it the Princeton professor made a strong case for fiscal stimulus during this kind of recession. Of course they also say the central bank should do everything it can, but they no longer argue that monetary policy will be a "game changer" that sparks a quick recovery when the economy is suffering from this type of recession.

In Japan as well, finance minister Taro Aso, who understands the private sector has stopped borrowing because of balance sheet problems, has stated clearly that BOJ monetary policy will not be effective unless the government keeps borrowing and spending until the private sector resumes borrowing. That is why fiscal stimulus constitutes the second "arrow" of Abenomics, as will be discussed in a later chapter.

In Japan, however, only a tiny handful of academic economists understand this point, and the Abe administration's economic adviser, Professor Koichi Hamada, is unfortunately not among them. He actually objected to Aso's statement, noted above, that monetary policy will not work without fiscal policy. Hamada's argument that monetary accommodation will work even without fiscal stimulus is correct if we assume, as orthodox economics does, that the private sector has a healthy balance sheet and always seeks to maximize profits. But this has not been the case in Japan since the bubble collapsed in 1990 or in the West since 2008.

FIGURE 2.2 Post-1933 U.S. Money Supply Growth Made Possible by Roosevelt Administration's New Deal Borrowing

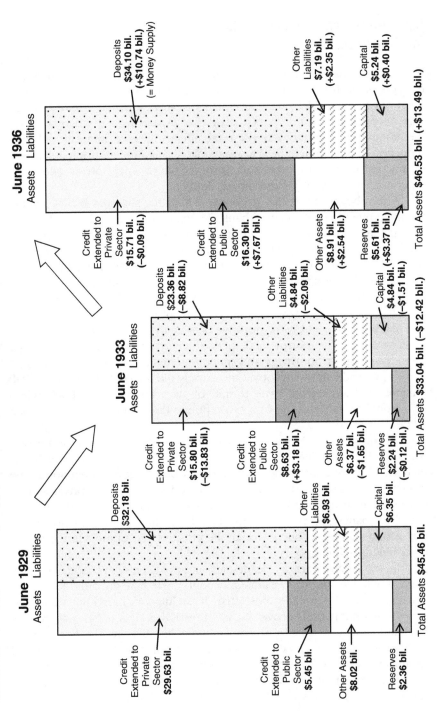

June 1929
Assets   Liabilities

Credit Extended to Private Sector **$29.63 bil.**

Credit Extended to Public Sector **$5.45 bil.**

Other Assets **$8.02 bil.**

Reserves **$2.36 bil.**

Deposits **$32.18 bil.**

Other Liabilities **$6.93 bil.**

Capital **$6.35 bil.**

Total Assets $45.46 bil.

June 1933
Assets   Liabilities

Credit Extended to Private Sector **$15.80 bil. (−$13.83 bil.)**

Credit Extended to Public Sector **$8.63 bil. (+$3.18 bil.)**

Other Assets **$6.37 bil. (−$1.65 bil.)**

Reserves **$2.24 bil. (−$0.12 bil.)**

Deposits **$23.36 bil. (−$8.82 bil.)**

Other Liabilities **$4.84 bil. (−$2.09 bil.)**

Capital **$4.84 bil. (−$1.51 bil.)**

Total Assets $33.04 bil. (−$12.42 bil.)

June 1936
Assets   Liabilities

Credit Extended to Private Sector **$15.71 bil. (−$0.09 bil.)**

Credit Extended to Public Sector **$16.30 bil. (+$7.67 bil.)**

Other Assets **$8.91 bil. (+$2.54 bil.)**

Reserves **$5.61 bil. (+$3.37 bil.)**

Deposits **$34.10 bil. (+$10.74 bil.) (= Money Supply)**

Other Liabilities **$7.19 bil. (+$2.35 bil.)**

Capital **$5.24 bil. (+$0.40 bil.)**

Total Assets $46.53 bil. (+$13.49 bil.)

Source: FRB, "Banking and Monetary Statistics 1914–1941" (1976): pp. 72–79.

Japanese Monetary Policy Has Relied on Fiscal Policy for Past 20 Years

In that sense, the effectiveness of Japan's monetary policy has been largely dependent on fiscal policy for the past 20 years. Private businesses have been paying down debt since around 1998, leaving the government as the sole remaining borrower. An expansion of government borrowing boosts the money supply and by extension the effectiveness of monetary policy. A reduction of government borrowing would shrink money supply regardless of any actions taken by the BOJ. In other words, fiscal policy effectively determines the size of Japan's money supply.

When the private sector experiences balance sheet problems, neither the government nor the central bank can tell businesses and households to stop paying down debt. The private sector, facing a debt overhang, must work down its debt as quickly as possible. And if the government does not respond correctly with fiscal stimulus, the economy will enter the kind of destructive deflationary spiral that the United States experienced from 1929 to 1933, with income falling from $1,000 to $900 to $810 and so on.

There is only one way for the government to arrest this vicious cycle, and that is to do precisely the opposite of what the private sector is doing. In other words, it must borrow and spend the surplus savings that the private sector is no longer borrowing and spending. That is what Japan chose to do in the end. And that is why the money supply did not contract and why GDP remained at bubble-peak levels in spite of the evaporation of ¥1,500 trillion in national wealth and the loss of corporate demand equal to more than 20 percent of GDP.

The only reason Japan did not experience its own Great Depression was that the government continued to borrow and spend. Because banks increased their lending to the government by buying government bonds, the money supply increased and the unborrowed savings of the private sector did not remain trapped in the banking sector. Figures 1.11 and 2.1 show that the Japanese economy has presented a strange new world for ortho-dox economic theory, one in which the effectiveness of monetary policy is determined by fiscal policy.

But the Japanese media, academics, and politicians have largely refused to acknowledge this. The vast majority continue to take the orthodox stance that fiscal stimulus is little more than wasteful pork-barrel spending and that the economy will recover only if the BOJ adopts a more aggressive monetary policy stance. Hence monetary policy became the first "arrow" of Abenomics, as discussed in Chapter 4. But people like Bernanke and Krugman who were formerly the key proponents of this view have changed their tune and are now stressing the importance of fiscal policy in balance sheet recessions and issuing warnings about a fiscal cliff.

A look at developments in the West since 2007 shows there were initially high expectations of monetary policy. My book *The Holy Grail of Macroeconomics* was published in English in April 2008, five months before Lehman Brothers failed. But apart from the Aso administration in Japan, the only party that understood its importance at the time was the Chinese government (a Chinese-language edition was published in November 2008). Many Chinese economists actually read my first English book *Balance Sheet Recession—Japan's Struggle with Uncharted Economics and Its Global Implications*, published in 2003, and were aware of the importance of fiscal policy in such crises. This is part of the reason why China was first among the G20 nations to launch a large-scale fiscal stimulus program in the aftermath of the Lehman bankruptcy.

In the West, meanwhile, academic economists saw the GFC as an opportunity to prove their new theory on the omnipotence of monetary policy. The Fed and the Bank of England slashed interest rates faster than ever before, and within 15 months of Lehman's failure most countries had taken rates down to all-time lows. The speed of their actions was based in part on criticism of the BOJ for taking five years to bring interest rates down to near-zero levels after Japan's bubble collapsed in 1990. (When the BOJ was actually cutting rates from 1990 to 1995, of course, there was not a single person in Japan or anywhere else who criticized it for being too slow to ease policy.)

The Fed and the Bank of England also embarked on massive QE programs around this time. Their policies were based on advice from academic economists who believed the United States had overcome the Great Depression with monetary policy and who argued the central bank could boost economic growth even when interest rates were at zero by buying up assets. The remark by Paul Fisher of Bank of England mentioned in Chapter 1 demonstrates the confidence these economists had in monetary policy at that time.

While these programs do appear to have lowered long-term interest rates in the United States and the United Kingdom by several tens of basis points, these policies delivered a modest economic stimulus at best, even after taking into account the impact of the lower interest rates. Despite an aggressive increase in the amount of Fed-supplied liquidity, private credit—a measure of the amount of money flowing from banks into the private sector—is only 3 percent higher in the United States (Figure 1.7) and is actually 15 percent lower in the United Kingdom (Figure 1.9) than six years ago, when Lehman went under. With so little money coming out of the banking system, the inflation rate has also stayed low or fallen in both countries. These indicators suggest that—just as balance sheet recession theory predicts—the funds supplied under QE remain trapped in the financial system amid a lack of borrowers.

Balance Sheet Recessions Triggered by Borrower-Side Problems, Financial Crises Triggered by Lender-Side Problems

The previous section is not meant to suggest that monetary policy has no role to play after a bubble bursts. On the contrary, monetary policy has a huge role to play. This is because when an asset bubble collapses it can cause two problems: a balance sheet recession, which is a borrower-side problem, and a financial crisis, which is a lender-side problem. A financial crisis erupts when the value of assets owned or held as collateral plunges after a bubble bursts, leaving financial institutions holding large inventories of problem loans. When many banks have the same problem at the same time, financial institutions that are worried about the potential failure of other institutions lend out as little as possible. Such defensive actions by individual institutions have the potential to render the entire financial system—and with it the settlement system—completely dysfunctional.

The system becomes dysfunctional because each day banks receive hundreds of thousands of requests from depositors to make payments to depositors at other banks. Since these payment decisions are made entirely by the depositors, a bank cannot be sure in advance that the payments it makes to other banks will equal the payments it receives from other banks at the end of the day. Some banks will receive more than they pay out, and others will receive less than they pay out.

In order to ensure that banks can meet their payment requests, an inter-bank market was created whereby banks experiencing excess inflows will lend out the excess to banks experiencing excess outflows, thereby allowing the latter to make necessary payments. Since total outflows and total inflows must sum to zero in a banking system, the risk that one or more banks will be unable to make their payments is minimized as long as banks trust each other and the interbank market is operating smoothly.

When a nationwide asset price bubble bursts, however, many if not most banks end up having the same bad-loan problem at the same time. When Bank A knows that Bank B has a major nonperforming loan problem and vice versa, neither will want to lend excess funds to the other via the interbank market.

During such crises, the entire financial system can collapse unless the central bank steps in, fulfills its role as lender of last resort, and provides financial institutions with the funds they need for settlement. Providing liquidity at such times is a basic obligation of any central bank. No one expects this liquidity to boost inflation or stimulate the economy—the funds are being supplied to avert a collapse of the settlement system at the heart of the economy. In the aftermath of the Lehman failure, central banks in the developed economies injected funds in response to the resulting financial crisis (this was dubbed QE1 in the United States), and those funds played a key role in preventing the collapse of the settlement system. The problem is not with QE1, which was a response to the financial crisis, but rather with QE2 and subsequent programs meant to stimulate the macroeconomy.

Bernanke Himself Says QE2 Unlikely to Have Major Macroeconomic Benefits

It was on the day after the midterm congressional elections in the United States in November 2010 that the Bernanke Fed unleashed a second round of QE, dubbed QE2. With heavy resistance from the Republicans making it increasingly difficult for the government to sustain the fiscal stimulus needed to fight the balance sheet recession, the Fed wanted to send a signal that it would do whatever it could to support the economy with monetary policy. The fact that the U.S. inflation rate had slipped below 1.5 percent also prompted Bernanke, whose greatest fear was deflation, to take action.

The Fed chairman published a piece explaining this policy in the November 4, 2010, *Washington Post* titled, "What the Fed did and why: Supporting the recovery and sustaining price stability." This document leaves the impression that even Bernanke did not expect QE2 to have much of a macroeconomic impact. He writes that QE2 will consist of "purchasing additional long-term securities, as [the Fed] did in 2008 and 2009," but at the same time acknowledges that the previous policy had "had little effect on the amount of money in circulation"—that is, that it did not produce an increase in bank deposits or other components of the money supply.

The primary objective of monetary accommodation by the central bank is to increase the supply of money available for the private sector to spend and boost the economy when that money is actually spent. Yet the Fed chairman is saying from the outset that the money supply will *not* increase. At the end of the piece, Bernanke even admits the Fed cannot solve all of the economy's problems by itself.

That is obviously true during a balance sheet recession, when the private sector is seeking to minimize debt. For the liquidity supplied by the central bank under QE to flow into the real economy and boost the money supply, someone has to borrow and spend it. But in 2010, there were no private borrowers in the United States, even at zero interest rates (this is illustrated in the Chapter 3).

Real Aim of QE2: Portfolio Rebalancing Effect

If that is the case, why did the Fed implement QE? The answer is that it had high expectations for the policy's portfolio rebalancing effect.

The portfolio rebalancing effect refers to the phenomenon in which the Fed raises the price of a given asset (longer-term Treasury securities in this case) by buying it, which prompts private investors to shift investment funds to less richly priced assets, pushing up the price of those assets. Rising asset prices will buoy the private sector, and if that leads businesses and households to spend more, the economy may improve. In effect, the Fed hoped QE would boost the economy via the wealth effect. Since the balance sheet recession began with a steep fall in asset prices, a monetary policy that lifts asset prices might, it was thought, help to combat the recession.

Between November 2010 and June 2011 the Fed purchased a total of $600 billion in longer-term Treasury securities—an amount almost equal to the total amount of new government securities issued during this period—with the expectation of generating a portfolio rebalancing effect. This $600 billion was indeed a huge injection of liquidity when required reserves in the banking system totaled only about $130 billion.

From a macroeconomic perspective, the Fed's purchases of Treasury securities mean that while individual financial institutions can buy and sell government bonds, they cannot in aggregate add to their holdings of Treasurys, since the entire supply of newly issued securities is being bought up by the Fed. In addition, since the U.S. private sector as a whole was deleveraging during this period, even if investors individually could buy and sell U.S. private sector debt, they could not increase their holdings of these assets in aggregate. With all newly issued government debt being acquired by the Fed and the private sector no longer borrowing, U.S. investors who had to invest new household savings and deleveraged funds from the corporate sector had only a few asset classes to choose from: stocks, commodities, foreign currency assets, and real estate.

Of the four asset classes, real estate was still an unknown quantity when QE2 was unveiled in 2010: after all, a bubble had just collapsed and uncertainty continued to cloud the market. The "pretend and extend" policy—an October 2009 directive from the authorities that banks roll over commercial real estate loans that would ordinarily have been called in—had barely managed to stabilize the commercial real estate market. House prices, meanwhile, continued to fall. That left stocks, foreign assets, and commodities. And all three appreciated markedly in the wake of QE2.

In terms of foreign assets, there were few attractive, high-yielding investment opportunities available when most of the Western economies and Japan faced balance sheet recessions. Funds therefore flowed into the emerging economies, where yields were high and demand for funds plentiful. Adding to the allure of these markets was the fact that many of them had adopted sound economic policies in the wake of the Asian currency crisis 10 years earlier.

Can Higher Share Prices under QE2 Be Justified on DCF Basis?

This development was clearly attributable to the portfolio rebalancing effect of QE2. The problem, however, is that asset prices should reflect the future earnings an asset is expected to generate. The appropriate price for an asset (i.e., its discounted cash flow, or DCF, value) is the total future earnings stream discounted by a given interest rate.

Bubbles are bubbles because they push asset prices to levels substantially above the DCF value. After a bubble bursts, investors tend to focus almost exclusively on assets' DCF value because during the bubble, they ignored that value and were then burned badly by the subsequent collapse. The reason why house prices in the United States and the United Kingdom continued to fall for three years after the central banks of both nations embarked on QE is that market participants in both nations believed QE would not be able to lift the DCF value of real estate. The other three asset categories, however, responded to QE.

Put differently, the central bank's attempt to generate a portfolio rebalancing effect is bound to create bubble-like conditions or at the very least a liquidity-driven market in certain asset classes. The question is whether the higher asset prices brought about by the Fed's QE can be somehow justified using the DCF yardstick. In other words, can the real economy keep up with the resulting gains in asset prices? If it cannot, the bubble will eventually burst, and the situation will be worse than if QE had never been implemented to begin with.

QE2 a Big Gamble for Bernanke

Viewed in this light, QE2 and QE3 represented a major gamble for Bernanke. They were a bet by the Fed that higher share prices under QE would drive a wealth effect that would boost the economy, with the resulting growth in real demand providing support for asset prices and dispelling concerns about a bubble. However, this is the reverse of the standard pattern in which improvements in the real economy drive asset prices higher. It is almost like putting the cart before the horse.

The portfolio rebalancing effect may have some impact if investors completely ignore DCF values, as they tend to do during a bubble. But when they are looking closely at DCF values, a delay in the economic or earnings recovery can trigger a market correction, extinguishing the portfolio rebalancing effect.

Since DCF calculations rely to a large extent on human judgment, not everyone will arrive at the same result. During the U.S. housing bubble, for example, then-Fed chairman Alan Greenspan said repeatedly that house prices had not diverged substantially from their DCF values and were not in a bubble. *The Economist*, in contrast, argued that U.S. house prices had climbed far above their DCF values and were in a bubble.[4] In the end, the magazine was right.

QE Undermined U.S. Leadership in G20

Bernanke's decision to force through QE, however, came at a huge international cost. It undermined U.S. leadership in the G20 and at other international forums. The U.S. agenda, including the push for Chinese currency reform, suffered a huge setback as a result.

Many countries became increasingly suspicious that the U.S. decision to adopt a policy that clearly would have only a limited impact on the domestic economy was actually intended to achieve a stealth devaluation of the dollar. Those fears were on full display at the G20 summit in Gyeongju, Korea, in mid-October 2010. Emerging countries also worried that QE would lead to capital inflows and that the resulting currency appreciation and potential for asset price bubbles would complicate the management of their economies.

Despite the concerns voiced at that meeting, however, Bernanke declared on November 3 that the Fed would go ahead with QE2. That decision deepened the rift between the United States and the rest of the world. Whereas the United States had originally hoped to fence in China on the issue of currency manipulation, it was China that ended up surrounding the United States and completely undermined the latter's leadership in the G20. China's Xinhua Agency is said to have described the United States as being outnumbered "19 to 1" at this meeting, although the actual number appears to have been 18 to 2. The United States and the United Kingdom, where Milton Friedman's monetarist theories had carved the strongest foothold, were both in favor of QE, while the rest of the G20 were circumspect or outright opposed to it.

The isolation of the two leading Anglo economies at the meeting signifies that their perceived attempt at currency devaluations with QE were viewed as a greater problem than the China's RMB by the international community. This marked a major shift in the international economic debate.

Japan's leading business daily, the *Nikkei*, reported that the agreement reached at the 2010 summit was unprecedented in that the G20 actually sanctioned the use of capital controls and currency intervention in response to QE2, which had already been announced by the United States.

---

[4] *The Economist*, "The Global Housing Boom: In Come the Waves," Special Report, June 16, 2005. www.economist.com/node/4079027.

Until then the United States had always been a champion of free-market economics and a fierce opponent of capital controls and currency intervention. At this meeting, however, the United States was forced to acquiesce to the use of these policies by other countries so that they could defend themselves against the QE shock. Otherwise, the United States could have found itself completely isolated within the G20 framework it had helped create.

Overnight, Bernanke's decision to pursue QE against the objections of other nations destroyed the U.S.-led international consensus against capital controls and currency intervention that had been in place for more than half a century. Not only was the United States unable to make any progress on the issue of the RMB, but its efforts to achieve a more open, market-based global economy were stopped in their tracks. That was the first price the nation paid for QE2.

QE with No Income Effect Harms Other Countries

The media in the United Kingdom, which had its own QE program, were generally supportive of Chairman Bernanke, but their arguments, too, were less than convincing. The *Financial Times'* Geoff Dyer, for example, wrote that it made no sense to criticize the United States for engaging in bold monetary accommodation when China had done the same, producing not only a domestic recovery but an asset bubble as well. What he neglected to mention is that China's policy easing was effective because it was backed by healthy loan demand. That is why the nation's money supply increased so sharply and why inflation accelerated, sending both GDP and imports markedly higher.

By October 2010, China's non-oil imports were already 18.4 percent above their pre-Lehman peak reached in May 2008, whereas the U.S. non-oil imports were still 4.1 percent below the pre-Lehman peak reached in June 2008. In view of the fact that China's non-oil imports fell 42.9 percent as a result of the Lehman shock compared with a 30.0 percent decline in the United States, the subsequent Chinese recovery was remarkable indeed.

Trading partners will generally not object if a recession-hit country uses monetary accommodation to boost domestic demand. Even if such a policy effectively devalues that country's currency, the adverse impact on trading partners will be more than offset by the resulting increase in domestic demand. For them, the benefits of a healthy economy more than outweigh the cost of having to compete with a cheaper currency.

Monetary accommodation in the United States and the United Kingdom has pushed down the value of the dollar and the pound but lifted domestic demand only marginally, as the sluggish growth in the money supply and employment demonstrates. The only impact of the U.S. and U.K. QE programs from an external perspective, therefore, has been a depreciation of the two currencies. Within three months of the Lehman Shock, the dollar fell 18 percent against the yen, and the pound sterling fell 23 percent against the Euro. Many nations were alarmed by this, seeing in it the potential start of a round of competitive currency devaluations.

Dollar-Buying Intervention by U.S. Authorities Would Have Produced Different Outcome

Martin Wolf, also in the pages of the *Financial Times*, wrote that the Fed must do everything it can to support the domestic economy, but that forex policy lies outside its remit. But if the United States had wanted to avoid being isolated within the G20, then-Treasury secretary Timothy Geithner—who was responsible for forex policy—should have intervened on behalf of the dollar to cancel out the QE-fueled slide in the U.S. currency. That way the United States would not have found itself outnumbered "19 to 1" at the summit, and the nation's leadership role in the G20 organization would have been preserved along with its right to speak out against Chinese currency manipulation.

In the end, QE2 led the G20 to sanction the use of inward capital controls and currency intervention in response to U.S. actions. This reflects a breakdown of the global financial consensus against capital controls and government intervention, a view that had been dominant for more than half a century.

Inward Capital Controls Help Keep Bubbles Fueled by Hot Money in Check

Of course this is not entirely a bad development. The creation of market-based international financial rules, an effort spearheaded by the United States, has created major problems in many economies. The recent financial crisis was just one example of problems caused by runaway markets.

There have been many cases, including the 1997 Asian currency crisis, in which ignorant and incompetent overseas investors lacking even a basic knowledge of host country economies and legal structures invested large amounts in emerging markets, creating bubbles in the process. These investors then panic when the unexpected occurs and take their money home, plunging the emerging economy into a debt crisis.

In the past the prevailing belief against capital controls often prevented emerging countries at the receiving end from controlling these dangerous inflows of hot and ignorant money. Furthermore, it was always the emerging market borrowers who had to go through painful adjustment processes at the end, not the lenders in the developed world who created the problem in the first place.

In the future, however, many more countries are likely to establish restrictions on foreign capital inflows, with Brazil and South Africa already trying to do so. This in itself need not be a bad thing. The risk is that what should be the last resort of capital controls and intervention will become the first resort, thereby increasing the likelihood that these policies will be misused.

QE Represents Government Intervention in Asset Markets

Inasmuch as quantitative easing is an attempt to lift asset prices, it represents a form of market intervention and in essence is little different from currency intervention. While the asset being purchased is government bonds instead of currency, the two policies are identical in that they represent an effort to alter prices determined by the market.

The distinction between QE and currency intervention is further blurred during a balance sheet recession, when the impact of QE is largely limited to a devaluation of the national currency. QE1, implemented in the immediate aftermath of the Lehman collapse, was aimed at restoring a functioning financial system and to that extent did not center on government manipulation of market prices.

With QE2, in contrast, Chairman Bernanke declared in no uncertain terms that the policy was aimed at influencing asset prices—in effect, that it represented government intervention in the markets. At the November 2010 meeting of the G20, China, Brazil, Germany, and other countries argued that if the United States insisted on intervening in the bond market, they should be given the authority to intervene in the currency market to defend themselves, and ultimately they obtained this authority. With the surfeit of investment funds in the markets today, currency intervention and controls on capital inflows are not necessarily a bad thing, especially for emerging economies where large and ignorant capital inflows from abroad can easily spark bubble-like conditions.

Operation Twist Lowered Long-Term Rates, but to No Effect

QE2 was adopted in the face of international criticism in order to raise the price of U.S. stocks and other assets. Although it coincided with a bottom in house prices, share prices fell sharply again in July 2011, sparking widespread disappointment.

The Fed responded in September 2011 with Operation Twist, under which the central bank sold $400 billion in short-term government bonds while buying an equivalent amount of long-term paper—the goal being to bring long-term interest rates down now that short-term rates were almost at zero. The goal of the program was to further reduce the yield on the 10-year Treasury note, which had already fallen below 2 percent. This program relied on the established view that the U.S. economy was more sensitive to long-term than to short-term interest rates. But while that may have been the case historically, there was little basis for arguing that Operation Twist would have a significant economic impact in 2011.

The argument that reducing bond yield to, say, 1.7 percent from 1.9 percent would suddenly light a fire under the economy is hardly convincing when lowering it to 1.9 percent had done nothing at all. If there were any sectors in the U.S. economy that were still responsive to lower interest rates, they should have picked up when the 10-year yield fell to an all-time low below 2 percent. A 10-year yield of less than 2 percent was itself a historical anomaly. That it failed to boost asset prices or the economy was a clear indication that something else was wrong. Simply pushing rates lower without trying to determine what is wrong cannot be expected to produce meaningful results.

The 1.8 percent-ish yield on the 10-year note prevailing in September 2011 was roughly the same as the all-time low of 1.85 percent recorded during the Great Depression. And the key similarity between these two periods was that the private sector had stopped borrowing. The bubble collapse that began with the New York stock market crash in October 1929 destroyed asset values while leaving debt intact, prompting the U.S. private sector to move collectively to minimize debt. That was the start of the Great Depression. Financial institutions used the funds returned to them as borrowers paid down debt to buy government bonds since there were no willing borrowers in the private sector, and the yield on the 10-year Treasury note dropped to 1.85 percent as a result.

Private-sector finance is in exactly the same state today as it was in the 1930s. After the housing bubble burst in 2007, businesses and households moved collectively to minimize debt, and money that could no longer be lent to the private sector was invested in U.S. Treasury securities instead, driving down long-term interest rates. This is also what had happened in Japan a little over a decade earlier. The 10-year Treasury yield stood at just under 2 percent before Operation Twist began, which is exactly what the 10-year Japanese government bond (JGB) was yielding at the end of 1997.

Long-term rates continued to fall in Japan until the 10-year JGB yield dropped to 0.43 percent on June 11, 2003. Yet Japan's private sector, still focused on repairing its balance sheet, did not respond at all to these ultra-low rates, and the economy did not improve.

Fed officials probably felt that implementing Operation Twist in this environment was better than doing nothing at all, but few expected it to lead to major improvements in the situation. Three out of 10 FOMC members actually voted against Operation Twist, and one of them, Dallas Fed President Richard Fisher, said in no uncertain terms that the Fed had done everything it could with monetary policy and the onus was now on fiscal policy.

The market did not take a particularly favorable view of the Fed's action, either, and bid shares down upon hearing the announcement. While the Fed's purchases of residential mortgage-backed securities (MBS) definitely lifted that market, Operation Twist provided on the whole only a modest fillip to the economy.

Operation Twist Provided Only Limited Economic Boost

It also had at least three negative effects. First, it squeezed bank earnings by flattening the yield curve. Banks earn their money by borrowing short and lending long, so a flatter curve directly reduces their income. With many U.S. banks in 2011 still facing a variety of problems, the squeeze on earnings resulting from Operation Twist may have had a significant impact at the margin.

A second adverse effect of Operation Twist was that it became increasingly difficult to see where the 10-year Treasury note *should* be trading. This further undermined the benchmark long-term yield's role as indicator, which had already been weakened by the Fed's long-term bond purchases under QE. As noted in Chapter 1, distortions in long-term interest rates are undesirable because they represent an important message from the market during a balance sheet recession.

A third adverse impact of Operation Twist was that the Fed's implementation of QE and Operation Twist diverted attention from the fiscal policy that was essential during this kind of recession. Inasmuch as Chairman Bernanke has also been arguing in favor of fiscal stimulus since 2010, Operation Twist was probably a desperate measure undertaken only because the prospects for fiscal stimulus had grown increasingly dim after the Republicans won control of the House of Representatives. But a fundamentally ineffective policy will not work no matter how aggressively it is implemented. In that sense, it would have been far better for the U.S. policy debate if Chairman Bernanke had said "monetary policy has done what it can, and now it is up to fiscal stimulus" instead of pushing ahead with monetary policy out of desperation.

But as chairman of the central bank and head of monetary policy, Mr. Bernanke may not be able to go that far in his public remarks. In Japan, too, no BOJ governor made a public case for additional fiscal stimulus when balance sheet problems had effectively brought private-sector borrowing to a standstill and the only way to expand the money supply was for the government to borrow and spend the money no longer being borrowed by the private sector.

Bernanke Admits the United States Faces Same Problems as Japan

The following year, in September 2012, the Fed responded to continued sluggishness in the U.S. economy by unveiling QE3. At the Jackson Hole monetary conference held on August 31 of that year, Bernanke attempted to justify the Fed's monetary policy up to that point. He gave his own assessment of policy and launched QE3 based on that assessment.

In his speech the chairman said that, with the exception of Japan, there were no precedents to fall back on when considering the current recession. In effect, he acknowledged that the problems faced by the United States today are the same as those that confronted Japan over a decade ago.

Bernanke went on to emphasize that the Fed's unorthodox monetary accommodation had had a significant impact while admitting it was very difficult to measure. He claimed QE—and particularly the Fed's purchases of longer-term securities—had lowered the yield on the 10-year Treasury note by 80–120 basis points, which he said was meaningful economically. In effect, he argued, this 80–120 basis points reduction in long-term rates had boosted GDP by 3 percent, which would indeed be a highly commendable outcome. But there are a number of problems with these figures.

First, the Fed estimates its purchase of $1.7 trillion in bonds lowered long-term rates by 80–120 basis points, but as Bernanke himself admits the lack of historical precedent makes this figure difficult to estimate. The econometric models used to estimate the impact of policy are constructed based on past data. With no precedents, it is nearly impossible to determine what would have happened to the 10-year Treasury yield if the Fed had not bought the bonds it did.

Fed Overestimates Impact of Quantitative Easing

The Fed is probably overestimating the impact of QE in two ways.

First is Bernanke's assertion that QE lowered long-term interest rates by 80–120 basis points. Although the Fed only bought bonds when QE1 and QE2 were in effect, interest rates did not rise in other periods, either. If interest rates were determined entirely by the supply and demand of bonds, they should have risen when the Fed was not buying. But they did not, which implies Treasury yields might have fallen substantially from pre-Lehman levels even without the Fed's purchases.

The reason is that the U.S. private sector as a group was saving an average of 6 percent of GDP during this period in spite of zero interest rates. If the private sector is not only not borrowing but is actually paying down existing debt at a time of zero interest rates, private savings have nowhere to go but the government, which is the sole remaining borrower. That is the chief reason why Treasury yields fell to such unprecedented levels.

This phenomenon was first observed in Japan, where the 10-year JGB yield had already fallen below 2 percent before the BOJ began its first experiment with QE in 2001. The adoption of QE in 2001 did not lower interest rates significantly, nor did its discontinuation in 2006 raise them significantly.

"Lower Long-Term Rates = Higher GDP" Formula Does Not Hold during Balance Sheet Recession

Next consider Bernanke's assertion that this 80–120 basis points decline in long-term rates lifted U.S. GDP by 3 percent. As the Fed chairman himself admits, this estimate is based on conventional econometric models. In other words, the Fed is using the relationship between long-term interest rates and GDP measured *prior to the balance sheet recession* to assert that an 80–120 basis points fall in long-term rates lifted GDP by 3 percent. While this figure *may* be accurate under ordinary conditions, it is useless during a balance sheet recession, when the private sector is focused on repairing damaged balance sheets and is striving to minimize debt. This is because businesses and households will not step up borrowing or investment simply because interest rates have fallen.

Proof is offered by the fact that after the bubble collapsed in 2007, the economy remained in a slump even though long-term U.S. interest rates had fallen nearly 400 basis points at one point. The price of housing, the sector that should be the most sensitive to interest rates, continued to slide until 2012 in spite of the lowest interest rates in history.

A 400 basis points drop in long-term interest rates would ordinarily give the economy an unprecedented boost and even spark inflation. Yet exactly the opposite has occurred in Japan for over 20 years (since 1990) and in the United States and the the United Kingdom for over five years (since 2008). Viewed in this light, Bernanke's assertion that Fed policy provided a major support for the economy by lowering long-term rates clearly overestimates its effectiveness.

Fed Has Also Underestimated Costs of QE

In this speech Chairman Bernanke not only discussed the benefits of the Fed's monetary accommodation but also touched on the costs. Perhaps unsurprisingly, he seems to have overestimated the former while under-estimating the latter.

For instance, Bernanke acknowledged the risk that large purchases of Treasury securities could distort the market's price-discovery function but said as yet there had been "few problems." However, the loss of the price signal provided by long-term interest rates as a result of central banks' massive QE programs has severely undermined national policy debates, in effect making it harder for governments to address balance sheet recessions properly.

This harkens back to the discussion in Chapter 1, which noted that a decline in government bond yields at a time of large fiscal deficits is a signal from the market to the government that it is not only acceptable but also *preferable to* run big deficits—that doing so does not present a major economic burden. When rates rise, on the other hand, the market is telling the government that budget deficits are weighing on the economy by crowding out private borrowing and investment.

For example, the 10-year government bond yield in Japan had dropped below 2 percent even before the BOJ embarked on its first round of quantitative easing in 2001. This was interpreted as a clear signal from the market that the nation's fiscal deficits were not burdening the economy and enabled the government to confidently maintain its fiscal stimulus. The Obuchi and Mori administrations were able to administer bold fiscal stimulus to overcome the economic crisis triggered by the Hashimoto government's deficit-reduction program largely because the domestic bond market indicated its support with low interest rates.

Unorthodox Monetary Policy Distorts Signals from Bond Market

But few are willing to take the bond market's signals at face value following the massive government bond purchases of the post-2008 Fed and the Bank of England (BOE) and post-2013 BOJ. Even if the bond market presents low interest rates to signal that fiscal stimulus is needed to fight a balance sheet recession, most people—and particularly the committed proponents of fiscal consolidation—will say the deficit must be reduced because interest rates are artificially low and would actually be much higher if the central bank were not a major buyer.

Assume (1) a U.S. economy where the Fed is not buying bonds and the 10-year Treasury yield is at 2.2 percent and (2) one where central bank buying had sent the 10-year yield down to 1.7 percent. The economy would benefit greatly if policymakers faced with the first scenario decided that a 10-year yield of 2.2 percent was low enough to justify fiscal stimulus. But if they were confronted with the second scenario and decided that, instead, deficit-*reduction* efforts were needed because the actual yield was almost certainly higher than 1.7 percent, it would be a major blow for an economy mired in a balance sheet recession.

All else being equal, of course, a 1.7 percent yield on the 10-year note should be better for the economy than a 2.2 percent yield. But during a balance sheet recession, when the private sector is extremely insensitive to interest rates, the incremental benefit of a drop in interest rates from 2.2 percent to 1.7 percent may be very limited. If an interest rate differential of 50 basis points had such a stimulative effect, the economy would have picked up long before interest rates fell to 2.2 percent. But that has clearly not been the case in Japan, the United States, or the United Kingdom.

In the end, the risk is that the Fed's QE and Operation Twist programs have obscured the voice of the bond market that is so critical during a balance sheet recession, thereby increasing the already significant obstacles to fiscal stimulus in a peacetime environment. The risk that the bond market's voice is not reaching the ears of policymakers and politicians is perhaps the biggest initial drawback of QE and Operation Twist.

Needless QE Acts as Drag on Financial Institutions

The qualifier "needless" is used here because balance sheet recessions are characterized by a massive surplus of private savings, and these funds are bound—outside the Eurozone, at least—to end up in bonds issued by the government, the sole remaining borrower. Left to their own devices, yields on government debt will fall steadily, just as they did in Japan prior to 2001.

During a balance sheet recession, when the private sector as a whole is saving and paying down debt, it is borrowers that are in shortest supply. Having the central bank join private financial institutions as a lender to the government—the sole remaining borrower—can hardly be a positive for the economy at such times.

Naturally, if the central bank's lending prompts the government to borrow *more*, it would help ease the bottleneck. But central bank buying can cause the most important indicator for deciding whether the government should increase or decrease its borrowing—the yield on government debt—to lose most of its informational content. As a result, a government that needs to increase borrowing may end up pursuing fiscal consolidation instead. In this way, government bond purchases by the central bank can have a detrimental impact on the overall economy.

The damage can be substantial—policymakers in recent fiscal debates in Japan, the United States, and the United Kingdom, have not viewed low government bond yields as carrying information crucial to deciding whether fiscal policy should be tightened or relaxed.

In addition, central bank purchases of government bonds at a time when the private sector is striving to minimize debt end up flattening the yield curve, making it even more difficult for the private sector to invest surplus funds. That also complicates the recovery efforts of financial institutions hurt in the bubble collapse, as noted above, and can prolong a credit crunch.

In the same Jackson Hole speech, Chairman Bernanke claimed Fed purchases of Treasury securities had substantially reduced the effective cost of financing the government's deficits. Over the past three years the Fed has returned a much larger than normal $200 billion in interest income on its bond holdings to the Treasury. However, as this would otherwise have become interest income for the private sector, it is not necessarily a positive for the economy, particularly when the need to nurse banks back to health is taken into account. If this $200 billion in interest were to become income for the private sector and most of it were used to fund consumption or investment, the U.S. economy would receive a corresponding boost. If this $200 billion were used to pay down debt, it would have shortened the time it takes for the United States to come out of balance sheet recession.

Why Fed Embarked on QE3 Two Months before Presidential Election

With the economy still struggling, the Fed unveiled QE3 just two months before the November presidential election in 2012. At the time, many domestic analysts asked why the Fed, which is supposed to be politically neutral, would undertake this kind of bold action at such a politically sensitive time. Republican candidate for president Mitt Romney and his running mate Paul Ryan both objected to QE3 for this reason.

The most likely answer is that the Fed wanted to be able to say it had done everything it could to avert the so-called fiscal cliff scheduled to arrive on January 1, 2013. The Fed may well have decided that politicians would be unable to address the fiscal cliff during this politically charged season and therefore chose to do everything it could to shore up the economy ahead of the January 1 deadline.

Chairman Bernanke probably knew it would be hard for politicians to address the crisis so soon after the election. For the Fed, making use of all the tools at its disposal would certainly be preferable to being grilled later on about why it had stood by and done nothing when it was obvious politicians would be unable to act. As will be discussed in Chapter 3, however, Chairman Bernanke clearly stated that monetary policy would not be able to offset the blow of deficit-reduction efforts. He warned that while the Fed had done everything it could, the U.S. economy would still incur substantial damage if the fiscal cliff were not averted.

Post-Bubble Wage Growth Nearly Identical in the United States and Japan

In response to broad-based criticism that QE is not working, monetary authorities in the United Kingdom and the United States have responded that at least they succeeded in preventing the kind of deflation seen in Japan. However, it is nonsense to compare conditions in these two countries just a few years after the bubble burst to those in Japan, where more than 20 years have passed. The more appropriate comparison would be between Japan and the West at the same points in the post-bubble era, and that reveals that the United States and the United Kingdom are following almost exactly in Japan's footsteps.

Wage inflation offers a better basis for comparison than price data since the latter are heavily influenced by external factors such as exchange rates (the yen climbed to then-record 80 yen to the dollar in April 1995 from 160 when the bubble burst in 1990). On this measure, Japanese wages (base pay) rose at an annualized rate of 3.28 percent during the bubble period from 1987 to 1991, while from 1992 to the end of 1996 they grew by 2.01 percent a year. When we look at total cash wages, which include bonuses (a major component of Japanese salaries), wage growth slowed from 3.70 percent during the bubble years to 1.63 percent in the five years after the bubble's collapse. In the United States, meanwhile, hourly wages rose at an annualized rate of 3.4 percent from 2006 to 2008, while since the bubble burst they have been edging up by 1.9 percent a year.

Conditions in Japan were far from deflationary in the first few years after the bubble collapsed. Wages rose at almost the same rate as wages in the United States today. And this was achieved without the QE programs implemented in the United States and the United Kingdom. That suggests QE has done less to avert deflation in these two economies than its proponents would have us believe.

The "Inconvenient Truth" of the Real Cost of Quantitative Easing

The U.S. housing market finally began to pick up five full years after the bubble burst in 2007, and four since the Fed had taken interest rates down to zero. A number of factors contributed to the turnaround, including a sharp decline in the supply of new housing, a substantial drawdown of existing home inventories, a sharp increase in purchases by institutional investors, a gradual pick-up in the economy, and historically low mortgage loan rates.[5]

---

[5] As market observers have noted, however, there remains a dearth of first-time homebuyers taking out mortgages. This is consistent with the fact that the U.S. household sector in aggregate continues to save more and borrow less, as shown by the

The private sector also made meaningful progress in repairing its balance sheet during those five years. Unlike the Eurozone and the United Kingdom, both of which fell off the fiscal cliff, Bernanke's desperate warnings helped the United States avoid the fiscal cliff, which sustained the flow of income to the private sector and allowed it to use that income to repair its balance sheets. Aggressive investment in the shale gas sector also contributed to the recovery.

Seeing the improvement in these indicators, Chairman Bernanke announced on May 22, 2013, that the Fed would begin scaling back its bond purchases under QE3 starting in early autumn and end such purchases altogether by mid-2014. That announcement roiled the Treasury market, sending the 10-year Treasury yield 70 basis points higher at one point. This marked the first time that U.S. authorities and market participants confronted the real cost of quantitative easing—that is, the problems that would not have been encountered absent QE.

To get a better idea of the scale of the problem, it should be noted that excess reserves at U.S. banks amounted to 19.8 times the value of statutory reserves in May 2014 (Figure 2.3). The corresponding multiples for the United Kingdom and Japan were 10.6 and 14.5, respectively. Despite this massive growth in excess reserves, the money supply has not increased much and inflation has not taken hold because the private sector is not borrowing. But once businesses and households complete their balance sheet repairs and resume borrowing, the money multiplier will turn positive at the margin, and the textbooks suggest that the U.S. money supply and prices could expand by as much as 20-fold.

An increase in lending of that magnitude would naturally require banks to bolster their capital, but the technique of securitization would make it possible to work around this constraint to a significant extent. That means we are looking at a potential inflation rate of 2,000 percent. The authorities will therefore need to bring excess reserves back down to the level of statutory reserves or sterilize them before inflation kicks in. But in the United States that would require either reducing bank reserves to 1/20th of their current level in a worst-case scenario or paying interest on excess reserves, which amount to $2.5 trillion as of April 2014.

If the Fed chooses to drain excess reserves, it will have to sell assets to reabsorb the liquidity. And since QE has been carried out largely via the purchase of long-term securities, the asset the Fed will have to sell is long-term securities.

The central banks of the United States and the United Kingdom currently hold more than 30 percent of their governments' outstanding long-term bond

---

flow-of-funds data illustrated in Chapter 3. This supports the speculation that the housing market recovery in 2013 had been driven more by investors than by real demand.

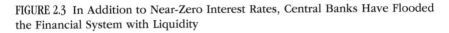

FIGURE 2.3 In Addition to Near-Zero Interest Rates, Central Banks Have Flooded the Financial System with Liquidity

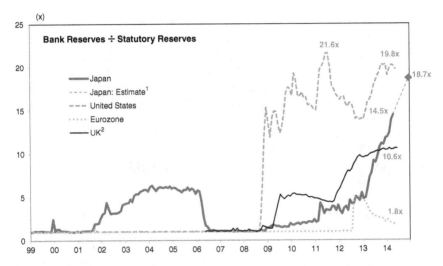

Notes: 1. Estimates are based on the assumption that required reserves will increase by 3 percent a year and bank reserves constitute 88.8 percent of financial institution's current deposit holdings with the BOJ. 2. The BOE suspends reserve requirements in March 2009. The post–March 2009 figures are based on the assumption that the original reserve requirement is still applicable.

Source: Nomura Research Institute, based on BOJ, FRB, ECB, and BOE data.

issuance, according to the IMF's April 2013 *Global Financial Stability Report.* Long-term interest rates in both countries could rocket higher if the central bank dumped these bonds onto the market. The fact that the mere mention of a tapering by Chairman Bernanke on May 22, 2013, was sufficient to send the 10-year yield up to 3 percent gives some idea of the magnitude of the potential market dislocation were the Fed to actually *sell* its long-term bond holdings.

BOJ's First Round of QE Was Easy to Wind Down Because It Was Conducted in Money Market

Of all the QE programs implemented so far, only one—the BOJ's first experiment with QE, carried out from 2001 to 2006—has been successfully wound down. This was possible because the BOJ, which anticipated the problems associated with exiting QE, implemented its QE program from 2001 to 2006 via the purchase of three-month bills issued by commercial banks.

The BOJ ultimately injected liquidity equal to six times statutory reserves, but moved to mop up these funds in 2006 as signs of a recovery in the economy and loan demand appeared. The BOJ drained the liquidity from the banking system simply by choosing not to reinvest the proceeds of maturing bills.

To redeem the maturing bills held by the BOJ, commercial banks transferred funds from their current accounts at the BOJ to the Bank, which reduced excess reserves. Because the BOJ did not reinvest the funds transferred in this manner, all of the bills held by the Bank were redeemed over a three-month period, fully absorbing the excess reserves that had been created. As the supply and absorption of liquidity was limited to the short end of the curve, there was little if any impact on the long-term bond market or long-term interest rates.

Redemption of Central Bank Bond Holdings Will Not Reduce Commercial Banks' Current Accounts

This time, however, the central banks in the United States, the United Kingdom, and Japan have injected funds by buying long-term *government* bonds. (The Fed is also purchasing MBS.)

Even though the Fed has already indicated that it will hold onto those bonds until they mature, implementing QE via long-term government bonds creates two problems that did not exist in Japan during 2001 to 2006. First, the bonds acquired will not mature for much longer—5 or 10 years in some cases. If the need to tighten monetary policy arises before the bonds mature, the Fed will be forced to raise rates that much faster. Second, because the bonds were issued by governments, their redemption will only reduce the government's balances at the central bank and not the excess reserves in commercial banks' accounts at the central bank.

To see this, assume that the Fed held onto the bonds until maturity. In this case, principal payments for the maturing government securities held by the Fed will be paid by the issuer—the government—to the Fed, with the necessary funds withdrawn from the Treasury's account at the Fed. This transaction has no effect on private financial institutions' accounts at the Fed and therefore will not reduce the excess reserves that have accumulated in those accounts. But the QE cannot be considered unwound until excess reserves, which currently amount to some 20 times statutory reserves or 2.5 trillion dollars, are removed. Otherwise, the risk is that the U.S. money supply and prices would ultimately increase to 20 times their current level.

Government Issue of Refunding Bonds to Private Sector Would Absorb Excess Reserves

In reality, the Treasury's account at the Fed is not that large, and the government will have to procure the funds from the private sector to make the redemption payments. To do so, it will either issue new refunding bonds or raise taxes.

If the government were to issue refunding bonds to the private sector to fund the redemption of the long-term bonds, the commercial banks that bought those refunding bonds would transfer the purchase price from their current accounts at the central bank to the government's account there, effectively draining excess reserves.

If the government were to raise taxes to redeem the bonds, that would also result in the private sector transferring that amount to the Treasury balances at the Fed from the commercial banks' accounts at the Fed, effectively draining reserves.

A tax increase would weigh on the economy by reducing private sector income, while the issuance of refunding bonds would do the same by lifting interest rates. In practice, most of the money for redemption will probably come from the issuance of refunding bonds.

Redeeming Fed Bond Holdings Has Same Effect as Issuing Deficit Bonds

Although refunding bonds ordinarily do not push interest rates higher because their proceeds are returned to the owners of maturing government bonds in the private sector, when Treasury securities are held by the Fed, the principal payments go to the Fed and not to the private sector. This means the private sector has to come up with *new* savings to purchase refunding bonds for those bonds held by the central bank. The economic impact of this refunding bond therefore, is the same as if the government had issued new bonds to fund a fiscal deficit. This also means the adverse impact of issuing the refunding bonds on the market will be the same as if the Fed chooses to sell the bonds it has acquired.

Fed Chair Janet Yellen has stated in her May 7, 2014, remarks[6] that it will probably take five to eight years for the Fed to drain the excess reserves and return its balance sheet to a more normal footing. If the $2.5 trillion in reserves is drained steadily over a five-year period, this will be equivalent to issuing $500 billion in new Treasury securities each year. As of April 2014, the Congressional Budget Office was estimating a deficit of $492 billion or 2.8 percent of GDP for the federal government in FY14, which ends in September 2014. This means the upward pressure on interest rates in the Treasury market would go from a situation in which the fiscal deficit was running at 2.8 percent of GDP to the equivalent of one in which the fiscal

---

[6] Reuters, "Could Take 5–8 Years to Shrink Fed Portfolio: Yellen," May 8, 2014. www.reuters.com/article/2014/05/08/us-usa-fed-yellen-idUSBREA470QE20140508.

deficit was double that, or 5.6 percent of GDP. Moreover, this state of affairs would continue for five years.

And if private loan demand has recovered at that point in time, it would force the federal government to issue new bonds totaling 5.6 percent of GDP when private loan demand has already picked up, potentially pushing interest rates sharply higher and causing severe crowding out.

While the Fed's pledge not to sell its bond holdings appears to have reassured the market, the government will have to issue new bonds in amounts equal to the maturing bonds held by the Fed. Whether the bonds are sold by the Fed or the government, therefore, the adverse impact on supply and demand will be identical.

The redemption of MBS will lead to a reduction in excess reserves since the money used to redeem these securities ultimately comes from the private sector.

Strength of Private Loan Demand Different at Start and End of QE

Some reading this will probably want to argue that there is nothing to worry about since the funds injected to the private sector by the Fed under QE can be used to purchase the refunding bonds issued by the government.

But when the Fed bought those bonds during the balance sheet recession, the government was the sole remaining borrower, and as a result government bonds carried a high premium. When the Fed is winding down QE, on the other hand, the balance sheet recession will be over and private borrowers will be starting to emerge. Since the need for private investors to buy government bonds has diminished, the price of those bonds is likely to have fallen substantially. If the government or Fed tries to sell bonds at such a time, the price they receive will almost certainly be far less than what the Fed paid several years ago.

Paying Interest on Excess Reserves Would Enable Rate Hikes . . .

Instead of removing the excess reserves, the central bank also has the option of sterilizing them by paying interest on them so that bankers have less incentive to lend. Chairman Bernanke said at a press conference in September 2013 that "We can raise interest rates at the appropriate time, even if the balance sheet remains large for an extended period"[7]—that is, even without draining the funds supplied under QE.

---

[7] Board of the Governors of the Federal Reserve System, "Transcript of Chairman Bernanke's Press Conference September 18, 2013," p. 23. www.federalreserve.gov/mediacenter/files/FOMCpresconf20130918.pdf

New York Fed President William Dudley then said on May 20, 2014,[8] that the Fed is currently considering various methods of paying interest on excess reserves, taking into account both interest expense and flexibility. He said three options are being considered: (1) reverse repos, in which the Fed lends its securities to financial institutions to temporarily drain funds from the financial system, (2) having commercial banks make term deposits at the Fed, or (3) paying interest directly on the excess reserves.

The interest expense incurred under these three methods would vary, and that difference might be significant at a time of zero interest rates like today. However, the difference would be largely insignificant once the economy returns to normal and private loan demand recovers, sending interest rates higher. When that happens the Fed will need to be prepared to make tens to hundreds of billions of dollars in interest payments each year no matter what method is used.

This is because, unlike today, where there is a shortage of borrowers in spite of zero interest rates, a phase when the central bank is trying to raise interest rates is generally one in which the private sector has completed its balance sheet repairs, private loan demand is picking up, and inflation is becoming a concern. At that point, lending rates are likely to be much higher, and the central bank would have to pay a similar rate of interest on excess reserves if it wanted to stop banks from lending out the money. That would remove the incentive for commercial banks to make (risky) loans to businesses and households and, as Bernanke noted, would enable the Fed to raise rates and prevent inflation from accelerating without having to drain excess reserves from the system.

But Cost Could Be Prohibitive

The problem is the cost of this policy. FOMC members have indicated that the Federal Funds rate should eventually return to the normal level of around 4 percent. Excess reserves amounted to about $2.5 trillion in April 2014. Four percent of $2.5 trillion amounts to $100 billion, and that is how much the Fed would have to pay in interest each year. As the Fed's profits and hence its remittances to the U.S. Treasury would decline by an equal amount, the federal budget deficit would be $100 billion higher than it is today for each and every year until the excess reserves are removed from the system. And all these additional expenses are incurred only because the Fed had implemented QE.

---

[8] William C. Dudley (2014), "The Economic Outlook and Implications for Monetary Policy," remarks before the New York Association for Business Economics, May 20, 2014. www.newyorkfed.org/newsevents/speeches/2014/dud140520.html

Many in the United States will complain bitterly about the banks being given $100 billion in guaranteed, risk-free profits each year at taxpayers' expense for *not* lending money to the private sector. The distributional impact of QE could not be worse in this sense.

If the Fed did not sell the bonds, a rise in interest rates to 4 percent from zero at present would also translate into massive capital losses on the Fed's long-term bond holdings. According to the International Monetary Fund (IMF) report published on April 18, 2013, the Fed's losses under the most likely rate hike scenario would amount to about 3 percent of GDP,[9] or about $500 billion. This figure represents the additional cost to the Fed of raising interest rates without mopping up the excess reserves it has supplied to the financial system.

The capital loss would be a one-time event. If the Fed holds the bonds to maturity it will receive the full principal payment, so there may not be any actual losses. Indeed the real reason for the Fed's reluctance to sell its bond holdings may be due to the fact that it cannot afford to realize those massive capital losses. After all, the Federal Reserve System was capitalized at just $50 billion in April 2014, and speculation regarding the Fed's solvency could undermine confidence in both the Fed and the dollar during this process.

Some of the more optimistic academics and market participants (perhaps those who have profited from QE?) continue to argue that central bank losses are meaningless and can be ignored. They argue that as long as the central bank conducts monetary policy responsibly, whether it is making money or losing money is irrelevant. But there is no historical precedent to suggest how the dollar or the Treasury market might react if massive losses leave the Fed facing technical insolvency. In particular, we do not know how the Chinese, Arabs, and other large foreign holders of dollar assets would react. This is an entirely unknown quantity.

After all, it is only since the "Nixon shock" of 1971, when the United States abandoned convertibility between the dollar and gold, that people around the world have been forced to accept paper currencies not backed by gold. This is a first in human history. And it is only 45 years ago in a 5,000-year history. The United States also experienced an unprecedented bout of inflation in the 10 years after Nixon closed the gold window. This painful experience forced central bankers to behave "as though [they] were on the gold standard," in the words of Alan Greenspan.

Maintaining trust in the Fed and the dollar among both market partic-ipants and the general public following such large losses would probably require a temporary injection of government capital, adding further to the federal deficit.

---

[9] International Monetary Fund, "Unconventional Monetary Policies—Recent Experi-ence and Prospects," April 18, 2013, p. 27. www.imf.org/external/np/pp/eng/2013/041813a.pdf

Whether these costs are high or low is a matter of opinion, but they *will* increase the fiscal deficit and could become a major political issue at some point. The *Financial Times* already warned in an article titled "Fed losses bolster QE criticism" published on March 15, 2014, that the unrealized losses of $53.2 billion reported by the Fed on its securities portfolio may trigger a political backlash against the U.S. central bank.

Cost of Winding Down QE Has Yet to Be Properly Analyzed

The IMF report noted above also indicated other costs of quantitative easing. For instance, the IMF suggested that low interest rates under QE would delay necessary structural reforms at banks and in the economy, that banks would lose their sensitivity to risk, resulting in more bad loans in the future, that the interbank market would effectively become dysfunctional, and that the central bank's balance sheet could be impaired. But there has been almost no detailed macroeconomic analysis of what might happen to an economy when QE is discontinued.

Research by the IMF and other organizations touches on the subject of risk management at commercial banks, but tends to discuss in only the vaguest terms the macroeconomic cost of QE, such as the slower recovery caused by the spike in long-term interest rates when the policy is discontinued. This may be because the IMF has been a QE proponent from early on.

The IMF report noted above, for example, says that given the potential for a surge in interest rates, the central bank should engage in close dialogue with the market and focus on the policy duration effect or forward guidance when winding down QE. But having a nice talk is hardly a sufficient prescription given the magnitude of the problems that could result when a central bank holding 30 percent of outstanding long-term government bonds has to either sell or face redemptions of those securities.

When the long-term rates went up in response to Janet Yellen's first congressional testimony on February 11, 2014, many in the market as well as in the media commented that her communication skills are not as good as those of her predecessor.

But the key reason why Bernanke was seen as being such a good communicator—at least until May 22, 2013—is that he was generally bearing good tidings in the form of more quantitative easing, which of course the market welcomed. QE at a time of weak private loan demand and a sluggish economy is harmless and will always be welcomed by a market addicted to it.

But when it came time to start winding down this policy, on May 22, 2013, Mr. Bernanke's heralded communication skills failed to prevent a sudden surge in long-term interest rates or corresponding damage to emerging markets and the U.S. housing market. This is not an issue that can be addressed via better communication with the market. Far from it.

Debate over Winding Down QE Sparks "Bad" Rise in Rates

For example, Chairman Bernanke tried to meet the demand for a closer dialogue with the market by declaring the Fed will not begin raising rates for a substantial period of time after ending its purchases of long-term bonds. This statement was probably intended to prevent the kind of turmoil witnessed in the spring of 1994, when the Fed surprised the markets by raising rates. In effect Bernanke was trying to reassure market participants that any future tightening would be telegraphed in advance. Nevertheless, the yield on the 10-year Treasury note surged from 2.3 percent to 3.0 percent after Bernanke said on June 19, 2013, that the Fed might scale back its asset purchases. U.S. mortgage loan rates (30-year fixed) also climbed from 3.35 percent at the time of a May 2 survey to more than 4.5 percent in late August, according to Freddie Mac.

While this surge in long-term rates had the short-term effect of prompting potential homebuyers to rush ahead with their purchases, the U.S. housing market has lost its forward momentum since those purchases were completed in autumn 2013.[10]

Moreover, the fact that this surge took place without any marked improvement in U.S. economic indicators suggests that the increase in rates that began in June was not a benign rise driven by an economic recovery but rather a "bad" increase triggered by expectations of deteriorating supply and demand conditions in the bond market as QE is unwound.

"QE Trap" Appears Increasingly Likely

This rise in long-term rates starting in June 2013 apparently came as a major shock to the Fed, and at the press conference following the September FOMC meeting Chairman Bernanke said, ". . . the rapid tightening of financial conditions in recent months could have the effect of slowing growth, . . . a concern that would be exacerbated if conditions tightened ever further." This suggests the FOMC was taking the situation very seriously and was worried it could deteriorate further.

The Fed was probably concerned that if interest rates rose this much when it had yet to do anything, an actual decision to wind down QE could

---

[10] Reuters, "Highlights: Fed Chief Yellen's Testimony to Congressional Committee," May 7, 2014. www.reuters.com/article/2014/05/07/usa-fed-highlights-idUSL2N0NS1L020140507

send rates even higher and cause conditions to worsen accordingly. As a result, the FOMC decided not to start reducing its bond purchases in September 2013, as initially anticipated.

If the winding down of QE pushes up interest rates by causing bond market participants who are wary of deteriorating supply/demand dynamics to demand a higher risk premium, the interest-rate-sensitive sectors that have driven the U.S. economy thus far—housing and automobiles in particular—could suddenly cool. That could give the Fed cold feet once again and prompt it to announce a temporary halt or postponement of the QE removal process.

Conditions would probably stabilize if that led to a modest fall in interest rates, as occurred in September 2013, but interest rates could rise again if economic indicators pick up and spur renewed talk of QE removal. That would put the brakes on the recovery and force the Fed to go slow again in an on-again, off-again policy that could easily continue for an extended period of time. As this would never have happened without QE, the Fed is finally at the point where it has to start confronting the real costs of the policy.

Long-term interest rates would never have risen this far so early in the recovery if the Fed had not implemented QE, and without the rise in interest rates the economy would have embarked on a smooth recovery. But now long-term rates could rise every time the Fed talks about winding down QE, throwing cold water on the recovery and complicating the Fed's efforts to bring the policy to an end. Japan, the United States, and the United Kingdom may find themselves unable to escape from this "QE trap" for many years because they carried out QE in the long-term government bond market.

Their predicament is illustrated in Figure 2.4. Countries that undertook QE via the purchase of long-term bonds initially saw a larger drop in long-term rates than non-QE countries, and to that extent their recoveries arrived sooner (t_1). But once the economy starts to recover, the bond market, fearing the central bank will move to drain excess reserves by either selling long-term bonds or stop re-investing the proceeds of maturing bonds (i.e., forcing the Treasury to sell refunding bonds), pushes long-term rates sharply higher, which weighs on interest-rate-sensitive sectors like automobiles and housing and slows down the recovery. Now the central bank becomes more reluctant to tighten policy because it fears a slowdown of the economy. Consequently, the economy picks up again, but as attention once again focuses on the need to mop up excess reserves, long-term rates climb again. This cycle is the "QE trap."

In countries that did not engage in QE, the decline in long-term rates occurs more gradually, and the economic recovery itself unfolds a little later (t_2). But here both the markets and the central bank can relax because there is no need for the latter to drain massive amounts of excess reserves when the economic rebound commences. The eventual rise in long-term rates is

FIGURE 2.4 United States May Be Facing a QE "Trap"

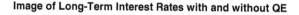

Image of Long-Term Interest Rates with and without QE

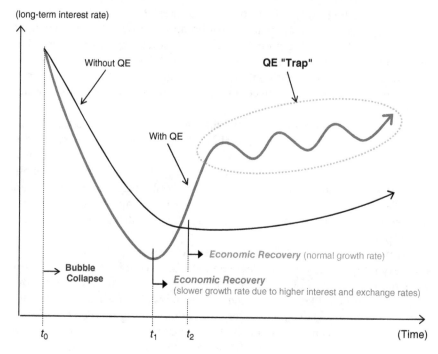

therefore far more gradual than in a QE country. Once the economy starts to pick up, non-QE countries are therefore likely to have higher GDP growth rates because interest rates are lower. This is illustrated in Figure 2.5.

This risk of long-term rates going higher than warranted by economic fundamentals was in the mind of New York Fed president William Dudley when he said on May 20, 2014, that the sequence of the FOMC's current plan for the post-tapering era—first ceasing the reinvestment of principal payments and then raising the policy rate—should be reversed.[11] He says rates should be raised *before* the Fed stops reinvesting principal payments. This remark was obviously driven by concern about a sudden deterioration in bond supply/demand dynamics when the Fed stops reinvesting those principal payments from maturing bonds and the Treasury is forced to issue new refunding bonds as noted above. Mr. Dudley argues a worsening of bond market conditions could potentially trigger a rise in long-term interest

---

[11] William C. Dudley, "The Economic Outlook and Implications for Monetary Policy," remarks before the New York Association for Business Economics, May 20, 2014. www.newyorkfed.org/newsevents/speeches/2014/dud140520.html.

FIGURE 2.5 United States May Be Facing a QE "Trap"—GDP

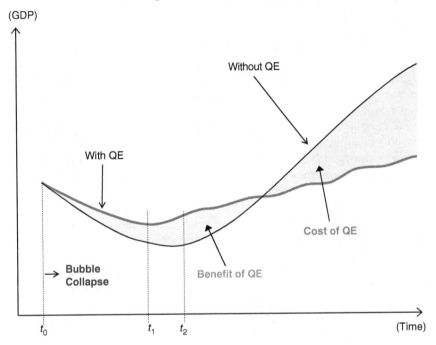

Image of GDP with and without QE

rates, tying the Fed's hands by preventing it from hiking short-term rates. But unless it stops reinvesting the principal payments it will never be able to drain the excess reserves from the banking system. This could also mean that the QE trap will continue for a long time.

I have long described quantitative easing as a policy that is fun while going forward but absolutely terrifying coming back. The September 2013 drama over a Fed tapering marked the beginning of the trip back.

Continued QE Trap More Likely Than Hyperinflation

If the funds supplied under the central bank's easing program could be mopped up in one or two operations—a kind of monetary shock therapy—the Fed may be tempted to do so. For example, if the excess reserves in the banking system is 20 percent of required reserves, one-time Fed selling of bonds can probably absorb the entire amount. But now that the Fed has created reserves equal to 20 times statutory reserves, it will be exceedingly difficult to drain this liquidity from the system.

Historically, all countries that created liquidity on this scale ultimately faced hyperinflation and a redenomination of the currency, wiping out the wealth of hard-working savers. This time, however, the money supply has not increased much and inflation has not emerged so far because there has been no private loan demand.

From this point onward, the scenario of a continued QE trap—in which long-term rates remain higher than warranted, and as a result, the economy remains less than fully vibrant—is more likely than hyperinflation. This is because a central bank that has engaged in QE is far less tolerant of inflation than a bank that has not.

A central bank that has undertaken QE has already supplied huge amounts of liquidity to the markets during the recession. These funds are harmless during a balance sheet recession, when there is no private loan demand and the money multiplier is negative at the margin. But once the private sector completes its balance sheet repairs and resumes borrowing, they have the potential to generate tremendous inflation. Thus the central bank that supplied the funds and the markets that received them become increasingly nervous and vigilant as the economy starts to pick up. This is the new normal.

Having implemented a massive quantitative easing program, the Fed must never be perceived by market participants as having fallen behind the curve on inflation. Once it gives that impression there is no telling how far long-term interest rates might rise, with serious implications for both the United States and the global economy.

To avoid this sort of problem, a central bank that has implemented QE must move to tighten policy much sooner than one that has not. As a result, long-term interest rates will remain higher than warranted by the economic fundamentals and the private sector will continue to worry about a further increase in long-term rates, making it difficult for the economy to return to a normal footing.

The first evidence of this intolerance at the Fed came in December 2013, when the U.S. central bank began tapering its asset purchases despite an inflation rate of just 1.1 percent. The second salvo was fired when Janet Yellen suggested in March 2014 that a rate hike could come as early as spring 2015. By continuing to indicate it may start tightening sooner than the market expects, the Fed hopes to solidify the impression that it will never fall behind the curve on inflation and thereby minimize any increase in long-term interest rates driven by inflation concerns.

In contrast, a central bank that has brought interest rates to zero but no QE can sit back and relax as private loan demand picks up and drives an economic rebound. Rate hikes need to be considered and implemented—gradually—only after the economy approaches full employment and prices and wages have started to rise. In this case there is no reason for the central bank or the markets to fear an economic recovery—it can be welcomed with open arms.

A central bank that has only employed orthodox easing methods will also face a rise in long-term rates if it is seen as falling behind the curve on inflation, but—all else being equal—the increase will be far milder than in a country where the central bank has injected massive amounts of liquidity via the long-term bond market.

BOJ Found Itself in Same Position in 2006

This phenomenon of a central bank being forced to tighten sooner than it would normally do because of QE was also observed in Japan in 2006.

In the spring of that year, then-BOJ governor Toshihiko Fukui announced the Bank would begin winding down the world's first QE program, which had begun in 2001. Although Japan's economy was inching toward recovery, the trend was not particularly strong, and some criticized the decision to bring the policy to an end as being premature.

However, Japanese businesses were showing signs of a pick-up in borrowing (as opposed to debt pay-downs) for the first time in a decade, and it was widely claimed that they had finally finished repairing their balance sheets. Many foreign holders of Japanese equities were also demanding that Japanese managers boost ROE by raising leverage now that their balance sheets were clean. But if Japanese companies had listened to those demands and started borrowing money en masse, bank reserves—equivalent at the time to about six times statutory reserves—could have fueled a dramatic increase in lending. In theory, at least, both the money supply and prices could have increased sixfold.

That is why Governor Fukui started winding down QE sooner than the market expected. The actual process, as explained earlier, was completed quickly because the Bank had chosen to limit the assets it purchased to three-month bills issued by commercial banks in order to avoid the QE trap.

Like the BOJ in 2006, Fed Chair Yellen is trying to keep a step ahead of the market in winding down QE. However, she is likely to face quite an ordeal—not only has the Fed created excess reserves equal to 20 times statutory reserves, versus a maximum multiple of six for the BOJ in 2001 to 2006, but it supplied most of those funds in the long-term government bond market.

Fed Admits That Supply and Demand Matters, Too

In a speech on November 19, 2013, Bernanke said QE had succeeded in lowering long-term interest rates by altering the supply and demand structure for long-term bonds. In other words, the Fed's aggressive buying of long-term bonds had made these bonds "scarcer and hence more valuable," driving down yields. He also declared that this downward impact on long-term rates was separate from forward guidance, with which the Fed tries to manage market expectations by pledging not to raise short-term rates for an extended period of time.

But if that is the case, a reduction in the Fed's purchases of long-term bonds (or actual sales of the same either by the Fed or the Treasury) will reduce the scarcity value of those securities, making them less valuable and raising their yields—regardless of how much the Fed insists that it will not raise the policy rate in its forward guidance. This is precisely what happened starting in June 2013. This means talk cannot fix the actual deterioration in supply and demand. In that sense, the FOMC's expectations that forward guidance can prevent a rise in long-term rates are unrealistic.

Fed Changes Course Despite a 1.1 Percent Inflation Rate

At the same time, based on the FOMC's logic, QE *should be* wound down while private loan demand is still weak and forward guidance is still in effect, that is, while the Fed can still credibly pledge to keep the policy rate at zero. This is because there are limits to how far long-term rates can rise when the yield curve is anchored at zero at the short end based on low inflation rate and weak private loan demand.

On the other hand, if the Fed waits until the inflation rate reaches 2 percent or private loan demand recovers, it will be forced to hike short-term rates. When that happens, the yield curve will lose its anchor, and long-term rates could potentially see an explosive rise. The U.S. central bank's decision at the December 2013 FOMC meeting to scale back its asset purchases under QE3 was probably based on this logic.

The December tapering announcement was particularly significant because it came at a time when U.S. inflation was running at just 1.1 percent. Chairman Bernanke—the same man who pushed for a 2 percent inflation target as soon as he became chairman of the Fed and was responsible for QE1, QE2, Operation Twist, and QE3—went ahead with tapering despite what he must have seen as modest inflation.

This rate of 1.1 percent is only slightly higher than the level around 1.0 percent that sparked fears of deflation at the end of 2010. At the time, the Fed was so worried about deflation that it rolled out QE2 in the face of heavy international criticism at the Seoul G20 meeting. Yet in December 2013, the Fed decided to begin *scaling back* quantitative easing even though inflation had slipped to around 1 percent, which is precisely where it was when QE2 was announced. In other words, the Fed chose to ease up on the monetary accelerator at a time when traditional inflation targeting theory held it should be keeping the throttle wide open.

The Fed's very different reaction this time can be attributed to (a) improvements in the real economy, symbolized by the fall in the unemployment rate; and (b) a growing realization among policymakers of the magnitude of the problems involved in winding down QE.

Traditional Phillips Curve Relationship No Longer Holds

On the first point, improvements in the unemployment rate have consistently exceeded Fed expectations since the spring of 2012 even as the U.S. inflation rate fell from 2 percent to just over 1 percent. According to orthodox economics, a decline in inflation to levels low enough to spark deflation concerns implies a rise in the unemployment rate. But recently the opposite has been true in the United States.

This means the traditional Phillips curve relationship between the inflation rate and the unemployment rate is no longer valid. Ironically, the U.S. inflation rate had fallen since QE3 was unveiled in the second half of 2012 even as the Fed has increased the amount of liquidity it injects into the market by nearly 50 percent.

There is no reason to insist on the 2 percent inflation rate prescribed by the traditional Phillips curve if the unemployment rate is dropping meaningfully in spite of falling inflation. At the same time, the decline in inflation at a time of bold monetary accommodation also implies that the Fed has no tools capable of raising the inflation rate to 2 percent.

That the unemployment rate is falling and the economy continues to improve at a time when the central bank has no effective policy tools at its disposal also removes any rationale for insisting on the traditional recommendation of a 2 percent inflation target.

In view of the above it would not be surprising if the Fed had decided to shift its policy emphasis to minimizing the future costs of winding down QE while it still could.

If the Fed wants to drain excess reserves while private demand for funds is still weak in order to avoid the QE trap, it has one more tool at its disposal. That is to admit that quantitative easing neither contributed to growth in the money supply nor gave a meaningful boost to the macroeconomy.

The adverse impact of winding down QE could be mitigated if the Fed announced that the policy had not been as effective as initially hoped. Indeed, San Francisco Fed president John Williams demonstrated empirically in a 2013 paper[12] that QE had not had a significant impact. While interest

---

[12] John C. Williams, "A Defense of Moderation in Monetary Policy," *Journal of Macroeconomics* 38 (2013): pp. 137–150.

rates would still rise during the process of draining reserves from the system, the increase—and the resulting negative effects—would be smaller if people realized the policy was not all that effective to begin with.

But if the Fed continues to pat itself on the back by claiming, as Chairman Bernanke did in his speech at Jackson Hole in 2012, that QE has been effective, the market will be that much more wary when the time comes to wind down the policy, and the corresponding economic impact will be that much greater.

Upcoming Chapters in QE Saga

Viewed in this light, the saga of quantitative easing is very long indeed. The adoption of QE during a balance sheet recession is only the first chapter. The second chapter began in May 2013 when the Fed started to talk about tapering. With private loan demand still weak, that has led to relatively little pressure or tension. However, the second chapter marks the start of the QE trap, and long-term rates could surge when the Fed tries to wind down the policy, causing the economy to slow and complicating the central bank's efforts.

The problem will become much more pressing once the private sector completes its balance sheet repairs and businesses and households resume borrowing. That will necessitate monetary tightening, the third chapter in the QE saga. If the Fed chooses not to sell the bonds, it will have to pay a high rate of interest on excess reserves while simultaneously incurring heavy capital losses on the long-term bonds it holds. The higher interest payments by the Fed means a correspondingly larger budget deficit for the federal government. The government may also have to inject temporary capital to enable the Fed to absorb those losses. At the same time, the Treasury will be selling redemption bonds to pay for the maturing bonds held by the Fed, which are effectively new money bonds that would, together with a larger deficit, put upward pressure on long-term interest rates.

And if the Fed fails to tighten, the money supply could expand rapidly—excess reserves are, after all, equal to 20 times statutory reserves—sparking worries about hyperinflation and leading to a further surge in long-term rates.

Capital Injection Could Also Be Threatened If Blame Shifts to Fed

On the political side, the preferred outcome at that juncture would be for the U.S. Congress to move quickly to inject capital temporarily into the central bank and declare that the government will not let the Fed become insolvent even if it moves to tighten monetary policy. But by the time that becomes a political issue things may not be that simple, since there will probably be talk of holding the Fed accountable for its actions. The large interest payments the Fed will be making to the banks, which would become a significant source of budget deficit for the federal government, may also come under attack.

Politicians—mostly Republican—who have opposed QE from the start would almost certainly take this opportunity to criticize the central bank, threatening its independence. Chairman Bernanke admitted in a speech on November 19, 2013, that such a scenario could have "reputational costs and possibly increase risks to the Federal Reserve's independence."

Yale Professor Emeritus Koichi Hamada, an economic advisor to Japanese prime minister Shinzo Abe, says any losses incurred by the central bank can be made good with money printed expressly for that purpose.[13] But these large capital losses at the central bank would happen at a time when market participants were worried about inflation. Printing money to cover the losses at such a time would only stoke more inflation fears.

Sales Should Start with Bonds Maturing Soon

As soon as these political and distributional issues hit the front pages, it would become clear to everyone that the excess reserves must be removed as quickly as possible, and the QE saga will enter its fourth and final chapter. The Fed should start mopping up excess reserves by selling long-term bonds with fast-approaching maturity dates, which are effectively short-term bonds. The sale of such bonds is unlikely to have a significant impact on long-term rates. Those sales of short-dated paper would still generate some capital losses for the Fed, but that would be worth it, if it enabled the Fed to mop up these highly problematic excess reserves.

Another possibility is that the Fed persuades the Treasury to refrain from issuing long-term debt and concentrate issuance instead at the short end of the curve while the Fed winds down QE. The Fed would then sell its long-term bond holdings and purchase an equivalent amount of short-term debt, essentially a reversal of Operation Twist. The impact of this operation on long-term interest rates would be quite limited if the Treasury agreed to curb issuance of long-term bonds during the process.

The Fed's bond portfolio would then consist mostly of short-term paper, enabling the central bank to sell short-term paper to mop up excess reserves

---

[13] *Nihon Keizai Shimbu*, "Kinyu Kanwa 'Deguchi Senryaku no Shinpai Muyo' Hamada Koichi Shi ni Kiku," electronic version, March 21, 2013. www.nikkei.com/article/DGXNASFL210I9_R20C13A3000000/.

in the money market. This two-stage approach could substantially curb the impact of winding down QE on the long end of the curve. It could also minimize associated market turmoil if market participants perceived it in that way.

Other possible methods of sterilizing the excess reserves include raising the statutory reserve ratio, capital ratio, or liquidity ratio that banks must satisfy. But such measures will also put upward pressure on interest rates. While ultimately some combination of these measures is likely to be adopted, the preferred way to minimize the impact on the yield curve in general and on the long-term sector in particular would be for the Fed to work with the Treasury as an issuer of U.S. government debt.

Final Cost of QE Can Be Calculated Only at End of Fourth Chapter

The end of the fourth chapter is unlikely to come for many years, but only then will it be possible to calculate the total cost of quantitative easing. Economists making that calculation will need to compare conditions then to a scenario in which the central bank had not implemented QE and the economy had recovered smoothly without the need to address the problem of massive excess reserves.

Their likely conclusion will be that with QE the economy sees a slightly shallower recession and slightly earlier recovery in the first chapter, but that benefit is completely negated by the crisis and turmoil of the second through fourth chapters. Moreover, the economic recovery beginning in the second chapter is likely to be weaker than if QE had never been implemented, as illustrated in Figure 2.5.

Economists will probably conclude that by addressing balance sheet recession with QE instead of the preferred tool of fiscal stimulus, the authorities brought upon themselves the harmful side effects of the second through fourth chapters.

Theoretical Debate on QE Has Focused Entirely on Benefits and Ignored Costs

In light of the above, it is obvious that removing QE is likely to be a very difficult and expensive undertaking. However, academic economists who led the United States, United Kingdom, and Japan into QE never told the public how to come out. Indeed there has been shockingly little theoretical research or debate on how to wind down QE in spite of the fact that it is a massive challenge confronting the BOJ, the Fed, and the BOE alike.

Many academic papers have been written on the benefits of quantitative easing since Japan confronted the so-called zero lower bound more than a decade ago, but almost none have discussed the costs and risks involved in ending these policies. In other words, they talked only about chapter 1 of the four-chapter saga. This is the height of professional irresponsibility and is comparable to arguing that fiscal stimulus will lift the economy while completely ignoring the fiscal deficits and other problems it brings. The QE was indeed a leap in the dark.

Making matters worse is the fact that most of the academic research published on quantitative easing is written from the perspective of what central banks can do *after* confronting the zero lower bound. What has been missing all along is an examination of why economies have not recovered after central banks took interest rates down to zero.

This is a problem that has characterized the broader discipline of economics in recent years. In effect, most of the analysis produced by academic economists starts with the assumption that some sort of "external shock" has dislodged the economy from its normal path but never tries to analyze the nature of the shock itself. When Paul Krugman proposed an inflation target and quantitative easing as remedies for Japan's deflation, he famously said that it did not matter *why* Japan was experiencing deflation.[14]

But if private-sector balance sheet adjustments are the reason why the economy has not recovered even after the central bank has taken interest rates down to zero, no amount of QE will increase the money supply, since the money multiplier will remain negative at the margin as long as those adjustments continue. And monetary policy cannot lift the economy without growth in the money supply and credit, which is why the economy has responded so poorly to QE thus far. In other words, there is no reason why QE should produce an economic recovery during a balance sheet recession.

But the money multiplier will turn positive once the private sector completes its balance sheet repairs and starts borrowing again. Once that happens, the whole situation is turned upside down as the central bank is forced to absorb all the liquidity it supplied just when the economy is starting to show signs of recovery. That pushes the economy into a QE trap.

While the political blame for the QE saga in the United States can be placed at the feet of the Democrats who acquiesced to it, it should also be remembered that QE2, Operation Twist, and QE3 were all adopted as next-best policies when Republican intransigence prevented the government from administering the first-best policy of fiscal stimulus. In that sense both parties share equally in the blame.

---

[14] Paul Krugman, "It's Baaack: Japan's Slump and the Return of the Liquidity Trap," *Brookings Papers on Economic Activities* 2 (1998): p. 172.

Ultimately, the leaders of the two parties will protest vociferously that economists only discussed QE's first chapter and neglected to mention the rest of the story.

Central Banks Should Establish a New Reaction Function to Drain Reserves

Ordinarily, the sooner the recovery arrives, the better for everybody. But for monetary authorities that have engaged in QE, a gradual recovery—and particularly a gradual rebound in private loan demand—is preferable to a quick turnaround. An abrupt recovery could prompt the Fed to raise rates quickly lest it create inflation and an asset bubble. That could cause long-term rates to skyrocket, with severe implications for the interest-sensitive sectors that have driven the economy up to this point.

In contrast, a gradual recovery in private loan demand would allow the authorities to drain excess reserves over time, thereby minimizing the kind of "bad" rise in rates noted above. Here, too, interest rates would rise more than they would have without QE, but the increase should be limited as long as underlying private loan demand remains weak.

If higher long-term interest rates appear to weigh on the U.S. economy, all the Fed would have to do is leave short-term rates at zero for a longer period of time. In this case the rise in long-term rates would keep a lid on inflation, thereby removing the need for the Fed to rush ahead with a normalization of short-term rates.

Once market participants recognize that the Fed has a reaction function—that is, that it will respond to an unwarranted increase in long-term rates due to a winding down of QE by extending the zero interest rate horizon—any increase in long-term rates is likely to be limited as long as short-term rates are anchored at zero.

The Fed should therefore give priority to draining liquidity from the system and extending the zero interest rate policy to address any resulting economic weakness due to higher long-term rates. Doing so would effectively minimize the eventual rise in long-term interest rates.

In this sense, I disagree with William Dudley, who argued for higher short-term rates before ending reinvestment. If the Fed follows the approach outlined by the New York Fed president—that is, raising short-term rates first and then draining liquidity—the possibility of a spike in long-term rates would increase since short-term rates would not be anchored at zero.

It will not be easy under any circumstances to reduce by 95 percent the liquidity that was injected into the system with the Fed's purchase of long-term government bonds. But if a moderate rise in long-term rates due to the winding down of QE succeeds in keeping inflation in check and enables the Fed to keep short-term rates at zero, the eventual increase in long-term rates need not be particularly destructive.

Recent indicators suggest that inflation is picking up in the United States and Japan and a housing bubble is developing in the United Kingdom. This means the Fed, the BOJ, and the BOE need to move quickly to wind down quantitative easing while they still can.

Emerging Markets Need Inward Capital Controls to Protect against QE

As noted earlier, countries such as China, Brazil, and Germany strongly objected to QE2 and similar policies from the outset because they knew QE would complicate domestic policymaking. The use of QE by the developed economies encourages global capital to flow into emerging markets with their comparatively high interest rates, creating bubbles in the process. When the developed economies then move to wind down QE, the capital flows out again, leaving the emerging economies to deal with depreciating currencies and inflation. This, at least, was their concern. And recent events suggest their fears were fully justified.

At the St. Petersburg summit in September 2013 the G20 leaders declared the emerging economies could address this kind of volatility with appropriate macroeconomic policies and structural reforms, but this was worse than nonsense. It is precisely the countries that have implemented the right macro policies and structural reforms that will attract the largest capital inflows, the sharpest asset price inflation, and the greatest subsequent difficulties in administering domestic policy.

If the advanced economies insist on implementing and then winding down QE policies, the emerging markets need to make full use of controls on inward capital flows to insulate themselves from hot money flows originating in the developed world. Despite the G20's sanctioning of such controls at the Seoul meeting in 2010 as mentioned earlier, countries like Brazil and Indonesia do not appear to have made full use of this tool over the subsequent three years. If they had done so and had succeeded in restricting capital inflows from the West, they would not have experienced the kind of difficulties reported since May 2013.

Their failure to do so is attributable in part to the extreme political unpopularity of restricting inward capital flows. After all, such inflows lift asset prices, make people wealthier, give domestic businesses access to low-cost funding, and help keep inflationary pressures in check. Everyone except the exporters struggling against the headwind of a strong domestic currency is happy in such an environment. Erecting restrictions on capital inflows, even if necessary for stable growth in the longer term, requires a gutsy decision by politicians. And in most cases that decision is put off or diluted because the status quo is so nice and comfortable.

One authority that has kept a stringent watch on inward capital flows is the central bank of Taiwan. Its governor, Perng Fai-nan, has become a rather unpopular figure at some foreign financial institutions as a result. But it was because he had the courage to check capital inflows that Taiwan's economy emerged from the currency crisis of 1997 and the more recent GFC without major damage. The lesson here is that in a world where the developed economies are implementing QE at will and without consulting others, authorities in emerging markets must have the courage to restrict—and if necessary prohibit—capital inflows.

The rise in U.S. interest rates starting in May 2013 occurred simply because the Fed said it *might* reduce its bond purchases under QE3. If the Fed actually begins to dismantle QE, interest rates are likely to rise further and become increasingly unstable, as noted in the discussion on the QE trap. Both the United States and the emerging markets affected by its actions are entering uncharted waters.

Japan Should Learn from Pioneers in QE Using Long-Term Bonds

The Fed decided to begin tapering despite an inflation rate of just 1.1 percent in consideration of a variety of potential future problems. In Japan, BOJ Governor Haruhiko Kuroda on April 8, 2014, declared the BOJ had no intention of giving in to market participants' demands for additional easing in response to the poor performance of Japanese equities since the beginning of the year. He also surprised many by expressing the view that Japan's deflationary gap was almost gone.

If the deflationary gap has in fact disappeared and the economy is close to full employment, further monetary accommodation would be not just unnecessary but also downright dangerous. Kuroda's comment, therefore, signals a major turning point for the policy debate in Japan, which has been predicated for the past 20 years on the assumption of a large deflationary gap.

Japan's bank reserves currently amount to some 14 times statutory reserves, a multiple expected to rise to nearly 18.7 by the end of 2014. Japan will then face the question of how to wind down a QE program that has become as large as that of the United States today.

The Fed has begun tapering its asset purchases with inflation at just 1.1 percent because it realizes the magnitude of the problems involved in winding down QE. The BOJ also needs to think about whether it should continue easing until the inflation rate actually rises to 2 percent.

The IMF report noted above singled out Japan and warned that if the BOJ was late in winding down quantitative easing and was perceived as falling behind the curve on inflation, the Bank could incur losses amounting to 7.5 percent of GDP, which would be greater than the worst-case losses for the Fed or the BOE. Since the capital of BOJ is only about ¥6 trillion while the above losses would amount to ¥36 trillion, this is a very serious risk indeed.

Until now Japan has always been the pioneer in the field of balance sheet recessions, and since 2008 Western countries have strived to learn from its experience. But when it comes to QE, the United States and the United Kingdom were the first to implement this policy in the long-term government bond market, and Japan would do well to monitor their markets' response, and particularly everything that has happened since May 22, 2013. If the conclusion reached is that QE should be wound down before it is too late, Japan needs to act without hesitation.

As of June 2014, Governor Kuroda continues to declare he will keep QE in place until the inflation rate hits 2 percent. One reason why Mr. Kuroda maintains his tone is that Japan also has the consumption tax hike scheduled for October 2015 to deal with, and the BOJ governor probably does not feel he can change course until that obstacle has been cleared. Indeed, if anything can delay the BOJ action and make everything more difficult in the future, it will be the delay induced by the consumption tax issue.

On the other hand, the governor has commented repeatedly on the Japanese economy's supply shortfall. He even indicated since April 2014 that Japan has reached full employment.[15] These remarks can be interpreted as laying the groundwork for the change in policy direction that will eventually be necessary.

The BOJ's monetary accommodation since the end of 2012 has brought about a weaker yen and provided a major fillip to the stock market (this is discussed in detail in Chapter 4), but if policymakers bask in their success and forget to properly time the dismantling of this policy, Japan could find itself in the very difficult situation warned about by the IMF.

Financial and Capital Markets during Balance Sheet Recessions

The Treasury market's sharp reaction to Chairman Bernanke's remarks on May 22, 2013, suggested it had become a liquidity-driven market in which

---

[15] Bank of Japan, "Sousai Teirei Kisha-Kaiken Youshi, 2014 Nen 4 Gatsu 8 ka (Summary of the Governor's Press Conference)," April 8, 2014.

participants were betting on the continuation of quantitative easing. In other words, interest rates were being determined less by economic fundamentals than by the question of whether QE would continue.

It is important to note that the term "liquidity-driven market" has different implications during a balance sheet recession. In an ordinary liquidity-driven market, central bank easing has produced a sharp expansion of the money supply that can finance both consumption and investment. In contrast, the liquidity-driven market in those economies suffering from balance sheet recessions has been driven by the *assumption* that the money supply will eventually expand.

In other words, today's market is being fueled not by actual growth in the money supply but by the hope that money supply would eventually grow based on the growth in the monetary base, which is one step before the money supply. This is a crucial distinction. In an ordinary (i.e., non-balance sheet recession) economy, as the central bank eases policy by lowering interest rates and expanding the monetary base, the private sector responds by increasing its borrowings, thereby expanding the money supply. Growth in the money supply and credit eventually boosts economic activity and prices, prompting people to invest in shares or real estate.

In the second half of the 1980s, for example, the BOJ cut the official discount rate to what was then an all-time low of 2.5 percent, prompting individuals and businesses to take advantage of the low rates to borrow and invest. The money supply grew, the economy expanded, and asset prices surged higher.

In Europe, the European Central Bank (ECB) took its policy rate down to what was then a record low of 2 percent in 2003, leading households and businesses across Europe to borrow and invest and eventually fueling a massive housing bubble. In the United States, too, many borrowed aggressively to invest in housing after Alan Greenspan took the federal funds rate down to a post-war low of 1 percent in 2003.

Today, however, businesses and households afflicted with balance sheet problems are not only not borrowing but are actually increasing their savings in spite of policy rates that are substantially lower than those of the bubble era. As a result, private credit in the Western economies has been flat ever since Lehman went under—even in the relatively healthy U.S. economy. Since 2008, private credit expanded by 6 percent in Japan and by 2 percent in the United States, but decreased by 2 percent in the Eurozone and by a huge 15 percent in the United Kingdom (Figures 1.7 to 1.10). Inflation remains so low in these countries because money supply growth has been tepid in spite of all the central bank–supplied liquidity.

The sluggish expansion of the money supply and credit indicates that the money available to the private sector to spend has increased only modestly. That is what makes the situation today so different from conditions during the bubble days, when the money supply in Western economies was expanding rapidly in response to central bank accommodation. While the current market has been described as a liquidity-driven market fueled by QE, the money supply—the money actually available for the private sector to spend or invest—has grown very slowly.

Balance Sheet Recession Brings Special Kind of Liquidity-Driven Market

However, one sector of the economy experiences a sharp increase in the funds at its disposal during a balance sheet recession, even if the money supply and credit available to the rest of the economy remain constrained. And that sector is the financial sector.

This happens for the following reasons. First, the businesses and households who would ordinarily be borrowers have not only stopped borrowing but are actually increasing their savings or paying back debt. Second, the people who would ordinarily be savers continue to save as they always have. Moreover, the funds supplied by the central bank under QE are eventually entrusted to the private sector fund managers as well. The parties who sold bonds to the central bank had been using them as savings vehicles, and the fact that those assets changed from bonds to cash did not mean they would suddenly be consumed. This means investment managers in financial institutions find themselves facing huge inflows of funds from newly generated savings in the household sector, deleveraged funds from the corporate sector, and fresh money from the central bank implementing QE.

Under ordinary circumstances, monetary accommodation expands the money supply throughout the economy, while during a balance sheet recession monetary accommodation only increases the funds entrusted to investment managers.

Seeing these huge fund inflows, many investors have conflated QE-fueled base money growth with actual money supply growth or have acted based on the assumption that the money supply will eventually increase. But the only part of the economy awash in funds is the corner populated by investment managers. In the real economy, the private sector is not borrowing, the money supply is not expanding, and the economy remains in a slump.

Investors who are able to see the broader picture would remain cautious until the private sector is ready to borrow again. Those who do not see the overall picture would remain bullish because they expect QE will boost the money supply in a textbook fashion and by extension the economy. It is this latter group of investors that has caused some asset prices to race ahead of the real economy in recent years.

Is Inflation of 1–2 Percent Too Low?

The Fed began looking for a way to wind down QE in May 2013, but many are still saying the Fed should keep QE3 in place now that U.S. inflation has fallen to the dangerously low territory of just above 1 percent.

The Fed target of a 2 percent inflation rate is based on statistical analysis showing that 2 percent inflation leads to optimal growth in real GDP. That would imply that recent U.S. inflation is too low and that the Fed should leave its easing policies in place for longer.

It should be noted that 2 percent target does not necessarily mean prices going up 2 percent per year. One shortcoming of price data is that they do not properly reflect the deflationary impact of technological innovation (i.e., the fact that products offering the same level of performance can now be bought for less). Some therefore argue that an official inflation rate of around 2 percent may be effectively equal to zero, which suggests the recent U.S. inflation rate of just above 1 percent is indeed cause for concern.

Does Inflation Improve People's Standard of Living?

The view that a certain amount of inflation is good for the economy because it encourages people to spend money is probably correct. But that does not necessarily imply the monetary authorities should target an inflation rate for at least two reasons. First is the question of how much people's standard of living will actually improve because of inflation-induced increase in expenditures. Second is the matter of whether the central bank can justify the costs of such a policy.

Regarding the first, people who would ordinarily prefer to focus on their profession may find themselves forced to consider buying real estate as a hedge against inflation. Such purchases do in fact get money moving through the economy and, if they lead to higher real estate prices, can give a further boost to economic activity via the wealth effect.

But this comes at a major cost. This stems from the fact that the time these people would otherwise have spent on their profession must instead be devoted to real estate investment, a field in which they have little or no expertise. This is important because both economic growth and the development of civilization in general have been made possible by an increasingly sophisticated division of labor that allows people to maximize their expertise and productivity.[16]

---

[16] This question was discussed in detail in the appendix to my earlier book, *The Holy Grail of Macroeconomics* ("Thoughts on Walras and Macroeconomics," pp. 295–308).

It was the invention of money that made this division of labor possible, and it is the ability to buy other goods and services with money income earned in one's own specialty that allows people to focus on sharpening their skills.

Inflation worries destabilize the value of the money serving as the foundation for this division of labor. That makes it more difficult for people to focus on their specialties, thereby diminishing the productivity gains resulting from the division of labor. As an example, assume that a software developer at an IT firm buys an apartment as an inflation hedge and encounters a problem with a tenant. If the effort expended on resolving this problem causes her to lose focus on her profession, her contribution to society's economic development will also diminish. In other words, inflation worries distract people from their specialties, with negative implications for the division of labor that has driven the development of civilization.

Moreover, the fact that she bought something she would not otherwise have purchased implies she was unable to buy something else that she would have preferred. This raises the possibility that spending during an inflationary period may produce less satisfaction or happiness per dollar than it would during a noninflationary period. In other words, expenditures may have increased because of inflation worries, but those expenditures may not have been the preferred use of money. This means the satisfaction and utility obtained from a given unit of expenditure may be significantly less when it is driven by inflation concerns.

Absence of Inflation Concerns May Have Lifted Utility of Consumption in Japan

If it were possible to determine how much of a nation's GDP actually enhanced people's utility, we might find that countries such as Switzerland and Japan, which have enjoyed extended periods of low inflation, actually have a higher share of GDP that is directly linked to people's satisfaction and happiness than countries with higher inflation rates, such as the United States and the United Kingdom.

The same would be true of deflation. If Japan were facing severe deflation, the value of money would not only become unstable, but the real value of debt would rise sharply—something noted by economist Irving Fisher in the 1930s—leading to further economic weakness. In that sense, both inflation and deflation are distractions that detract from meaningful economic growth. However, the modest deflation Japan experienced prior to the GFC, which consisted of annual declines in consumer prices of less than 1 percent a year, probably posed no such concerns.

Freed from having to worry about inflation, Japanese consumers bought exactly what they needed or wanted, and the amount of satisfaction or utility derived from each yen spent was probably quite high. Not having to worry about inflation also saved time and eliminated unnecessary concerns and headaches over the past 20 years. The utility derived from Japanese consumers' ability to completely ignore inflation may not show up in the GDP statistics, but it was probably significant.

This kind of approach may be alien to orthodox economics with its focus on headline GDP growth. But as the developed societies age—and as some, like Japan, start to shrink—aggregate GDP growth will become less important than per capita GDP growth and particularly the *quality* of that growth.

In such a world, any distraction that prevents people from maximizing their unique talents within society's division of labor must be eliminated. The notion that the central bank should target a 2 percent inflation rate just because that is the level of inflation that maximized GDP growth in the past will have to be reviewed if not discarded if it is preventing people from maximizing their time on their chosen field of specialization.

QE Should Not Be Pursued Any Further Given Difficulty of Winding It Down

The argument that the Fed should engage in further QE to lift the inflation rate from the current level of 1.42 percent should also be judged against the massive costs entailed in winding down the policy—that is, the QE trap.

There are two problems in particular. One is that QE implemented during balance sheet recessions has little impact on either prices or the real economy. The other issue is that as soon as private loan demand starts to pick up the authorities will be forced to drain or sterilize excess reserves, which could entail a surge in the fiscal deficit and interest rates weighing heavily on the recovery, as described above.

Once the cost of removing the QE is fully taken into account, the price for maintaining or expanding QE simply because the U.S. inflation rate is currently running below 2 percent is very high indeed.

Economics is a very young science, and as such it has been extremely prone to fads. During the 1950s and 1960s, economists were fascinated by the possibility of fine-tuning the economy with fiscal policy, with many believing that Keynes has finally found the cure to end all recessions. When that led to inflation and stagflation in the 1970s, money supply targeting became all the rage. But the Fed's experiment with it from October 1979 did not produce the result expected by its proponents. Then came the inflation targeting, first proposed in the 1990s as a remedy to the deflation in Japan, and now adopted by many nations facing similar threats. My hunch is that this fad will subside also, especially when the full cost of QE needed to achieve the target in a balance sheet recession, the cause of deflation, is finally made known.

QE a Problematic Byproduct of Balance Sheet Recessions

In a sense, QE is a problematic byproduct of a balance sheet recession. It is a "byproduct" because there is no reason why a policy like QE would be proposed anytime other than during such a recession. If this were an ordinary recession, there would be no need for QE since the economy would have responded long before interest rates hit zero. If the authorities understood that a balance sheet recession is rooted in a shortage of borrowers, they would not have expanded QE—which is designed to increase the number of *lenders*—to the extent they did. And they were able to keep on expanding QE because there is no apparent harm from doing so *during a balance sheet recession.*

The world is turned upside down when the private sector completes its balance sheet repairs and returns to the textbook world of profit maximization. Now the massive excess reserves sloshing around in the banking system suddenly become a major problem, and both the markets and the authorities become extremely nervous as the central bank prepares to drain these reserves from the system. Now that Fed Chair Yellen has indicated that the QE would be unwound in the next five to eight years, everyone must get ready for the rough and uncharted ride to normalcy.

CHAPTER 3

The United States in Balance Sheet Recession

T he last chapter pointed out that the United States was able to maintain relatively robust economic growth by quickly abandoning the agreement made at the Toronto summit in 2010. But the road was not an easy one. The U.S. economy had been in a balance sheet recession since 2008, but a lack of understanding of the problem led to numerous policy missteps at the beginning.

The officials in charge of economic policy today, however, fully understand the risks of balance sheet recessions. Consequently, the United States is in a much better position than Europe, where policymakers are completely unaware of the rare economic sickness that is infecting their economies.

Figure 3.1 shows flow-of-funds data for the United States. The line for the household sector, the driver of the recent housing bubble, was below zero during the bubble, which means households borrowed more than they saved, while after the bubble burst households began saving more each year in spite of zero interest rates. As U.S. households were described as the key source of final demand to the global economy, the sudden increase in their savings triggered a sharp slowdown in both the U.S. and the global economies. After 2007 U.S. households no longer lived up to their decades-long reputation as perennial borrowers.

The corporate sector, meanwhile, scaled back its borrowing in the aftermath of the Internet bubble collapse in 2000, and when the housing bubble burst in 2007 it became a net saver as companies started increasing savings and paying down debt. Their increased savings in 2010 is also attributable in part to the severe funding difficulties they faced when the GFC brought on a destructive credit crunch starting in 2007. This point will be described in detail with reference to Figure 3.4, but companies that have gone through a credit crunch tend to hold large amounts of cash or liquid securities in self-defense to avoid a repeat of that painful experience.

FIGURE 3.1 United States in Balance Sheet Recession—U.S. Private Sector Saved on Average 6 Percent of GDP since 2008

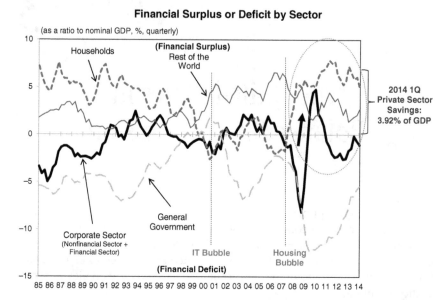

Financial Surplus or Deficit by Sector

Note: All entries are four-quarter moving averages. For the latest figures, four-quarter averages ending in 2014 Q1 are used.

Sources: FRB; U.S. Department of Commerce.

Even though the extent of private sector deleveraging, at nearly 4 percent of gross domestic product (GDP) for 2014 Q1 on four-quarter moving average basis, is a cause for serious concern, officials from the White House down to the Federal Reserve now understand the risks of balance sheet recessions. Key U.S. officials—ranging from Fed chairman Ben Bernanke to leading academic economist Paul Krugman—have read my book, and their policy proposals and contributions to the ongoing policy debate reflect an understanding that the United States is in the grip of a balance sheet recession. I have also been told that at the Council of Economic Advisers (CEA), which advises the president on economic policy, one of the books new staff members are required to read is *The Holy Grail of Macroeconomics.*

Consequently, the U.S. response to the balance sheet recession over the past few years has provided an example for the rest of the world. In particular, the decision by officials at the Fed and the White House to use the expression "fiscal cliff" to warn against premature fiscal consolidation kept the United States from making that mistake, unlike the Japanese in 1997 and the Europeans after 2010.

When a nation has run a $1 trillion-plus deficit for four straight years, demands for deficit-reduction measures should come as no surprise. Yet the United States managed to avoid such policies, which is crucial during a balance sheet recession, because officials argued that fiscal consolidation at that point in the economic cycle would have devastating consequences. Thanks to their efforts, the United States has staged a comparatively robust recovery with industrial output now above the previous peak of 2008 in spite of the large blow to the economy after Lehman Brothers failed. This compares favorably with the level of industrial production in the Eurozone (now at 2003 levels), the United Kingdom (1993), and Japan (2003)—although it should be noted that Japanese output would probably be substantially higher if not for the 2011 earthquake. Moreover, the strong U.S. economy has recently driven marked improvements in the fiscal deficit. In other words, by averting premature fiscal consolidation with warnings of a "fiscal cliff," the United States was able to sustain the recovery's momentum, which is now paying handsome dividends in the form of smaller deficits.

Rating Agencies Need to Be More Tightly Regulated

No one could claim that things in the United States have gone smoothly. There have been numerous policy missteps and a great deal of confusion, particularly in the immediate aftermath of the Lehman failure.

The roots of the crisis can be traced to former Fed chairman Alan Greenspan, who refused until the end of his term to acknowledge that the United States was in a housing bubble, even as the situation spiraled out of control. In his testimony before Congress, Greenspan was asked by politicians on both sides of the aisle whether housing was in a bubble, and he repeatedly said no. Ordinarily the central bank governor should be the first to sound the warning about a bubble, but in this case the brakeman left his post. Greenspan's denial of the bubble and his inability to stop or even slow it eventually plunged the U.S. economy into an unprecedented crisis.

The immediate trigger of the financial crisis was a new financial instrument called the collateralized debt obligation (CDO), which packaged a pool of subprime mortgages into a new security. Rating agencies, which traditionally were responsible for monitoring the quality of financial instruments traded in the market, gave in to the temptation of short-term profits and issued a slew of AAA ratings for these securities. Because of their actions, instruments that could be understood and evaluated by only a tiny handful of investment professionals were sold to a mass audience of global financial institutions.

So not only did the Fed chairman fail to put on the brakes, but the private-sector organizations that should have done the same opened up the throttle. When the U.S. housing bubble finally burst and the problems with CDOs surfaced, many global financial institutions—including, of course, most U.S. institutions—found themselves facing life-threatening problems.

The financial crisis would never have occurred if the rating agencies had not given such high ratings to CDOs containing subprime loans and other securitized products. The reckless securitization that occurred would have been impossible without the cooperation of the rating agencies, which makes them as responsible for the crisis as former chairman Greenspan.

This problem of the rating agencies was a new twist that did not feature in the Great Depression of the 1930s. Prior to the Great Depression, U.S. banks relied solely on collateral when lending money. But as that collateral lost much of its value in the depression, both banks and the authorities began to recognize the limitations of this approach and the importance of credit checks and ratings. Thus the hard lessons of the Great Depression greatly expanded the role played by credit ratings and rating agencies.

The recent tragedy, however, was caused by reckless behavior by these same rating agencies. Inasmuch as the CDOs that triggered the crisis were so complex that it would have taken a team of a dozen mathematicians working full time for three weeks to determine the risk characteristics of a single CDO, only institutions able to maintain such a team of quants should have been allowed to buy them. In other words, they should have been deemed ineligible for a credit rating, since a rating implies a product is suitable for purchase by ordinary investors. Such a restriction would also have prevented rating agencies from giving overly generous ratings to these instruments to win more business.

The role of the rating agencies should have been to ensure that securities being traded on the markets upheld certain standards of quality and to apply the brakes as necessary to prevent those markets from spinning out of control. However, it was found out after the fact that there were no brakes. Rating agency regulation must be reviewed and tightened to prevent this from happening again.

Why Was Lehman Allowed to Fail?

When a large number of financial institutions confront the same toxic CDO problem at the same time, the authorities—as discussed in Chapter 1—must treat it as a systemic crisis and address it using policies that are completely different from ordinary, market-based resolutions. In other words, they must put in place policies designed to save everybody because this is a 95 percent problem, not a 5 percent problem.

Unfortunately, the Treasury secretary at the time, Hank Paulson, possessed neither the relevant concepts nor the expertise needed to apply them, and as a result the authorities let Lehman Brothers—the first bank at which problems surfaced—go under. It was this action that triggered the global financial crisis (GFC). Of particular importance were Paulson's opening remarks to a meeting held at the New York Fed the weekend before Lehman failed. He stated that the government had no intention of using taxpayer money to rescue Lehman. Attending this meeting were Timothy Geithner, then serving as head of the New York Fed, and the leaders of key financial institutions who had gathered because they believed letting Lehman fail would have monumental consequences. But after the Treasury secretary's opening remarks, the financial system lurched toward collapse.

Lehman, after all, was not alone. The vast majority of Western financial institutions held CDOs whose value had collapsed. Each bank knew its rivals held the same distressed securities, but no one knew just how far the prices of those securities might fall.

That led to two problems. First, other private institutions would not rescue Lehman without a government backstop because they could not get hold of a reliable estimate of the losses the bank was carrying. A backstop refers to a government pledge to bear any losses above a certain threshold. With a backstop, private institutions know in advance the maximum potential loss they will have to bear if they take over a distressed company in these circumstances. Starting from this figure, they would then add other costs related to the rescue and compare that to the potential benefits of rescuing Lehman. If the cost-benefit analysis is such that management feels it can make a convincing case to shareholders, the deal will be done.

If the authorities thought a failure of Lehman Brothers would entail significant damage to the broader economy, the correct response would have been to adjust the value of the backstop as necessary to find someone in the private sector to rescue the firm. Robert Steel, who served as undersecretary for domestic finance at Treasury, had supervised the rescue of Bear Stearns six months earlier. He possessed the necessary acumen to deal with this kind of situation and had successfully persuaded JPMorgan to acquire the failed firm by providing an appropriate backstop. Thanks to his efforts, the fallout from that failure was modest.

But Steel left government in July that year, leaving Paulson, who lacked both the necessary acumen and experience, to deal with the Lehman crisis. And Paulson declared that there would be no backstop. With no reliable estimate of the final losses at Lehman, no other private sector institution could come to its rescue. As a result, the investment bank went under when the markets opened the following Monday.

The second problem was that with so many financial institutions facing the same problems at the same time, the collapse of Lehman Brothers led all of them to wonder who might be next. Consequently they went to extreme lengths to protect themselves by stashing away cash and liquid securities.

But a financial system functions only when institutions are willing to lend to each other, as explained in Chapter 2. And to keep the economy going, it must also lend private savings to those who can use them.

When many banks confront the same problem at the same time, Bank A has no idea when Bank B might go under, and Bank B feels the same about Bank A. Under these circumstances, no institution will lend funds to the interbank market, and the financial system as a whole will become completely dysfunctional, sparking a credit crunch. After Lehman went under, not only did the stock market plunge, but nonfinancial corporations that could no longer obtain financing were forced to sell off financial assets and use the proceeds to fund day-to-day operations. This will be discussed in detail with reference to Figure 3.4.

One logical consequence of this is that the post-Lehman tightening of banking regulations in the West centering on too-big-to-fail and systemically important financial institutions (SIFIs) is missing the point. The most serious crises happen when all banks face the same problem at the same time. Their size and interconnectedness are of secondary importance. In such cases the authorities must be given the power to rescue the entire system, even if that entails dubious business transactions (such as the continued lending to Mexico after August 1982 mentioned in Chapter 1). Unfortunately, Paulson was incapable of shifting his thinking from an orthodox market-based approach to the kind of approach needed to save the 95 percent.

The global synchronous financial crisis then developed into a global economic crisis as U.S. businesses laid off a total of 8 million employees. The mass job cuts were difficult to avoid given the funding crisis these companies faced at the time. Since then, U.S. businesses have been criticized for holding large quantities of unproductive financial assets. However, their stance is largely explained by the destructive credit crunch and funding crisis they experienced from 2007 to 2009. Any corporate treasurer or financial officer who lived through a credit crunch of that magnitude would subsequently build up a large cash pile to prevent a repeat of those events.

Another major policy misstep during the crisis was that the Federal Reserve, which is charged with maintaining financial system stability, did not (could not?) stop Paulson's actions. If the Fed had understood that allowing Lehman to fail would have such severe consequences, it should have pulled out all the stops to prevent Paulson from pushing Lehman to bankruptcy, just as former chairman Paul Volcker had done with Mexico during the Latin American debt crisis discussed in Chapter 1. Apparently, however, the Federal Reserve no longer has anyone who remembers how the 1982 Latin American debt fiasco was handled. In other words, the Fed has lost its institutional memory of how to recognize and deal with a systemic banking crisis.

Sources have told me that New York Fed president Geithner tried to take action but was unable to secure the cooperation of Bernanke and

Paulson in Washington, with the end result being the debacle we saw. Indicators at the time were already pointing to major systemic problems in the U.S. financial system, and numerous commentators—myself included—had issued warnings. It is extremely unfortunate for the global economy that the U.S. authorities did not heed those warnings and move to avert a Lehman bankruptcy.

TARP Prevented Bank Failures but Also Created Turmoil

Problems surfaced at AIG only hours after Lehman failed, and this time Paulson, perhaps realizing the severity of the situation, did an about-face and decided to rescue AIG. Soon after came what was essentially a taxpayer-funded rescue of the banks in the form of the Troubled Asset Relief Program (TARP). Here as well, however, the authorities made two mistakes. First, Paulson and Bernanke thought the problem could be addressed with the government purchase of bad assets. At the time I tried to convince a senior Treasury official that that would be totally insufficient and that capital injections were needed, but there was as yet little sense of urgency among the authorities. Conditions deteriorated rapidly, however, and by the time TARP was actually implemented a few weeks later it had become a direct injection of capital. Unfortunately, precious time had been lost, and the program's name stayed the same in spite of the major changes to its substance.

Another problem with TARP was that Paulson and Bernanke told the taxpayers' representatives in Congress that the program was needed to end the credit crunch at the banks but did not explicitly specify an end to the credit crunch as a condition for banks' return of the TARP funds. Consequently, banks started paying back the money they had borrowed the next year, after the worst of the crisis had passed, even though the credit crunch continued for an extended period of time after that.

TARP helped keep leading U.S. banks out of bankruptcy by forcing them to accept an injection of government funds. But the banks, unhappy with the conditions attached to the funds by the authorities, paid the money back even though the credit crunch, the original justification for taxpayer approval of TARP funds, was still in force.

The chink in the authorities' armor that made this possible was the remark by Timothy Geithner, who by then had become Treasury secretary, that banks capable of raising fresh capital on their own could pay back the government. What the Treasury Secretary should have done is require banks to demonstrate an increase in lending over a specified duration (e.g., three years) before allowing them to pay back the funds. Because of this misstep, banks returned the government's money even as the credit crunch continued to weigh on the U.S. economy for an extended period of time. That, in turn, left many ordinary Americans extremely suspicious of Washington's motives.

In Japan, the Hashimoto administration's pursuit of fiscal consolidation in 1997 led to simultaneous weakness in the yen and Japanese stocks that was referred to at the time as the *nihon-uri* or "sell Japan" phenomenon. Falling share prices hit the numerator of Japanese banks' capital ratios while the sliding yen hit the denominator, and the resulting decline in capital adequacy ratios nearly stopped lending in its tracks in the autumn of 1997 and Japan experienced its first credit crunch in half a century.

The crunch was quickly addressed by the government in February 1998 with the passage of a law enabling capital injections. Although the initial Japanese plan attached no conditions to the capital injection, Washington objected to it. As a result, the final legislation contained numerous conditions, including an inspection process that was little more than a "people's trial," with prosecutors to be sent in to expose the bank's dirty laundry.

The entirely foreseeable outcome of this requirement was that not one bank chose to participate in the program, and not a single yen of taxpayer money found its way to distressed banks (this 100 percent rejection was never reported in the Western press however). This is because banks could also meet the new capital adequacy targets by reducing lending. As a result, the credit crunch got worse, and the Japanese economy continued to weaken.

The ruling party quickly realized its mistake and scrapped the conditions demanded by Washington to encourage banks to participate in the program. The first modest capital injections were finally carried out at the end of March 1998. These injections stopped credit conditions from deteriorating any further, while a second, much larger round of capital injections conducted a year later, in March 1999, resulted in dramatic improvements in the situation, something confirmed by the Bank of Japan's (BOJ) *Tankan* survey (Figure 1.18).

Another factor hastening the resolution of the credit crunch was the Japanese authorities' decision to require banks to use newly injected government capital to support lending instead of writing off nonperforming loans (NPLs). Banks were instructed to dispose of their NPLs over time using period earnings.

These examples demonstrate that when executive compensation and a variety of other conditions are attached to capital injections, either (1) the banks will reject the infusions outright, as they did in Japan, or (2) if forced to accept the money, as they were in the United States under TARP, they will quickly find ways to return the money and all the attached strings. Placing banks in that position is likely to postpone the end to the credit crunch, causing a corresponding delay in the economic recovery.

TARP played an important role inasmuch as it prevented the worst-case scenario of a string of failures at large U.S. banks. However, the authorities' decision to allow banks to pay back the government without first ending the credit crunch—which Paulson and Bernanke had promised Congress the program would do—deeply undermined the credibility of U.S. financial authorities in the eyes of the public. This was a very unfortunate outcome that could have been avoided if the authorities had only learned from Japan's experience.

The point here is that when the government is faced with both NPL problems and a nationwide credit crunch at the same time, it must fix the latter first with a capital injection because a lack of credit can quickly kill the entire economy. The government should work on improving the health of individual banks only after the systemic risk is addressed. This sequencing is important because if the authorities try to fix both problems at the same time, chances are high that they will get neither.[1]

U.S. Authorities Changed Course with "Pretend and Extend"

At the same time that U.S. authorities adopted tougher banking regulation in the form of the Dodd-Frank Rule and more recently the so-called Volcker Rule, they substantially eased the rules governing NPL write-offs in the autumn of 2009. This succeeded in preventing the plunge in commercial real estate prices from threatening the solvency of the U.S. banking sector.

By the autumn of 2009, U.S. commercial real estate prices had fallen an average of 43 percent from their autumn 2007 peak (Figure 3.2), causing the outstanding balances on many real estate loans to exceed the value of the underlying collateral. Banks could not roll over these loans since they were prevented from lending an amount greater than the value of the pledged collateral. The decline in property prices also caused many loans to violate loan-to-value (LTV) covenants even when the outstanding loan balances were less than the value of the collateral.

If banks had followed the rules and refused to roll over commercial real estate loans that no longer satisfied LTV covenants, a massive crisis could have resulted, incapacitating a banking sector and an economy already shaken to their foundations by problems in the housing sector.

Moreover, the need to roll over many of these loans—which had grown so massively during the bubble period—meant the authorities and banks had to act quickly. The U.S. economy would have undergone a second financial crisis if banks had not been allowed to refinance commercial real estate loans.

---

[1] This is explained in greater deal in Richard Koo, *The Holy Grail of Macroeconomics: Lessons from Japan's Great Recession* (Singapore: John Wiley & Sons, 2008, Chapter 7).

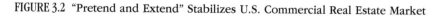

FIGURE 3.2 "Pretend and Extend" Stabilizes U.S. Commercial Real Estate Market

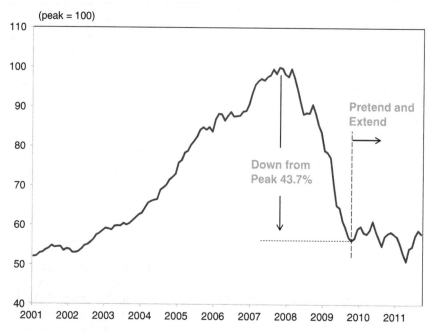

Note: This index discontinued in September 2011.
Sources: Moody's Investors Service; Haver Analytics.

This recognition led the authorities to change their stance dramatically. They declared that if banks had reason to believe the value of the commercial property backing the loans had fallen more than warranted, they would be allowed to roll over the loans (i.e., the authorities would not treat them as nonperforming). This decision was laid out in the Policy Statement on Prudent Commercial Real Estate Loan Workouts (better known as "Pretend and Extend"), which was jointly released on October 30, 2009, by the Federal Reserve, the Federal Deposit Insurance Corporation (FDIC), and the Office of the Comptroller of the Currency. Under this policy, banks were allowed to roll over loans on which the outstanding balances exceeded the value of the underlying collateral as long as the borrower had long-term contracts with high-quality tenants and rents appeared unlikely to fall substantially.

This signaled a major shift in the position of U.S. authorities, which until then had been urging banks in an orthodox fashion to dispose of their NPLs as quickly as possible. Until October 2009, they did not understand that a quick resolution of NPLs is the preferred response only when the problems are small relative to the size of the overall financial system, but not when the problems are large. It also indicated a reversal in the views of Secretary Gei-thner, who initially had insisted the United States would avoid a drawn-out, Japan-like recession by forcing banks to dispose of their bad assets quickly.

Faced with a nightmare situation in the commercial real estate sector, the U.S. authorities effectively abandoned their orthodox plans for the early disposal of NPLs. Instead, they decided to allow banks to roll over their bad loans—just as the Fed had instructed U.S. lenders to do during the Latin American debt crisis of 1982 and Japanese authorities had instructed its banks to do in 1998—and gradually address the problem over time using period earnings.

This was extremely fortunate as it signaled that, one year into the GFC and the new administration, the authorities were finally confronting the real-ity of the situation. U.S. commercial real estate prices stabilized following this directive in the autumn of 2009 and then entered an upturn that has continued to this day. Today, nobody is talking about the problems in the commercial real estate sector, even though in 2009 they were fully expected to become the next flashpoint of the financial crisis after housing.

Like myself, former Fed chairman Paul Volcker was also of the opinion that the only option for the United States given the magnitude of the prob-lems was to move ahead slowly and put time on its side. In the beginning his views were also ignored.

Fiscal Stimulus Shifts from "Three Ts" to "Three Ss"

Turning to the real economy, Lawrence Summers, the first director of the National Economic Council (NEC) under President Obama, initially argued that a large "jolt" of fiscal stimulus would be enough to prime the economy's pump and put the U.S. economy back on a growth trajectory. When making a case for fiscal stimulus in 2008, he said it should be "timely, targeted, and temporary," then known as the "three Ts."

While a single jolt of stimulus might be enough to restart economic activ-ity and pull the economy out of an ordinary recession, it is not the answer during a balance sheet recession, which will continue until the private sector completes its balance sheet repairs—that is, until it finishes deleveraging. As long as that process is under way the government must keep administering fiscal stimulus.

During such a recession people choose to save more and pay down debt in spite of zero interest rates in order to remove the debt overhang. As a result, the number of willing borrowers for the newly saved and deleveraged funds drops sharply, leaving the economy with a large pool of unborrowed savings that leaks out of the economy's income stream. The government must continue borrowing and spending that unborrowed savings until the private sector is ready to borrow if it wants to stop the leakage from developing into a deflationary spiral. Accordingly, "timely, targeted, and temporary" stimulus was not enough to deal with the problems confronting the United States.

Summers soon realized the problems with the three Ts and changed his tune and said in a speech in July 2009 that what the U.S. economy actually needed was "speedy, substantial, and sustained" stimulus. This marked a major step forward in his understanding of the crisis. He also declared in no uncertain terms that the U.S. recession was no different qualitatively from Japan's, and that the experiences of the United States in the 1930s and of Japan more recently indicated premature fiscal consolidation during such a recession could be extremely dangerous. Summers also cited the deleveraging of the private sector—a process required for the future health of the economy—as a reason why fiscal stimulus must be sustained.

Summers' switch from the "three Ts" to the "three Ss" was important because it indicated he had begun to understand what a balance sheet recession was. Until then, the only member of the Obama administration to have mentioned the dangers of premature fiscal retrenchment was Secretary Geithner. Summers did not commit himself to that extent at the beginning and seemed to hope the $787 billion stimulus package passed in February 2009 would be enough to restart the economy.

President Obama, also assuming initially that the "three Ts" would be enough, began his first term with a pledge that a leader must never make during a balance sheet recession—namely, he promised to halve the fiscal deficit over the next four years. This sort of statement is totally counterproductive from the standpoint of forward guidance for fiscal policy, as explained in Chapter 1. Fortunately, Summers' subsequent warning about the danger of premature fiscal consolidation with three Ss prevented the Obama administration from implementing the initial pledge.

In summary, although the U.S. authorities made some mistakes and created unnecessary confusion when the financial crisis first erupted, they adopted within one year after the Lehman collapse all the right policies to address a balance sheet recession. Fiscal stimulus shifted from the "three Ts" to the "three Ss," and the management of the financial crisis moved from quick disposal of bad loans to the more pragmatic approach of capital injection and "pretend and extend." This is the main reason the U.S. economy is now in far better shape than those of the United Kingdom or Europe.

Obama Has Yet to Disclose the Name of the Disease

In spite of the government's dramatic shift in the right direction, President Obama has yet to explain why these policies are necessary. While he says there would have been terrible consequences if they had not been adopted, he has done very little to explain why they are the *right* policies for the United States today. As a result, average Americans have not been told that they are confronting a balance sheet recession. In particular, they have not being told that, while they are doing the right thing by individually repairing their balance sheets, collectively they are weakening the economy by deleveraging. With the president still not telling them that they are facing a fallacy-of-composition problem, they ask why the government must continue racking up huge fiscal deficits.

The Republican party took advantage of this explanation vacuum and garnered a fair bit of support by focusing attention on the budget deficit and the problem of "big government," which, they argue, runs counter to the notion of self-responsibility that is one of the founding principles of the United States. The Tea Party faction is particularly opposed to big government, and its uncompromising stance on this issue has made it difficult for the Republicans as a group to find common ground with the Obama administration in many areas. As a result, while the administration has come up with the correct response for a balance sheet recession, many of the proposed measures have yet to be implemented because of opposition from the Republicans.

The fiscal stimulus needed to address a balance sheet recession is a fairly expensive course of treatment. The cost appears even greater because the stimulus must continue for an extended period of time. To win public approval for this costly treatment, the government needs to tell the public exactly what sort of disease it is confronting. Yet the Obama administration has not even told the American public the name of that disease.

This is the equivalent of a doctor treating a patient for pneumonia, which is many times more expensive than treating a common cold, without telling the patient what she has. Not surprisingly, the patient and her family will be upset when they receive a huge bill for what they thought was just a bad cold. In the United States, the patient has been treated for pneumonia and is definitely on the mend but is now objecting to further medication because it seems unnecessarily costly.

If the concept of balance sheet recessions had existed for decades and if most undergraduates had been exposed to it during their college years, a single mention of the term by the president would probably have sufficed for people to recall that fiscal stimulus was needed to address this kind of recession. Once doctors agree that a patient is suffering from pneumonia, their opinions on how to treat it are unlikely to diverge significantly. A patient with pneumonia will therefore be treated in basically the same way anywhere in the world.

Unfortunately, balance sheet recession theory has yet to gain that kind of currency, and as a result no politician has explained the full extent of the disease to the public, perhaps because the risks involved in doing so are too great. But without a full explanation, it will be difficult to win their support for costly medication.

Most of the spending under the $787 billion stimulus package enacted in 2009 ended two to three years later, and the measures that were supposed to follow that package were scaled back significantly because of Republican opposition, delaying a U.S. recovery. The deficit-reduction measures totaling 3 percent of GDP that were scheduled to take effect at the start of 2013 (i.e., the so-called fiscal cliff) were largely avoided, but the spending cuts and tax increases that *were* implemented have been a major drag on the recovery. Without them the United States would have been in much better shape than it is now.

Bernanke's "Fiscal Cliff" Warning Saved the U.S. Economy

Against this backdrop, it was extremely fortunate for the United States that Fed chairman Bernanke issued such strong warnings about the fiscal cliff of both 2012 and 2013. By preventing the United States from falling off that cliff, Bernanke averted the tragic outcome of premature fiscal consolidation seen in Japan in 1997 and in Europe and the United Kingdom since 2010. In that sense, the United States is the only nation to have learned from Japan's experience and put its lessons into practice.

Initially, however, even the Fed chairman was a believer in the power of monetary policy, to the extent that he called himself a disciple of Milton Friedman. Ten years ago Bernanke, then a professor at Princeton, was one of those who objected most strenuously when the BOJ said there was little a central bank could do after taking interest rates to zero. He also appeared to hold a very optimistic view of the Lehman bankruptcy initially, saying that while GDP would take a small hit the situation should improve in a year or so. He appears to have believed that conditions would improve if the Fed quickly cut rates to zero, and he did so faster than any Fed chairman in history.

The speed of the Fed's rate cuts probably owed something to the earlier argument in the West that the Bank of Japan had been too slow to lower interest rates. But even though the Fed cut rates at the fastest pace in history, the economy did not pick up as Bernanke expected. The reason was simple enough: the problem with the U.S. economy was a lack of borrowers. Borrowers were disappearing because their balance sheets had been impaired by the collapse of an asset price bubble, and that was not something that could be resolved by a rapid decline in interest rates.

Chairman Bernanke recognized that and changed his stance around 2010, although it was not until his Humphrey-Hawkins testimony before

Congress in July 2011 that I was able to confirm this with my own eyes. By then some members of Congress had begun to worry that the U.S. economy had fallen into the same balance sheet recession as Japan, and I was asked to testify with the chairman of the Fed.

Ordinarily the Fed chairman is the only person who presents testimony at these twice-yearly events, but several members of the private sector had been summoned that day in light of the severity of the recession. Chairman Bernanke was scheduled to testify in the morning followed by the rest of us in the afternoon, but we were seated next to him and had the chance to hear him speak.

My knowledge of Japan's experience over the previous 15 years left me unable to agree with Chairman Bernanke's monetarist approach. My previous book, *The Holy Grail of Macroeconomics*, pointed out a number of problems in his research on the Great Depression as indicated in Chapter 2. That day, however, we were sitting together for three hours, so I signed a copy of the book and gave it to him. The Fed chairman took one look at it and said he didn't need another copy, as he had already read it and found the sections on Japan to be very useful. Still, I wondered whether he had really understood the book, which after all was quite critical of his earlier academic work.

But all my doubts vanished when his testimony began. He said it would be dangerous for the government to pursue deficit-reduction efforts at this point in time. This was the same Fed chairman who until the previous year had been saying the fiscal stimulus of 2009 had played its role but now it was time for the government to pursue fiscal consolidation while the Fed supported the economy with monetary policy.

Even more surprised by the chairman's stance were the Republican members of Congress present that day. Believing the Chairman to be generally sympathetic to their cause, they repeatedly asked him to give his view of their proposed deficit-reduction measures. However, the chairman refused to acknowledge the need for such measures and instead reiterated the view that, while necessary in the longer run, fiscal consolidation should not be pursued now.

Chairman Bernanke's concerns about premature fiscal consolidation were highlighted most clearly in the debate a year later over the tax hikes and spending cuts planned for January 2013. His views were laid out in the strongest of terms at a press conference on April 25, 2012. First, *New York Times* reporter Binyamin Appelbaum noted the Chairman's claim that the Fed could do more if it wanted to. He then asked why, with inflation under control and unemployment expected to remain high for several years, the Fed was not doing everything it could *now*. Chairman Bernanke responded by saying that using monetary policy to lift an inflation rate already running above the Fed's 2 percent target would reduce the unemployment rate only "slightly" and that the FOMC's view was that such a move would be "very reckless." Bernanke also said it was because the Fed had established a reputation as an inflation fighter over the past 30 years that it had been able to ease policy so aggressively over the past few, and that it was not wise to risk tarnishing that reputation for "quite tentative and perhaps doubtful" improvements in the real economy.[2]

In other words, the Fed chairman was acknowledging that the real economic impact of further monetary accommodation would be "quite tentative and perhaps doubtful." If that was the case, it made no sense for him to say there were "additional tools" at the Fed's disposal. Oddly enough, Bernanke's response—that risking the asset of the Fed's credibility as an inflation fighter for "quite tentative and perhaps doubtful gains" would be "very reckless"—was identical to how the Bank of Japan responded to similar demands for further policy accommodation over a decade earlier. His focus on the Fed's credibility marked a sharp shift in his stance from the time when, as "Helicopter Ben," he showed little concern for the central bank's reputation.

Bernanke Declared Monetary Easing Could Not Offset Impact of Fiscal Cliff

The Fed chairman's realization that monetary policy had been rendered impotent was made even clearer by the next question, which concerned the fiscal cliff. Dow Jones reporter Kristina Peterson noted that Bernanke had warned Congress about the fiscal cliff and proceeded to ask how the Fed would respond if Congress did not take action to avoid it.

The Fed chairman's categorical response left a lasting impression: "There is . . . absolutely no chance that the Federal Reserve could or would have any ability whatsoever to offset that effect on the economy."[3] This marked a huge turnabout from his position until 2009, which was that any negative economic impact from fiscal consolidation could be neutralized with monetary policy. His strong opposition to fiscal consolidation was most likely based on the understanding that both GDP and the money supply were dependent on the scale of the government's fiscal stimulus now that U.S. businesses and households had become net savers in spite of zero interest rates.

---

[2] Board of the Governors of the Federal Reserve System, "Transcript of Chairman Bernanke's Press Conference" (April 25, 2012), pp. 7–8. www.federalreserve.gov/mediacenter/files/FOMCpresconf20120425.pdf.
[3] *Op. cit.*, p. 8.

Fall from Fiscal Cliff Triggered Japan's Deflation

At the same meeting, the Fed chairman asserted the United States had succeeded in avoiding deflation by carrying out the policies he himself had proposed to the Bank of Japan more than a decade before. But monetary theory requires an increase in the money supply for monetary policy to vanquish deflation, and money supply growth in the United States has not picked up substantially since quantitative easing began.

And whereas Japan, a huge current account surplus nation until a few years ago, had a strong currency for many years, the current account deficit countries of the United States and the United Kingdom saw sharp drops in their effective exchange rates following the collapse of Lehman Brothers and the GFC. This is probably a key reason why the United States and the United Kingdom did not experience deflation in spite of unemployment rates that were much higher than those recorded in Japan.

Despite the deflation, Japan's unemployment rate never exceeded 5.5 percent (it stood at 3.5 percent in May 2014), and GDP never fell below its bubble-era peak. In the United States, meanwhile, the unemployment rate climbed into double-digit territory at one point and GDP fell substantially from its high. All this is to say that it makes little sense to compare Japan, which kept GDP at or above its bubble peak but experienced a modicum of deflation, and the United States, which avoided deflation but suffered significant real-economy damage.

Moreover, the deflation that did exist in Japan was minor at best. Consumer prices were falling less than 1 percent a year until the GFC, and that minimal fall in prices was due in part to the opening of the domestic market to imports.

Japan's deflation had two main causes. One was the downward pressure on prices caused when Japanese firms collectively shifted production overseas following the yen's rise to 79 against the dollar in 1995. The other was the Hashimoto administration's premature decision to pursue fiscal consolidation in 1997, which tipped the economy into a double-dip recession and led to five consecutive quarters of negative growth.

The first of these represented the correction of massive price disparities between Japan and other countries (*naigai-kakakusa*) that had attracted so much public attention in the 1990s. Prior to that, Japan's domestic markets had been protected by import duties and a variety of nontariff barriers, forcing Japanese consumers to pay much higher prices for a wide range of goods than their counterparts elsewhere in the world. From around 1995, however, Japanese companies began bringing in products they had sourced overseas, which helped tear down the nontariff barriers erected against imports and sparked a process of convergence between domestic and international prices. This phenomenon, known in Japanese as *kakaku-hakai* or price destruction, was responsible for much of Japan's deflation and caused the phrase *naigai-kakakusa*, once heard on a daily basis, to be forgotten. This is a reminder of just how high Japanese domestic prices used to be relative to international prices before 1995.

The United States, which experienced a sharp depreciation of the dollar in the wake of the GFC, did not suffer from the first of these problems. However, the nation has yet to inoculate itself against the second: the risk of premature fiscal consolidation coming from Republicans and particularly from the Tea Party.

The fiscal cliff of January 1, 2013, was estimated at 3 percent of GDP, which coincidentally was the same size as the Hashimoto administration's disastrous ¥15 trillion deficit-reduction plan in 1997 that pushed Japan into a double-dip recession. And Japan began to experience deflation only after the double-dip recession. In that sense, the United States was extremely fortunate that it has so far managed to avoid falling off the cliff.

If the United States is to avoid a Japan-style deflation, it needs to put the fiscal cliff behind it—and not just for one or two years but for as long as the private sector needs to repair its balance sheet. Once the private sector finishes repairing its balance sheet and starts borrowing again, deficit-reduction efforts by the government will not lead to the kind of economic meltdown seen in Japan in 1997 or in Europe more recently.

The United Kingdom, Spain, and many other European countries have fallen off the fiscal cliff and will require a great deal of time to restore their economies to pre-crisis levels of activity (see Chapter 5). The fact that the Eurozone is pushing ahead with more fiscal consolidation and bad loan disposals based on orthodox market fundamentalism will only delay the recovery.

U.S. Households Still Repairing Balance Sheets

How is the real economy in the United States? As noted above, the household sector continues to increase savings despite zero interest rates, and the economy is showing all the signs of a balance sheet recession, just like Japan over the past 20 years.

Figure 3.3 shows changes in the U.S. household sector's financial assets and liabilities since 2000. The white bars show trends in financial assets. When these bars rise above the zero centerline, it indicates the household sector increased its financial assets during that period, while a white bar below the centerline means households drew down their financial assets.

The shaded bars, meanwhile, indicate trends in financial liabilities. The scale is arranged inversely, so that a shaded bar below the zero centerline means the household sector increased its financial liabilities, while a shaded bar above the centerline indicates it reduced its liabilities by paying down debt.

FIGURE 3.3 U.S. Households Are Still Saving More Than Borrowing at Zero Interest Rates

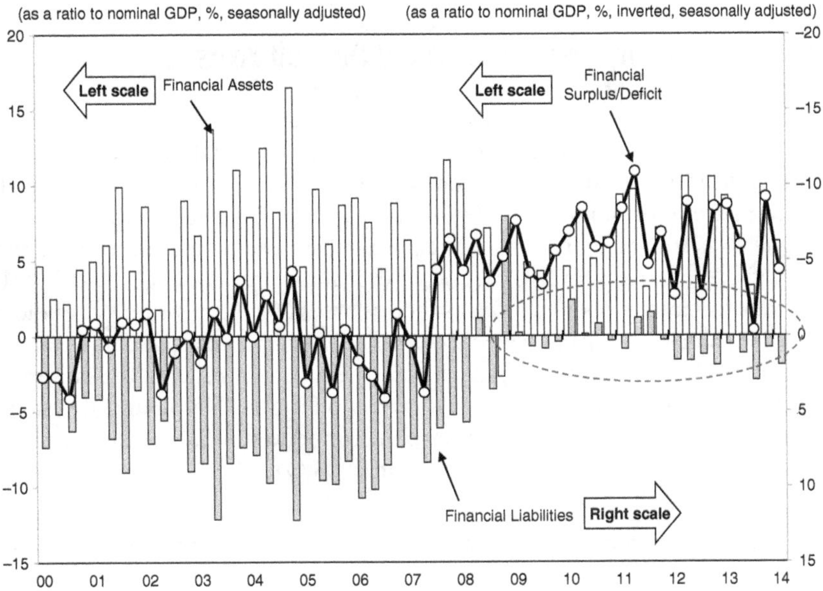

Note: Latest figures are for 2014 Q1.

Sources: Nomura Research Institute (NRI), based on flow of funds data from FRB and the U.S. Department of Commerce.

The broken line in the graph shows the net financial surplus or deficit (i.e., net savings) of the household sector, defined as the change in financial assets less the change in financial liabilities. A value greater than zero implies that growth in financial assets exceeded growth in financial liabilities during the given period (financial surplus), while a value less than zero means the increase in financial liabilities outweighed the increase in financial assets (financial deficit). While this line is essentially the same as the graph for the household sector in Figure 3.1, the latter uses a four-quarter moving average to highlight the medium-term trend, whereas Figure 3.3 shows seasonally adjusted values for individual quarters to present a clearer view of recent trends.

Figure 3.3 shows that U.S. households have run a financial surplus for 27 consecutive quarters starting in 2007 Q3. Furthermore, the shaded bars, which were deep in negative territory during the bubble days, have often been positive since the GFC. Although the latest numbers indicate that households are starting to borrow money again (shaded bars below zero), there is still a net financial surplus. As interest rates were at zero during most of these 27 quarters, U.S. households have in fact been minimizing debt and maximizing savings. The reasonable conclusion to draw is that U.S. households are still in the midst of balance sheet adjustments.

Nonfinancial Corporate Sector Faced Difficult Years in the Wake of GFC

The nonfinancial corporate sector was also in financial surplus for eight quarters during the first two years of GFC—that is, it is saving more—in spite of zero interest rates, as shown in Figure 3.4. Despite reportedly being financially stronger than households, U.S. businesses were forced to draw down financial assets for five consecutive quarters, from 2008 Q1 to 2009 Q1, in order to pay suppliers, creditors, and workers (see the white bars below zero in Figure 3.4). This reflects the extreme financing difficulties many firms faced during the credit crunch. This period, starting with the failure of Bear Stearns, marked the height of dysfunction for the U.S. financial system, which explains the sudden sharp drop in corporate fundraising activity (i.e., the shrinkage in financial liabilities) from 2008 Q1.

FIGURE 3.4 U.S. Nonfinancial Corporations Suffered Greatly during the First Two Years of GFC

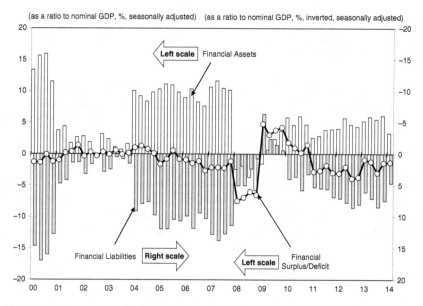

Note: Latest figures are for 2014 Q1.

Sources: NRI, based on flow of funds data from FRB and the U.S. Department of Commerce.

For four successive quarters beginning in 2009 Q1, the U.S. corporate sector reported negative growth in financial liabilities as companies paid down debt in spite of zero interest rates (shaded bars above zero in Figure 3.4). During this period, in other words, the corporate sector was minimizing debt in order to repair its balance sheet. These five-plus-four quarters must have been a living hell for many U.S. corporations. Subsequently the efforts to reduce liabilities came to an end and borrowing slowly picked up.

U.S. Companies Hit Far Harder by GFC Than by Collapse of Internet Bubble

Interesting in this regard is the different response of nonfinancial corporations to the collapse of the housing bubble in 2007 and the Internet bubble in 2000. Growth in both financial assets and financial liabilities plunged when the Internet bubble burst, but there was no financial crisis, and the corporate sector as a whole did not pay down debt (no shaded bars above zero) or draw down financial assets to make payments (no white bars below zero).

When the housing bubble collapsed, in contrast, businesses drew down financial assets for five consecutive quarters, and after that they paid down debt for four straight quarters in spite of zero interest rates, underlining the magnitude of the recent financial shock relative to the Internet bubble collapse. U.S. companies laid off 8 million employees and the unemployment rate rose sharply, but that was partly in response to the severe financial problems they faced including a vicious credit crunch. It is because of that painful experience that they continue to accumulate financial assets even today in spite of zero interest rates.

After the collapse of the Internet bubble, which involved much milder adjustments, it still took 12 quarters, or a full three years, for corporate sector behavior to return to pre-bubble norms. As the shock this time was much greater, it will probably take at least a few more years for U.S. companies to stop accumulating savings and resume borrowing money to expand their businesses.

Can U.S. Corporate Sector Become Economic Engine?

The chief cause of Japan's recession was that firms with impaired balance sheets moved to minimize debt. In the United States the corporate sector has a comparatively healthy balance sheet, which has led some to believe it could lead the economy out of recession. On the other hand, the ability of U.S. businesses to lay off workers more easily than firms in Japan and Europe makes them more sensitive to final demand. But substantial improvements in final demand cannot be expected when the U.S. household sector, the source of final demand, is not only not borrowing but is actually increasing savings at a time of zero interest rates. U.S. businesses confronting this highly unusual household behavior on a day-to-day basis for the past six years are unlikely to move aggressively to expand their operations until household behavior changes.

The fact that the household sector is a net saver in spite of more than six years of zero interest rates has probably come as a particular shock to businesses, as it implies that this is no ordinary recession. If the current slow growth is here to stay, some U.S. businesses may find they need to reduce their leverage in response. In other words, leverage ratios predicated on the assumption of a quick return to pre-bubble growth rates may have to be adjusted downward.

Long-Term Rate "Conundrum" Kept Housing Bubble Alive

Another reason companies are cautious is that they were burned in the Internet bubble just a decade earlier. Although they had largely finished repairing the damage to their balance sheets from the Internet bubble by the end of 2003, they were not yet ready to start borrowing when the housing bubble arrived.

Because companies did not borrow aggressively, long-term rates rose only 0.6 percent even as Fed Chairman Greenspan raised the federal funds rate by 4.25 percent from 1 percent in 2004 to 5.25 percent in 2006.[4] Low and stable long-term rates then gave an extended lease on life to the housing bubble sparked by Greenspan's decision to take the fed funds rate down to 1 percent in 2003.

Chairman Greenspan tried to guide the economy through the aftermath of the Internet bubble collapse with a housing bubble inflated by 1 percent interest rates. That bubble was supposed to have died a natural death as long-term rates rose if businesses had resumed borrowing money after they finished repairing balance sheets.

But because of the post-bubble debt trauma, they did not borrow, keeping long-term rates low. Fed Chairman Greenspan labeled this low long-term rate a "conundrum," because he could not understand the corporate behavior. The resultant low long-term rates allowed the housing bubble to continue expanding for another two years, with disastrous results.

This is also why U.S. corporate balance sheets remain relatively clean even after the recent bubble collapse. In a sense they *benefited* from the post-Internet bubble trauma because it discouraged them from aggressively leveraging up later in the decade.

---

[4] The last two increases were made under Chairman Bernanke.

Put differently, although the bursting of the Internet bubble in 2000 had opened a large hole in corporate balance sheets, households responded eagerly to the Greenspan Fed's 1 percent interest rates and helped inflate the housing bubble. That, in turn, pulled the U.S. economy out of the slump that followed the collapse of the Internet bubble (and 9/11).

However, household balance sheets took a huge hit when the housing bubble burst in 2008, and the corporate sector also incurred heavy damage from a financial crisis that included a severe credit crunch triggered by the Lehman bankruptcy. Business managers who have lived through a credit crunch tend to develop a lifelong aversion to borrowing, and that painful experience is why U.S. businesses remain as cautious as they are.

Post-2007 Fed in Similar Position to BOJ in 1990s

A big difference between conditions after the housing bubble and those after the Internet bubble is that, in the latter case, the U.S. economy had a household sector that was still responsive to low interest rates. Today the entire private sector is either nursing balance sheet wounds incurred when the housing bubble burst or struggling with the debt trauma as a result of GFC and is no longer responsive to monetary accommodation.

In that sense, the conditions faced by the Fed since 2008 have been similar to those confronted by the BOJ in the 1990s. In Japan, the simultaneous rise and collapse of two bubbles—one in real estate and one in stocks—meant there was no longer any part of the economy that would respond to low interest rates. It was as though the U.S. had experienced the Internet (equity) bubble collapse of 2000 and the real estate bubble collapse and GFC of 2008 at the same time. That is why Japan, and now the United States, have taken so long to recover.

Flow-of-Funds Data Suffer from Poor Accuracy

Many economists, including Chairman Bernanke of the Fed, worried that across-the-board cuts in government spending starting in the spring of 2013 would lead to significant economic weakness. But the economy not only did not stall, but also the deficit for the fiscal year ending in September 2013 came in at just 4.1 percent of GDP, down substantially from the previous-year figure of 6.8 percent. If the government deficit is shrinking while the private sector is continuing to save, it would seem the U.S. economy should be weaker than it is. Why the discrepancy? Here we face the limitations of flow-of-funds data in general and peculiar features of the U.S. statistics in particular.

Compiling flow of funds requires a massive amount of data. Estimating nonfinancial corporations' financial assets, for example, requires the central bank to sum up the cash, equities, derivatives, and all other financial assets held by all private sector companies. The BOJ, for example, states that it uses more than 7,000 data series to compile the flow of funds statistics. This is an overwhelming task, and it naturally requires a variety of estimation and sampling procedures with their attendant problems. It also means frequent revisions as better numbers are collected later from tax and other authorities. That means later numbers might paint a picture of the economy that is very different from the earlier numbers. And that is what happened in the U.S. recently.

Figure 3.5 shows the financial balance of the U.S. corporate sector through 2013 Q2 as reported by the Fed in September 2013. According to these data, the corporate sector has been consistently in a financial *surplus* since 2009.

When the net savings of the household sector, which had been hit hard by the housing bubble collapse, were added, the U.S. private sector appeared to be saving 6–10 percent of GDP from 2008 onward in spite of zero interest rates, a very alarming development.

FIGURE 3.5 Data through 2013 Q2 Show U.S. Corporate Sector Running Steady Financial Surplus in Contrast to Subsequent Releases

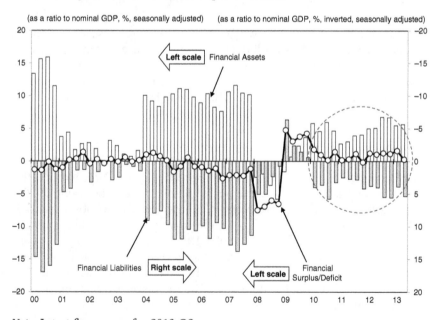

Note: Latest figures are for 2013 Q2.

Sources: NRI, based on flow of funds data from FRB and the U.S. Department of Commerce.

At the end of 2013 the Fed updated this series with the results for 2013 Q3. These revised numbers showed the corporate sector running a financial deficit in 2011 but a substantial financial surplus for the rest of the post-Lehman period.

The flow-of-funds data through end-2013, released in March 2014, indicated the corporate sector was still running a financial surplus all the way to 2013 Q4, and when households and financial institutions were added, the broader private sector was saving an alarming 7.8 percent of GDP for 2013.

Bad Data Were Good for Policy Debate

Faced with these frightening figures showing both businesses and households saving massive amounts in spite of zero interest rates since the beginning of the GFC, former Fed Chairman Ben Bernanke coined the phrase "fiscal cliff" to emphasize the dangers of a situation in which the government stopped borrowing and spending at a time when the private sector was no longer borrowing.

But the flow-of-funds data through 2014 Q1, released in early June 2014, contained major revisions suggesting the corporate sector has actually been running a financial *deficit* since 2011 Q1 (Figure 3.1)!

This means the financial surplus of the private sector was much smaller than was initially thought. In 2014 Q1 businesses and households were saving 3.9 percent of GDP according to the revised data. This represents a major shift from the 7.8 percent of GDP for 2013 Q4 that had been indicated by the previous data.

Even if the corporate sector is running a modest financial deficit, however, the financial surplus of the household sector remains large enough that the private sector as a whole continues to run a financial surplus. In other words, the balance sheet recession remains in force. That means government fiscal stimulus is still necessary, although perhaps not to the extent previously thought. Instead of the fiscal cliff being 1,000 meters high, in other words, it was actually about 500 meters high.

Despite the large revision, the earlier data ultimately had a positive impact on U.S. policy. Fed Chairs Bernanke and Yellen were moved to action by the earlier data, which showed both households and corporate sectors saving at a time of zero interest rates. Hence they issued strong warnings about the fiscal cliff when the Republican opposition was pushing for fiscal retrenchment.

It was because of these warnings that the original austerity policies scheduled to be implemented in January 2013 were scaled back substantially, which in turn made possible today's comparatively strong U.S.

economy. In that sense it was fortunate that the earlier data overstated the size of the private sector's financial surplus.

The revised data also help explain why the U.S. economy continued to grow in spite of tax hikes and spending cuts in 2013. Given the earlier data, it seemed odd that the U.S. economy had not slowed more sharply in response to the government's austerity measures. The forecasts published by the government and the Fed at the time also anticipated a larger slowdown in response to these measures.

But the revised data indicate that the U.S. private sector's financial surplus has shrunk substantially, from the peak of 9.8 percent of GDP in 2010 Q1, to 3.9 percent in the latest figures. This reduction in private savings was able to offset much if not all of the negative impact of the austerity measures.

Estimated Correctly, Private Sector Financial Surplus Continues to Shrink

There are certain peculiarities to the U.S. data as well. Flow-of-funds data for any nation, which show the financial surplus or deficit for the household, nonfinancial corporate, financial, and government sectors along with the "rest of the world," should add up to zero. But they do not in the case of the United States. This means some if not all of the entries in the U.S. flow of funds data have problems with accuracy.

With so many estimation and sampling challenges, it is something of a miracle when these five values sum to a figure approaching zero. What happens is that most countries employ a variety of adjustments and re-estimations to ensure they add up to zero in the end. In Germany, for example, I was told that it is very difficult to obtain accurate data on the corporate sector because German companies, both large and small, are active not only throughout Europe but around the world. Data for the corporate sector are therefore said to be substantially less robust than those for the household or government sectors. In order not to distort the relatively accurate data available for other sectors, a Bundesbank statistician told me that any residuals are assigned to the corporate sector, which already suffers from the least accurate data. As a result, German corporate sector data undergo the largest and most frequent revisions.

In Japan, the BOJ actually publishes a table indicating which entries in the flows of funds data are more robust than others. Of the three categories indicated it is no surprise that those data coming directly from primary sources are considered most robust.

In the United States, too, the data for different sectors are characterized by varying degrees of accuracy. A Fed statistician told me that the Fed's data-gathering capabilities are second to none, but if the resulting figures do not add up to zero, the Fed would rather release the original numbers as-is rather than massage the numbers until they do.

The same Fed statistician also told me that of the five sectors—household, nonfinancial corporates, financials, government, and overseas—the figures for the government and overseas sectors are the most accurate because primary data can be used as-is. Fed statisticians can simply use monthly trade and current account data for the overseas sector and fiscal balance data for the government sector and need not make any further estimates. Revisions to the data for these two sectors have also been the smallest and the least frequent.

Because the data for these two sectors are relatively accurate, subtracting the sum of the two from zero gives a fairly accurate estimate of the U.S. private sector as a whole. While it is impossible to break down the resulting figure into households, operating companies, and financial institutions, the important thing in terms of balance sheet recession theory is to know what the private sector as a whole is doing, and this figure is sufficient for that purpose.

Figure 3.6 shows trends in the private sector calculated (1) using this method and (2) simply by summing up the individual figures for households, operating companies, and financial institutions in Figure 3.1.

FIGURE 3.6 There Are Gaps between the Two Definitions of "Private Sector" in the U.S. Flow-of-Funds Data

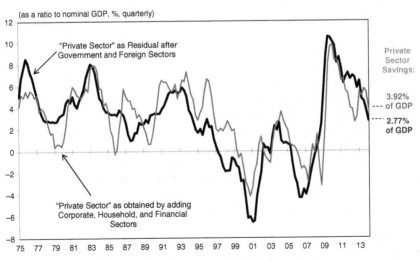

Note: For the latest figures, four quarter averages ending in 2014 Q1 are used.

Sources: FRB; U.S. Department of Commerce.

Figure 3.6 shows that there have been a number of large divergences between these two approaches in the past, reflecting inaccuracies in the data. For example, the financial surplus as calculated by the first approach has been falling after peaking in 2009 at 10.6 percent of GDP, but the financial surplus under the second approach was not shrinking much until the June 2014 revisions are introduced.

This means the first calculation presents a better picture of the actual state of the U.S. private sector long before the revisions upgrade the accuracies of the second calculation. Those using the U.S. data therefore should use both calculations to see where the U.S. private sector is going.

Recovery in U.S. Private Sector Demand for Funds May Outpace Japan

It was argued in Chapter 2 that central banks trying to unwind QE would find it easier to do so with a slow recovery in demand for funds. What is the likelihood that private demand for funds in the U.S. will recover gradually, as opposed to rapidly? Japan's experience points to this possibility. The corporate balance sheet problems at the root of Japan's recession had been largely rectified by 2005, but the subsequent rebound in loan demand was extremely sluggish.

One reason was that many companies, after 15 years of balance sheet repairs consisting mostly of paying down debt, had become highly averse to the idea of taking on new debt. Japanese managers even coined a new term, *cash flow management*, to describe their mindset. In the West this phrase would suggest the management and investment of the cash flows generated by corporate activity. In Japan, however, it was used to mean something very different.

Specifically, it referred to the practice of borrowing no money and paying for everything—including capital investment—using only the cash generated by the business. This practice came in response to the traumatic experience of repairing balance sheets following the bubble collapse in 1990 and to the painful credit crunch they faced starting in 1997. This style of management continues to be practiced even today, 24 years after the bubble collapsed and despite almost 20 years of zero interest rates. As a result, growth in private loan demand has been tepid even though corporate balance sheets are pristine and banks are willing to lend at the lowest interest rates in history.

The same phenomenon was observed in the United States after the 1930s, as people who had gone through the Great Depression—another traumatic balance sheet recession—refused to borrow money for the rest of their lives.

The question is whether the same thing could happen in the United States today. Flow-of-funds data indicate that the U.S. household sector remained a large net saver through 2014 Q1, the latest quarter for which data are available, in spite of zero interest rates. This indicates that U.S. households do not think their balance sheets are clean enough or their savings sufficient. This is a far cry from the state of affairs up to 2007, when U.S. households were quite willing to take on huge amounts of debt.

Meanwhile, U.S. house prices rebounded sharply in the first half of 2013. In fact, they have taken only five years to rebound when Japanese house prices needed 15 years to do so, suggesting that improvements in the U.S. may proceed faster than in Japan. This difference is due in no small part to Chairman Bernanke's warning about the fiscal cliff since 2011, which helped prevent a double-dip recession triggered by premature fiscal consolidation. In contrast, Japan experienced a severe double-dip recession in 1997 because of premature deficit-reduction efforts. As noted in Chapter 1, yields on commercial real estate in Japan had recovered by the start of 1997 to levels that were attracting international investors, and land prices were in the process of putting in a bottom on demand from foreign investors. But then the Hashimoto administration embarked on its premature deficit-reduction efforts, sending the economy into a double-dip recession and causing land prices to fall another 50 percent. Inasmuch as the United States is making an active effort to avoid the mistakes Japan made in 1997, private loan demand is likely to recover sooner than it did in Japan.

Housing Market Strength during the First Half of 2013 May Have Contained Temporary Factors

Since autumn 2013, however, residential investment has "stalled out," to use New York Fed President William Dudley's words, in spite of low interest rates and favorable demographic trends.[5] The Case-Shiller house price index also shows that house prices stopped rising in autumn 2013 (Figure 1.1). Possible factors cited by Dudley included heavy student loan debt that had left some university graduates unable to buy homes, continued tightness in mortgage credit, and a rise in interest rates from their lows.

Although many people believe the housing market recovery that began late in 2012 reflected the true state of affairs and that the slump since autumn 2013 is only a temporary interlude, the reverse is also possible. After all,

---

[5] William C. Dudley, "The Economic Outlook and Implications for Monetary Policy," remarks before the New York Association for Business Economics, May 20, 2014. www.newyorkfed.org/newsevents/speeches/2014/dud140520.html.

except for the rise in interest rates starting June 2013, all of the housing-negative factors noted by Dudley are specific to the post-GFC era. Even the high interest rates seen since the middle of 2013 are still very low by historical standards.

In other words, it is difficult to argue that the housing market has slowed temporarily because of the recent appearance of these factors. It may instead be the housing market strength seen in the first half of last year that was due to temporary factors.

One possibility is that those who were both willing and able to buy but were waiting to confirm a bottom in the market all made their move toward the end of 2012. Purchases of houses by institutional investors definitely picked up sharply in late 2012.[6]

A sudden influx of buyers after five years of inactivity would naturally drive house prices higher. But the market could be expected to lose momentum once that spurt of buying is over given the relatively modest gains in income and employment. Even when house prices were rising sharply in 2013, many noted that there were relatively few first-time buyers.

Thus the housing market recovery in 2013 H1 may have been a temporary phenomenon that was not backed by meaningful improvements in the fundamentals. In addition to housing, bonus depreciation provisions and extended unemployment benefits also expired at the end of 2013. This means growth prior to the end of 2013 received an artificial boost from temporary factors that cannot be expected to continue. People, myself included, have a tendency to view bad news as temporary and good news as permanent, but it may be that the strength seen in 2013 was at least partly due to temporary factors.

There is no question that the U.S. private sector is making steady progress in its balance sheet adjustments, and while house price increases have slowed down they are no longer at the rock-bottom levels seen for a time. In that sense conditions are clearly improving. Still, the argument can be made that the strong momentum seen in the housing market and elsewhere in 2013 were somewhat temporary in nature.

Fed's Reputation Falls to Earth

Chairman Bernanke made a number of mistakes when the GFC first erupted. Soon afterward, however, he rallied the troops around the "fiscal cliff"

---

[6] RealtyTrac, "All-Cash Share of U.S. Residential Sales Reaches New High in First Quarter Even as Institutional Investor Share of Sales Drops to Lowest Level Since Q1 2012," staff report, May 5, 2014. www.realtytrac.com/content/foreclosure-market-report/q1-2014-us-institutional-investor-and-cash-sales-report-8052.

slogan and prevented the government from pursuing premature fiscal consolidation, thereby keeping the United States from repeating the errors of Japan in 1997 and the Eurozone since 2010. Bernanke and his successor Janet Yellen are currently the only central bank heads who have spoken in no uncertain terms about the dangers of premature fiscal consolidation. Both the United States and the global economy were very fortunate to have someone like Bernanke and Yellen in charge of the Federal Reserve at this critical juncture.

On the other hand, U.S. politicians have harshly criticized the Fed, charging that former Fed chairman Alan Greenspan overlooked the formation of a bubble and that Chairman Bernanke failed to prevent the GFC in spite of his mandate for maintaining financial system stability. The February 11, 2010, edition of the *Wall Street Journal* actually spoke of the Fed in the following terms: "A driver with a record of accelerating cars into ditches may not be the best person to test a new braking system." This poor assessment was underscored by the fact that Bernanke had received the lowest-ever percentage of "yea" votes in his reconfirmation hearings in January 2010. Mistrust of the central bank and the desire for a "second opinion" are also the reasons for the Congress to invite me and other private-sector representatives to testify alongside Bernanke in 2011.

As someone who served as a doctoral fellow of the Board of Governors in Washington and as an economist with the Federal Reserve Bank of New York many years ago, I find it disheartening to see what has happened to the Fed's reputation within the United States. A central bank chairman forced to defend his institution under such circumstances must argue that the Fed has more tools at its disposal—even if monetary policy has lost much of its effectiveness. If Bernanke were to admit that the central bank were powerless, the Fed would only come under more criticism and could be forced to do things it would not otherwise have had to. The situation could grow far worse if politicians were to start demanding reckless policies capable of turning the dollar into confetti. To prevent that outcome, a central bank governor facing a balance sheet recession is almost forced to say that there is more that can be done in order to maintain monetary policy initiative.

The Bank of Japan's honest admission more than 10 years ago that there was nothing more it could do led to merciless bashing by people both inside and outside the country. Ironically, Bernanke was at the head of this mob. The worst-case scenario in Japan was avoided only because the Liberal Democratic Party (LDP) administration at the time included people like Kiichi Miyazawa and Taro Aso who understood the limitations of monetary policy and tried to protect the Bank. In the United States, where the economy has remained weak for five years and the unemployment rate remains at elevated levels, a similar comment by the Fed chairman would probably find few defenders in Congress or the administration. Although QE1 was a traditional case of a central bank operating as a lender of last resort, Bernanke's decisions to embark on QE2, Operation Twist, and finally QE3 were almost certainly driven in part by the need to defend the institution of the Fed.

The challenge now is how to overcome the impending QE trap as the U.S. private sector begins to show signs of health. Of course a clean and healthy balance sheet is no guarantee that the private sector will resume borrowing. For that to happen, the sector will have to overcome its debt trauma, a process that may take years if the Japanese example is any guide. Because the U.S. has managed to avoid falling off the fiscal cliff so far, demand for funds in the United States should recover sooner than it did in Japan, but it could still take much longer than most people are hoping for. If in fact the private sector's demand for funds remains weak in coming years, that should be viewed as an opportunity to unwind QE, not to extend it.

CHAPTER 4

The Great Potential of Abenomics

A benomics, the colloquial name for the economic policy of the Abe administration in Japan, consists of three "arrows"—(1) bold monetary accommodation by the Bank of Japan (BOJ), (2) flexible fiscal stimulus, and (3) structural reforms. After being launched late in 2012, Abenomics enjoyed a five-month honeymoon with the markets, helped by favorable coincidences that dramatically changed the economic landscape. The markets' initial enthusiasm was based on the prospect of bold quantitative easing (QE) by the central bank. Although this honeymoon ended in May 2013, the policy still has great potential, and if that can be properly leveraged, Japan should be able to put the long balance sheet recession and its aftereffects behind it for good.

First, the honeymoon: The markets began to pay attention to Abenomics when Shinzo Abe was elected leader of the Liberal Democratic Party (LDP) and then led the party to victory in the general election on December 16, 2012. That kicked off a ferocious decline in the yen and a corresponding rise in the Japanese stock market. Share prices had risen 80 percent by May 2013, and the yen dropped by more than 20 percent against the dollar. This dramatic stock market rally and currency depreciation produced a major change in the Japanese economic environment.

Some said these developments were proof Abenomics was working, but closer examination suggests they were actually due to an extremely fortunate combination of circumstances. It was foreign investors, after all, who drove the yen lower and Japanese stocks higher. Between December 2012 and December 2013, net purchases of Japanese equities by foreign investors totaled ¥16.7 trillion, while Japanese retail investors were net sellers to the tune of ¥9.3 trillion and Japanese institutional investors sold ¥6.7 trillion more than they bought.

New York hedge funds and other foreign investors shifted huge quantities of money to Japan upon the announcement of Abenomics, selling the yen and buying Japanese equities. Most domestic investors—and particularly

the institutional investors who know the Japanese economy better than anyone else—did not follow in the foreigners' footsteps and chose instead to
stay in the domestic bond market.

And domestic investors were not alone. The Abe-led LDP did not win
that many votes in the general election held on December 16, 2012. While it
garnered a majority of the seats, the third-party factions combined won more
votes than the LDP. In fact, the LDP's percentage of the vote at 27 percent
was almost the same as when it had been unseated by the Democratic
Party of Japan (DPJ) in the previous general election. There are actually
surveys from the time confirming that a majority of voters did not expect
the economy to improve under Abenomics, and most Japanese investors
stayed in the bond market for the same reason.

The behavior of domestic and foreign investor groups diverged in part
because of factors unique to the latter. Before coming to Japan, New York
hedge funds, anticipating a further deterioration of conditions in the Eurozone, had placed large bets on a collapse of the euro. That, it turned out,
was not to be. In spite of all the commentators in the United States and
United Kingdom media arguing it was only a matter of time before the euro
crumpled, European Central Bank (ECB) President Mario Draghi's pledge in
the summer of 2012 to do "whatever it takes" to defend the euro prevented
a collapse and threatened to create major losses for investors who had bet
heavily against the single currency.

Many of these funds showed no interest whatsoever in Japan as long
as they were betting against the euro. Many of them are my firm's clients in
real life, and I can testify that Japan held no fascination at all for them until
the autumn of 2012.

But just as they began to find themselves squeezed by the euro's unexpected resilience, Japan's new prime minister pledged to erect an inflation
target and engage in bold monetary accommodation. Hedge funds, seeing
this as an opportunity to redeem themselves, closed out their short positions
in the euro and moved money to Japan. The funds covered their shorts in
periphery bonds, sending yields sharply lower, and bought Japanese stocks
with the proceeds, driving them higher. Thus their response was good news
for both Europe and Japan.

This chain of events suggests the hedge funds did not spend a great deal
of time studying the situation in Japan beforehand. Indeed, the impression
received in conversations with them is that they found their backs up against
the wall in the Eurozone and decided Japan was the only way to save the
day. Had they not been in such a bad way in Europe, they might not have
reacted as aggressively as they did to the announcement of Abenomics. This
was extremely fortuitous for the Abe administration.

Although most of the market moves took place before any new policy
measures were actually implemented, foreign investors were excited by the
fact that the government set an inflation target jointly with the Bank of

Japan. The appointment of Haruhiko Kuroda in March 2013, who argued for aggressive QE to overcome deflation, added to their enthusiasm. The "quantitative and qualitative easing" (QQE) program unveiled on April 4, 2013, under which the BOJ pledged to double the monetary base, sparked expectations that Japan was about to do something amazing.

BOJ Already Had a Massive QE Program in Place

The impressions created by Kuroda's easing announcement were very different in Japan and overseas. A look at Western newspapers at the time reveals a general sense of awe in response to the announcement that the BOJ planned to double the monetary base, which had already been far larger than those of Western economies (as a percentage of GDP) for an extended period of time. This is highlighted in Figure 4.1, which compares the size of the monetary base in Japan, the United States, the United

FIGURE 4.1 Kuroda BOJ Shocks the World by Announcing It Will Double Japan's Already Substantial Monetary Base

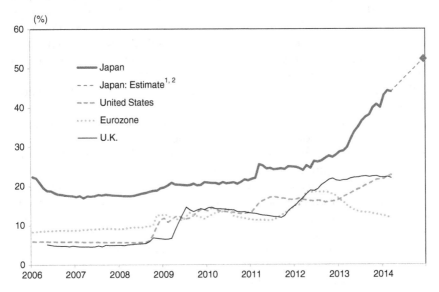

Notes: 1. Estimates are based on the assumption that Japan's nominal GDP will increase by 3.3 percent a year, which is the GDP growth outlook of the Japanese government for FY2014. 2. All figures, including the BOJ's monetary base target for the end of 2014, are seasonally adjusted by Nomura Research Institute.

Sources: Nomura Research Institute (NRI), based on BOJ, Cabinet Office, Japan, FRB, U.S. Department of Commerce, ECB, Eurostat, BOE, and ONS data.

Kingdom, and the Eurozone over time. Despite three rounds of quantitative easing, the U.S. monetary base was smaller in gross domestic product (GDP) terms than Japan's had been during the tenure of Kuroda's predecessor, Masaaki Shirakawa. Overseas finance experts were shocked to hear the new BOJ governor was planning to double it from that already high level. The announcement of QQE therefore lent further momentum to the weak yen/ strong equities trend.

It bears repeating that Japan's monetary base was already several times larger as a percentage of GDP than those of Western economies even before the announcement. This difference is due in part to cultural factors. Both individuals and companies in Japan tend to hold much more money in the form of cash and bank deposits. Cash is part of the monetary base, and compared with Western economies, where credit card use is prevalent, it is still used for a substantial percentage of transactions in Japan.

Another key difference is that when Western companies—and U.S. firms in particular—experience an increase in cash or bank deposits on hand, they immediately try to invest it in money market instruments or some other financial asset to enhance their yield. They may well hire someone with a business school degree to find the best way to invest and manage revenue coming into the firm. In practice that means the money seldom stays in the bank for long. They want to keep only slightly more than the absolute minimum there while investing the rest in capital and financial market instruments.

Japanese firms, on the other hand, do not immediately invest new bank deposits or cash in higher-yielding financial instruments. Their position is that they have a core business to take care of, and that trying to achieve higher yields on the firm's spare cash is not an acceptable use of limited management and entrepreneurial resources.

This is not necessarily the wrong approach—in fact, focusing the energy of the most qualified people on the core business has enabled Japanese companies to create the outstanding products they are known for. Assigning employees to cash management and investment operations channels corporate resources away from the core business. Assuming that management and entrepreneurial resources are the single most valuable resource a company has, the Japanese style of management, which devotes finite business resources to the core business and does not worry if bank balances grow a little bigger than is optimal, is not necessarily a bad thing. But it explains why the nation's bank deposits and monetary base were so large to begin with relative to those of the United States and Europe.

This cultural difference contributed to overseas observers' surprise over Abe's pledge to expand the monetary base and Kuroda's plan to double it. Domestic investors, on the other hand, were used to this state of affairs and were not particularly surprised by the announcements. This was one major difference.

Why Didn't Japan's Institutional Investors Follow Their Overseas Counterparts?

That begs the question of why Japanese institutional investors did not participate in the Abenomics-inspired move in the markets. The reason is that they, more than anyone else in Japan, have to confront the symptoms of a balance sheet recession on a daily basis.

Japanese banks and institutional investors are the first receptacles for both corporate debt repayments and new household savings and must find places to invest those funds. The institutional investors responsible for investing pension fund and life insurance reserves in most countries are also limited by law in the amount of currency and principal risk they can take on, as explained in Chapter 1.

Many countries have adopted such rules to prevent large losses of principal caused by managers taking on excessive currency and principal risk. Hence managers cannot invest all of their funds in foreign assets or domestic equities and must allocate a certain amount to domestic borrowers.

But since the private sector as a whole is saving in a balance sheet recession, there are no domestic borrowers. And the money keeps flowing in. Much of the 7.3 percent of GDP currently being saved by Japan's private sector makes its first stop at these institutions. Every day they struggle to find domestic borrowers and, failing to find them, are forced to buy bonds issued by the only domestic borrower left standing—the government. Having experienced this struggle on a daily basis for the past two decades, they understand better than anyone that there is no reason why a BOJ pledge to engage in more aggressive quantitative easing (QE) should lift the economy. After all, an absence of borrowers means the money multiplier is zero or negative at the margin, and without growth in the money supply there is no reason why the economy should pick up or why inflation should rise.

The bond market is the right place to be for an investor who believes that monetary accommodation cannot produce inflation, because the alternative of investing in equities carries with it the risk of being forced to sell on disappointment. This, briefly, was the reaction of the domestic institutional investors, who understood there was no private demand for funds in Japan.

Indeed, Japan's deflation is due entirely to the absence of private borrowers. If there were businesses and households willing to borrow, the money multiplier would have remained positive, the money supply would have surged, and inflation would have accelerated long before interest rates had to be lowered to zero. In other words, Japan's "lost 20 years" and its deflation are attributable to the shortage of private borrowers. And those borrowers are absent because of the horrendous balance sheet problems they faced following the bursting of the bubble in 1990 and its aftereffects. Japan's institutional investors have long understood that efforts to tackle deflation were bound to fail unless the authorities tackled the balance sheet problems first.

The BOJ engaged in QE under strong political pressure once before, from 2001 to 2006, when it created excess reserves equal to six times statutory reserves. This was the first time in history a central bank had deliberately created so much liquidity in order to accelerate inflation. But contrary to the reflationists' theoretical arguments, the money supply did not grow and inflation did not pick up.

The yen actually rose quite sharply and became a major problem in 2003 and 2004.The good relationship between Japanese prime minister Junichiro Koizumi and U.S. president George W. Bush enabled Japan to undertake what was then the world's largest-ever currency intervention, with the government selling a total of ¥35 trillion in those two years to keep the yen from appreciating further. In the first year alone it sold ¥30 trillion. And this was despite a massive QE program under a zero-interest-rate regime. In the end, nothing went as theory predicted because there were no private-sector borrowers, which meant the QE generated almost no increase in the money supply (Figure 1.10). The sluggish reaction of the U.K. and U.S. economies to QE up to 2012 also made Japanese investors more cautious. Following the GFC the Fed created bank reserves equal to 20 times statutory reserves under QE, while the corresponding multiple for the United Kingdom was about 10. Inflation in both countries was running at about 2 percent, which is where the BOJ's Kuroda set his target, and real interest rates were negative. Yet when Abenomics was launched in December 2012, both countries had an unemployment rate of 7.8 percent,[1] versus 4.3 percent in Japan. Fed chairman Ben Bernanke has pledged to discontinue QE once the U.S. unemployment rate falls to 6.5 percent, but unemployment in Japan was already far below that level when Abenomics began at the end of 2012.

Further, in spite of this massive increase in bank reserves in the United States and the United Kingdom, the U.S. recovery has been modest at best, while the U.K. economy actually fell into a double-dip recession at one point. These two examples demonstrate that conditions will not improve simply because the inflation rate is near 2% and real interest rates are negative, and that is another reason why Japan's institutional investors stayed in the bond market.

Yen Fell and Stocks Rose Because Japan's Institutional Investors Stayed in Bond Market

This decision actually prolonged the Abenomics honeymoon. As long as Japanese institutional investors remained in the Japanese government bond

---

[1] Later revised to 7.9 percent in the United States and 7.7 percent in the United Kingdom.

(JGB) market and helped keep interest rates low, foreign investors felt it was safe to continue buying local equities and selling the yen.

The risks of buying Japanese equities will increase once Japanese interest rates start to rise. That would also raise the possibility of a resurgent yen, forcing investors to think twice about selling the currency. If Japanese interest rates had risen while U.S. and U.K. rates remained low, the yen could easily have appreciated against those currencies, undermining expectations of corporate earnings growth driven by a weak currency and drastically reducing the appeal of Japanese equities. However, interest rates did not rise because Japanese institutional investors stayed in the bond market. Reassured foreign investors continued to buy Japanese stocks and sell the yen.

Their behavior also prompted an inflow of Japanese retail investors into the stock market starting around February 2013. Institutional investors might understand that the absence of borrowers in a balance sheet recession results in a negative money multiplier and prevents the money supply from growing. But such theory is likely to go over the heads of retail investors. They simply joined the bandwagon because share prices had been rising and the media were trumpeting the arrival of inflation. As a result, the Nikkei Average climbed 80 percent from its lows, and the yen plunged to 100 against the dollar from the high 70s.

This stock market rally and the accompanying fall in the yen were attributed to Abenomics, but in fact they were also the result of Japanese institutional investors staying put in the bond market. In that sense, the Abe administration truly had luck on its side. It was only because the people who really understood the economy remained in the JGB market that foreign hedge funds and domestic retail investors were able to move the stock market as much as they did.

Honeymoon Altered Japan's Economic Landscape

An 80 percent rise in share prices will naturally alter the domestic mood. There was a growing sense starting in March and April that something was finally about to give the Japanese economy a push in the right direction. Such a reaction is only natural after an 80 percent advance by the stock market. And with the yen down as well, more people began to think inflation might finally reappear in Japan.

By April, television talk shows were pushing the idea that inflation was just around the corner even though there was no inflation and in fact not even any *signs* of inflation. It is said that people will start to believe anything if it is repeated a hundred times, and with the media talking incessantly about inflation being "just around the corner" people started to think that perhaps there was something to the rumors. In that sense, the Abenomics honeymoon definitely had a positive impact on sentiment, via what might be called a "talk show effect." And this represented a major shift for Japan's economy.

The "talk show effect" was important because Japanese companies had largely finished paying down debt by 2005, leaving them with pristine balance sheets. Still businesses did not borrow, even though banks were willing to lend money at the lowest interest rates in history.

There were two reasons for this. The first was their debt trauma—a determination not to go through such a painful deleveraging experience ever again. The second was the lack of investment opportunities in Japan's mature economy. The debt trauma is a psychological phenomenon observed when an economy emerges from a balance sheet recession. It is very different from the actual balance sheet problems found in the United States, the United Kingdom, and Spain today, where rules prevent banks from lending to businesses and households with insolvent balance sheets.

Japan's businesses and households did not finish repairing their balance sheets until around 2005, which prevented them from borrowing even if they wanted to. Since then, they could have borrowed money but chose not to because of an aversion to debt formed over 15 painful years of paying it down after the bubble collapsed. The same sort of trauma was observed in the United States in the aftermath of the Great Depression. Having lived through a debt hell beginning in 1929, American businesses and households promised themselves they would never again go into debt. And most of them never did. The United States private sector refused to borrow even after its balance sheet returned to health with the help of massive fiscal stimulus during the Second World War.

It took the country 30 years from the start of the Great Depression in 1929 for long- and short-term interest rates to return to the average level of the 1920s. It was not until 1959 that both long- and short-term interest rates in the United States returned to the 1920s average of 4.1 percent.

Abe and Kuroda tackled this psychological problem with a kind of psychological warfare—in effect, they did something shocking enough to persuade people that inflation was actually going to pick up. And once the television talk shows jumped on the bandwagon, the national psyche began to change.

Bond Market Reaction Ended Abenomics's Honeymoon

While the government's decision to address this psychological problem with a psychological operation deserves praise, the problem was that the talk show audiences included lenders as well as borrowers. This is the other side of the double-edged sword of inflation targeting. A problem arises if the institutional investors representing the lenders also see these shows and start to worry about inflation. Their assets, after all, consist largely of JGBs, which at the time were yielding just 0.8 percent in the 10-year sector. An inflation rate of 2 percent would cause the prices of those 10-year bonds to crash. If lenders, too, began to anticipate inflation, they would have to sell their JGB holdings to avoid massive losses.

That selling commenced soon after QQE was implemented, sending the 10-year bond yield—which had initially dropped below 0.40 percent— almost 70 basis points higher to 1.00 percent in May 2013. The surge in long-term rates was accompanied by rapid corrections in the equity and forex markets. Up to that point investors had been buying Japanese stocks and selling the yen based on the assumption that Japanese interest rates would not rise, but now that they had, such positions would have to be unwound. That sent Japanese equities lower while boosting the yen.

USD/JPY fell back into the 90s after climbing to 103, and the Japanese stock market dropped about 20 percent. Stocks and the yen then entered a period of range-bound trading that continued until this writing (June 2014). This reaction by the bond market signaled a clear end to the honeymoon enjoyed by Abenomics from December 2012 through May 2013.

Private Sector Continues to Save after One Year of Abenomics

What will happen now that the Abenomics honeymoon is over? The policy still has great potential. After all, it was only the first of the policy's three "arrows"—the BOJ's bold monetary easing and foreign investors' positive reaction to it—that produced this honeymoon. There are still two arrows remaining.

The second arrow of fiscal stimulus has been criticized by orthodox economists as "more of the same," if not excessive, given that Japan already has public debt in excess of 200 percent of GDP. But as discussed in Chapter 1, Japan's private sector is saving over 7 percent of GDP at a time of zero interest rates. The latest flow-of-funds data show that in spite of all the talk about the economic improvements brought about by Abenomics, the net savings of Japan's nonfinancial corporations in 2014 Q1 amounted to 6.3 percent of GDP (Figure 4.2), far more than the 1.5 percent of GDP being saved by the household sector (Figure 4.3), although the household sector's financial surplus probably shrank more than usual in Q1 on the surge in demand ahead of the April 1 consumption tax hike.

The textbooks tell us that companies will rush to borrow money and expand their businesses when interest rates are at zero. That companies in Japan continue to do precisely the opposite in spite of pristine balance sheets suggest they are still suffering from a major debt trauma.

FIGURE 4.2 Japan's Nonfinancial Corporations Continue to Run Financial Surplus

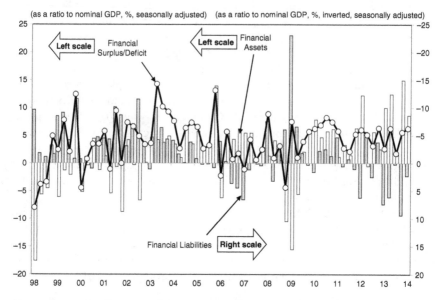

Notes: Seasonal adjustments by NRI. Latest figures are for 2014 Q1.

Sources: NRI, based on flow of funds data from the BOJ and Cabinet Office, Japan.

As Figure 4.2 shows, the behavior of Japanese companies has improved compared with the late 1990s and early 2000s, when balance sheet problems were at their worst. The shaded bars—which are on an inverse scale and represent change in financial liabilities—were above the zero centerline until 2005 Q1. In other words, Japanese companies were reducing their debt overhang by paying down debt during this period.

Over the past several years, in contrast, the shaded bars have spent more time below the zero centerline, indicating that some companies are taking advantage of zero interest rates to increase their borrowings, albeit on a modest scale. On the whole, however, growth in financial assets, indicated by the white bars above the zero centerline in the graph, continues to exceed the increase in liabilities, resulting in a persistently large financial surplus for the corporate sector.

Japan's Growth over Last Year Attributable to Fiscal Policy

So while corporate behavior has improved in Japan, the chief cause of the nation's economic woes—the fact that the corporate sector continues to save far more than it spends—persists even today, a year after the adoption of Abenomics. The fact that the household and corporate sectors together

FIGURE 4.3 Japanese Households Still Characterized by Financial Surplus

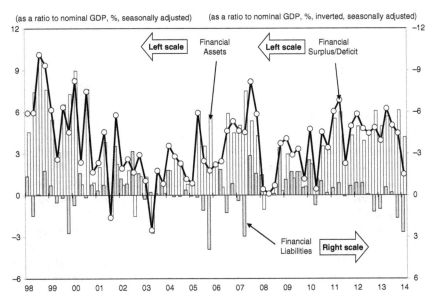

Notes: Seasonal adjustments by NRI. Latest figures are for 2014 Q1.

Sources: NRI, based on flow of funds data from the BOJ and Cabinet Office, Japan.

are still saving 7.3 percent of GDP a year means GDP will contract by an equivalent amount unless the government and the rest of the world are willing to borrow and spend that amount. Since Japan's current account balance is now close to zero, it is up to the government to borrow and spend the private sector's savings surplus.

The fact that the private sector remains a huge net saver in spite of the BOJ's zero interest rates and quantitative easing policies also means that the sharp improvements in the economy over the past year are attributable largely to the second arrow of Abenomics—fiscal policy—and that the effect of monetary policy has been limited to a weaker currency and an indirect wealth effect via higher stock prices. In other words, the key reason Japan's economy is doing better than last year is that the government borrowed and spent private savings amounting to 7.3 percent of GDP, which suggests conditions have yet to return to normal.

A majority of economists and pundits both inside and outside Japan remain unaware of the huge scale of private sector saving and have criticized the second arrow as a continuation of the massive fiscal stimulus that has failed to produce a recovery over the years. But in fact it was only because of that stimulus that Japan was able to avert a depression for the past two decades, as explained in Chapter 1.

Finance minister Taro Aso is one of the few politicians who understand this mechanism, which is why he has been charged by the prime minister with the task of looking after the economy. As he understands that Japan's private sector is a huge net saver at a time of zero interest rates, the first thing he did as prime minister in 2008–2009 and as finance minister in the Abe administration was to compile a program for fiscal stimulus. He understands that withholding fiscal stimulus at a time when the private sector is a huge net saver despite zero interest rates is simply not an option.

The greatest mistake in Japan's fiscal policy over the past two decades was former Prime Minister Ryutaro Hashimoto's pursuit of austerity in 1997, but subsequent administrations—with the exception of the Obuchi and Aso governments—also prolonged the recession unnecessarily by failing to deliver proactive fiscal stimulus. Their fiscal stimuli were always behind the curve, and the first Abe cabinet in 2006–2007 was short-lived because he delayed the economic recovery by focusing on structural reform when the problem was actually with balance sheets. This time, fiscal policy features prominently in the government's economic policy, reflecting the bitter experience of the first Abe cabinet. The first supplementary budget was passed by the Diet in January 2013, and numerous other measures have been implemented since then.

Can the Abe Administration Overcome the Trauma of Balance Sheet Recession?

The second arrow of Abenomics is fiscal stimulus, but it actually consists of two components. The first is government expenditures, which are crucial when the private sector is saving 7.3 percent of GDP at a time of zero interest rates. Without government spending, the Japanese economy could stall yet again.

The second component is the investment tax credit and accelerated depreciation allowances that were implemented in January 2014. These measures are intended to produce a change of heart among business managers still averse to borrowing. The plan was to designate the first few years as a time for treating this trauma, after which the special measures could be retired in favor of a general cut in the corporate tax rate. Based on this thinking, the policy adopted at the start of 2014 allows businesses to immediately write off 100 percent of investments made through March 31, 2015, and to write off 50 percent of any investments made between then and March 31, 2016.

The government has received about 10,000 applications for the investment tax breaks in just over four months (through end-May 2014), an indication that these policies are working. However, their impact is not expected to show up in the flow-of-funds data for some time yet.

It should be noted that additional borrowings by businesses are not always necessary: reduced savings will have the same macroeconomic impact. With Japanese (and U.S.) businesses sitting on a huge cash hoard, the first changes may actually show up in the form of reduced financial asset accumulation instead of an increase in financial liabilities.

A resumption of borrowing and spending would set everything moving in the right direction. Since a trauma, once overcome, loses its power over the patient, this could represent a true opportunity for Japan to emerge from the long recession. And once private loan demand picks up, there will be no need for the government to continue its fiscal stimulus because private borrowing will take up the slack and keep the economy going.

It is also important not to underestimate the depth of this psychological problem. A trauma will continue until it is well and truly overcome. As indicated earlier, after the U.S. economy went haywire in 1929, it was not until 1959, fully 30 years later, that interest rates returned to normal levels—that is, to the average level of the pre-Depression 1920s. Even though corporate and household balance sheets had been cleaned up thanks to New Deal spending and the astronomical fiscal stimulus occasioned by World War II, it took until 1959 for the private sector to resume borrowing money. That gives some idea of just how severe this kind of trauma can be. In Japan as well, 24 years have passed since the bubble collapsed and yet there is still no sign that interest rates are ready to return to normal.

Japan does have one advantage over the Depression-era United States: Its GDP—and consequently its income—has never dropped below the levels recorded at the peak of the bubble. Because the private sector has been able to use that income to pay down debt, conditions have not been quite as painful as they were in the United States.

In the Depression-era United States, some 46 percent of GNP evaporated because of the Hoover administration's mistaken policies, creating a horrible situation in which Americans had 46 percent less income with which to pay down debt. In Japan, in contrast, stable incomes enabled people to continue paying down their debt. Still, many businesses failed during this period, and many people lost their jobs. The end result was that millions of people—perhaps tens of millions—had to rethink their future plans and aspirations, resulting in a trauma that lives on today.

During World War II the U.S. economy recovered almost immediately as the government undertook fiscal stimulus on a truly astronomical scale. Japan's government was forced instead to administer stimulus piecemeal, and only after the economy had weakened, prolonging the recession and making people increasingly cautious. It is good that the Abe government is finally trying to tackle this problem, but there is no easy cure for this kind of trauma.

In 2011 the United States, which had been plunged into a balance sheet recession by the global financial crisis (GFC), implemented an accelerated depreciation program of the kind now being replicated by the Japanese government. The Obama administration's policy enabled businesses to immediately write off 100 percent of fixed investment undertaken in 2011, and to write off up to 50 percent of any investments made in 2012. Together these measures are thought to have provided meaningful support for the U.S. economy. The United States deserves praise for having taken just three years to implement this policy, while Japanese businesses had to wait 24 years after the country entered a balance sheet recession. On the other hand, the fact that Japan's private sector has already repaired its balance sheet means the program is likely to be even more effective than it was in the United States, where businesses and households were still undertaking balance sheet repairs in 2011.

In terms of policy calibration, it is difficult to estimate in advance the extent of policy actions needed to treat this kind of trauma. The situation would be different if there had been numerous balance sheet recessions in the past and there were statistical data to indicate the likely consequences of certain policy actions. But such data simply do not exist because balance sheet recession is a rare economic phenomenon that occurs only once every several decades. The last one was the Great Depression of the 1930s.

So we do what we can. The team led by finance minister Taro Aso is doing its best to tackle these balance sheet recession–specific problems, demonstrating that Japan is finally getting down to business and trying to enact the kinds of policies that will bring an end to two decades of recession. The Abe administration is in fact the first Japanese government that has tried to tackle this psychological trauma head-on.

The Trauma of the Balance Sheet Recession Will Be the Last Effect to Go

To add some historical context, the Aso administration in 2008–2009 was supposed to have implemented the above measures to address this trauma. The prime minister understood that Japan's only remaining problem was the aversion to debt and knew that it must be dealt with somehow. Soon after he became prime minister, Aso began laying the groundwork for a system of accelerated depreciation allowances and investment tax credits, ideas that were then picked up by the media. These policies are a focused solution to the debt trauma in that they promise lower taxes only to people who undertake investment. Unfortunately, Lehman Brothers failed just as debate on these policies began, forcing the government to make an emergency economic package its first priority.

Japan experienced a 34.7 percent drop in industrial output—the largest of any major country—during the GFC. This was largely due to the concentration of its production and exports in durable goods, demand for which collapsed in the wake of the GFC. Lehman went under on September 15, 2008, and by February 2009 Japanese industrial production had plunged to 1983 levels, wiping out 25 years of output gains in the space of just five months. In comparison, industrial production in the United States, where the crisis originated, only fell back to 1997 levels (Figure 1.4). Japan suddenly found itself suffering from massive overcapacity, rendering an accelerated depreciation program and investment tax breaks meaningless. Hence nothing more was heard of them.

Prime Minister Aso prevented the Japanese economy from sinking any further with the fiscal stimulus package that was needed at the time, but was still defeated in the next election, which brought the DPJ into power for the next three years. During this period no policymakers asked what should be done about a private sector that was not borrowing money in spite of zero interest rates. On several occasions I was invited by Diet members, including some senior politicians from the DPJ, to talk about balance sheet recessions. Under the DPJ government, however, it was difficult to tell whom to talk to, to get things done. Ultimately no such measures were implemented and the time was wasted.

Nevertheless, desperate efforts by the private sector drove a gradual recovery in Japanese output, and by January 2014 production had rebounded to 2004 levels. Moreover, the extreme strength in the yen that had continued through the end of 2012 finally corrected as U.S. hedge funds responded to the first arrow of Abenomics. The time is ripe, therefore, for the government to implement measures aimed at resolving Japan's debt trauma.

The first arrow of Abenomics has provided a kind of psychological cover fire for the second. Real estate prices started to rise in the spring of 2013 on the assumption that inflation might finally be on the horizon. In that sense, the Kuroda BOJ's QQE has provided an atmosphere conducive to the second arrow of Abenomics—fiscal stimulus—which is also being used to tackle the debt trauma.

Focus of Structural Reforms Must Shift from Lenders to Borrowers

The third arrow of Abenomics is structural reform. This component is designed to address the second reason why Japanese companies are not borrowing and investing in Japan: the lack of investment opportunities in a mature economy. The purpose of the reforms is to open up investment opportunities through deregulation and market-opening measures so that businesses will want to invest in Japan. If the anti-trauma measures of the second arrow are the "push," the reforms of the third arrow are the "pull."

The term *structural reform* has been used to mean a depressingly wide range of things over the years. Moreover, the vast majority of pundits and economists both inside and outside Japan are unable to distinguish between balance sheet problems and structural problems, and when orthodox monetary and fiscal policy do not produce the expected results they are quick to call for structural reforms without giving further thought to the possibly that they may be actually facing balance sheet problems instead. But balance sheet problems, not structural problems, were chiefly responsible for the recessions in Japan in 1990, following the collapse of the Heisei bubble, in Germany in 2000, after the telecom bubble burst, and in the Eurozone in 2008, following the collapse of the housing bubble. This mistaken diagnosis caused these recessions to last far longer than necessary.

On a positive note, the structural reforms being proposed by the Abe administration appear to be different from past efforts and seem to be headed in the right direction. For instance, former prime minister Junichiro Koizumi called repeatedly for structural reform and coined a famous slogan stating that there could be no economic recovery without it. The initiative that Koizumi pushed hardest for was the privatization of the ¥200 trillion postal savings system. At that time a substantial portion of the nation's savings was deposited with the Postal Savings Agency, with most of that money being invested in public sector entities and government bonds. The primary objective of privatization was to draw this money back into the private sector.

But if Japan has lacked one thing over the past 20 years, it is (private) borrowers, not lenders. Koizumi tried to increase the number of lenders to the private sector, but with no private *borrowers* this initiative could never have had a positive economic impact. I opposed it from the outset, arguing it would entail serious costs while providing no benefits.

The costs stemmed from the fact that the Postal Savings Agency's expertise was in buying government bonds, not lending to the private sector. For know-how on lending to the private sector one had to go to Japan's commercial banks, credit unions, and *shinkin* banks. If an agency without such know-how is privatized and forced to start lending to the private sector, the only way it can possibly compete is on the basis of price. In other words, it will have to lend at lower rates than its rivals to gain a foothold in the industry.

Japanese lending rates were already so low that banks were unable to earn reasonable risk-adjusted returns. The only way the privatized Postal Savings Agency could compete was by offering even lower rates of interest. And since it had no bad loans at the time, it had room to expand such lending substantially. Private-sector financial institutions that were lending to businesses and households based on expertise accumulated over the years could potentially be "crowded out" of the picture, giving the Postal Savings Agency a dominant market position.

Having been forced out of the market, private-sector financial institutions would then have no choice but to buy government bonds, since government was the only remaining borrower. The result would be a ridiculous situation in which private financial institutions with expertise in lending to the private sector were forced to buy government bonds, while the Postal Savings Agency, whose only expertise was in buying government bonds, was lending to the private sector. The latter's lack of lending know-how would almost certainly create large amounts of bad loans down the road, since the interest rates it was charging did not properly reflect the risk being assumed. In that sense, the privatization of the Postal Savings Agency was not an answer to the problems Japan confronted and should not have been rushed through at the time.

In contrast, nearly all of the structural reforms being proposed under Abenomics are aimed at increasing the number of *borrowers*. By deregulating the agriculture, energy, environmental, and health-care sectors, the Abe administration hopes to open up these markets and create new investment opportunities, thereby deepening the pool of borrowers. It is the right kind of structural reform for the problems Japan faces today. The Trans Pacific Partnerships (TPP) trade initiative that Abe is pushing also represents an attempt to increase the number of borrowers by opening up Japanese markets.

Is Japan's Slump Due to Shrinking Population or Balance Sheet Problems?

The actual Japan Revitalization Strategy announced in June 2014 is a 124-page document covering many areas, the content of which is beyond the scope of this book. For businesses and investors—whether domestic or foreign—considering investing in Japan, two areas probably attract the most attention from a macroeconomic perspective: demographics and immigration policy. After all, the biggest reason companies hesitate to invest in Japan is the declining population. I have been told by countless global investors and fund managers over the past 10 years that they could never invest in a country whose population is headed toward extinction.

It is difficult to accept the argument that Japan, still the third-largest economy in the world, does not rate as an investment destination because of something that may or may not happen hundreds of years from now. Nevertheless, the declining population is in fact perceived as being one of the underlying factors in Japan's economic slump. And some

Japanese companies *are* moving their production facilities overseas, where markets are growing, instead of staying put in the shrinking domestic market.

Japan's shrinking and aging population and its closed door to immigrants appear as a huge negative from the standpoint of countries like the United States or the United Kingdom, where immigration has made a tremendous economic contribution. California's Silicon Valley, for example, would be unable to function without immigrants from Taiwan, India, and China. And London has remained so competitive as a financial center because it attracts talented people from around the world in what has been dubbed the "Wimbledon effect."

It therefore comes as little surprise that fund managers who have succeeded in such places—many being immigrants themselves—will ask whether Japan, with its aging population and shrinking economy, really has a future. As it was these same foreign investors who supported Japanese share prices from the 1990s through Abenomics, their concerns have serious implications for Japanese asset prices.

There are two issues here. First is whether demographics alone can explain Japan's economic slump. Second is whether the government is taking measures to increase the low birthrate and encourage immigration.

Slump in Domestic Demand Was Due to Balance Sheet Recession, Not Decline in Working-Age Population

Kosuke Motani's best-selling 2010 book, *The True Face of Deflation* (Japanese; Kadokawa Shinsho), argues that the decline in domestic demand can be explained by the slump in Japan's working-age population. The data he draws on to support his thesis go beyond standard measures of domestic demand such as retail sales to include data series directly linked to economic activity, such as the number of automobiles sold and the volume of water consumed. All of these indicators turned down in the second half of the 1990s, mirroring trends in Japan's working-age population, according to the author. Motani carefully examined the data for individual prefectures and confirmed that the only prefecture where domestic demand has continued to expand is Okinawa, which is also the only prefecture where the working-age population has continued to grow.

Motani's very accessible book presents some fascinating data and contains a number of useful indicators and analyses. That said, I cannot accept his argument that the decline in the working-age population is sufficient to explain Japan's economic slump. This is because most of the phenomena cited by Motani are attributable to the balance sheet recession.

Personal Financial Assets Have Already Been Invested Somewhere

First, Motani argues that the most important economic stimulus for Japan will be to persuade households to spend their ¥1,500 trillion in personal financial assets, most of which are held by senior citizens, or to gift those assets to the younger generation to spend. However, this ¥1,500 trillion is not just sitting in a warehouse as a stack of banknotes. Most of the money has already been entrusted to financial institutions, which have lent the money to someone else who has then spent it.

This implies that if the government encourages people to invest some of this money elsewhere, the people and businesses who have been borrowing and spending it up to now will no longer be able to do so and will have to cut back on consumption and investment. Since earmarking some of this ¥1,500 trillion for use in another sector will take the money away from someone who is borrowing and using it now, there is no reason the economy as a whole should benefit. Such a policy will work only when the money has been sitting in a bank in the form of unborrowed savings or lying in a vault somewhere as cash.

No matter how old the population grows or how many assets the elderly accumulate, domestic demand will not suffer as long as their financial assets are lent out by financial institutions and eventually spent.

Corporate Debt Pay-Downs Weighed on Consumption and Investment

But after the Heisei bubble collapsed, businesses and households began paying down debt in spite of zero interest rates in order to repair their balance sheets. This unusual situation, in which private companies refused to borrow money, not only weakened aggregate demand, but also caused ultra-low interest rates to become entrenched and threw into turmoil the retirement plans of the elderly, many of whom had intended to supplement some of their day-to-day living expenses with interest income. Having lost that income and lacking any other revenue sources, they were forced to protect their principal by cutting back on consumption.

The working-age population also suffered from a sharp drop in the yields available on deposits, pensions, and life insurance due to the lack of borrowers, and people were suddenly faced with the need to save more in preparation for their retirements. This had the effect of constraining personal consumption, particularly from the second half of the 1990s onward, a period that coincides with the decline in the working-age population noted by Motani.

For instance, long-term interest rates were at 5 percent to 6 percent prior to the Heisei bubble. Assuming senior citizens had financial assets worth ¥1,000 trillion that were earning 5 percent, that money would have generated annual interest income of ¥50 trillion a year, or 10 percent of Japan's current GDP. That money would have had a huge impact on Japan's economy if spent.

Short-term interest rates are at zero today and long-term rates at 0.6 percent, so ¥1,000 trillion invested in 10-year JGBs generates income for senior citizens of only ¥6 trillion a year, a decline of ¥44 trillion. This loss of income has weighed heavily on the consumption activity of both senior citizens and the working generation.

Under ordinary circumstances, senior citizens consume but do not produce, so a growing population of seniors tends to reduce the deflationary gap and stoke inflationary pressures. In Japan, however, businesses' aversion to debt leaves them unwilling to borrow even at zero interest rates, while senior citizens, shorn of their interest income, seek desperately to protect their principal. The aging of the population has therefore become a deflationary, instead of an inflationary, force. The real source of the problem is not the aging population itself but rather the fact that balance sheet problems have left the private sector unwilling to borrow. That unwillingness, in turn, has depressed interest income, forcing senior citizens to do whatever they can to protect their principal.

Real Bottleneck in Japan's Economy: Lack of Loan Demand at Private Companies

The chief priority for Japan's government should be to mobilize tax breaks and other available incentives to get private-sector companies borrowing again. If this can be achieved, the other problems are not that daunting. The investment tax credits and accelerated depreciation allowances implemented in January 2014 as part of the second arrow of Abenomics are extremely important in this sense.

Once companies resume borrowing and spending, the ¥1,500 trillion in financial assets will be put to use for the private sector, and if interest rates rise as a result, it will become easier for senior citizens to spend money. The working-age population will also be able to build a retirement nest egg without having to save as much as it does now.

A recovery in private demand for funds would also make it possible for the government to engage in fiscal consolidation via tax increases and spending cuts without depressing GDP, since the private sector would quickly step in to borrow and spend the money no longer being borrowed by the government. Then and only then will the government be able to tackle the problem of fiscal deficits. In short, what Japan lacks more than anything else is private borrowers. Removing this bottleneck is essential to the normalization of the economy.

Balance Sheet Recession Has Taught Japanese How to Be Frugal

Other examples cited by Motani in his book include the fact that per capita water usage peaked in 1997 and has fallen steadily since then. However, this can probably be explained by the mass shift of production overseas following the yen's climb to extreme levels in 1995. The amount of water used to manufacture products naturally fell as factories moved overseas.

In addition, the behavior of Japanese consumers was fundamentally altered when expectations of high economic growth and ever-rising land prices collapsed after the bursting of the bubble. Until then people had been consuming based on the assumption their salaries would continue to rise every year. When they realized around 1995 that assumption was no longer valid, they suddenly became more cautious.

Until the early 1990s, for example, it was common practice in Japan to buy a new automobile every two or three years. Japan's used car dealers were not only selling vehicles with so little mileage on them as to be unthinkable in the West, but were selling them at astonishingly low prices. The cars themselves were the best made in the world and could be driven for easily another decade or two, which led to heavy demand for them in Southeast Asia and the former Soviet Union.

But after the economy fell into a balance sheet recession, incomes stopped rising and then started to fall, at least for some. People began using products longer and stopped buying new cars so often. This was the chief reason why the domestic auto market stopped growing and then began to steadily contract. Another reason why domestic auto sales fell nearly 2.6 million units from the peak was the appearance of so-called parking police a few years earlier, as their crackdown on parking violations had further diminished the already sparse merits of owning an automobile in a Japanese city.

The United States had its own golden era in the 1960s, and when the economy slumped in the 1970s people stopped buying a new car every two years. The same thing happened in Japan in the second half of the 1990s.

When I returned to Japan in 1984 after 17 years in the United States, it was difficult to find shops that would repair shoes or clothing, and it was almost impossible to find stores selling used clothes. As long as the economy continued to grow so quickly, shoes and clothes were seen as things to be replaced, not repaired. When I had items that needed mending I actually took them back to my parents' home in San Francisco and had them tended to at a neighborhood shop. Today, on the other hand, there are so many repair shops in Japan that it is a wonder they all manage to stay in business. The number of used clothing stores has also exploded.

All these phenomena are byproducts of the long recession and proof that the Japanese have finally become intelligent, "ordinary" consumers in the Western sense of the word. While this should be welcomed inasmuch as it means less wasteful spending, it came as a major shock to the retailers whose business models were predicated on the kind of consumer behavior exhibited during the boom years.

The decline in the working-age population noted by Motani is neither a necessary nor a sufficient condition for a slump in domestic demand. However, a cessation of borrowing by the private sector at a time of zero interest rates is a sufficient condition. At the core of this problem is the fact that while businesses have finished cleaning up their balance sheets, the bitter experience of paying down debt over the years has left them averse to borrowing. Consequently they refuse to borrow even though interest rates are at zero and bankers are willing to lend. Overcoming the debt trauma is therefore a necessary condition for a full-fledged recovery in Japan's economy.

Is Japan Really Closed to Immigration?

Neither the new Revitalization Strategy nor the Basic Policies released on the same day contain anything that might relieve investors' concerns on the second issue, that is, government efforts to address the low birthrate and encourage immigration. The government remains extremely reluctant to discuss immigration policies, noting specifically in the introduction to its Basic Policies that "the increased utilization of foreign workers does not constitute an immigration policy." Nor are there any indications that this stance might change in the future, with the Revitalization Strategy noting that "the policy of accepting foreign workers will be designed so as not to be misconstrued as an immigration policy."

Motani also notes that Japan has only about 1.7 million foreign residents, including illegals, when Koreans with permanent residence in Japan are excluded. The number is increasing by about 60,000 a year and has risen by about 600,000 over the past decade when exchange students are included in the tally. This figure of 1.7 million represents just 1.3 percent of a total population of 130 million and, as Motani points out, will be far from sufficient to stop or reverse the aging of Japan's population, even if it increases substantially.

For instance, he notes that in the five years from 2005 to 2010 alone, Japan's working-age population shrank by 3 million, or about 600,000 a year. Replacing these people with foreign workers would require the government to increase current levels of immigration tenfold, which is both socially and logistically unrealistic.

As many overseas investors and business executives are themselves immigrants, both the official statements above and Motani's numbers will only serve to worsen their impressions of Japan.

Japanese Economy Would Cease to Function without Foreigners

The problem with the official statements and statistics is that they paint a picture that is very different from the reality. While it is little known outside the country, foreigners—and those from China in particular—are now active participants in many sectors of Japan's economy. A huge number of retail establishments, from restaurants to department stores, are now staffed by foreigners speaking fluent Japanese. In the wake of the March 2011 earthquake and tsunami, many local companies faced a severe labor shortage when these workers temporarily returned home. The June 4, 2011, edition of the influential business weekly *Shukan Diamond* actually featured a special report on the economic impact of the mass departure of foreign workers following the March 2011 disaster at the request of their families.

Recent policy proposals pointedly ignore the contributions of these foreigners, even though many of them speak polished Japanese and are full-fledged members of local society. The only relevant reform in the government's June 2014 growth strategy is an extension of the "Technical Intern Training Program" from three years to five.

Abenomics was supposed to encourage domestic and foreign businesses and investors to invest in Japan by improving perceptions of the country. If so, the government needs to send out the message that it is tapping the skills of these foreign workers by highlighting their contributions as integrated members of Japanese society. Recent statements, however, have failed to do so.

The number of foreigners who have learned to speak Japanese and who respectfully participate in local society has increased tremendously over the past 15 to 20 years. The government's unwillingness to highlight their contributions is very unfortunate, not only for the country but also for Abenomics.

If the government cannot acknowledge these people's contributions or even their existence, the private sector will need to do more to inform investors outside Japan. When foreign businesspeople and investors visit the country, for example, they are typically taken to expensive Western eating establishments or sushi restaurants costing upward of ¥10,000 a person. If instead they were taken to cheaper "revolving sushi" shops or the kind of ordinary restaurants and supermarkets that locals frequent, they would be able to see for themselves the huge number of foreigners who staff these establishments.

Additionally, while they may be working in convenience stores and revolving sushi restaurants today, some of them will no doubt start businesses in Japan once they save up an initial investment. In fact, they are almost certainly more likely to start businesses than a similarly aged group of Japanese. Few ethnic groups in the world are as enterprising as the Chinese. While such activity has yet to be confirmed, it is not hard to envision a world 10 years from now in which many of Japan's new start-ups are being founded by Chinese who came to the country as exchange students.

Investors make the long trip to Japan because they want to learn more about the country. If they spend more time in establishments for locals, they will find out that Japanese society has opened up a great deal during the past 15 years and that many foreigners have become a part of it.

On the subject of demographics, it has long been understood that Japan needs to increase the number of childcare workers if it hopes to reverse the decline in birthrates that is constraining the economy. Yet the problem is not that there is a shortage of such workers, but rather that they are paid so little that even those holding the necessary certifications tend to switch professions.

Money is needed to resolve both this problem and the shortage of nurses to look after the elderly. But the government's obsession with budget deficits is preventing it from enacting the measures needed to solve this problem. Public concerns about the falling birthrate and aging population will persist until compensation for both professions improves.

Agricultural Reforms a Major Step for LDP Government

Although the Revitalization Strategy suffers from the problems discussed above, it also contains some groundbreaking reforms of the sort that would have been unthinkable previously, including major changes to the nation's agricultural policy.

The lack of agricultural reform in Japan has long been attributed to the existence of Japan Agricultural Cooperatives, or JA, rather than to the farmers themselves. It is reportedly much cheaper for farmers to buy products from the neighborhood home improvement center than to buy from JA, even though the latter is supposed to be looking out for their interests. An attempt to reform JA in the Strategy represents a major decision for the LDP, which has long relied on the rural vote.

The revised Japan Revitalization Strategy also mentions the TPP, which is now considered part of the third arrow. The fact that the TPP negotiations have gotten bogged down because of opposition from the agricultural sector may be one reason why the Abe government has chosen this opportunity to compile a series of agricultural reforms.

Unlike the critics and pundits who spend their days talking, politicians cannot enact reforms without careful consideration of how much political capital they have and how long it will take to overcome the opposition. In that sense, the Abe administration deserves praise for having the courage to tackle the thorny issue of agricultural reform.

Structural Reforms Are Microeconomic Policies That Take Years to Work

Each structural reform proposal unveiled by a Japanese government is greeted by criticism from the media and pundits who claim it does not go far enough. Some foreign investors even threatened to crash the Japanese stock market by unloading their holdings unless the Diet passed reform bills more quickly.

But structural reforms typically take many years to work because they operate at the microeconomic level. In effect, they encourage people to change their behavior by altering the incentive structure. For instance, one person might respond to a reform by leaving her employer, going back to university to acquire an MBA, and then starting her own company, a process that could take many years.

U.S. president Ronald Reagan and U.K. prime minister Margaret Thatcher embarked on their famous structural reforms at the start of the 1980s. But the benefits of Reagan's supply-side reforms were not felt until the Clinton administration, more than 12 years later. It makes no sense to expect today's structural reforms to produce change overnight. It typically takes many years—and often a decade or more—for structural reforms to have an impact. As such, there is no reason why such reforms should move share prices today.

Scale of Structural Reform Is Also Important

There are many areas in which Japan could benefit from structural reform. The risk is that the announcement of detailed proposals will lead disappointed investors and businessmen to ask, "Is that all there is?" There have been numerous cases in which the initially announced reforms seemed much bigger and more substantial than they turned out to be when the details were revealed. The devil is truly in the details.

One reform being proposed is an easing of restrictions on the amount of floor space a building can contain relative to the size of the land underneath it. The macro-level impact of this reform would be very different depending on whether it is implemented only in certain parts of Tokyo or in cities across the country. If the latter, Japan could well experience a revival of the double-digit growth last seen during the late 1960s.

Compared with their counterparts in other developed countries, Japan's urban residents have high incomes but live in extremely small, crowded dwellings. People with similar incomes elsewhere live in larger homes and apartments and enjoy a higher standard of living. Japan's housing situation is so bad because the country makes poor use of its land. The potential demand for better housing is so great that if this problem could be addressed with changes to the floor-space regulations described above, the Japanese economy could easily post double-digit growth for the next decade. Restricting the reforms to certain parts of, say, Minato or Shibuya ward in Tokyo would mean the loss of another opportunity to address this pressing issue.

A variety of proposals have been made and the prime minister is following up on them, but the final reforms may still be disappointing. The hope is that Abe's approach to the reforms will provide enough "pull" to persuade more businesses to invest in Japan.

We Should Not Expect More Good Fortune

What sort of risks does Abenomics entail? In addition to the possibility that the third arrow will turn out to be insufficient when the details are finally unveiled, the first arrow—which was responsible for the Abenomics honeymoon—also has some major potential risks, not least among them the QE trap. This also begs the question of what should be done with the first arrow now that the honeymoon is over.

The first arrow was definitely the driving force behind the honeymoon, inasmuch as foreign investors jumped on the bandwagon and helped spur outsized stock market gains and a heavy devaluation of the yen. But when considering future approaches, we should remember the expression "Don't push your luck too far" and not automatically expect past good fortune to continue. No one could have predicted what happened between December 2012 and April 2013, since no one in Japan thought foreign investors would join together and ride the trade for as long as they did.

However, additional accommodation by the BOJ in anticipation of further economic gains risks disaster. The notion that the economy will improve if only inflation can be generated suffers from what economists call a time inconsistency problem.

In an ordinary recovery, the labor market approaches full employment as the economy expands. Wages then start to rise, as do prices. People begin to anticipate inflation, which lifts interest rates. There is no problem when the rise in interest rates is the result of a recovery. As the economy is already rebounding when interest rates start to climb, the government's tax revenues are expanding. A recovery in an economy depressed as long as Japan's has been could produce a tremendous surge in tax revenues. Any increase in government bond yields or debt issuance costs would be more than offset by the growth in tax receipts, enabling the government to address this problem without difficulty.

The situation from the standpoint of financial institutions is similar. This kind of rise in interest rates implies a recovery in private loan demand, and lending to the private sector will always generate higher returns than lending to the government, which earns the lowest possible rate of interest. Once banks are able to obtain adequate returns by lending to the private sector, they will be able to absorb any capital losses on their government bond portfolios as interest rates climb.

Hence there is no problem with this kind of inflation and rising interest rates—it is the standard pattern of a traditional economic recovery. Rising interest rates rooted in a recovering economy and resurgent private loan demand are therefore a favorable or "good" interest rate increase.

There are two reasons Japan's economy could be derailed from this positive scenario. The first is that reflationists like Kuroda are trying to reverse the order of this process. The second is the QE trap mentioned in Chapter 2.

On the first point, the BOJ governor has said in so many words that since the problem with the economy is deflation, it will recover as soon as inflation takes hold. But bond yields would rise if market participants really expected the BOJ's reflationary policies to produce inflation, since no one would be willing to hold 10-year bonds yielding 0.6 percent at a time when prices were rising at 2 percent a year. And bonds can be sold with a single phone call—a trade takes as little as two minutes.

In contrast, it takes time for the real economy to respond to inflation. Most people will not change their behavior until they confirm that prices are actually rising. And if someone does decide to buy, say, real estate as an inflation hedge, he will have to decide where to buy, inspect the properties that are on the market, and negotiate a loan with a bank. He might also have to spend time convincing his spouse. All of this takes time. Meanwhile, bond trades can be executed in a matter of minutes.

If market participants really expected the Kuroda BOJ to do whatever it takes to generate inflation, bonds would be the first assets to be sold, and interest rates would rise. The value of government bonds held by domestic financial institutions would fall as rates rose, resulting in large capital losses. But the private credit extended by these financial institutions would still be depressed because it takes time for both borrowers and lenders to get ready. In other words, the capital losses would come first, and because they are not offset by a corresponding increase in profits they would have the potential to create a capital shortfall, preventing the bank from lending. A sharp rise in interest rates would also weigh on demand for funds, and already anemic growth in the money supply and credit would grow even weaker. The first arrow of Abenomics would effectively self-destruct.

The government would suffer from a similar problem. As interest rates rose, the cost of issuing new debt would increase sharply, and tax revenues would remain depressed since the real economy has yet to recover. The higher bond yields would lead to a chorus of calls for fiscal consolidation, which has already happened. When Japanese government bond yields surged in April 2013 and ended the honeymoon, a number of private economists joined David Lipton, first deputy managing director of the International Monetary Fund (IMF), and—of all people—BOJ governor Haruhiko Kuroda in calling for fiscal retrenchment. If this chorus were to become a crescendo, the second arrow of Abenomics would be crushed. And if the government is unable to administer fiscal stimulus at a time when Japan's private sector is still a net saver, the money supply would stop growing and the economy could re-enter a deflationary spiral. A situation like this—where inflation concerns drive interest rates higher ahead of any improvement in the real economy—is a "bad" rise in rates and is particularly dangerous during a balance sheet recession.

The sharp upturn in interest rates in April 2013 that ended the Abenomics honeymoon meant that the BOJ's job was done and that the BOJ governor need not—must not—do any more. Japan has been very lucky so far, but doubling down on the first arrow in expectation of further good luck could wipe out all the gains made up to now.

Until Kuroda became governor, the BOJ had always been concerned about this scenario, in which inflation concerns appear first and send interest rates higher. The question now that he has gone ahead with QQE is how to manage this risk.

Even if the BOJ is able to keep long-term rates from rising on expectations of higher inflation, it will soon face the second problem of the QE trap. From both a theoretical and a practical perspective, therefore, Japan's policymakers need to prepare themselves for a scenario in which a "bad" rise in interest rates precedes a "good" rise, as this is a real possibility under QQE.

Kuroda May Be Trying to Close Gap between Expectations and Reality ...

On April 8, 2014, Governor Kuroda announced that additional quantitative easing would not be necessary because Japan's deflationary gap was about to disappear and the economy was on the brink of achieving full employment. His remarks were greeted with surprise at a time when the lagging performance of Japanese equities in the global market had raised hopes of further accommodation from the BOJ.

The argument that the deflationary gap has almost closed is based on the BOJ's own analysis, and a fair number of private- and public-sector research organizations alike would beg to differ. Nevertheless, there are growing indications that the slack in some parts of labor market is disappearing. For example, the government has been finding it difficult to get public works projects started on time because of a shortage of construction workers and delays in delivery of materials attributable to a lack of truck drivers.

Much of the labor shortage is probably attributable to the fact that few young people today want to become truck drivers or construction workers. Another contributing factor is the rapid shrinkage in Japan's working-age population.

It may be possible to address the shortage of construction workers by importing laborers from abroad—one is reminded of the many Iranians who came to work in Japan in the bubble era of the late 1980s. However, truck drivers must pass a driving test in Japanese. At least in these sectors, therefore, wage increases are long overdue.

For the economy as a whole, however, there is a long way to go before the deflationary gap disappears—after all, the Japanese private sector is still saving 7.3 percent of GDP a year in spite of zero interest rates. Simply normalizing this situation could lead to substantial growth in GDP.

Many people in Japan believe they could achieve more if only the macro environment were a little better. Recently a friend told the story of how an advertisement for a staff position at his company attracted 150 applicants—including graduates of the University of Tokyo. This anecdote suggests that while unemployment may be low, there are still many people who are not satisfied with their current jobs.

If so, why did Mr. Kuroda choose to comment on an issue that is still open for debate? He may have wanted to reduce the gap that has opened up between expectations of monetary policy, which have grown so large under Abenomics, and the reality.

There are a number of gaps involved here. One is the labor market mismatch between the skills required by employers and those possessed by job seekers. Eliminating this gap will be essential if Japan is to realize its remaining economic potential, but that will require an entirely different kind of growth strategy for education and training. And this is not something that can be achieved with monetary policy.

Another gap is the disparity between the actual costs of winding down quantitative easing—what I have dubbed the QE trap—and the market's estimate of those costs, which is essentially zero since most market participants have completely ignored the issue.

During the past few years, market participants and the media in the United States, Europe, and Japan have called for more quantitative easing whenever the economy appears to weaken somewhat or share prices begin to slip. The frequency of those calls around the world suggests some parts of the global market have become completely addicted to QE.

Winding down QE entails huge costs, as explained in Chapter 2, with the resulting pain not unlike what an addict experiences when trying to give up his habit. It would come as no surprise if monetary authorities sought to adopt policies that would ease this pain by avoiding or minimizing the QE trap. In other words, Kuroda's remarks on the deflationary gap may actually have been meant to signal that the economy has already picked up and that market participants should not expect too much more from monetary policy.

That is not to say the BOJ will alter its policy any time soon—any adjustment will almost certainly require proof that the economy succeeded in absorbing any adverse impact from the April 2014 consumption tax hike and possibly even the second hike planned for October 2015. Any sign of economic weakness is likely to delay changes in policy.

Indeed, if anything worries the BOJ governor, it should be the delay in monetary policy normalization caused by the need to cushion the impact of two consumption tax hikes. If the resulting deferral causes the Bank to fall behind the curve on inflation, it could spark a sharp increase in long-term rates and the kind of massive capital losses warned about by the IMF in its April 18, 2013, report.

To avoid this devastating scenario, the government should be ready to implement additional fiscal stimulus (or postpone the tax hike) so the BOJ will not feel the need to remain accommodative when the inflation outlook suggests that it should be tightening.

BOJ and Government Must Stress That Inflation Overshoot Will Not Be Tolerated

Only the BOJ governor knows whether his comment on the deflationary gap was intended to prepare the markets for an eventual unwinding of quantitative easing. But given that it took the Fed half a year to begin tapering its asset purchases after first broaching the subject on May 22, 2013, it would not be surprising if Kuroda has begun laying the groundwork for an eventual reduction in the BOJ's asset purchases.

One signal the BOJ and the government could give to prepare the market is to declare they will target an inflation rate of 2 percent but will not under any circumstances tolerate an overshoot in which inflation rises substantially above this level.

By doing so, the BOJ and government would remove the market's concern that the current path leads eventually to a plunging yen and runaway inflation. Removing these worries would substantially reduce the risk of a steep rise in long-term interest rates.

BOJ Had Weapon to Prevent JGB Crash during Balance Sheet Recession

Japan's public debt reached 240 percent of GDP. In spite of oft-repeated warnings starting nearly 25 years ago that this pace of debt accumulation would spark a JGB market crash, there has been no crash. There are two reasons why. First, fiscal deficits incurred during a balance sheet recession are a result of mistakes made by the private sector during an asset price bubble, which means they can be financed without difficulty (unless the country in question is a member of the Eurozone) because of the self-corrective mechanism described in Chapter 1.

Another reason is that if the government bond market were to be attacked by outside speculators during a balance sheet recession, the central bank would be able to buy as many bonds as necessary to support the market. Since the money multiplier is negative at the margin during such a recession, the central bank cannot create inflation no matter how many bonds it buys. If speculators try to knock the bottom out of the JGB market with targeted selling, the BOJ can simply respond with aggressive buying on a scale sufficient to wipe out the short sellers. Once the speculators have been annihilated and the market stabilizes, the Bank can gradually sell the bonds it bought back to Japanese institutional investors.

Under ordinary economic conditions the central bank must never buy government bonds to quash speculators, but during a balance sheet recession it can. In effect, countries in balance sheet recessions have a way to defend themselves—as long as they do not belong to the Eurozone.

But how would such potential short sellers react if BOJ purchases of JGBs sparked inflation concerns, leading to a "bad" rise in interest rates? The BOJ's first responsibility in such a situation would be to quell inflation concerns. But to do so it would have to sell JGBs—not buy them—to absorb excess liquidity. In other words, the central bank would have lost a key defense against a crash in the JGB market.

The BOJ's attempts to lift the inflation rate with massive purchases of government bonds were a highly risky endeavor from the outset. Moreover, the Bank will have to deal with the QE trap when the economy finally starts to recover. That is why the BOJ should unwind QE before inflation takes root, just as the Fed started tapering its asset purchases in December 2013 when the U.S. inflation rate was only 1.1 percent.

The first arrow of Abenomics has been highly successful, benefiting from both an announcement effect and sheer good luck. But the BOJ needs to be much more careful now that the honeymoon is over.

No One Has Criticized Japan for Currency Manipulation

One thing that is not likely to change even after the honeymoon is the weakness in the yen. For many years there was constant upward pressure on the yen from Japan's large trade surpluses. However, Japan became a trade-deficit nation in 2011 and is now running substantial deficits. In addition to all the damage from the March 2011 earthquake, the country faces a rapidly aging population and a hollowing out of domestic industry. These conditions should have produced a weaker yen sooner, but the Japanese currency remained extremely strong through the end of 2012. Newly elected prime minister Abe then unveiled Abenomics and along with it a program of bold monetary accommodation. That, coupled with a timely reaction by U.S. hedge funds, finally broke the yen's back, and the Japanese currency tumbled over 20 percent in just five months.

In the past, such a rapid depreciation of the currency would almost certainly have elicited criticism from G7 or G8 members claiming manipulation. And in fact these past experiences caused FX market participants to worry that senior Western officials would open up with a barrage of criticism. But they never did. Although German Chancellor Angela Merkel appears to have grumbled a bit, she did not do so officially, probably because Japan is now a trade-deficit country.

In the 22 years from the time the bubble collapsed until 2012, Japanese prime ministers, finance ministers, and deputy vice finance ministers repeatedly tried to jawbone the yen lower but were ultimately unsuccessful because Japan was running one of the world's largest trade surpluses. When it tried to boost the economy by devaluing the yen while running a trade surplus, trading partners running a deficit with Japan naturally objected, arguing it was exacerbating already large global imbalances. Official statements like that cause a quick reaction from the currency market in the direction of a stronger yen, frustrating Japanese authorities' attempts to guide the yen lower.

One of the international "rules" for economic policy is that a trade-surplus nation—which by definition has surplus savings—should use those savings to stimulate domestic demand and boost the economy during a recession. Trade-deficit nations, on the other hand, have a savings shortfall, so it is considered acceptable for them to devalue their currencies and tap external demand to bring their trade accounts into balance.

For 40 years Japan ran one of the world's largest trade surpluses and did not have the option of addressing recessions by devaluing its currency.

Now that it is posting trade deficits, however, no one can complain when it pushes down the value of the yen because the practice is in accordance with international rules.

Japan Supported Global Economy for Four Years after Lehman Collapse

There is more to this story than meets the eye. The yen was as strong as it was for the four years through end-2012 in part because of the Japanese government's commitment to the international agreement reached in 2008. Two months after Lehman Brothers failed, the G20 held an emergency meeting in Washington where the 20 member nations essentially agreed not to start a currency war (then-prime minister Taro Aso was Japan's representative). Although the G20 members pledged explicitly not to engage in the kind of competitive devaluations seen in the 1930s, the only country to observe that pledge in the end was Japan.

The other countries availed themselves of the back-door approach to devaluation offered by quantitative easing and devalued their currencies en masse. The United Kingdom, the United States, and Europe all engaged in aggressive accommodation. The Swiss undertook massive official interventions on the forex market aimed at reducing the value of their currency. Because Japan did not join them, the yen soared against these currencies.

Japan's prime minister at the time was Taro Aso, and business leaders complained to him that if the yen remained so absurdly strong it would put them out of business. But he refused to budge because he was a student of history and had learned the lessons of the Great Depression. The global economy and trade collapsed during the depression of the 1930s because the key surplus country—the United States—took the position that being a creditor nation entailed no responsibilities. In fact, it did not even see itself as a creditor nation. When debtor nations responded to the recession by devaluing their currencies, the United States quickly followed suit. A debtor nation running a trade deficit has no choice but to devalue its currency, but if a creditor nation running a trade surplus does the same, the debtor will be forced to devalue again. In the 1930s this led to so-called competitive devaluations that ultimately forced the world's trading nations to erect protectionist trade barriers to defend themselves. Global trade then fell by two-thirds in an unprecedented collapse of economic activity.

When Lehman Brothers went under, Japan was running a large trade surplus and was one of the world's largest creditor nations. Prime minister Aso knew from his study of history that the global economy would collapse if Japan were to engage in the same behavior as debtor nations, so he made the conscious decision not to follow in their footsteps. It was an extremely unpopular decision, and the LDP lost power to DPJ in the general election of August 2009.

However, the first finance minister in the DPJ administration, Hirohisa Fujii, was also a student of history and of exactly the same mind as Aso. It was because he understood the lessons of the 1930s that he did not give in to the urge to devalue the yen, and the Japanese currency remained strong as a result.

For Japan to make a stand for the global economy and global trade at that point in history was a noble act and the right thing to do. This sacrifice was particularly significant given what would have happened if Japan had followed in the footsteps of the United States and the United Kingdom. Yet almost everyone outside Japan took it for granted.

A global currency war was averted because prime minister Aso of the LDP and finance minister Fujii of the DPJ both had a deep appreciation of history and chose not to join the fight to the bottom. Their efforts prevented a 1930s-style collapse in global trade, and over the next four years the U.S. economy managed to pick up. Europe dug another hole for itself with self-inflicted policy errors, as will be discussed in Chapter 5, but even there the situation had improved compared with the desolate outlook after the Lehman collapse.

In the meantime, Japan not only lost its trade surplus, but fell deeply into deficit as the strong yen destroyed its competitiveness. About half the deterioration in the trade balance was due to increased energy bills from the nuclear power plant shutdown, but the other half was due to the lost competitiveness of its manufacturers.

Four years later the LDP returned to power in Japan. Newly installed prime minister Abe declared his intention to lower the value of the yen, and overseas hedge funds were happy to lend him a hand. Although this elicited complaints from the U.S. auto industry for the first time in many years, officials in the United States and elsewhere remained remarkably quiet. This was because finance minister Aso made a strong case before the G8 and G20 that Japan was the only country that had observed its promise four years ago not to engage in a currency war, while everyone else had used the back-door approach of QE to drive their currencies lower. It was only because Japan did not join them that a currency war had not broken out. Japan paid a major sacrifice over this four-year period as it went from running large trade surpluses to large trade deficits, he said, and should be allowed to do what everyone else had done now that global economic conditions had improved. He ended by daring anyone to complain or rebut his position. No one did, perhaps because Aso's participation in the G20 meeting four years earlier as prime minister lent added weight to his argument.

The yen is likely to remain weak given the events of the past four years and the fact that Japan is now a huge trade-deficit nation. Barring some catastrophe in the Western economies, the probability of the yen rising to 70, say, or even 85 against the dollar is quite small.

Real Effective Exchange Rate Does Not Fully Express Japanese Firms' Pain

Some have argued that if the real effective exchange rate is used as a yard-stick, the yen was never that strong and was actually far weaker in the post-Lehman period than in 1995, when the nominal USD/JPY rate fell to 79.

The concept of the real exchange rate is as follows. If inflation is higher in the United States than in Japan, U.S. producers are becoming less compet-itive relative to Japanese producers even if the nominal exchange rate stays the same. The yen is therefore viewed as having fallen against the dollar in real terms.

The bilateral real exchange rates so calculated are then added together using the actual amounts of trade as weights to obtain the real effective exchange rate.

Japan experienced zero or mild deflation from 1995 until the present while prices rose in the United States and other trading partners. Conse-quently, the yen's real effective exchange rate is actually much lower today than it was in 1995.

But there are two problems with this argument. One is that when the yen rose into the low 80s against the dollar in 1995, it stayed there for only four months. This time, in contrast, the yen's extreme strength has lasted for more than four years, with far more severe consequences for Japanese industry. Making matters worse is the fact that Taiwan, Korea, and China have since emerged as serious competitors. Hence Japan has paid a very high price.

A second problem is that Japanese exports now consist almost exclu-sively of durable goods and intermediate or capital goods for the same. This is a problem because the prices of durable goods have not increased at all in either Japan or in the world, including the United States.

When calculating the real effective exchange rate, nominal exchange rates are adjusted using a comprehensive measure of inflation like the CPI. But the exchange rate calculated in this way does not reflect the pain Japanese producers are feeling because Japan's exports consist largely of durable goods, and the selling price of those goods in foreign markets has not increased. In other words, both domestic and foreign inflation rates are zero as far as Japanese exports are concerned. This means the *real* real effective exchange rate faced by Japanese exporters is almost identical to the nominal exchange rate, which was hovering at all-time highs in the four years through the end of 2012. Exporters incurred heavy losses as a result.

Of course U.S. firms seeking to export durable goods to Japan have an even greater problem. Their manufacturing costs are rising by about 2 percent a year because of domestic inflation, but the price at which those products can be sold in Japan has not risen at all. That is why U.S. automakers start to complain at the slightest hint of yen weakness, with Japan being cast as the villain as soon as the story is picked up by the media or a certain type of politician. But those arguments have lost some of their sting now that Japan is also running a trade deficit.

U.S. automakers, their representatives in Congress, and the U.S. Trade Representative previously wielded so much influence because Japan was running one of the world's largest trade surpluses, and there was an international consensus that it was unacceptable for such a country to exacerbate global imbalances by devaluing its currency. That is why Japan was unable to boost external demand during the first 22 years of its balance sheet recession by pushing the currency lower. In June 1999, Japan's Ministry of Finance ignored Western warnings and tried to weaken the exchange rate—then at 117 to the dollar—to 122 with a massive intervention in the forex market. However, the move was vigorously opposed by then-Treasury secretary Lawrence Summers, and the yen surged to nearly 100 in spite of the ¥3 trillion intervention.

But now Japan is a trade-deficit nation. While it continues to post a surplus with the United States, it is already running deficits with Europe. Trading partners have no basis for criticizing a trade-deficit nation that tries to reduce its deficit with a currency devaluation.

The current range of 95 to 105 is probably the most comfortable level for US$/JP¥, all things considered. Now that Japan's nuclear power program has been shut down, further weakness in the yen is probably best avoided as the negative economic impact of rising energy costs could start to outweigh the benefits of a cheaper yen. Compared with the yen's pre-Abenomics extremes, an exchange rate of 95 to 105 would still provide a significant boost to the economy and to the domestic mood.

Although it was the advent of the Abe administration that triggered the yen's decline, there are two basic reasons why the yen stabilized at this level without reversing. One is Japan's trade deficit, and the other is the huge sacrifice Japan made over the four years starting in 2008 to save the global economy.

Rising Fiscal Deficits Caused by Change in Corporate Behavior

At the risk of digressing from the topic of Abenomics, some are arguing that with the public debt as large as it is, Japanese investors will no longer be able to absorb all of their government's debt issuance a few years from now.

They cite the growth in the public debt as a percentage of Japan's personal financial assets, which totaled ¥1,630 trillion at end-March 2014.

While personal financial assets should naturally be taken into account, this approach can cause us to lose sight of the nature of the problem facing Japan. The public debt has grown to its current size because of a change in behavior at Japanese *businesses*, not households.

This should be clear from the flow-of-funds data in Figures 1.15a and 1.15b, which show a near-perfect inverse correlation between corporate sector savings and the fiscal deficit. The coefficient of correlation between (1) nonfinancial corporations' financial surplus/deficit as a percentage of GDP and (2) general government's financial surplus/deficit as a percentage of GDP from FY1980 to FY2013 was –0.815. When private financial institutions are added to the mix, the negative correlation rises to –0.867.

All of the periods in which businesses increased their savings coincide with recessions. In other words, the direct cause of Japan's fiscal deficits has been companies' decision to increase savings in spite of zero interest rates, which triggers a recession by widening the deflationary gap in the private sector.

Businesses behaved in that way because from 1990 to 2005 they were busy repairing balance sheets damaged in the bubble's collapse. From 2008 onward, they were trying to protect themselves against the global financial and economic crisis spawned by the failure of Lehman Brothers.

In both cases, the growth in corporate savings came first—only then did the economy weaken and the fiscal deficit increase. The implication, already noted in Chapter 1, is that domestic financial institutions have all the unborrowed private savings needed to finance the fiscal deficit.

Expressed differently, it is only because private companies are saving so diligently that the economy weakened to the extent it did, and without that weakness the government would not have needed to run such large fiscal deficits. This cause-and-effect relationship is exactly the opposite of that observed in Greece, where fiscal deficits were caused by profligate governments. The difference between the two is obvious from the interest rates on government debt.

A fiscal deficit in ordinary economic times leads to the crowding out of private borrowers as both the public and private sectors try to borrow from a limited pool of private savings, sending interest rates higher. As the government steps into the queue and borrows money the private sector had hoped to borrow, it distorts the allocation of resources and can have a negative impact on broader economic growth, just as the economics textbooks teach. But the chief cause of the ongoing recessions and deficits in Japan, the United States, and in Europe is the private sector's decision to increase savings at a time of zero interest rates in order to repair balance sheets damaged by imprudent behavior during the bubble. Unless the government borrows and spends these unborrowed savings, they will remain trapped within the banking system—since there are no other borrowers—and generate a deflationary gap.

Government borrowing under such circumstances does not distort the allocation of resources. If the government did not borrow and spend this money, the result would be unemployment, which is the worst possible form of resource allocation.

During this type of recession, the private-sector fund managers responsible for investing these funds will beat a path to the door of the government—the last borrower standing—lifting the price of government bonds and driving down yields.

This kind of fiscal deficit, which results from mistakes in the private sector, is "good" in the sense that it supports economic activity and money supply, helps businesses and households repair their balance sheets, and leads the economy to recovery. That is clearly reflected in the low yields on government bonds.

The fact that these fiscal deficits are rooted in a change in corporate behavior also implies that deficit-reduction efforts are bound to fail unless businesses resume borrowing. Once they do, GDP will be sustained even if the government embarks on fiscal consolidation efforts because the businesses will step in to borrow and spend the private savings that the government is no longer borrowing. And as long as GDP is sustained, the deficit-reduction efforts will be successful. When fiscal problems stem from excess savings in the *corporate* sector, there is little point in judging the sustainability of public finances by looking at the savings of the *household* sector.

How Should Japan's Tax System Be Reformed?

The consumption tax rate is to be raised to 10 percent by 2015 in two stages, under an agreement reached by the ruling DPJ coalition and the opposition LDP in the summer of 2012. The first increase, from 5 percent to 8 percent, was already implemented in April 2014, and the second is scheduled to take place in October 2015.

While not part of Abenomics, this arrangement may be convenient for Japanese politicians on both sides of the aisle, who understand that at some point Japan must raise its consumption tax rate. However, it also poses massive economic risks at a time when the private sector is still a large net saver in spite of zero interest rates.

Japan will eventually have to raise the consumption tax, but this issue has traditionally been the third rail of Japanese politics: all prime ministers who increased the tax lost their jobs soon afterwards. Given the stigma attached to it, the bipartisan agreement probably represents the best chance politicians will ever have to raise the consumption tax because it enables them to put half the blame on others.

From an economic standpoint, however, raising taxes at a time when the private sector is saving 7.3 percent of GDP is a suicidal act that could destroy the nascent recovery, just as the Hashimoto administration's consumption tax hike quashed the rebound in 1997. That government went ahead with the consumption tax hike because it saw that real GDP was growing at an inflation-adjusted rate of 4.4 percent, the highest of any G7 nation. In the event, however, the tax hike sent Japan's economy into a deflationary spiral and caused it to contract for five consecutive quarters, a postwar record.

The reason for the collapse was twofold. First, the previous year's GDP data had been boosted by government demand in the form of reconstruction efforts following the Hanshin-Awaji earthquake, which devastated the city of Kobe, the author's birthplace. Second, the private sector had not only stopped borrowing but was saving to the tune of 6 percent of GDP in spite of interest rates that had already fallen to near-zero levels. The government's decision to embark on fiscal consolidation at a time when the private sector had stopped borrowing effectively left no one to borrow and spend private savings and tipped the economy into a deflationary spiral.

Fiscal Stimulus Introduced to Offset Consumption Tax

There is no economic reason to raise the tax rate when the private sector is a net saver at a time of zero interest rates. However, raising the consumption tax rate in line with the bipartisan agreement reached in 2012 is *politically* advantageous. Indeed it marks one of the rare occasions on which politicians actually wanted to raise taxes.

As part of its bid to raise the consumption tax, the government correctly decided to administer a ¥5.5 trillion fiscal stimulus in January 2014 to offset the economic blow of the first tax increase.

This was not a particularly costly operation. The consumption tax hike in 1997 was accompanied by decisions to shelve a large-scale supplementary budget, abolish a special tax cut, and raise taxpayers' share of social security costs. Those four measures were expected to have a combined fiscal hit of ¥15 trillion. This time there is only the consumption tax hike to offset. The cost of offsetting the blow to the economy this time would be about half that.

Assuming the estimate that a 1 percentage point increase in the consumption tax rate will increase tax revenues by about ¥2.5 trillion is accurate, a fiscal stimulus of ¥6 trillion to ¥7.5 trillion should be sufficient to counterbalance the impact, ignoring any psychological factors. The government has already enacted ¥5.5 trillion in stimulus, and more may be on its way for the second tax hike if the economy shows signs of stalling.

The game plan here is that the ¥5.5 trillion fiscal stimulus, which includes the long-awaited accelerated depreciation allowances and investment tax credit, will both keep the economy from collapsing and finally cure the debt trauma of Japan's private sector. Once businesses and households are ready to borrow, the fiscal stimulus will be allowed to expire while the higher consumption tax rate is left in place.

Current Corporate Earnings Based on Massive Fiscal Deficits

Although the lack of corporate borrowers has been the key bottleneck in the Japanese economy, domestic business groups such as Keidanren continue to call for deficit-reduction efforts. Not only is there no basis for their argument, but they would be the greatest losers if the government actually followed their advice and cut the deficit.

As representatives of their shareholders, business executives would have the right to criticize the government if it were fiscal deficits that had pushed interest rates higher and crowded out private investment. In that case, deficit-reduction efforts would lower interest rates and boost private investment, having a positive impact on both the broader economy and on individual businesses.

But this argument holds no water at a time when interest rates are at zero. That government bond yields have fallen as far as they have is a solid indication that fiscal deficits have *not* been a burden on the private sector. In fact, deficit-reduction efforts under these conditions would inflict the greatest damage on the private sector itself as the economy would fall into a deflationary spiral and incomes plummet. A substantial portion of recent corporate earnings is actually attributable to the support for aggregate demand provided by the government as it borrows and spends the unborrowed savings of the private sector.

But individual business executives feel justified in demanding the government put its fiscal house in order because they cannot see this support unless they are direct recipients of orders from the government. If the government were to listen to their demands it would be tremendously detrimental both to their shareholders and to the economy as a whole.

Working Down Public Debt Will Require Bold Policies to Lift Japan's Growth Rate

Given all the consternation caused by lifting the consumption tax rate a mere 3 percentage points, it is natural to be concerned about Japan's ability to work down the public debt, currently valued at 2.4 times GDP.

The debt grew so large because for the past 20 years the authorities, the media, and academic economists have refused to lend their support to the only medicine that works during a balance sheet recession—fiscal stimulus—because they do not understand that Japan is in a balance sheet recession. When the government *has* engaged in fiscal stimulus, these groups have continuously argued that it should be followed by deficit-reduction efforts, thereby undermining the forward guidance effect of the spending.

With the exception of the Obuchi administration, which declared it would not try to chase the two hares of economic recovery and deficit reduction at the same time, and the Aso administration, which had to deal with the GFC, every Japanese government before the current Abe administration has followed policies that tried to achieve both goals, and it is because of their greed that the balance sheet recession has lasted as long as it has.

In so doing Japanese governments have tried to adhere to numerous resolutions on fiscal consolidation over the past two decades—despite the fact that such promises can never be fulfilled during a balance sheet recession. Not once did they meet their deficit-reduction targets. Instead, the repeated tapering of fiscal stimulus only prolonged the recession, which increased public debt.

Now the question is what to do about Japan's massive public debt. Trying to trim it using the standard approaches of tax hikes and spending cuts will require a dizzying amount of time. Some are even afraid it is too late no matter what Japan does. That may be true if the menu of policy options is limited to tax hikes and spending cuts. Moreover, the problem of the past 20 years—a corporate sector that is saving instead of borrowing in spite of zero interest rates—has yet to be resolved. This issue alone will probably take at least a few years to resolve using the kind of investment tax breaks and accelerated depreciation programs implemented in January 2014.

Fiscal consolidation will become possible only after the problem of the private sector's unborrowed savings is addressed, and many shudder to think about how large the public debt will be by then. But such a reaction can lead to a vicious cycle in which debt fears prevent the government from administering the necessary anti-trauma measures.

Once it is acknowledged that the problem grew as big as it did because policymakers pursued the orthodox approach of simultaneously chasing the two hares of deficit reduction and economic recovery, resolving the issue will require an entirely different approach. Tax hikes and spending cuts alone will not work because they depress economic activity.

Indeed, one of the biggest dangers countries face when coming out of balance sheet recessions is the temptation to raise various taxes to reduce the huge public debt that has accumulated during the downturn. Such indiscriminate tax increases can easily sap "animal spirits" and nip the private sector's nascent recovery in the bud, resulting in a stagnant economy for years to come. Although this is by no means an exclusively Japanese problem, people in Japan have to be most alert to this risk given the size of their public debt. What Japan needs instead is bold policies to lift the growth rate.

Incentives Needed to Restore Japan's Economic Vitality

Here we come back to the government's growth strategy, the third arrow of Abenomics. Before such policies are implemented, Japan needs to discuss what kind of country it could or should be. The fact that many local industries have already moved to China and other emerging economies means the menu of policy options for boosting Japan's growth rate is increasingly limited.

Abe's exhortation to "take back Japan" does not imply a restoration of Japan's golden era. After all, most of the industries of that era have already left for emerging economies with much lower wages. What the slogan really calls for is a restoration of Japan's economic vitality, which will require incentives capable of getting people excited again. But any such incentives must take into account what Japan is actually capable of. No matter how motivated people are, the vision is unlikely to be realized if the necessary conditions for success are not in place.

From this perspective, Japan actually has a number of sectors in which China and other emerging economies will have a difficult time overtaking it. In addition to its well-known advantages of advanced technology and quality control, Japan has other cultural and geographical strengths that include exceedingly low crime rates, clean water and air, a kind, polite and punctual people, and a bountiful natural environment with four seasons. By positioning itself as, say, the Switzerland of Asia and focusing on its highly advanced manufacturing sector, its sophisticated services, and a tourism industry that draws on the nation's natural beauty, Japan could once again become a globally competitive economy.

Japan is also likely to attract increasing interest from Asia's rapidly growing middle and upper classes simply because it is geographically close and has many things to offer that they cannot find at home. Additionally, Asians' appreciation for Japan's low crime rates and the politeness and kindness of its people is likely to increase as they grow wealthier.

More Effective Land Utilization Could Propel Growth

There are a number of obstacles to realizing the potential described above, including high taxes and the high cost of urban housing. The latter is attributable to unreasonable restrictions on building footprint and square area as a percentage of land area, which have constrained the supply of residential and commercial space and made Japan one of the world's least efficient users of land, as mentioned earlier. This is a problem that the structural reforms of Abenomics' third arrow definitely need to address in order to boost growth and raise the nation's standard of living.

The third arrow is set to include a review of the building restrictions. But as mentioned above, the question is how broadly any changes will be applied—if limited to a small area, the macroeconomic impact of such measures would be far less than if they were applied in cities around the country. Incidentally, the issue of poor land utilization was first discussed at the Structural Impediments Initiative talks between Japan and the United States in 1991, but the topic was soon forgotten after the United States' attention was diverted by Saddam Hussein's invasion of Kuwait and the first Gulf War.

Japan Needs Bold Tax Reforms Modeled on U.S. and Hong Kong Systems

Lowering the high tax rates that are Japan's other main shortcoming would seem to contradict the goal of trimming the national debt with higher taxes. Here Japan needs to decide what sort of country it wants to be and then determine which taxes should be raised and which should be cut. If Japan is to position itself as the Switzerland of Asia and pursue development by attracting Asian money, it will need to lower its income tax rates, even if that requires raising the consumption tax.

Ronald Reagan tried similar supply-side reforms in the United States 35 years ago. At the time, Americans were growing increasingly panicked as they watched Japanese manufacturers of home appliances and electronics, steelmakers, semiconductor makers, and shipbuilders that had emerged in the 1970s take business away from local companies. The United States, once the world's undisputed industrial leader and the home of the American dream, was now being pursued by Japan. Some even said the nation might have to return to its roots as an agricultural producer if Japan continued to steal away its industrial base.

While Japanese management techniques became all the rage at U.S. business schools, policymakers launched a wide range of measures intended to keep Japanese imports in check. These included the Super 301 provisions of the Trade Act of 1974, a devaluation of the dollar via the Plaza Accord of 1985, and a wide range of gentlemen's agreements.

The conclusion eventually reached was that the only way to fend off someone who is chasing you is to run faster. This approach, manifested in supply-side reforms, revived the U.S. economy with large income tax cuts and major incentives for private enterprise.

Japan's industrial base, much like America's then, is rapidly being lost to China and other emerging economies, and bold supply-side reforms will be needed if the nation is to fend off these competitors. Reagan aroused criticism by running large budget deficits, but they were almost laughably small in comparison to Japan's deficits today. Japan also faces issues Reagan never had to face, including an aging population and problems stemming from the balance sheet recession. Hence it needs to act even more boldly than the United States did with Reaganomics.

An excellent model would be the tax system of Hong Kong, thought by many to be the world's best example of a supply-side economy. The top income tax rate in Hong Kong is 17 percent, which translates to about 15 percent of net income. The city-state levies no taxes on capital gains or dividend income and has no inheritance tax.

Hong Kong has been able to grow to its current form in spite of numerous challenges because this tax system maximized incentives for people to work and invest. Hong Kong is also the world's most efficient user of land, which has enabled it to function well despite an extremely high population density. Additionally, its per capita income on a purchasing power parity basis surpassed that of Japan in 2013.

There were some in the Reagan era who said the United States should look to Hong Kong's tax system for inspiration. The United States also made gifts from foreigners to U.S. citizens tax-free in an attempt to attract more capital from abroad.

Taiwan, which like Japan has lost much of its industry to China, slashed its inheritance and gift tax rates to 10 percent several years ago. That bold move prompted a great deal of capital to return to Taiwan after years of steady outflows.

Policies Need to Change Perceptions of Japan at Home and Abroad

The world's view of Japan would be shaken to its foundations if the Abe government were to announce it was lowering the top income tax, corporate tax, and inheritance and gift tax rates to 20 percent while raising the consumption tax rate also to 20 percent.

At home these changes would serve as a potent supply-side incentive, sharply reducing the number of loss-making firms and drastically curtailing the kind of unnecessary and inefficient expenditures made mostly for tax reasons. They would also accelerate the transfer of financial assets from senior citizens to the younger generation. These tax cuts would not only ensure broad-based improvements in the efficiency and productivity of Japan's economy but would also lift inward investment by foreigners and encourage wealthy Japanese to repatriate their capital.

It is said that few countries are as resistant to bold reforms as Japan, and lowering the top tax rate to 20 percent may sound like something out of a science fiction novel. But the state of the public finances means more audacious ideas like this will be needed if the nation is to find a way out of its predicament.

Balance sheet recessions happen only once every several decades because they are triggered by nationwide asset price bubbles, which themselves are extremely rare events. When they do occur, the government needs to administer sufficient fiscal stimulus from the outset and sustain that stimulus until the private sector resumes borrowing. If the government refuses to do so and tries instead to chase the two hares of deficit reduction and economic recovery—as Japan has done over the past two decades and the Eurozone since 2010—the recession will only grow longer and deeper. Ultimately the public debt will expand to the kinds of levels seen in Japan today.

Despite the size of Japan's national debt, the fact that this kind of recession occurs at most once every several decades means the authorities have plenty of time to reduce the deficit before the next balance sheet recession. Since the people who lived through the bubble and the subsequent balance sheet recession will never make the same mistake again, the next bubble and balance sheet recession will not occur until after they are dead and their experiences have been forgotten.

In other words, if the government adopts a 30- or 40-year horizon, it will have time to employ all its tools to boost economic efficiency and growth—including fundamental reforms to the tax system. But if it tries to address the public debt problem in the abbreviated space of just five or ten years, the government risks delivering another blow to the economy.

Japan had to rely largely on trial-and-error in the beginning because no economics text even mentions the phenomenon called a balance sheet recession. And for a long time the country made the mistake of trying to chase two hares at the same time. Because of these missteps, Japan's per capita GDP is now less than Singapore's, and on a purchasing power parity basis it has been overtaken by Taiwan and Hong Kong. But now that we know what a balance sheet recession is and how it functions, there is no reason for Japan to make the same mistake again.

For the first time since the Meiji Restoration of 1868, Japan is being chased by China and other emerging economies, which means it has little time left in which to implement necessary reforms. The United States drew on Japan's lessons from the 1990s to successfully avert its own fiscal cliff.

Now Japan needs to draw on America's experiences in the 1970s when it was chased by Japan and quickly implemented the supply-side reforms needed to restore incentives for people to work and invest.

Japan must regain lost time by compiling a bold growth strategy based on its comparative advantages and a thorough understanding of balance sheet recessions including the debt trauma that follows.

CHAPTER 5

Euro Crisis—Facts and Resolution

The unfolding euro crisis offers a perfect opportunity to apply the teachings of balance sheet recession theory. The concept of balance sheet recessions is essential to understanding this crisis from both a macroeconomic (weakening economy) and a microeconomic (widening competitive gap) perspective, but in Europe there are far fewer people who understand this theory than in Japan, the United States, or the United Kingdom.

The crisis erupted when Greece's fiscal profligacy was revealed. But the real tragedy was that countries in balance sheet recessions—the opposite of the state Greece was in—were forced to respond in the same way as Greece, tipping them into deflationary spirals. Events unfolded in this way for two reasons. First, the Maastricht Treaty that underlies the euro is a defective document that makes no allowance for countries in balance sheet recessions. Second, the plurality of government bond markets within the same currency zone means that the self-corrective mechanism for balance sheet recessions functions poorly, if at all, in the Eurozone.

As noted in Chapter 1, the Eurozone, too, experienced a massive housing bubble. This bubble burst in 2007, as Figure 1.2 shows, prompting businesses and households in the affected countries to begin deleveraging and triggering numerous balance sheet recessions. Fiscal stimulus is essential to overcoming such recessions, and in 2009 Eurozone governments moved to provide such stimulus under an agreement reached at the emergency G20 summit in November 2008, soon after Lehman Brothers went under. The government spending that followed went a long way toward stabilizing and reviving the economies of the Eurozone.

However, Greece was plunged into fiscal crisis after it was revealed at the end of 2009 that the government had been hiding the extent of its fiscal deficits, and that forced other Eurozone nations to engage in deficit-reduction efforts as well. This was an extremely destructive turn of events because while the Greek government had been spending far more than was warranted by the country's private-sector savings, other Eurozone nations were characterized by huge pools of unborrowed private savings as businesses and households moved collectively to repair their balance sheets. In effect, the governments of these countries began cutting their deficits just when they needed to borrow and spend this unborrowed savings via fiscal stimulus.

At the time, almost no one in the West had any idea what a balance sheet recession was. As a result of an exclusive focus on the *size* of Greek's fiscal deficit instead of its causes, everyone—the Eurozone nations as well as the United Kingdom, the United States, and even Japan's Kan administration, which knew nothing about balance sheet recessions—changed course and embarked on fiscal consolidation so as not to become "the next Greece." This trend gained additional momentum in 2010 when the G20 agreed at the Toronto summit to reduce their fiscal deficits in half and again in 2011 as Eurozone countries adopted a new "fiscal compact" at Germany's urging. Although the United States realized its mistakes and quietly distanced itself from the Toronto agreement, the rest of the G20 continued to march to the wrong tune, which had particularly devastating consequences for the Eurozone.

Euro's Adoption Lowered Interest Rates Sharply

Why did this happen to the Eurozone? The control stick for this artificial currency was in the hands of the European Central Bank (ECB), which carried on the tradition of the German Bundesbank, famed for its inflation-fighting prowess. Its headquarters, like the Bundesbank's, was in Frankfurt. Many Eurozone members saw a steep drop in interest rates since the euro policy rate was essentially a continuation of Deutschmark rates.

The decline in rates was particularly sharp in the European periphery, and spectacularly so in Greece. As Figure 5.1 shows, Greece's 10-year government bond spread relative to Germany stood at 1,800 basis points in 1993 before starting a steady decline that took it down to several dozen basis points by 2001, when the country was admitted to the Eurozone.

Two factors contributing to this steep decline included (1) a substantial reduction in inflation risk due to the ECB's reputation as an inflation fighter and (2) the adoption of a common currency, which made it easy for foreign investors to buy the government debt of peripheral nations like Greece without concern for currency risk. Although Greek government bonds still carried credit risk, that amounted to just a few dozen basis points. This state of affairs continued until around 2008.

FIGURE 5.1 Eurozone Government Bond Spreads Relative to German Bunds

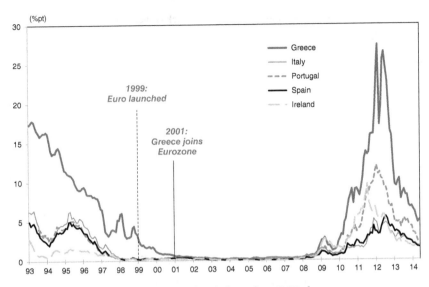

Source: Nomura Research Institute (NRI), based on ECB data.

Maastricht Treaty Acted as Constraint on Credit Risk

One reason credit risk declined was that the Maastricht Treaty contained a provision requiring member nations to cap their fiscal deficits at 3 percent of gross domestic product (GDP). It was thought that the risk of default by a Eurozone government would be extremely slim as long as this condition was satisfied. Greece therefore went from a situation in which 90 percent of its government debt was held by local investors at the end of 1994 to one in which 74 percent of its debt was owned by foreigners in 2007 (Figure 5.2).

With the exception of Greece, fiscal deficits in most Eurozone nations hovered around 3 percent of GDP until 2006 (Figure 5.3). The 3 percent rule was adopted because it was thought that managing an artificially created currency like the euro required a number of artificial conditions. One particular concern was that a Eurozone government would take advantage of the market's faith in the euro or the ECB to run up large budget deficits, eventually dragging down the credibility and value of the common currency. This concern proved to be well founded when Greece's fiscal deficits sparked a major sell-off in the euro.

This framework was fine as long as the market believed Greece was running fiscal deficits of around 3 percent of GDP. The crisis came when the new government that took power in the autumn of 2009 reported that the

FIGURE 5.2 Foreigners Owned 74 Percent of Greek Government Bonds in 2007

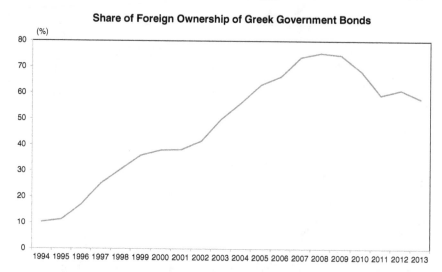

Source: NRI, based on the data from Bank of Greece.

FIGURE 5.3 Eurozone Fiscal Deficits

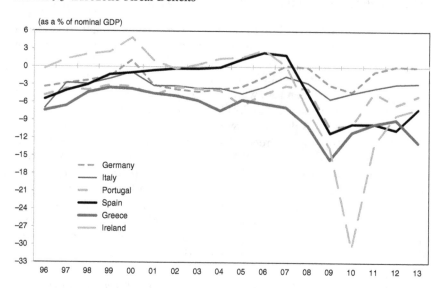

Source: Eurostat.

previous government had fudged its deficit data and that the actual shortfall was much larger. Greek government debt yields surged in the wake of that revelation, with the spread over German debt rising at one point to 2,500 basis points (bp) (Figure 5.1).

Greece Was Spoiled by Euro, and Germany Reacted Violently

Ultimately, joining the euro slashed Greece's debt issuance costs, and the government's commitment to fiscal discipline weakened markedly as foreigners aggressively bought the nation's debt. That was clearly the primary cause of the nation's crisis.

The people who designed the euro included the aforementioned clause in the Maastricht Treaty in an attempt to prevent Eurozone membership from allowing governments to run up large fiscal deficits. But Greece, as it turned out, got around that constraint by lying. Meanwhile, the media focused on the fact that German workers could not retire until the age of 67 while their Greek counterparts could stop working before they turned 60 and still receive a pension. This kind of coverage fueled a view in Germany and elsewhere that Greek society needed to be beaten into shape.

One influential German politician I interviewed in 2012 argued that fundamental reforms were needed because Greece was not a modern nation-state but a vestige of the ideas and systems of the Byzantine and Ottoman Empires. Greece's tax collectors were almost unimaginably incompetent. The German politician told the story of a friend who went to the local tax office to confess that he had an unreported swimming pool, only to be told that he need not report it since the paperwork for determining the additional property tax was too much trouble.

He argued that the deep influence of personal relationships in Greek-style democracy meant election results were not being determined via a healthy policy debate. He went on to say that Greece had been accepted into the Eurozone because it was the birthplace of Western democracy, but the decision had clearly been a mistake because little of that tradition remained. Another German politician said that regardless of what happened in the short run, Greece needed to rebuild its entirely uncompetitive economy in the longer term by leaving the euro and sharply devaluing its currency.

Such views were behind the opposition of Germany and some other countries to aid for Greece. From their perspective, there was no need to help out a lazy country that did not follow the rules. This view found form in the official German government stance that Greece and other periphery nations needed to carry out structural reforms, including efforts to reduce their fiscal deficits. Contributing to this stance was Germany's own experience with painful structural reforms around 2005.

Germans Believed Structural Reforms Required a Crisis

Structural reforms refer to the kind of measures Germany itself implemented from 1999 to around 2005—in particular, pension reforms and other policies intended to enhance labor market flexibility. These reforms had been very painful, but Germans saw them as the driving force behind the nation's resurgent competitiveness. German politicians I talked to said the country still had far to go in terms of structural reform. But based on the difficulties they themselves had experienced, they firmly believed now was the time for southern Europe to undertake similar reforms.

During the first half of the 2000s, when Germany was suffering from a severe recession and German firms were falling over themselves in a rush to move factories to low-wage countries in eastern Europe, there was still tremendous domestic political resistance to the reforms. The lesson from this experience was that such painful reforms are possible only in the midst of a crisis. Hence their view that the unfolding economic crisis in southern Europe offered a rare opportunity for fundamental reform.

This is why German chancellor Angela Merkel talks about the need for structural reforms every time something happens in southern Europe—in effect, her remarks are drawing on Germany's own very painful experiences. One German politician close to Merkel told me that while she is by no means opposed to the idea of assisting periphery countries, she would not sanction such aid without the structural reforms needed to close their competitive gap with the rest of Europe.

Inasmuch as the Germans see current conditions as presenting an opportunity for reform in southern Europe, they may see a further deterioration in conditions as offering an even greater opportunity. Additional economic weakness is therefore unlikely to lead them to call for a change of policy. Indeed, one reason why Germany has not altered its stance even as the euro crisis has deepened is that German policymakers continue to believe the crisis represents a chance for southern Europe to undertake the same structural reforms that Germany itself undertook around 2005.

While there is something to be said for this argument, the tragedy is that the only country in which the problems were caused by a profligate government whose spending greatly exceeded private savings was Greece. All the other peripheral nations not only observed the Maastricht Treaty deficit provision but actually had large pools of unborrowed private savings after 2008 because the bubble collapse had led businesses and households to focus on repairing their balance sheets. In other words, Greece was the only nation that had no domestic savings and required external assistance. Spain and Ireland, which were in the midst of balance sheet recessions, had more than enough private savings to finance their own fiscal deficits, as indicated in Figure 1.18.

Nevertheless, these two countries, along with Portugal and Italy, were lumped together with Greece and dubbed the "PIIGS" by callous and ignorant analysts. They were then forced to undertake the same structural reforms as Greece even though they suffered from an entirely different economic problem—a balance sheet recession. The structural reforms were the wrong policy for the wrong countries and made the situation far worse than it was.

Moreover, the Eurozone suffered from another inherent problem—the unborrowed savings of some countries were not flowing into their own government bond markets, thereby preventing the self-corrective mechanism from functioning. This point is discussed in detail later in this chapter.

German Balance Sheet Recession Eight Years before GFC Started the Crisis

The view held by the vast majority of Germans—that their current competitiveness is rooted in the painful structural reforms implemented in the early 2000s—is actually only half correct. The rest is due to the fact that the ECB's ultralow interest rate policy, which was intended to pull Germany out of a severe balance sheet recession following the collapse of the IT bubble in 2000, created bubbles in the European periphery.

As I mentioned in my previous book,[1] German households and businesses alike participated heavily in the global IT bubble that lasted from 1998 to 2000, and when the bubble burst the German economy fell into a severe balance sheet recession. Although very few Germans realized it at the time, Germany was only the second developed country to experience this type of recession in the postwar period (Japan was the first). Shares on the Neuer Markt, Germany's version of the Nasdaq, rose tenfold during the bubble before falling 97 percent (Figure 5.4), and the households and businesses that had invested heavily in IT firms incurred huge losses. The German economy was shaken to its foundations, and from 2000 onward the household and corporate sectors massively increased their savings, with their combined net savings amounting to 10 percent of GDP in early 2005 (Figure 5.5).[2]

---

[1] Richard Koo, *The Holy Grail of Macroeconomics: Lessons from Japan's Great Recession* (Singapore: John Wiley & Sons, 2008), pp. 35–37.

[2] Flow-of-funds data show Germany's corporate sector dramatically increasing its holdings of financial assets from 2006 to 2007, but according to a Bundesbank statistician, this reflects special adjustments made when the data for 2006 and beyond were rebased and does not reflect what actually happened at German companies.

FIGURE 5.4 Neuer Markt Collapse in 2001 Plunged Germany into Balance Sheet Recession

Source: Bloomberg, as of July 4, 2014.

FIGURE 5.5 German Private Sector Refused to Borrow after IT Bubble Burst

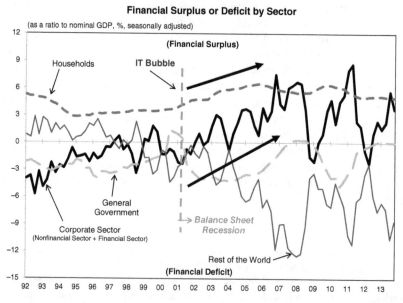

Notes: The assumption of Treuhand agency's debt by the Redemption Fund for Inherited Liabilities in 1995 is adjusted. All entries are four-quarter moving averages. For the latest figures, four-quarter averages ending in 2013 Q4 are used.

Source: NRI, based on the data from Bundesbank and Eurostat.

FIGURE 5.6 German Households Stopped Borrowing Altogether after IT Bubble

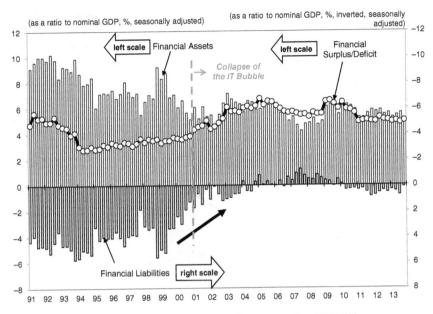

Notes: Seasonal adjustments by NRI. Latest figures are for 2013 Q4.

Source: NRI, based on flow of funds data from Bundesbank and Eurostat.

The flow-of-funds statistics for Germany's household sector (Figure 5.6) show that household behavior changed dramatically after the IT bubble collapsed—they effectively stopped borrowing. Up until 2000 German households were saving but still took out loans to buy houses. After the bubble burst, however, they ceased borrowing altogether, and from 2005 to 2009 they actually paid down existing debt. This sort of debt-averse behavior has continued until the present day.

With German households no longer borrowing, house prices did not respond at all to the ECB's drastic monetary easing, which started in 2001 and took the policy rate down to what was then a postwar low of 2 percent by 2003. In fact, German home prices continued to fall. Meanwhile, home prices in other Eurozone countries climbed higher as the central bank's ultralow interest rate policy produced textbook housing bubbles (Figure 1.2).

The increase in German corporate borrowings during the IT bubble years was almost as large as that seen during the reunification boom (Figure 5.7). The corporate sector sharply reduced its own borrowings after the bubble burst and pushed ahead with balance sheet repairs, ignoring

FIGURE 5.7 German Nonfinancial Corporations Also Deleveraged after IT Bubble

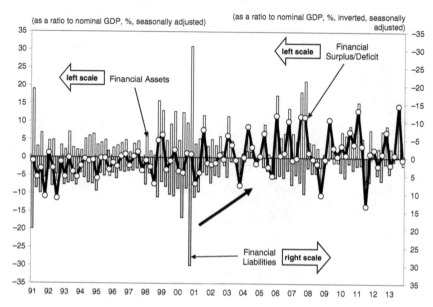

Notes: The assumption of Treuhand agency's debt by the Redemption Fund for Inherited Liabilities in 1995 is adjusted. Seasonal adjustments by NRI. Latest figures are for 2013 Q4.

Source: NRI, based on flow of funds data from Bundesbank and Eurostat.

the fact that the ECB had brought interest rates down to a postwar low of 2 percent.

These statistics also make it clear why the German economy did not recover from 2000 onward in spite of aggressive monetary accommodation by the ECB and why it was ultimately labeled the "sick man of Europe." There is no reason why the economy should have responded to the ECB's easing because there were no private-sector borrowers in Germany despite postwar-low interest rates.

Yet most German analysts were completely unaware of the tremendous impact the IT bubble's collapse had had on the German economy. I was invited to German research institutes and universities on six occasions in 2012 alone, and people were always surprised to see the graph in Figure 5.6. They had no idea that the German household sector had changed its behavior so dramatically in response to the bursting of the bubble. Without knowing that, it is impossible to hold a meaningful discussion about subsequent problems in the Eurozone.

German IT Bubble Brought about Euro Crisis

Post-2000 Germany was facing a classic balance sheet recession as the private sector moved collectively to minimize debt after its balance sheet was impaired by the collapse of an asset bubble. To keep the economy from deteriorating any further, the government needed to step in to borrow and spend the resulting increase in unborrowed private savings. But German policymakers at the time were unaware of the concept of a balance sheet recession[3] and in any case were prohibited by the Maastricht Treaty from running a fiscal deficit in excess of 3 percent of GDP. In fact, Germany itself was responsible for inserting that 3 percent clause into the treaty. The country was therefore unable to apply the necessary fiscal stimulus, and the economy continued to weaken.

As the German economy was the Eurozone's largest, a weak Germany meant a weak Eurozone. The ECB responded with bold monetary accommodation, taking short-term interest rates to 2 percent—lower than they had ever been under the Bundesbank—in 2003 (Figure 1.3).

At the time, ECB President Claude Trichet jokingly boasted of an ECB that had, under a French president, achieved interest rates lower than at any time the Germans were in charge of the Bundesbank. However, interest rates were at ultralow levels not because the ECB had succeeded in vanquishing inflation, as he seemed to imply, but rather because Germany was in a serious balance sheet recession.

As there were no borrowers and the private sector had shifted its priority to minimizing debt, Germany did not respond to the ECB's ultralow interest rates. In fact, the M3 money supply grew at just half the rates recorded in the rest of the Eurozone (Figure 5.8).

When the German economy did not respond to the ECB's easing, the dominant view domestically was that structural problems were to blame. This is exactly the same mistake that Japanese prime minister Junichi Koizumi made when he mistook a balance sheet recession for structural problems. In Germany, that mistake ushered in bold structural reforms spearheaded by then–prime minister Gerhard Schröder and known as Agenda 2010. But no matter how enthusiastically the nation implemented these reforms, the economy did not improve—and for the same reasons that the Japanese economy had not improved under Koizumi's leadership. Many Germans wanted to know why things were not getting better despite all the reforms. The answer is that while structural reforms have huge merits

---

[3] Joseph Ackerman, then the CEO of Deutsche Bank, did realize the importance of my first book *Balance Sheet Recession* soon after its publication in 2003 and featured it in one of his bank's report to its clients.

FIGURE 5.8 German-Eurozone (ex-Germany) Competitiveness Gap Has Macro (50.2 percent) and Micro (49.8 percent) Origins

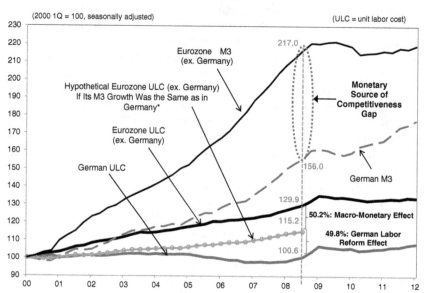

*Parameters obtained from the regression result of Eurozone ULC (ex. Germany) on Eurozone M3 (ex. Germany), log(Eurozone ULC[ex. Germany]) = 3.155506 + log(Eurozone M3 [ex. Germany]) × 0.318227, was then used to calculate what the Eurozone (ex. Germany) ULC might have been if its money supply growth was equal to those in Germany.

Source: NRI, based on ECB, Eurostat and Deutsche Bundesbank data.

of their own, they will not help an economy suffering from a balance sheet recession.

ECB's Rate Cuts Create Bubbles outside Germany

Meanwhile, the ECB's large rate cuts from 2001 onward created major asset bubbles in Eurozone countries that had already experienced a sharp fall in interest rates when they joined the zone. The periphery nations in particular enjoyed strong balance sheets because they had not participated in the IT bubble. From their perspective, it was the most natural thing in the world to respond to the ECB's ultralow interest rates—which were intended to rescue Germany—by investing in real estate. Economic theory tells us that when a central bank takes interest rates down to extremely low levels, a private sector with a healthy balance sheet can be expected to invest in real estate in anticipation of future inflation and asset price increases. The resulting European housing bubbles were driven by precisely the same mechanism as the U.S. housing bubble, which occurred when Fed chairman Alan Greenspan rushed to lower rates to the postwar low of 1 percent in response to the Internet bubble collapse, and they were also similar in scale.

Borrowing by households in Ireland, where the housing bubble was larger than anywhere else, increased dramatically as the ECB took rates down to 2 percent (Figure 5.9), the lowest rate in modern Irish history. Private sector balance sheets were clean at the time because Ireland had not participated in the IT bubble, and Irish households responded in textbook fashion to the rate cuts by borrowing and investing in property.

The same thing happened in Spain. Spanish households (Figure 5.10), traditionally frugal savers, were unable to resist the lure of 2 percent interest rates and began increasing their investment in housing. They, too, had sidestepped the IT bubble, so their balance sheets were clean when the ECB

FIGURE 5.9 Irish Households Increase Borrowing after IT Bubble and Begin Deleveraging in 2009

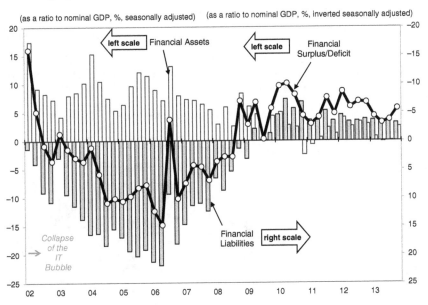

Notes: Seasonal adjustments by NRI. Latest figures are for 2013 Q4.

Source: NRI, based on flow of funds data from Central Bank of Ireland and Central Statistics Office, Ireland.

FIGURE 5.10 Spanish Households Increased Borrowings after IT Bubble and Are Deleveraging Today

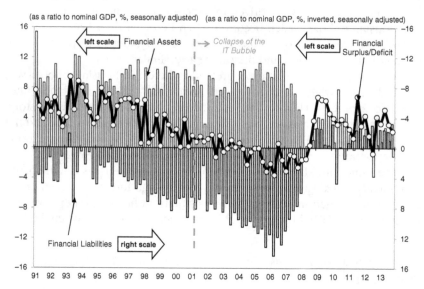

Notes: Seasonal adjustments by NRI. Latest figures are for 2013 Q4.

Source: NRI, based on flow of funds data from Banco de España and National Statistics Institute, Spain.

FIGURE 5.11 Germany Recovered from Post-IT Balance Sheet Recession by Exporting to Other Eurozone Countries

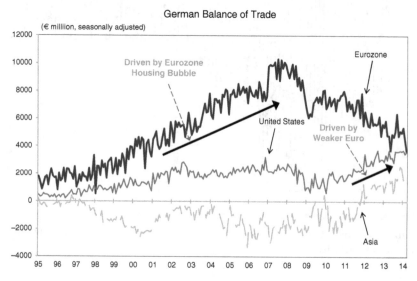

Source: Deutsche Bundesbank.

started cutting rates. As a result, they responded in textbook fashion to the ECB's dramatic easing of policy.

As countries outside Germany responded to the ECB's rate cuts by borrowing money and using it to buy property, their economies picked up dramatically, providing a major fillip to Germany. Eventually Germany was able to emerge from its balance sheet recession by boosting exports to these countries.

Germany had been running small trade surpluses until 2000, but in 2007 it overtook Japan and China to post the world's largest surplus. European Union (EU) markets were responsible for almost all the growth, with some two-thirds of all German exports destined for the Eurozone (Figure 5.11). Germany's trade surplus with the United States increased only slightly during this period, while its trade deficit with Asia actually widened. In other words, exports increased because other Eurozone economies were doing so well after the ECB eased monetary policy to save the German economy.

Misunderstandings Regarding Lack of Competitiveness in Southern Europe

Some in Germany argue that southern Europe suffers not only from the macroeconomic problem of fiscal deficits but also from the microeconomic problem of a lack of international competitiveness, and that addressing the latter issue will require either the kinds of structural reforms that Germany itself undertook or an exit from the Eurozone and a return to cheaper local currencies.

The large trade deficits of southern European nations when the crisis erupted would seem to support this argument. However, this argument is based on the mistaken assumption that the loss of competitiveness in these countries is due to policy missteps. If a country becomes uncompetitive because the authorities did not tighten monetary policy in response to inflation and wages have risen as a result, it needs to restore that competitiveness by devaluing the currency. This is something the countries of southern Europe did frequently in the pre-euro era.

This historical precedent leads some to call for southern Europe, and Greece in particular, to leave the Eurozone. But since the adoption of the euro the nations of southern and northern Europe alike have been operating under the same monetary policy, preventing them from tightening monetary policy even if they wanted to. The fact that wages and prices are too high in southern Europe—and their resulting lack of international competitiveness—is therefore attributable to ECB monetary accommodation and not to anything these countries have done.

Money Supply Growth Much Lower in Germany

If that is the case, why did such a wide gap in competitiveness open up between countries operating under a unified monetary policy? The reason is that the economies of Germany and other economies were not synchronized and experienced sharply different rates of money supply growth (Figure 5.8).

This happened because Germany was caught up in the IT bubble and fell into a severe balance sheet recession when the bubble burst in 2000. When the private sector stops borrowing money because of balance sheet problems, the money supply stops growing as the private money multiplier falls to zero or even turns negative at the margin. Government borrowing via fiscal stimulus is then needed for the money supply to expand, but in Germany that was constrained by the 3 percent limit on fiscal deficits in the Maastricht Treaty.

Although Germany did run a fiscal deficit slightly in excess of 3 percent of GDP on several occasions, it was hardly sufficient when the private sector was saving nearly 10 percent of GDP. Consequently, both the economy and money supply growth slumped. That led the ECB to lower its policy rate to a postwar low of 2 percent in 2003, but because there were no borrowers in the country, German money supply growth continued to stagnate, as did the price of housing and other assets. With slow money supply growth, wages and prices languished as well.

In contrast, southern European countries had steered clear of the IT bubble, and their private sectors had clean balance sheets and healthy demand for funds. Hence the decline in the ECB's policy rate to 2 percent produced a surge in borrowing and money supply growth. With the money supply growing rapidly, wages and prices rose as well.

So while the ECB's 2 percent policy rate had little impact in Germany, which was in a balance sheet recession, other countries with clean balance sheets responded vigorously to the central bank's accommodation, producing a large disparity in money supply growth and competitiveness. In other words, the lack of structural reform in the periphery that is emphasized by the Germans is by no means the only reason for the competitiveness gap. Much of it is due to the lack of synchronicity between Germany and the rest of Europe, and the fact that in post-2000 Europe only Germany was in a serious balance sheet recession.

German Reforms Responsible for Only Half of Competitive Gap

The three lines at the bottom of Figure 5.8 are an attempt to compare the competitiveness gap created by Germany's balance sheet recession with the gap due to the country's painful structural reforms.

First, M3 in the Eurozone (ex-Germany) expanded by 117 percent between the collapse of the IT bubble in 2000 and Lehman's bankruptcy in 2008 Q3. That growth led to corresponding increases in wages and prices. But in Germany, where the collapse of the IT bubble prompted the private sector to focus collectively on minimizing debt, the money supply grew only 56 percent over the same period, which served to depress price and wage inflation.

As a result, German inflation during this period was far lower than in other Eurozone nations. As the third line from the top in Figure 5.8 shows, unit labor costs (ULC) in the rest of the Eurozone rose from 100 (rebased) in 2000 to 129.9 in 2008 Q3, for an increase of 29.9 percent. In Germany, which is shown as the bottom line in Figure 5.8, they grew to 100.6, for an increase of just 0.6 percent. If we assume that German workers were no more competitive than their counterparts in the rest of the Eurozone in 2000, the implication is that by 2008 Q3 workers in the rest of the Eurozone were 29.3 percentage points more expensive than their German counterparts.

The next question is how much of this 29.3 percentage points gap was attributable to the microeconomic factor of Germany's painful structural reforms and how much was due to the macroeconomic factor of the nation's balance sheet recession. The following estimates suggest a roughly equal split between the two factors.

The money supply in the Eurozone ex-Germany grew 117.0 percent during this period, while unit labor costs rose 29.9 percent. The regression results shown at the bottom of Figure 5.8 indicate that each percentage point increase in the money supply increased unit labor costs by 0.318 percent. This means if money supply growth in the Eurozone ex-Germany had been the same as in Germany, unit labor costs in the rest of the Eurozone would have risen by 15.2 percent, not 29.9 percent. In other words, money supply growth was responsible for 14.7 percentage points (29.9 percent – 15.2 percent), or 50.2 percent, of the 29.3 percentage points gap in unit labor costs.

Meanwhile, unit labor costs in Germany rose only 0.6 percent during this period, which means that 14.6 percentage points (15.2 percent – 0.6 percent) of the 15.2 percent estimated growth in unit labor costs cannot be explained by money supply growth, and is instead attributable to Germany's structural reforms. This 14.6 percentage points is 49.8 percent of the total 29.3 percentage points gap.

Although this simplified calculation has a number of shortcomings, it provides a starting point for measuring the impact of the structural reforms vis-à-vis the impact of Germany's balance sheet recession. It suggests that while the microeconomic factor of German structural reforms was certainly important, they explain less than half (49.8 percent) of the overall gap in competitiveness. The remaining 50.2 percent is attributable to the fact that

Germany was in a balance sheet recession while the rest of the Eurozone was enjoying strong economic performance and money supply growth.

Performing the same analysis for Germany and Greece shows that German structural reforms can explain 52.6 percent of the gap in competitiveness between the two nations, while the remaining 47.4 percent is attributable to differences in money supply growth. The similarity of Greek results to those for the Eurozone (ex-Germany) suggests that while Greek wages did in fact rise substantially compared with those in Germany, the increase was not that different from the rest of the Eurozone (ex-Germany).

Ultimately the ECB lowered rates out of concern for Germany, but the German economy did not respond because it was in a balance sheet recession. Instead, the low interest rates fueled housing bubbles in countries on the European periphery, causing both GDP and the money supply in these nations to surge along with prices and wages. Germany finally succeeded in pulling itself out of the balance sheet recession by massively increasing exports to these countries.

Germany Benefited Most from Euro

Had Germany not been part of the Eurozone, the ECB would not have lowered rates as far as it did, and there would have been no reason for the housing bubbles in the periphery nations to expand to the extent they did. In that case, the only way Germany could have addressed its balance sheet recession—at a time when the economy was not responding to monetary policy—is by devaluing the Deutschmark, which was anathema to the Bundesbank, or administering a massive dose of fiscal stimulus, as Japan did in the past and the United States is doing today.

In that sense, Germany benefited more than any country from the euro. The only reason its fiscal deficits did not widen substantially after the IT bubble collapsed was that the ECB, in order to rescue Germany, created housing bubbles in other Eurozone countries that had sidestepped the IT bubble.

After Lehman Brothers went under, the housing bubbles burst and these countries fell into severe balance sheet recessions. Ironically, the Greek crisis that followed caused a sharp devaluation of the euro, giving another boost to German exporters. So while Germany's exports to the Eurozone fell in the wake of the euro crisis, as shown in Figure 5.11, the weaker euro lifted German exports to the rest of the world.

Germany is the only Eurozone country in which industrial output is now close to pre-Lehman levels, and the unemployment rate is at its lowest level since reunification 24 years ago. In that sense, Germany benefited significantly from its Eurozone membership in the wake of both the IT bubble collapse and the GFC.

After the housing bubbles burst in the periphery nations that had provided such an economic boost to Germany, their economies weakened and attention suddenly focused on their competitiveness. But people should question whether Germany is in a position to criticize these nations for being uncompetitive. After all, it was only because the ECB lowered short-term interest rates to 2 percent in an attempt to rescue Germany that these countries experienced asset price bubbles, lost their competitiveness against Germany, and ultimately fell into balance sheet recessions. It was not the policy choices of peripheral countries that produced this outcome.

The recessions and lack of competitiveness in the periphery are not the result of national idleness: They occurred because Germany, the first nation in the Eurozone to experience a balance sheet recession, was unable to use the fiscal stimulus needed to address such a recession and ECB monetary policy was forced to pick up the slack.

Around 2005 I told a senior ECB official it was unfair that although Germany had fallen into a balance sheet recession after participating in the IT bubble of its own volition, the ECB did not demand it administer fiscal stimulus; instead, the central bank was creating bubbles in other economies with monetary accommodation meant to rescue Germany. His response was "that is the meaning of a common currency—Germany cannot be allowed an exception on fiscal stimulus, so we must lift the entire Eurozone economy using monetary policy." The result of this approach is the Eurozone crisis we see today.

If Germany had addressed its balance sheet recession with fiscal stimulus, there would have been no need for the ECB to ease monetary policy to the extent it did, and hence the competitive gap between Germany and the periphery nations would not have grown as large as it did.

This lack of synchronicity will persist as long as some countries in the Eurozone are suffering from balance sheet recessions while others are not. To get around it, countries in balance sheet recessions must be urged to administer fiscal stimulus so that the ECB need not engage in excessive monetary accommodation, resulting in the creation of bubbles elsewhere in the Eurozone. If Germany wants to avoid a bubble from an excessively low ECB policy rate, it should be the one telling peripheral countries to implement fiscal stimulus.

One More Mutual Dependency between Germany and Eurozone Periphery

A financial look at the euro crisis reveals another mutual dependency. In what is to some extent an inevitable development, German and French banks were by far the biggest lenders to the periphery nations.

When the collapse of the IT bubble sparked a balance sheet recession in Germany, both the household and the corporate sectors became net savers—for example, they were running financial surpluses (Figure 5.5). By 2005, for example, Germany's private sector was saving 10 percent of GDP in spite of postwar-low interest rates. The German government was running a fiscal deficit slightly in excess of 3 percent of GDP, but Maastricht Treaty constraints prevented it from borrowing more. Since the private sector was saving 10 percent of GDP but the government was borrowing only 3 percent to 4 percent of GDP, that left German financial institutions with unborrowed savings equivalent to 7 percent of GDP that could not be invested locally.

The only option for German banks was to lend the money overseas. And one of the first places they turned was the European periphery, where housing bubbles had fueled strong economic growth. Not only did these markets offer ample loan demand and high interest rates, but there was no currency risk for the lenders because these countries were also in the Eurozone.

Japan experienced a similar collapse in domestic loan demand in the 1990s during its balance sheet recession, but because the Japanese government administered ample fiscal stimulus and funded it by issuing large quantities of debt, there was no need for Japanese banks to look overseas. Instead, they were able to invest the private sector's unborrowed savings domestically, in JGBs, without taking on any currency risk.

German banks, on the other hand, were unable to invest the unborrowed savings domestically because the government did not want to run larger fiscal deficits. That forced them not only to lend to the Eurozone periphery and Eastern European countries but also to buy collateralized debt obligations (CDOs) consisting of U.S. subprime loans. Many German lenders found themselves in this situation, and their actions exacerbated the housing bubbles in the United States and the Eurozone periphery. German banks later suffered a major blow when the housing bubbles in the Eurozone periphery burst and subprime mortgage problems surfaced in the United States.

Ultimately, because there was a massive supply of unborrowed savings in Germany during its balance sheet recession and the German government, in order to keep its fiscal deficits within the Maastricht-imposed ceiling of 3 percent of GDP, refused to take up the slack, German manufacturers were forced to depend on exports to periphery countries while German banks relied on loans to the same markets. Thus the government's inability to serve as the borrower and spender of last resort when necessary created large distortions in both the real economy and the financial system.

Germany succeeded in pulling out of its own balance sheet recession because the ECB created bubbles in other countries with aggressive monetary accommodation. However, those bubbles started to collapse in 2007, plunging the periphery countries into severe balance sheet recessions. *That is the primary cause of the euro crisis.*

Spain's Vicious Balance Sheet Recession

A look at Spain's household sector since 2007 shows that since the housing bubble burst, Spanish households—much like their U.S. counterparts—have stopped borrowing in spite of interest rates that are the lowest in the history of the Eurozone (Figure 5.10). Spanish households increased their borrowing in just two of 20 quarters from 2009 Q1 onward and paid down debt in the remaining 18. In the 19 years from 1990 through the end of 2008, Spanish households had collectively paid down debt in just one quarter—1993 Q2—and at the time Spanish interest rates were far higher. This serves as a reminder of just how unusual current conditions are for Spain.

Meanwhile, Spain's corporate sector was forced to draw down financial assets for eight consecutive quarters starting in 2008, when housing bubbles burst and banking sector problems surfaced in the United States and Europe, as shown by the white bars below the centerline in Figure 5.12. Since 1990 there had been only one quarter—1992 Q1—in which Spanish businesses were forced to draw down financial assets, and interest rates then were much higher than they are now. This highlights the severity of the financing problems companies faced starting in 2008.

Spain's corporate sector also paid down debt for three consecutive quarters starting in 2009 Q2, a time when Spanish interest rates were at all-time lows. In other words, Spanish businesses in 2009 were both paying down debt and drawing down financial assets to a massive degree. 2009 was the first year since this data became available in which Spain's corporate sector collectively paid down debt, reflecting the severity of balance sheet problems since 2007 and the resulting financing difficulties for businesses.

The behavior of Spanish firms started to return to normal around 2010, but the Greek crisis elicited calls for the government to reduce the fiscal deficit, and as soon as the government embarked on a path of fiscal consolidation the economy fell into a double-dip recession. Spanish businesses were again forced to draw down financial assets and trim existing debt, a highly undesirable combination that has continued to the present.

From peak to trough, household sector borrowings fell by 5.58 percent of GDP between 2007 Q3 and 2013 Q3, and corporate sector borrowings dropped by 17.78 percent of GDP. Together, the private sector's net savings increased by a stunning 23.36 percent of GDP (Figure 5.13). Private demand equal to more than 20 percent of GDP effectively vanished as people who had been borrowing large sums to invest in housing suddenly stopped and began saving instead. The result was a vicious deflationary cycle. Spain's

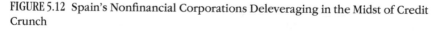

FIGURE 5.12 Spain's Nonfinancial Corporations Deleveraging in the Midst of Credit Crunch

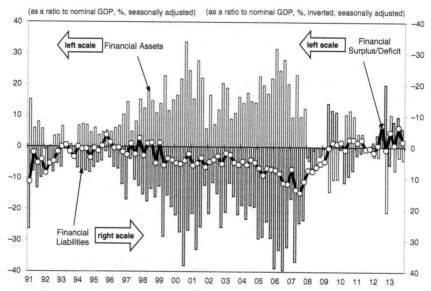

Notes: Seasonal adjustments by NRI. Latest figures are for 2013 Q4.

Source: NRI, based on flow of funds data from Banco de España and National Statistics Institute, Spain.

unemployment rate stood at 25.1 percent in May 2014, and the rate for people aged 25 and under was an astonishing 54.0 percent, figures similar to those seen in the United States during the Great Depression.

Ireland's Household Sector Forced to Pick Up Pieces after Massive Housing Bubble

Ireland's household sector has exhibited similarly large changes in behavior since the nation's massive housing bubble burst in 2007. As the broken line in Figure 5.9 shows, Irish households were running a financial deficit equal to as much as 14.8 percent of GDP (2006 Q2) during the bubble years as they borrowed money to invest in property. After the bubble burst the situation reversed, and by 2010 Q2 they were running a financial surplus equivalent to 10 percent of GDP. This change alone represents a loss of demand equal to 25 percent of GDP, underscoring the severity of the trials faced by the Irish economy.

FIGURE 5.13 Spain in Balance Sheet Recession: Spanish Private Sector Increases Savings Significantly after Bubble

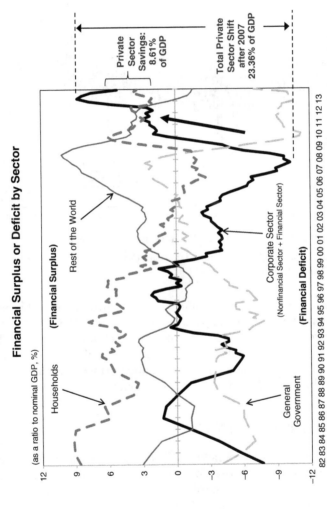

Financial Surplus or Deficit by Sector

Notes: All entries are four-quarter moving averages. For the latest figures, four-quarter averages ending in 2013 Q4 are used.

Sources: Banco de España and National Statistics Institute, Spain.

FIGURE 5.14 Irish Nonfinancial Corporations Are Also in Financial Surplus

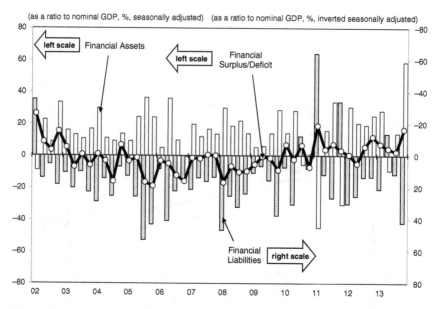

Notes: Seasonal adjustments by NRI. Latest figures are for 2013 Q4.

Source: NRI, based on flow of funds data from Central Bank of Ireland and Central Statistics Office, Ireland.

As the shaded bars in Figure 5.9 show, Irish households not only stopped borrowing but began paying down debt in 2009 Q2 and have done so ever since in spite of the lowest interest rates in modern history. Although Irish house prices are finally showing signs of stabilizing, they have fallen 50 percent from their autumn 2007 peak, and balance sheet adjustments for the affected households are expected to continue.

Irish Businesses Remain Net Savers

Ireland's nonfinancial corporations (Figure 5.14) also took on a great deal of debt during the bubble years of 2005 to 2008, but from 2010 until the end of 2013 they ran a financial surplus in 13 out of 16 quarters in spite of the lowest interest rates in the nation's modern history.

The increase in private savings from the bottom in 2008 Q2 to the peak in 2010 Q4 was equal to 38.0 percent of GDP, a high for the Eurozone. Moreover, this happened at a time when interest rates in Ireland were at an all-time low (Figure 5.15).

FIGURE 5.15 Ireland in Balance Sheet Recession: Irish Private Sector Increased Savings Significantly after Bubble

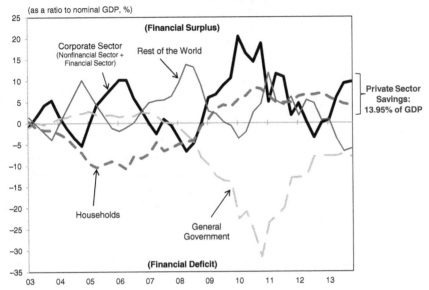

Financial Surplus or Deficit by Sector

Notes: All entries are four-quarter moving averages. For the latest figures, four-quarter averages ending in 2013 Q4 are used.

Sources: Central Bank of Ireland and Central Statistics Office, Ireland.

The increase in fiscal deficits over the same period amounted to 28.8 percent of GDP, which means the government borrowed and spent 76 percent of the private sector's unborrowed savings (28.8 percent divided by 38.0 percent), thereby returning this money to the economy's income stream. That still left a deflationary gap of more than 9 percent of GDP in an economy in the midst of a deflationary spiral. The government's subsequent deficit-reduction efforts caused the deflationary gap to widen even further. In other words, Ireland's fiscal deficits were far too small given the scale of the private sector's deleveraging efforts, and as a consequence Irish GDP fell as much as 20 percent from the peak in nominal terms and more than 10 percent in real terms. The unemployment rate climbed to 15.1 percent at one point but has recently fallen back to 12.0 percent. The Irish private sector's net savings in 2013 still amount to 13.95 percent of GDP even with near-zero interest rates, an indication the economy remains mired in a balance sheet recession.

Portugal's Balance Sheet Recession Began Quite Recently

Following the collapse of the European housing bubble in 2008, Portugal's household sector (Figure 5.16) started to reduce its borrowings, as shown by the shaded bars in the graph. Only in 2011 did the sector begin paying down debt in earnest, and it continues to do so today.

At the beginning of the global financial crisis (GFC), financing problems forced Portugal's nonfinancial corporations (Figure 5.17) to draw down financial assets in just one quarter (2009 Q1). Conditions were relatively normal for some time after that. But as Figure 5.17 shows, these firms were forced to reduce debt and draw down financial assets starting in 2011 Q4. That highly undesirable combination continues today.

The relatively stable conditions seen in the first half of the crisis in Portugal reflect the fact that the country did not experience a housing bubble of the scale seen in Spain and Ireland, and as a result private sector balance sheets did not incur nearly so much damage. During the second half, as the Eurozone crisis worsened, Portugal was carelessly if not maliciously lumped together with the four other "PIIGS" in spite of this key difference,

FIGURE 5.16 Portuguese Households, Unaffected by IT Bubble, Are Deleveraging Now

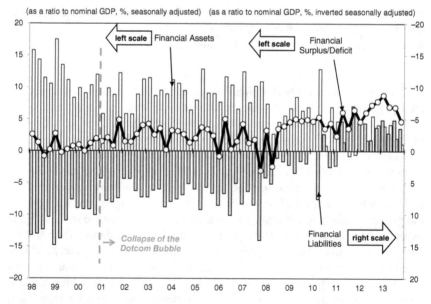

Notes: Seasonal adjustments by NRI. Latest figures are for 2013 Q4.

Source: NRI, based on flow of funds data from Banco de Portugal.

FIGURE 5.17 Portuguese Nonfinancial Corporations Deleveraging in Midst of Credit Crunch

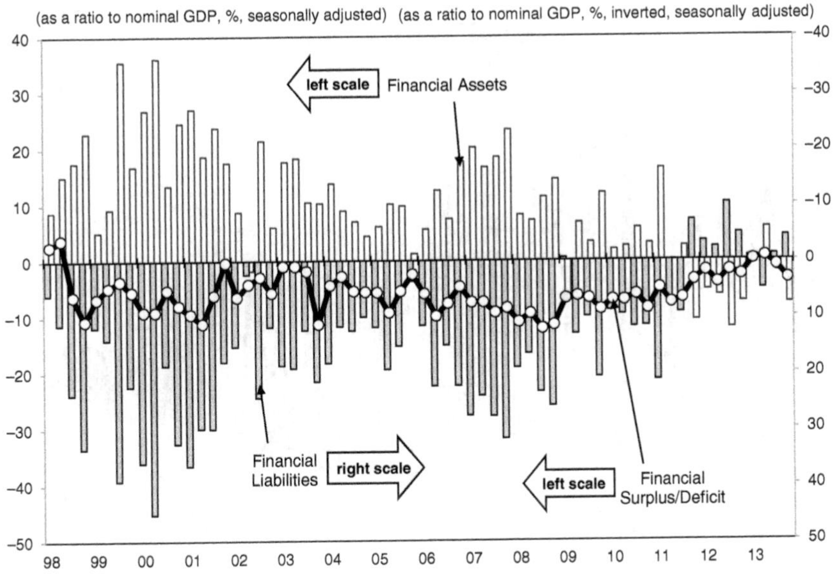

(as a ratio to nominal GDP, %, seasonally adjusted) (as a ratio to nominal GDP, %, inverted, seasonally adjusted)

Notes: Seasonal adjustments by NRI. Latest figures are for 2013 Q4.

Source: NRI, based on flow of funds data from Banco de Portugal.

complicating Portuguese banks' efforts to obtain funding and forcing them to cut back on lending. As a result, Portugal is now facing not only the borrower-side problem of a mild balance sheet recession but also the lender-side problem of a credit crunch. The fact that Portugal's household and corporate sectors are saving 7.49 percent of GDP at near-zero interest rates means they are still in difficult straits at the moment.

Italy Is in Same Position as Portugal

The same is true for Italy. The Italian household sector halved its borrowing starting in 2008, but until mid-2011 it followed the standard pattern of borrowing on one hand while saving on the other. This is probably because Italy's housing market was largely untouched by the bubbles seen elsewhere in the Eurozone, which meant the nation's private sector had no major balance sheet problems (Figure 5.18). Once Italy was dragged into the euro crisis in mid-2011, however, households not only stopped borrowing but actually began paying down existing debt in spite of the lowest interest rates in modern history.

FIGURE 5.18 Italian Households Stopped Borrowing in 2011

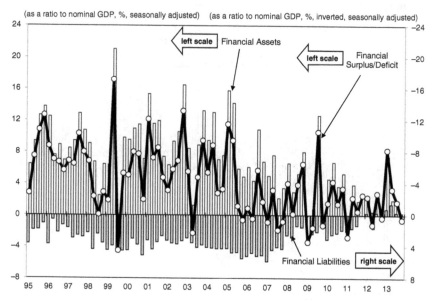

Notes: Seasonal adjustments by NRI. Latest figures are for 2013 Q4.

Source: NRI, based on flow of funds data from Banca d'Italia and Italian National Institute of Statistics.

Italian nonfinancial corporations were forced to draw down financial assets in 2008 and 2009 in response to the financial crisis, but conditions returned to normal in 2010. Starting in 2011 Q4, however, they liquidated financial assets for five consecutive quarters and reduced debt for eight straight quarters (Figure 5.19). As in Portugal, which also managed to avoid a housing bubble, this rapid deterioration in conditions in 2012 occurred because Italy's financial sector was sucked into the euro crisis.

In any event, a sharp increase in private savings was behind the recessions in all four countries, and government borrowings have been too small to stabilize the economies by offsetting the drop in demand from private-sector deleveraging. In Portugal and Italy, which did not experience housing bubbles and which only saw things go bad in the second half of the crisis, banking sector (i.e., lender-side) problems probably played a larger role than in those countries experiencing the borrower-side problem of a balance sheet recession.

With the private sectors in these countries collectively deleveraging and the money multiplier zero or even negative at the margin, there is no

FIGURE 5.19 Italian Nonfinancial Corporations Started Deleveraging in 2012 while Facing Credit Crunch

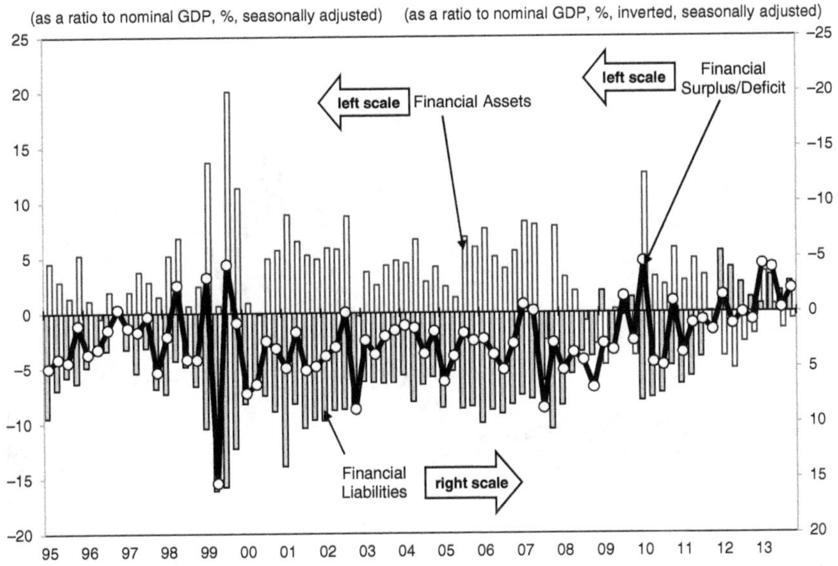

Notes: Seasonal adjustments by NRI. Latest figures are for 2013 Q4.

Source: NRI, based on flow of funds data from Banca d'Italia and Italian National Institute of Statistics.

reason why monetary policy should work. As expected, the Eurozone money supply has not grown much since the GFC in spite of massive injections of liquidity by the ECB (Figures 1.8, 5.8).

As long as this private-sector deleveraging process continues, fiscal stimulus is essential and fiscal consolidation will only prolong the recession. That Spain, Ireland, and Portugal are currently pursuing deficit-reduction efforts suggests they are making exactly the same mistake as Japan in 1997. What makes the situation in the Eurozone even more worrisome is that a large number of countries are making this mistake simultaneously.

Why the Polarization of Eurozone Government Bond Yields?

There is another Eurozone-specific problem that stands in these countries' way. Whereas government bond yields in the United States, the United Kingdom, and Japan, all of which are experiencing balance sheet recessions,

FIGURE 5.20 Peripheral Bond Yields Jumped on Destabilizing Capital Flows

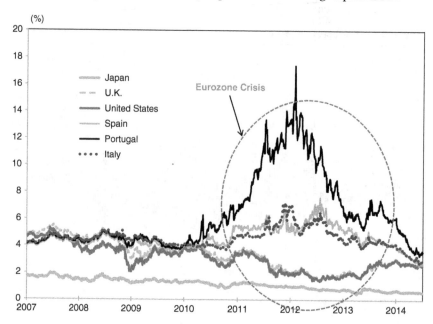

Note: As of July 4, 2014.
Source: Bloomberg.

have dropped to historical lows to provide support for fiscal stimulus, government bond yields in the periphery countries—which are also in balance sheet recessions—surged (Figure 5.20). This bifurcation of yields is attributable to certain conditions unique to the Eurozone.

During a balance sheet recession, which occurs when the private sector moves collectively to pay down debt or increase savings, the institutional investors responsible for investing private savings have only a limited range of investment options, as described in Chapter 1. The fact that the private sector as a whole is striving to minimize debt means that fund managers cannot, in aggregate, lend to their own private sector. Of course they have the option of buying domestic equities or foreign securities, but investors such as pension fund managers and life insurers are subject to regulations that prevent them from taking on excessive principal or currency risk.

These large institutional investors therefore tend to buy fixed income assets that are denominated in the local currency and offer safety of principal. The only asset satisfying those conditions in a balance sheet recession is domestic government bonds. Institutional investors therefore head en masse to their own government bond market, sending yields down to levels unthinkable under normal economic conditions. The steep drop in yields provides support for fiscal stimulus and thereby provides an important self-corrective mechanism during a balance sheet recession, as described in Chapter 1. This mechanism was first observed in Japan 20 years ago, and it has since been seen in such countries as the United Kingdom, the United States, and Sweden.

Eurozone Allows Investors to Buy Government Bonds of Member Countries with No Currency Risk

This self-corrective mechanism failed to operate in many parts of the Eurozone because institutional investors who think their own governments' fiscal deficits are too large can buy bonds issued by other, less fiscally challenged Eurozone governments without taking on any currency risk. This is because all government bonds in the Eurozone are denominated in the same currency, and there are 17 markets to choose from.

Additionally, the Eurozone periphery has been no exception to the rule that orthodox economists and pundits who do not understand balance sheet recessions ignore the size of private-sector savings and focus exclusively on the size of fiscal deficits. They assume, as did their counterparts in Japan 20 years ago, that large fiscal deficits imply the nation will collapse unless the government quickly takes action to right the fiscal ship. When investors in the country hear the media talk about the problems of large fiscal deficits from morning to night, they instinctively become wary of that country's bonds and turn instead to the government bond markets of Eurozone countries with smaller fiscal deficits.

Today Spanish pension funds and life insurers who are wary of Spanish government bonds can just as easily buy German or Finnish government bonds. That means Spain's large surplus of private savings will flow to Germany, causing Spanish government bond yields to rise. When that happens, the government panics because higher yields indicate that the market is shunning its bonds, which prevents it from carrying out the fiscal stimulus that is essential during a balance sheet recession. Even worse, it is forced to undertake deficit-reduction efforts, the single worst thing a government can do. Conditions then deteriorate further in what becomes a vicious cycle.

In November 2011 I had the opportunity to lead a seminar of large institutional investors in Madrid, and when I asked how many had moved funds out of Spain and into Germany, they all raised their hands. Their purchases contributed to a €345 billion increase[4] in foreign holdings of German govern-ment bonds from 2008 to 2011. Countries like Spain, Ireland, and Portugal that were experiencing balance sheet recessions watched as their rapidly growing private savings—the cause of those recessions—fled to Germany's government bond market, driving yields on their own debt higher and mak-ing it impossible for them to administer necessary fiscal stimulus. In other words, the self-corrective mechanism for balance sheet recessions does not function in the Eurozone.

If the German and Dutch governments were to borrow and spend the private savings of countries like Spain and Ireland, there would be no rea-son for the broader Eurozone economy to contract. Such actions would also provide an indirect boost to the economies experiencing an outflow of savings. However, the Maastricht Treaty's 3 percent deficit rule has kept Germany and the Netherlands focused on fiscal consolidation. As a result, the unborrowed savings of peripheral countries became the unborrowed savings of the broader Eurozone. The fact that the self-corrective mecha-nism no longer functions is a critical structural flaw in the Eurozone that needs to be rectified as soon as possible.

Eurozone-Specific Fund Flows Amplify Economic Swings

Until the GFC, Eurozone fund flows were moving in the opposite direction. As noted above, the collapse of the IT bubble in 2000 plunged Germany into a severe balance sheet recession, forcing local banks and other finan-cial institutions confronting a shortage of domestic borrowers to seek the higher-yielding government debt of southern European nations. These fund outflows from Germany fueled the housing bubbles in these countries.

This is an excellent example of the Eurozone's tendency toward highly procyclical fund flows in one direction or the other. During good times, investors seeking higher returns tend to send their money to economies experiencing bubbles, thereby exacerbating financial excesses. But once the bubbles burst the funds flee those economies, which are now in balance sheet recessions, and flow into markets at the other end of the boom-and-bust spectrum.

The problem with such shifts is that they are highly destabilizing and amplify swings in the real economy. Funds flow into countries that are experiencing bubbles and are in no need of further liquidity, pouring more fuel on the asset fire, while governments facing balance sheet recessions

---

[4] Although the data for 2012 and 2013 are available in Eurostat's *The Structure of Government Debt* series, those shown as of July 3, 2014 contain many inconsistencies and are therefore not used here.

must stand by and watch as the funds they desperately need go elsewhere, making it impossible for them to administer the necessary fiscal stimulus and accelerating the vicious cycle.

Meaning of "Fiscal Space" Differs Inside and Outside Eurozone

From around 2012 more people—including some among the Eurozone authorities—have come to understand that fiscal stimulus is essential during a balance sheet recession. Yet many of them continue to believe that fiscal stimulus is an option only for countries with "fiscal space," with deficit-reduction efforts remaining the only answer for the rest. A country with fiscal space is one that can safely issue government bonds and has a certain amount of leeway in its fiscal position. However, most are unaware that this term has a very different meaning depending on whether the country is inside or outside the Eurozone.

A balance sheet recession occurs when there are unborrowed private savings at a time of zero interest rates. By definition, such an economy has in its financial system unborrowed savings sufficient to fund the fiscal stimulus needed to close the deflationary gap. The unborrowed savings, after all, is the *source* of the deflationary gap.

The fund managers charged with investing those funds have no choice but to buy bonds issued by the government, which is the sole remaining borrower during a balance sheet recession, and that will provide the fiscal space required. Of course these investors can also shift funds overseas, but that entails currency risk, a major stumbling point for investors whose liabilities are denominated entirely in the local currency. Hence the balance sheet recessions in the United States, the United Kingdom, and Japan have led to a sharp drop in government bond yields, providing these countries with the fiscal space they need.

In the Eurozone, however, there are numerous government bond markets using the same currency, and flows of capital between them are completely free. Countries that would have more than adequate fiscal space if they did not belong to the Eurozone find the unborrowed savings of their private sectors fleeing for the government bond markets of other Eurozone members. Consequently, the fiscal space they had disappears.

Spain's private sector, for instance, is currently saving at the annual rate of 8.6 percent of GDP (Figure 5.13), an amount more than sufficient to finance the Spanish government's fiscal deficit, which amounted to 7.1 percent of GDP in 2013. If Spain were not a Eurozone member, it would have ample fiscal space and its government bond yields would have fallen sharply long ago. The same is true for Ireland and Portugal. And there would have been no crisis to begin with if government bond yields in these countries were as low as they are in places like the United States, the United Kingdom, and Sweden. The euro crisis, after all, was sparked by surging government bond yields in the periphery.

The reality, however, is that a substantial portion of both Spanish savings and foreign savings that entered Spain during the bubble days has fled for the perceived safety of foreign shores. That, coupled with fears about future capital outflows, has pushed Spanish government bond yields to levels far higher than corresponding yields in Japan, the United Kingdom, and the United States, where the risk of capital flight is much smaller.

The surge in bond yields and resulting lack of fiscal space has forced governments to undertake deficit-reduction efforts, plunging these economies into a deflationary spiral. That pushes investors to move even more money overseas, as rising unemployment rates increase the possibility of sovereign downgrades and even an actual default. The more money leaves the country, the worse the situation becomes.

Maastricht Treaty Is Defective and Should Be Revised Immediately

How should this Eurozone-specific problem be addressed? There are two main issues to consider. One is the fact that the Maastricht Treaty is a defective agreement that makes no allowance for balance sheet recessions. The other is the highly procyclical and destabilizing flows of capital between various Eurozone government bond markets.

Regarding the first, Spain's private sector (households + nonfinancial corporations + financial institutions) is currently saving 8.6 percent of GDP even with zero interest rates, but under the Maastricht Treaty the government can borrow and spend only 3 percent of GDP. The remaining 5.6 percent becomes a deflationary gap that causes the Spanish economy to contract. The Treaty makes no mention of what to do in a situation where the private sector is saving 8.6 percent of GDP in spite of zero interest rates. It presumes a textbook world in which the private sector is always trying to maximize profit and never considers a scenario in which the private sector is minimizing debt at a time of zero interest rates.

This is perhaps to be expected, as the concept of balance sheet recessions was unknown outside Japan when the details of the Treaty were being worked out in the 1990s. If policymakers had been aware of this risk and had incorporated it in the Treaty, the response of the ECB and the German government to the collapse of the IT bubble would have been very different indeed.

If the Treaty had requested if not required countries in balance sheet recessions to respond with sufficient fiscal stimulus to prevent any harm to the ECB's monetary policy or to other Eurozone nations, Germany would not have had to rely as much on exports, and the ECB would not have had to lower interest rates as far as it did to rescue Germany, creating housing bubbles in Spain and Ireland in the process. And if German banks had been able to invest in their own government's bonds, far less money would have flowed into Spanish government paper and U.S. subprime securities. In that sense, the euro crisis was caused in part by policy distortions under a Maastricht Treaty that makes no allowance for balance sheet recessions. This is something that needs to be rectified as soon as possible.

A 3 percent cap on fiscal deficits makes a certain amount of sense in an ordinary (non-balance-sheet recession) world. But countries recognized as being in a balance sheet recession should not only be freed from that constraint but should be encouraged *if not required* to administer adequate fiscal stimulus so that their economic weakness does not cause problems for the ECB or other members of the Eurozone. Only then will the Treaty be suitable for both balance sheet recessions and ordinary economic conditions.

In Practice, Fiscal Stimulus Requires EU and ECB Approval

As a practical matter, even if the governments of countries like Spain and Ireland realize that their economies are in balance sheet recessions, they will be unable to escape from the destructive path of fiscal consolidation unless the EU and ECB share that awareness and give their stamp of approval to fiscal stimulus. This is because capital flight to the German bond market would likely increase severalfold if periphery governments were to embark on such stimulus without official approval from the Europen Union (EU) and ECB.

As such, no matter how much individual countries understand the real cause of their recessions, no change in policy can be expected until international bodies such as the EU, the ECB, and the International Monetary Fund (IMF) officially recognize that these countries are in balance sheet recessions and that fiscal stimulus is the correct policy response. To make Maastricht "compliant" with balance sheet recessions, therefore, the EU and ECB need to sanction fiscal stimulus and provide support if necessary. In particular, an EU panel of experts should be asked to certify whether a country is in a balance sheet recession or not. If the country is so certified, it would be expected to implement sufficient fiscal stimulus with full support from the EU.

This clause to provide necessary support is extremely important because without it, investors may still prefer to take their money elsewhere. But it could also face strong resistance from Germany and other countries that may end up footing the bill. While Germany's concerns would appear at first glance to be quite reasonable, closer examination shows they reveal a lack of understanding of balance sheet recessions.

By definition, countries in balance sheet recessions have a massive pool of unborrowed domestic savings. If that savings flows to the local government bond market with the official approval of the IMF or the EU, there would be no need for fresh expenditures by the EU or Germany. What is needed, therefore is a mechanism to encourage the unborrowed private savings of countries in balance sheet recessions to stay in (or be returned to) those countries' government bond markets. That would restore the self-corrective mechanism for Eurozone countries in balance sheet recessions without imposing any additional burden on German taxpayers.

Ban on Buying Other Nations' Debt Ideal Way to Stabilize Eurozone

In other words, even with a revised treaty and the EU's blessing, fiscal stimulus would be impossible to administer if the unborrowed savings of countries in balance sheet recessions fled to other Eurozone bond markets, preventing those governments from issuing debt to fund stimulus measures.

This is the Eurozone's second structural flaw. A way must be found to overcome this Eurozone-specific problem of volatile capital flows among countries while maintaining fiscal policy freedom for national governments. I have proposed two solutions to this problem. One is an ideal solution that would eradicate the problem once and for all but would be politically difficult to implement. The other is a more pragmatic alternative that would be easier to implement.

The ideal solution is a rule that prohibits Eurozone governments from issuing debt to anyone other than their own citizens. Had this rule been adopted from the euro's outset in place of the 3 percent deficit cap noted above, the euro crisis would never have happened. Spanish investors would be prevented from investing in German government bonds; only Germans could buy those bonds. That would drastically reduce the Eurozone-specific problem of procyclical and destabilizing capital flight.

Adopting this rule in place of the 3 percent fiscal deficit cap would not only restore fiscal discipline but would also enable governments to respond properly to balance sheet recessions, as they would be able to administer the necessary fiscal stimulus as long as the public approved. And the public—who would be in the midst of paying down debt—should be able to understand the need for fiscal expenditures as long as the government explained to them how balance sheet recessions work.

This rule would also have prevented the Greek crisis, since the Greek government would be prevented from running deficits larger than its citizens are willing to finance with their own savings. Adopting this rule would restore fiscal discipline to national governments since they could not borrow any more than their citizens are willing to lend.

This would also have important implications for the rock-throwing demonstrators on the streets of Athens. The rule would effectively stop these self-proclaimed victims of the IMF and rich German and French bankers from protesting. If they want to protect public-sector jobs, they will have to persuade friends and family members to buy more Greek government bonds.

By preventing foreigners from buying government debt, this rule would also make fiscal policy an entirely internal affair. That would also prevent political and fiscal problems in individual member nations from roiling the broader Eurozone. If the Greek government were to go bankrupt, for example, only the Greeks would suffer, and the problem could be considered separately and apart from the broader Eurozone (although a provision would have to be made in the event of a default on Eurozone government bonds held by the ECB).

This would also put an end to the current situation in which an election or change of government in one country has the potential to throw the single currency into turmoil. As long as governments are allowed to sell debt only to their own citizens, fiscal policy becomes an entirely domestic issue, drastically reducing the likelihood of it harming the Eurozone as a whole. That would allow the ECB to focus on administering monetary policy for the broader Eurozone without worrying about election results or political developments in individual member nations.

Efficiency Gains from Single Currency Remain Intact

To preserve the efficiency gains from the adoption of the euro, this rule should be applied only to government bonds and not to private-sector debt. German banks would be free to buy Greek corporate bonds, and Spanish investors would be able to purchase German equities.

The improvements in economic efficiency resulting from the adoption of a single currency actually accrue to the private sectors of these countries. A larger single market creates more efficiencies. And as many economic agents with different views start to participate, the market grows deeper.

On the other hand, there is room for debate on whether the capital efficiency of the broader economy is improved when investors in one country buy the government debt of another country. It is difficult to see how global capital efficiency is improved, for example, when German investors buy higher-yielding Greek securities (unless the Greek government is using the money far more effectively than the German government). As such, limiting government borrowing to domestic savings would not undermine the capital efficiency benefits of having a single currency.

As for the question of how to distinguish between domestic and foreign financial institutions, those institutions that are subject to inspections by local financial authorities should be recognized as domestic financial institutions, just as under current banking regulation. This would enable the authorities to conduct asset checks at any time.

Martin Wolf wrote about my proposal in the *Financial Times* by saying it was an interesting solution but wondered how it could be enforced—in other words, how could the private sector be prevented from circumventing it? I agree that it would be difficult to enforce a rule that prevents the sale of government debt to foreigners in a financial market as tightly integrated as that of the Eurozone. There will always be someone who tries to circumvent the rules. But if the vast majority of financial institutions and institutional investors abide by it, conditions will change greatly.

For instance, if Spain's large institutional investors bought their own government's debt, yields would fall sharply and prices would rise. And if yields in countries like Spain and Ireland fell to the levels seen in the United Kingdom and the United States, the euro crisis itself—which was sparked by a surge in government bond yields—would come to an end. An increase in the price of Spain's government debt would also make the investment performance of other domestic investors who were not holding those bonds suffer by comparison, encouraging them to buy as well.

Upon hearing my proposal, people in Europe say that while the plan is rather extreme, it would have prevented the euro crisis had it been adopted from the outset. They also notice that my proposal challenges the frequently voiced notion that fiscal union is the only way to make the single currency work. The single currency would work without fiscal union as long as member countries' debt is sold only to their own citizens.

Another common reaction is that this rule is in effect a capital control, which is prohibited in the Eurozone, and that this hurdle would be hard to overcome. But this capital control would not result in efficiency losses because private-sector capital flows are not affected. Furthermore, the EU authorities' introduction of their own capital controls in the Cypriot financial crisis of 2013 demonstrated that rules are only rules and exceptions can always be made.

Others note that foreigners already hold substantial portions of the debt of all Eurozone nations, which would make it difficult to adopt such a rule today. However, this problem could be addressed with a transition period lasting five to 10 years—the question is only whether the authorities have the will. Adopting this single rule would surely be worth it if it could preserve the tremendous human achievement the euro represents.

Different Risk Weights Should Be Applied to Domestic and Foreign Government Debt

In the second half of 2012 I responded to the concerns noted above with a somewhat more pragmatic proposal calling for Eurozone financial institutions and institutional investors to apply different risk weights to the domestic and foreign government bonds in their portfolios. Specifically, I proposed that the risk weight for domestic government bonds should be kept at or close to the current figure of zero while assigning a significantly higher weight to the bonds of other governments.

The concept of risk weights has been widely adopted by financial regulators around the world since the Bank for International Settlements (BIS) capital rules for banks were introduced in the 1990s. Risk weights are based on the view that financial institutions should have to set aside more capital against riskier loans or investments.

The original purpose of this rule was to prevent financial institutions from taking on excessive risk, but the goal of my proposal is to see that Eurozone investors in government bonds face conditions as similar as possible to those confronting investors in countries outside the Eurozone such as Japan, the United States, and the United Kingdom. The justification for assigning a lower risk weight to domestic government bonds is that domestic investors have the best understanding of local economic conditions and the local bond market.

Investors in Japan, the United States, and the United Kingdom are able to buy financial instruments from all over the world, but a substantial portion of their funds ends up in domestic government bonds because of regulations limiting the amount of principal and currency risk they can assume. This ring-fencing of the domestic government bond market by foreign exchange risk has produced a sharp decline in government bond yields during the balance sheet recession, thereby providing these governments with the necessary fiscal space. If similar conditions could be created in the Eurozone, member countries would also enjoy enhanced fiscal space and see the self-corrective mechanism restored.

The assignment of different risk weights to domestic and foreign government bonds would only work for banks and institutional investors that are under the supervision of the monetary authorities. But if these investors began buying more domestic government bonds, yields would fall accordingly, creating the fiscal space these countries need. While this proposal, unlike my first, would not enhance fiscal discipline by making fiscal policy an entirely internal issue, it would be far easier to enact since risk weights already play a central role in financial regulatory efforts around the world.

Next-Best Alternative to Risk Weights Already in Place?

It would take some effort to make the two needed modifications under the Maastricht Treaty, which was designed with strong legal protections. However, an early review of the Treaty is essential given the severity of the balance sheet recessions in countries like Spain, Ireland, and Portugal. Now that Cyprus has provided a precedent for the authorities implementing rules that contravene the principle of free capital flows, it should be possible to take one more step and introduce different risk weights for government debt.

Unfortunately, the Eurozone policy debate has yet to reach that stage, but there are rumors that the authorities in periphery countries are unofficially requesting local financial institutions to buy their own governments' debt. If those rumors are true, it would represent a next-best alternative to an official risk-weight policy. Such suasion, even if unofficial, should be welcomed if it can help restore the self-corrective mechanism in these countries.

That said, it would be far more transparent for the authorities to introduce differentiated risk weights on an official basis and thereby ensure a dependable self-corrective mechanism.

Separation of Sovereign Risk and Banking Risk a Rejection of Self-Corrective Mechanism

Standing in the way of these proposals are recent efforts to integrate the Eurozone banking system and achieve a clear separation of banking risk and sovereign risk. These efforts are problematic because they could make it difficult for financial institutions to buy and hold their own governments' bonds.

Proponents of this approach say it makes no sense to pay different interest rates depending on whether one is standing on the Italian or the Austrian side of an Alpine ski resort, and that this kind of financial fragmentation should be resolved by separating sovereign risk from (unified) private banking system risk. At present, the owners of a resort on the Italian side of the border would pay a premium on top of the benchmark Italian bond yield, while on the Austrian side the owners would pay a premium on top of the benchmark Austrian bond yield, resulting in financial fragmentation despite the use of a common currency.

While this argument seems reasonable enough at first glance, we need to ask why the disparity in interest rates exists in the first place. If the gap in government bond yields is attributable to capital flight between government bond markets and lack of synchronicity between economies, there can be no solution to the underlying problem until these phenomena are properly addressed.

The yields on Spanish government bonds would have fallen substantially if Spain's unborrowed savings had been invested in them. That, in turn, would have lowered funding costs for Spanish banks and dramatically reduced the problem of fragmentation that has drawn so much attention. Additionally, reduced capital inflows to Germany from periphery nations would have kept long-term interest rates in Germany from falling as far as they have, further narrowing the interest rate disparity between Germany and periphery countries. In other words, the problem of financial fragmentation would largely disappear if the self-corrective mechanism were functioning—for example, if the unborrowed savings of countries in balance sheet recessions were invested in their own government bonds.

If the EU authority actually implements the idea of separating sovereign risk from banking sector risk, they will effectively be telling financial institutions not to hold debt issued by their own governments, which is a complete rejection of the self-corrective mechanism. By rendering useless the mechanism that automatically lowers government bond yields during a balance sheet recession, the deflationary spiral these nations are facing could intensify, further accelerating capital outflows.

If the authorities stay on this course, the Eurozone will need to create some other program to return the savings that have fled the periphery. If the domestic financial sector is incapable of or prohibited from channeling the nation's unborrowed savings into their own government bond market, the Eurozone itself will need to assume that role. In other words, it would have to absorb the unborrowed savings in periphery nations by issuing, for example, eurobonds and then return the funds to those nations. However, this would be very difficult from a political standpoint, with Germany perhaps most strongly opposed to the issue of eurobonds.

Germany's opposition is based on the argument that it would not be fair to use the same bond issue to finance the fiscal deficits of both Germany and Greece, where workers in one are ineligible to receive a pension until they turn 67 while employees in the other can retire before the age of 60. But if that is the case, Germany should reject the whole concept of separating banking risk and sovereign risk.

The policy the EU is currently considering would not only disable the self-corrective mechanism that is inherent in all economies experiencing balance sheet recessions, but—without a program to recirculate funds via the joint issue of eurobonds and so forth—could actually increase the amount of unborrowed savings (i.e., the deflationary gap) across the Eurozone.

The better option is for the EU to adopt different risk weights that would directly address the problem of unborrowed savings fleeing countries in balance sheet recessions, which triggered the ongoing euro crisis. Any policy that risks further exacerbating this problem by separating banking risk and sovereign risk must be avoided.

Joint Issue of Eurobonds Would Only Solve Half of Eurozone's Structural Defects

On the subject of the eurobond, many still believe fiscal union is essential and make the simplistic argument that the crisis occurred because the Eurozone unified its monetary policy but not its fiscal policy. But fiscal union could force countries in balance sheet recessions to adopt the same fiscal policy as countries that are not, making the problem worse. If the Eurozone does opt for fiscal union, it must be a union capable of accommodating nations in balance sheet recessions. But without a synchronicity of economies, that could be very difficult to achieve from a political perspective.

The view that the countries of the Eurozone should jointly finance the deficit by issuing eurobonds would certainly address one of the Eurozone's two structural flaws, but it would face significant political hurdles and would do nothing to address the second flaw.

The two structural defects are (1) the highly procyclical and destabilizing flows of capital between various government bond markets in the Eurozone, and (2) the Maastricht Treaty makes no allowance for balance sheet recessions.

The joint issue of eurobonds would solve the first problem by combining the 17 separate government bond markets in the Eurozone into a single market. If German savings and Spanish savings alike had to be invested in jointly issued eurobonds, the destabilizing, procyclical capital flows described above would be minimized. While this is a significant merit, the eurobond also has its problems, the largest of which concerns the political process used to determine how much debt to issue and how to allocate the proceeds among Eurozone members. Another question concerns what would happen if one of the issuing nations became unable to service its portion of the debt.

These are huge political problems that are unlikely to be easily resolved by 17 nations in different phases of the economic cycle. As mentioned earlier, if the fiscal deficits of two nations with pensionable ages of 58 and 67 are to be financed using the same jointly issued eurobonds, taxpayers in the second nation are bound to be unhappy. This would be particularly difficult to accept for Germany, which prides itself on its sound economic management, and in fact Chancellor Merkel has vigorously opposed the eurobond proposal.

Persuading Germany to agree to joint debt issues will require an acceptance of its demands, which are likely to include more aggressive deficit-reduction policies in the periphery nations. But in countries where the private sector is striving to minimize debt at a time of zero interest rates, a government attempt to do the same will only exacerbate the deflationary spiral resulting from the balance sheet recession. That would make the situation even worse and cast the Eurozone out of the frying pan and into the fire.

Draghi Unaware That There Are Two Kinds of Recessions and Fiscal Deficits

Understanding of balance sheet recessions at the EU, the ECB, and the IMF—the so-called "troika" that holds the key to a shift in policy stance—has definitely improved over the past few years. However, they are all starting from a low base. The IMF demonstrates the best understanding and has gone so far as to use the term *balance sheet recession* in some of its publications. Of the three members of the troika, the IMF has been the most reluctant to endorse fiscal consolidation and, in that sense, has presented the most realistic policy proposals.

The BIS, headquartered in Basel, Switzerland, has also come to a better understanding of balance sheet recessions. In fact, it used the concept in its 84th Annual Report, published on June 29, 2014, to describe the difficulties the developed world has confronted since the GFC. The "central bankers' central bank" even went on to argue that monetary easing is largely ineffective during balance sheet recessions, a point I have been making for the past 15 years.

What is difficult to understand is that ECB president Mario Draghi notes at each press conference following meetings of the Governing Council that Europe's economic weakness is attributable to necessary balance sheet adjustments in the private sector. In other words, he knows the private sectors in these countries are undertaking balance sheet adjustments yet continues to admonish governments to pursue tough deficit-reduction efforts. And he continued to hold that position even after peripheral bond yields fell back to very low levels in spring of 2014. In doing so, he is effectively ignoring if not rejecting the message emanating from the bond markets.

And he is not alone. Many more people are now aware that balance sheet adjustments are taking place, but few understand that during such phases the money multiplier turns negative at the margin, drastically reducing the effectiveness of monetary policy. And fewer yet understand that the government must act as the "borrower of last resort" during this type of recession in order to keep the economy and money supply from shrinking.

Even the BIS, which recognized the impotence of monetary policy during balance sheet recessions, remains silent on the need for fiscal policy at such times.

The ECB president seems to hold the orthodox academic view that there is only one kind of fiscal problem and one kind of recession. In an interview published in the July 21, 2012, edition of France's *Le Monde* newspaper, Mr. Draghi was asked whether fiscal consolidation and other long-term structural reforms would be able on their own to overcome short-term problems. He insisted they would and cited the example of Italy in 1992.

At the time, Italy was running a fiscal deficit worth 11 percent of GDP, but as soon as it committed itself to participating in the currency union, government bond yields started falling even before there was any improvement in the deficits (although it should be noted that government bond yields also fell sharply in Japan, the United States, and the United Kingdom around this time for reasons that had nothing to do with the European currency union).

But Italy's fiscal deficit in 1992, when private demand for funds was robust, had a completely different effect on the economy from that of Spain in 2012, when private-sector demand for funds was negative even at near zero-interest rates. When Italy undertook deficit-reduction efforts in 1992, the private sector quickly stepped in to borrow and spend the money the government was no longer borrowing. As a result, the economy did not weaken, and the budget deficit shrank substantially. The same phenomenon was observed in the United States under the Clinton administration starting in 1992, with the U.S. fiscal balance eventually moving into surplus. And in both countries, government bond yields began falling as soon as the government embarked on its deficit-reduction efforts.

In Spain, meanwhile, the economy turned south and the unemployment rate surged dramatically higher as soon as the government embarked on fiscal consolidation in 2010. With the nation's economy in a deflationary spiral, Spain's private savings fled to Germany, and Spanish government bond yields rose sharply in spite of the government's deficit-reduction efforts.

We can conclude from the above examples that there are at least two kinds of fiscal deficit: those that occur because of private sector mismanagement and those that occur because of public sector mismanagement (i.e., government or politicians). The two have very different characteristics, as noted in Chapter 1.

That the head of the ECB does not recognize this distinction is worrying. After all, the only way the economies of Spain and Ireland will start to move in the right direction is if the ECB and the EU give their official approval to fiscal stimulus while encouraging private savings to stay in those countries. Of course it may be that the clearly very intelligent Mr. Draghi understands all this, but is saying what he says out of consideration for German demands for structural reforms in the periphery nations. But if that is the case,

Germany bears much of the responsibility for the misdiagnosis that led to this crisis.

Outside of Greece, Capital Flight Is the Problem

For a number of years I have had discussions with authorities in the Eurozone. Most of the objections raised at these gatherings concern policy implementation. For example, participants will often argue that while fiscal stimulus might be necessary during a balance sheet recession, the government has no choice but to continue along the path of fiscal consolidation if the markets will not allow it. The German government official mentioned at the beginning of this chapter also argued that there is simply no way German taxpayers would sanction further fiscal stimulus in periphery countries with already sizable fiscal deficits.

While these objections may seem quite reasonable, it made no sense to presume how the markets would react when no one has actually tried. I stressed that with the exception of Greece, whose problems are indeed rooted in fiscal profligacy, all the other countries have huge pools of private savings, and that if those savings were to return to the domestic government bond market the ultimate cost to German taxpayers and the ECB would be zero. This perspective—that with the exception of Greece the periphery nations actually have deep pools of savings to draw upon—has been completely absent from the Eurozone policy debate until now.

For instance, Spain's private sector is saving a net 8.6 percent of GDP at a time when the government is running a fiscal deficit amounting to 7.1 percent of GDP. If those savings were to flow into the domestic government bond market, the nation would be more than capable of financing its own fiscal deficits without relying on external assistance from Germany or elsewhere.

Yet policymakers in Germany and the Nordic countries who have never seen the private-sector savings figures continue to issue extreme warnings about expanding fiscal deficits in the periphery nations. They arbitrarily assume that government bond yields in the periphery have risen because the private sectors in those countries are not saving enough. They also fear that delays in structural reforms will increase the ultimate cost to the taxpayers of Germany and other northern European nations. They simply do not understand that, with the exception of Greece, the essence of the problem is capital flight and not a shortage of savings.

The real question concerns how the market would react once these private savings numbers are brought into the policy debate. What if the EU and ECB came out and said something like this: "We have discovered a new kind of economic malady called a balance sheet recession during which the private sector minimizes debt instead of maximizing profits. Extensive analysis indicates that Spain, Ireland, and a number of other countries are in balance sheet recessions. As these countries also have a huge pool of private savings, we want those savings to stay in those countries to fund the fiscal stimulus they need. To that end, we will revise the Maastricht Treaty so that countries in balance sheet recessions can administer the fiscal stimulus they need. We will also introduce differentiated risk weights for holdings of domestic versus foreign government bonds to make sure that these countries have the fiscal space they require."

A statement of this sort from the Troika would probably change the way market participants perceive peripheral countries. And if the statement is accompanied by the two structural revisions mentioned, not only their perception but also their behavior is likely to change. Unfortunately, except for the BIS, the European authorities have not mentioned even once during the present crisis that this might be a different kind of recession.

It is difficult to envision market participants changing their stance and assessing policy using some yardstick other than deficit reduction unless the authorities, which play the role of physician in this analogy, do so first. In that sense, it is rather irresponsible for the authorities to claim that fiscal stimulus is impossible because "the markets would not allow it" without bothering to explain why that treatment is both feasible and necessary.

It would be one thing if the authorities did their best to explain the situation but the market refused to listen. But blaming the market for an inability to administer the proper treatment without even telling the market that the economy has contracted a different kind of disease is little more than an attempt to pass the buck.

Explaining Balance Sheet Recessions to the German Public

I have been warning ever since my 2003 book that if Japan, the United States, and Europe were to fall into balance sheet recessions, it would be the Eurozone, bound by the defective Maastricht Treaty, that would suffer the most.[5] That prediction became a reality with the current crisis. From the outset I have tried to explain to European policymakers and the public what a balance sheet recession is and how it must be dealt with.

As time has passed many people in European financial and business circles have come to realize the importance of the concept of balance sheet recessions. When I gave a speech in Madrid in November 2011, a

---

[5] Richard Koo, *Balance Sheet Recession: Japan's Struggle with Uncharted Economics and Its Global Implications* (Singapore: John Wiley & Sons, 2003), p. 234.

business leader stood up and said, "Spain should nationalize Richard Koo and enlist his help in solving the nation's problems." I did not know that human beings can be nationalized in Spain, but no matter how well-received my talks have been across Europe, in the end the response is always the same: "We understand what you are saying. Now please go and convince those stubborn Germans."

The next most common objection to my proposal after "the markets would never allow it" is "the German public would never allow it." The concern is that Germans who cannot retire with a pension until the age of 67 will ask why they should have to rescue a country where people can retire in their 50s. Germans also bear the cost of the so-called solidarity surcharge established after unification to help fund the reconstruction of Eastern Germany. That alone is a heavy burden, and many feel the last thing Germany needs is to take on the rescue of some unrelated periphery nation.

So I decided to try an experiment on an April 2012 business trip to Europe. I gave ordinary, "stubborn" Germans a no-holds-barred introduction to balance sheet recession theory to see how they responded. The whole idea sprang out of a telephone interview conducted a month before the trip with a reporter from the Berlin newspaper *T.A.Z.* This publisher was scheduled to hold an annual forum in Berlin on the same weekend as the conference I had been invited to. The left-leaning publisher had a focus on environmental issues, and the forum, held on a Saturday afternoon, was organized around the theme of "Seeking the good life" and was designed to appeal to the general public. Subjects ranged from gardening to nutritional supplements, and there was just one session on the economy.

I agreed to speak in order to try the experiment. However, a seminar on the famous German author Carolin Emcke was scheduled for the same time slot as mine, and the organizers of the event apologized in advance, saying I should not take it badly if few people showed up for my talk.

Even Germans Understand Need for Fiscal Stimulus If Properly Explained

When I arrived at the forum, however, I was greeted by a huge crowd, with many people upset that they had been turned away because of fire code rules.

For an hour and a half I told several hundred ordinary Germans that many Eurozone countries were currently in balance sheet recessions and that these countries required fiscal stimulus. The response was extremely positive in spite of the fact that the presenter was an unknown Asian economist speaking in English through a simultaneous interpreter.

Many people subsequently expressed their gratitude to me for showing that there was a different way to look at the Eurozone crisis. Some of the questions from the audience were quite perceptive, and I left with the sense that most had understood my message. To be honest, the organizers had had no idea how things would turn out—they were even worried I might be heckled. Nothing of the sort happened.

In November 2013 I was invited by the German Psychoanalytic Association (DPV) to talk about the euro crisis and balance sheet recessions in front of an audience of 500 German psychoanalysts at Goethe University–Frankfurt. The forum was held because the DPV was worried the extended Eurozone recession might lead to social and political disenchantment and unrest. Here as well the response was extremely positive. While the audience consisted of people far removed from the world of economics, they told me afterward that now they finally understood the essence of the problems being confronted.

These experiments demonstrated that when the problem is explained slowly and carefully, even "stubborn" Germans are capable of understanding the concept of balance sheet recessions. So in my experience, the excuse that "the German public would never allow it" is less than convincing. When the theory is properly explained, even Germans can appreciate the need for fiscal stimulus during a balance sheet recession.

Excessive Focus on Fiscal Deficits While Ignoring Growth in Private Savings

The above experiments also made it clear that most people in Europe are completely unaware that the private sectors of Spain, Portugal, and Ireland are large net savers in spite of near-zero interest rates. While they know these countries are running large fiscal deficits and require financial assistance from overseas, they do not know that businesses and households are actually saving much more now than they did during the bubble years.

In that sense, Ireland and the countries of southern Europe need to do more to let people both at home and abroad know that they are experiencing the single most distinctive characteristic of a balance sheet recession—namely, growth in private-sector savings at a time of zero interest rates.

Many are also surprised when I point out that one of the two key underlying causes of the euro crisis is that peripheral nations' private-sector savings are flowing into the German government bond market. They are also delighted to hear that all of these countries except Greece have sufficient private savings to finance their own fiscal deficits and that German taxpayers will not have to pay a single euro more as long as these savings can be channeled into their own government bond markets.

Lack of Private Loan Demand Biggest Problem for Germany

Over the past several years Germany has stressed the need for fiscal consolidation in other Eurozone nations, but it also has a big problem of its own—the same one that Japan has. The nation's private sector has effectively stopped borrowing money since the IT bubble burst (Figure 5.5) in 2000 in spite of near-zero interest rates. Net savings by Germany's household sector climbed to 6.5 percent of GDP in 2005 and has remained in the elevated range of 5 to 6 percent ever since.

The corporate sector, which under ordinary circumstances is a net investor, has frequently registered large financial surpluses (Figure 5.5). Even if we strip out financial institutions and look only at nonfinancial corporations (Figure 5.7), it is clear that these companies are not actively borrowing in spite of near-zero interest rates. Germany's flow-of-funds data for the corporate sector do suffer from some accuracy issues, as noted in Chapter 3, but on the whole, its borrowing activity has been anemic in spite of record low interest rates. This is similar to the situation in Japan. Japanese firms are still not borrowing despite record low interest rates and clean balance sheets, a legacy of the debt hell they went through after the bubble burst.

The only way for Germany to sustain economic activity at a time when households are saving but businesses are not borrowing even at zero interest rates is to (a) run fiscal deficits to absorb the private sector's excess savings or (b) continue to run a trade surplus with the rest of the world. For now it has chosen the second route, but neither is sustainable in the long run. Germany must either reduce household savings or increase corporate borrowing if it hopes to sustain the current level of economic activity over a long-term horizon.

It has been said that cultural factors make it extremely difficult to change household savings behavior with policy measures. If so, a government's only option is to induce changes in corporate behavior. But doing so will not be easy if German businesses—like their Japanese counterparts—have developed an aversion to borrowing in the wake of the bubble's collapse and are adamant they will never borrow again. The fact that the corporate sector has continued to sock away savings and pay down debt in spite of historically low interest rates suggests the German debt trauma—like that at Japanese firms—is quite severe. If German firms no longer want to borrow, the government needs to create incentives similar to the second and third arrows of Abenomics mentioned in Chapter 4 to overcome the trauma.

Germany Unlikely to Announce Stimulus Package

Until now the focus was on the question of how to keep private savings in the periphery nations from leaving those nations and how to persuade the governments of those countries to borrow and spend the money. In contrast, economists like Paul Krugman and Michael Pettis have argued that persuading Germany to spend more would increase the flow of money throughout the Eurozone. To be sure, there would be no reason for the broader Eurozone economy to decelerate if Germany borrowed and spent all the money flowing in from the periphery. But this is not a realistic proposal given the current state of the German economy.

Germany's unemployment rate is at a 20-year low, and industrial production is approaching its pre-Lehman peak. Even house prices are now rising. With overheating becoming a real concern, policymakers are worried if anything about inflation. It is unlikely that a government in these circumstances would accept outside demands to borrow and spend *more*.

Given the current economic situation in Germany, a far more realistic option would be to keep the savings of periphery nations within their borders and have the governments of those nations borrow and spend the money. And if the German private sector does in fact have an aversion to debt, the German government should take appropriate measures to resolve the trauma.

In June 2013, German Finance Minister Wolfgang Schäuble announced an interesting plan that could play a role in returning Spain's private savings to Spain. The plan calls for the government-owned development bank KfW to use its sovereign credit rating to raise money cheaply on the market and then lend that money at low interest rates to small businesses in Spain via a Spanish government-owned bank. Currently this program is capped at about €800 million, but until Spanish savings are encouraged to stay in Spain via the adoption of differential risk weights or other measures, this program should be aggressively expanded as a means of recycling Spanish savings back to Spain.

Disadvantages of Euro Exit for Greece

The portion of the competitive gap between Germany and Greece that is attributable to macroeconomic factors has already narrowed substantially. Since 2010, for example, the German money supply has increased substantially while the Greek money supply shrank as capital fled the country. Money supply growth rates for the two countries intersected in 2011 and have trended together since then (Figure 5.21).

The shrinking Greek money supply and falling employment have already led to a decline in unit labor costs of nearly 20 percent since the peak in 2010, and given the time lag between shifts in the money supply and their impact on prices and unit labor costs, further declines can be expected. As of June 2014, the gap in unit labor costs between the two countries had

FIGURE 5.21 "Competitiveness Problem" Attributable to Divergence of Eurozone Money Supply Growth

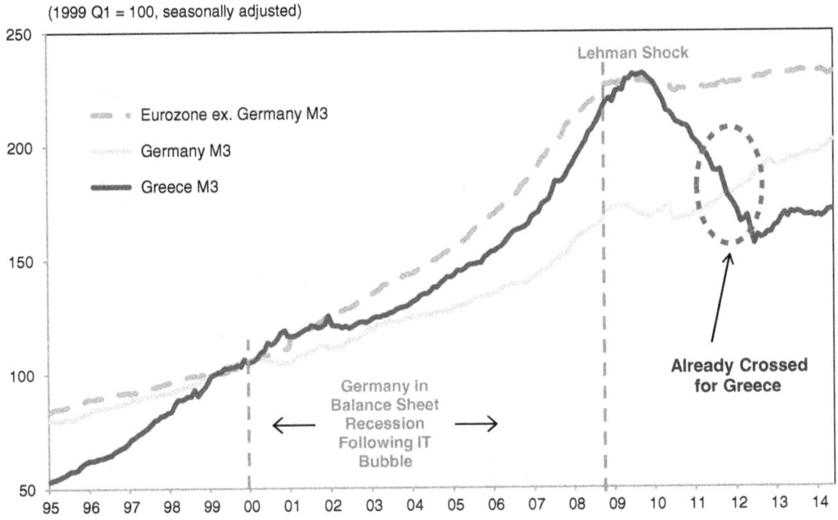

(1999 Q1 = 100, seasonally adjusted)

Notes: Growth in M3. Figures for Germany and Greece are seasonally adjusted by NRI.

Source: NRI, based on ECB, Deutsche Bundesbank and Bank of Greece data.

narrowed to less than half of the peak in 2009, and it is only a matter of time before it disappears altogether (Figure 5.22).

The fact that unit labor costs in the two countries are now approaching each other and that macroeconomic developments (i.e., money supply growth) are helping to close this gap undermines the case for a Greek exit from the euro. The main reason for a Greek exit was to restore competitiveness by devaluing the currency, but that has already been achieved to a large extent by the ongoing decline in unit labor costs. Had it not been for Germany's structural reforms, the competitive gap between the two economies might already have disappeared.

Argentina's Experience Also Suggests Euro Exit Would Have Few Merits for Greece

The impending closing of the gap in unit labor costs between the two countries is important because if Greece does choose to exit the euro, it will take a substantial amount of time before the nation overcomes the resulting turmoil.

FIGURE 5.22 Future Convergence of Eurozone Unit Labor Costs

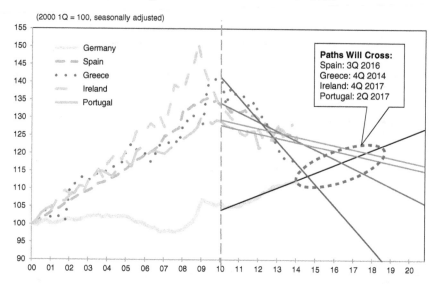

Notes: The figures for Greece are seasonally adjusted by NRI. Path of ULC growth was on the trend from 2010 Q1 to 2013 Q4.

Source: NRI, based on ECB's data.

The Argentine default in 2001 and the end of that country's dollar peg is frequently cited as a reference. Argentina had its own currency, the peso, but it still took more than three years for the resulting turbulence to subside, and the events continue to cast a shadow over the country. In 2012, more than 10 years after the default, one of the Argentinian navy's training vessels was impounded in Ghana, and the government is still engaged in a legal battle over the debt rescheduling of 2005.

When I visited Argentina in 2011 and 2013, I took the opportunity to ask local residents about the events of that time. People in the financial sector who had been forced to freeze customer bank accounts said it was an absolutely dreadful experience that they never wanted to go through again. In particular, those working at commercial banks told me that, with the general turmoil and complete breakdown of social order, they lived from day to day, fully expecting to be killed by mobs of people angry at being unable to withdraw their deposits. Some Western economists insist the adjustments were over quickly, citing data showing that Argentinian GDP resumed growing a year after the default. However, it took nearly three years for local residents to feel that the society and economy had stabilized.

When I asked Argentinians whether they thought Greece should follow down the same path, they answered that their country has always been rich in agricultural and natural resources and is capable of exporting any number of products given an appropriate exchange rate, but they had doubts as to whether Greece fell in the same category. Argentina's economic crisis began in 1998 and the default followed in 2001, but it was not until 2004 that GDP returned to 1998 levels. With Greece lacking Argentina's bountiful natural resources, the view there was that it would take Greece longer to recover. In addition, Argentina had its own currency, whereas Greece would have to adopt an entirely new currency, which could well extend the turmoil.

As a rule, transitions from weak to strong currencies tend to go smoothly and face relatively little opposition, whereas moves in the opposite direction are difficult to implement and often require heavy-handed measures such as deposit freezes and other capital controls.

If the disparity in unit labor costs between Greece and Germany is going to disappear soon, there is very little reason for Greece to exit the euro, as that would almost certainly lead to turmoil that could take a long time to settle. Furthermore, if Greek labor unions agree to further wage cuts in return for the promise of job security, the competitive gap between the two nations could be eliminated even sooner. Such an agreement would hardly come as a surprise given the nation's current unemployment rate of 27 percent.

A senior German government official I spoke with on a visit to Berlin in June 2012 already noted that Greek prices and wages were starting to become more competitive. If that leads to greater private investment in Greece, the economy will finally be ready to move to the next step.

Germany's Competitive Gap with Other Countries Will Also Disappear in a Few Years

Unit labor costs in both Ireland and Spain have also fallen markedly, as Figure 5.22 shows. This is a natural result of the fact that they are in severe recessions, with Spain's unemployment rate now in excess of 25 percent.

If we extrapolate the current trend in German unit labor costs outward from 2010 Q1, it will intersect with Greece's trendline in 2014 Q4, with Ireland's in 2017 Q4, with Spain's in 2016 Q3, and with Portugal's in 2017 Q2. The results of this kind of estimate vary greatly depending on the time frame used for the trend. With the exception of Ireland, however, an extrapolation of more recent trends suggests the labor cost gap with Germany may disappear even sooner. And in Ireland, unit labor costs have already fallen nearly 15 percent from their peak at end-2008. Labor costs there now may be quite competitive given that low wages were cited as one of the country's chief advantages in 2000.

In Germany, meanwhile, there are growing calls to rectify the excesses of the so-called tripartite labor agreement of 1999. This 1999 contract between the government, employers, and labor unions was designed to keep wage inflation *lower* than the rate of increase in labor productivity and thereby keep German businesses from moving production to Eastern Europe. It was this accord, along with other reforms described above, that enabled the nation to keep wage inflation in check. Even the Bundesbank, that inflation fighter par excellence, has said German wages should be allowed to rise in accordance with productivity gains.[6] Given that Germany's unemployment rate is at the lowest level since reunification and industrial output is nearly back to the pre-Lehman peak, it is only natural that wages should rise. The day when the competitive gap disappears will not be far off once German wages start to increase.

Draghi's LTROs Prevented Collapse of Eurozone Financial System

When an asset price bubble collapses, it can trigger both a balance sheet recession, which is a borrower-side problem, and a financial crisis, which is a lender-side problem. The former must be addressed with fiscal policy, because monetary policy is largely ineffective when the private sector is minimizing debt. In a financial crisis, on the other hand, rate cuts, liquidity injections, capital infusions, and asset purchases by the monetary authorities are essential tools.

The ongoing euro crisis is no exception to this rule. Its financial crisis is a systemic banking crisis in which many banks face the same problem at the same time. Many banks held toxic CDOs from the United States along with government bonds from the Eurozone periphery that had plunged in value because of capital flight. That, coupled with the collapse of housing bubbles across the Eurozone, led to bad loan problems that left banks distrustful of each other, prompting severe credit concerns across Europe from mid-2011. By the end of that year, the situation was so bad that financial institutions no longer trusted one another and would only deal with each other via the ECB.

As noted in Chapter 2, one of the fundamental duties of a central bank is to prevent a collapse of the settlements system by supplying liquidity as the lender of last resort. Examples include the BOJ's actions in 1997 when Sanyo Securities defaulted on the uncollateralized call market and the Fed and BOE's response to the collapse of Lehman Brothers in 2008. In both

---

[6] *Financial Times*, "Bundesbank Shows Signs of Yielding," May 9, 2012. www.ft. com/intl/cms/s/0/5a40a056-99fb-11e1-accb-00144feabdc0.html#axzz36xR8eEDr.

cases the central bank injected massive quantities of liquidity into the system to overcome the crisis.

As the euro crisis deepened in 2010, the Trichet ECB overcame German resistance to buy government bonds issued by periphery nations, but these purchases were limited in scale and did not have sufficient impact. Trichet perhaps believed too strongly the notion that the ECB had inherited the mantle of the Bundesbank and consequently felt obliged to be as tough on inflation as the German central bank had been. That stance helped delay the ECB's response to the financial crisis.

At the end of 2011, Trichet was replaced as ECB president by Mario Draghi, who eased policy aggressively with two Long-Term Refinancing Operations (LTROs) in December 2011 and February 2012, under which the Bank provided three-year loans at an interest rate of just 1 percent. Some €489 billion was supplied under the first LTRO, while the second operation relaxed the rules on eligible collateral, prompting 800 banks to borrow a total of €529.5 billion.

Italian and Spanish banks were the most active borrowers in both operations, but more than 400 German banks as well as the financial arms of corporations like Mercedes-Benz and Volkswagen availed themselves of the second LTRO. Most of the German institutions were small regional banks whose participation was made possible by the easing of collateral rules. This suggests that even in Germany, where the economy was comparatively strong, small financial institutions found themselves in difficult straits as a post-IT-bubble shortage of domestic borrowers forced them to invest in more risky foreign assets. It is estimated that they borrowed a total of €100 billion under the program. The funds supplied under the two LTROs went a long way toward stabilizing the Eurozone financial system and initially produced a sharp drop in Italian and Spanish government bond yields, reassuring investors across the Eurozone.

In that sense, the replacement of the orthodox Trichet with the more innovative Draghi as ECB president was a fortuitous event for the Eurozone. Draghi acted based on the assumption—which turned out to be correct— that the ECB could supply an unlimited amount of liquidity without creating inflation because the Eurozone was characterized by overcapacity and a lack of private loan demand.

In the summer of 2012 Draghi unveiled the "outright monetary transactions" (OMT) program, under which the ECB agreed to provide aggressive financial support for debtor nations meeting certain criteria. He also kept speculators in check by declaring the ECB would do "whatever it takes" to defend the euro. This announcement prompted many investment funds to stop shorting Eurozone bonds and head for Japan, as discussed in Chapter 4. The decision by financial institutions in peripheral nations to begin buying their own governments' debt (possibly at the request of local authorities) also helped stabilize the situation in the Eurozone, at least from a financial perspective.

"Grand Bargain" with ECB Is an Empty Promise

The next question is whether further increases in the liquidity supplied by the ECB would help drive a recovery in the Eurozone economy. The answer, unfortunately, is no. Many of the Eurozone countries are in the midst of balance sheet recessions, and most of the funds supplied by the ECB remain trapped in the banking system because there is no private demand for loans.

Unfortunately, many market participants and policymakers are still unable to distinguish between the lender-side problem of a financial crisis, where monetary policy is still effective and needed, and the borrower-side problem of a balance sheet recession, where monetary policy is ineffective. Many of them overestimated the impact of the LTROs and thought the ECB's actions would bring an end to the problems in the Eurozone. One senior official I spoke with in March 2012 went so far as to say that "there is no problem that €1 trillion cannot solve" and emphasized that the Eurozone had put the worst behind it. Another senior official said, "Now that the fiscal compact required for fiscal consolidation has been put in place and the ECB has acted, all that is left for the Eurozone is to carry out the structural reforms needed to support economic growth."

But none of these measures addressed the main cause of the ongoing recession—the fact that the private sector was striving to minimize debt because of balance sheet problems—and the economic slump continued. Moreover, Draghi continued to insist that the first priority for countries with debt problems was to win back the markets' trust with fiscal consolidation, and that other policies could wait until that was achieved. The ECB president's remark that "sequencing matters" reflected a concern that if the ECB reassured the governments of debtor nations by easing policy first, they might neglect to carry out the necessary deficit-cutting efforts.

But in a balance sheet recession, where the private sector is striving to minimize debt, the effectiveness of monetary policy is determined by the amount of fiscal stimulus delivered by the government, the last borrower standing. Under these conditions, it is physically impossible for central bank accommodation to offset the negative economic impact of the government's fiscal consolidation efforts, as emphasized by Bernanke in his April 25, 2012, interview on the fiscal cliff. If both the private and public sectors start to minimize debt, there will be no borrowers left, and no matter how much the central bank eases policy the money supply will not grow—and may even shrink—because the money multiplier has turned negative at the margin. With no growth in the money supply, there is no reason why the economy should improve. A "grand bargain" with ECB where the Bank would support debtor nations with monetary accommodation as long as they carry out deficit-reduction efforts is therefore something of an empty promise.

Double-Dip Recessions and the Eurozone's Bad Loan Problem

A banking system has two functions in an economy. One is to make sure that all the payments requested by depositors are made correctly and on time. The other is to make sure that all deposited savings are borrowed or invested. The first is required by the law governing banks, and the second is fulfilled by the need of individual banks to maximize profits.

The funding problems in the interbank market that prompted the ECB to implement the LTROs had to do with the first function. The banks' NPL problem, on the other hand, is an undesirable and unintended by-product of the second function. It becomes particularly acute following the bursting of a nationwide asset price bubble, and it is not something a central bank can remedy as a lender of last resort.

In a country like Spain, where the economy has entered a deflationary spiral and the unemployment rate has risen to 25 percent, banks are bound to face bad loan problems. With the exception of Ireland, where house prices stopped falling in 2013, housing prices in most Eurozone countries continue to fall, as shown in Figure 1.2, which implies that both banks' nonperforming loans (NPLs) problems and the private sector's balance sheet problems will continue to worsen. Moreover, many of the periphery nations have fallen into double-dip recessions, which during a balance sheet recession can lead many to desperation and prompt them to finally throw in the towel.

In Japan, the double-dip recession that began in 1997 abruptly raised the unemployment rate and exacerbated problems in the banking sector as people who had believed a turnaround in the economy was just around the corner finally gave up. Japan's unemployment rate stayed below 4 percent for seven years after the bubble burst, until 1997, in part because companies were doing everything they could to keep from laying off workers. But after the double-dip recession hit they started to reduce staff levels. Prior to 1997 Japan's banking problems were also quite localized (e.g., a loan scandal at two small credit unions and the failure of the *jusen* housing loan companies), but the double-dip recession in 1997 triggered the failure of Sanyo Securities, Hokkaido Takushoku Bank, and Yamaichi Securities, causing the financial crisis to quickly develop into a nationwide credit crunch.

Mr. Draghi's LTROs certainly provided an answer to the funding problems faced by Eurozone banks, but the region still has a major bad loan problem. In addition, the credit crunch remains severe as banks with substantial NPLs are unable to make new loans.

EBA's Lack of Understanding of Systemic Crises Leads to Rash Actions

The Eurozone is in the midst of a systemic banking crisis in which large numbers of banks face the same problem at the same time. In spite of this, the Eurozone's banking supervisor, the European Banking Authority (EBA), rashly demanded in 2011 that all Eurozone banks quickly bolster their capital adequacy ratios.

If only a handful of financial institutions are distressed and the majority of banks and operating companies are healthy, the latter can help recapitalize the former. But when a large number of banks are facing the same problem at the same time, they cannot raise fresh capital quickly because no one has surplus funds sitting around and the cost of funding at such times becomes exceedingly high. And expensive capital that could weaken the bank is no capital at all. In other words, when many banks face the same problem simultaneously, the government must either take the lead and recapitalize the banks or relax its capital adequacy rules so that banks can continue lending.

The United States faced this kind of problem when its housing bubble collapsed in 2007. The authorities there took the lead in recapitalizing commercial banks with the Troubled Asset Relief Program (TARP). And in the autumn of 2009, they instructed banks to "pretend and extend" even those commercial real estate loans that no longer met bank lending criteria to prevent loans from being called in. Essentially the authorities recapitalized the banks and relaxed the rules so that banks could continue lending.

The authorities adopted this pragmatic approach because the entire banking system could have collapsed if they had insisted on following market principles and banking regulations to the letter. They realized that during a systemic crisis, when large numbers of banks confront the same problem, an approach that runs contrary to market principles is required. It should be noted that both the TARP capital injection and "pretend and extend" are almost exact copies of the (much criticized) Japanese approach when the country faced a systemic banking crisis starting in 1997.

Unfortunately, the EBA demonstrated no such wisdom or understanding, as it made no distinction between an ordinary (i.e., localized) banking crisis and a systemic crisis. When the EBA insisted that all banks quickly increase their capital ratios, the only way banks could meet the new requirement was to cut back on lending, which further exacerbated the European credit crunch.

The impact was felt not just in Europe but also in the emerging economies, including Asia. Many European banks aggressively sold off overseas assets because regulators at home looked askance at European institutions that were reluctant to lend in their home markets. One of the reasons why the emerging economies lost momentum starting in 2012 was that the European banks providing funding for long-term projects in these countries (along with Japanese lenders) suddenly found themselves paralyzed by the EBA's demands.

Cypriot Bank Resolution Could Worsen Financial System Jitters

At a time when conditions in the Eurozone were rapidly deteriorating because of the EBA's rash actions, things got even worse when Dutch finance minister Jeroen Dijsselbloem, a market fundamentalist who declared no more taxpayers' money would be used to rescue financial institutions, became chairman of the Eurogroup of Eurozone finance ministers.

The Eurozone was in the process of creating the European Stability Mechanism (ESM) with €700 billion for the recapitalization of distressed banks. The ESM was to begin operation in 2014, but before that could happen Mr. Dijsselbloem took policy in an entirely different direction, declaring that troubled banks would be resolved according to market principles. When the Netherlands nationalized the failed lender SNSR on February 1, 2013, equity and subordinated debt holders were forced to bear the entire loss.

Soon after, in March 2013, the banking sector problems in Cyprus surfaced. The Eurogroup responded with a market-based "bail-in" that imposed a haircut on all large depositors while protecting small depositors holding less than the €100,000 covered under Eurozone deposit insurance. As a result, large depositors across the Eurozone started to question the safety of their own banks, making it even more difficult for bankers to lend.

Market fundamentalists in Japan had also argued strongly in favor of this bail-in approach over a decade ago, but some of us objected that using this approach for a single institution when all of the large banks had the same NPL problem and the same rock-bottom credit ratings would jeopardize the entire financial system by causing large depositors at all banks to worry. Shizuka Kamei, then serving as Liberal Democratic Party (LDP) policy chief, listened to our warnings and averted a major crisis with his decision to delay adoption of the deposit insurance cap.

No banks in Japan were resolved under this approach during the crisis even though one of its leading proponents, Heizo Takenaka, subsequently became financial services minister. Japan's banks were therefore able to stage a gradual recovery. Ironically, the only time a bail-in was used was when the Incubator Bank of Japan, founded by Mr. Takenaka's close friend Takeshi Kimura, failed in 2011 as a result of irresponsible management. As the bank did not have any demand deposits, it was decided that resolving it under the bail-in approach would not affect the broader financial system. The institution had relatively few assets, and when it was wound down the majority of Japanese banks had already returned to health. Under such conditions it makes sense to resolve a badly managed bank using this approach.

After Cyprus, it appears that Eurozone policymakers fell into one of two camps: those who insisted Cyprus was an exception and would not serve as a precedent, and those who said the use of bail-ins would become the standard approach going forward. However, large depositors are likely to remain uneasy unless the authorities declare in no uncertain terms that the ESM, and not Dijsselbloem's method, will provide the blueprint for dealing with future financial crises.

It is ironic that the United States, which is home to so many market fundamentalists, moved quickly to rescue the entire banking sector with pragmatic measures that included "pretend and extend" and a government recapitalization of distressed institutions, while Europe, with its large population of social democrats, chose to adopt a market-fundamentalist approach at the worst possible time.

Both balance sheet recessions, which occur when a large part of the private sector rushes to pay down debt in spite of zero interest rates, and systemic banking crises, which result when large numbers of banks face the same problem at the same time, are at heart fallacy-of-composition problems, and responding to them in the wrong way can cause conditions to deteriorate rapidly. Authorities confronting such a situation must follow the example of former Fed chairman Paul Volcker, who responded to the Latin American debt crisis in 1982 by allowing all banks to nurse themselves back to health over an extended period of time—an approach that ran counter to market-fundamentalist approaches.

Unfortunately, as the Dijsselbloem case shows, the Eurozone suffers from a demonstrated lack of knowledge concerning balance sheet recessions and systemic banking crises. Policymakers are treating a patient with pneumonia as if she had an ordinary cold, which has had and will continue to have severe implications for her prognosis. Ultimately, the greatest tragedy of the ongoing financial crisis in the Eurozone is that there has been no one like Paul Volcker with the knowledge and influence needed to deal with the situation properly.

The tax haven status of Cyprus means the scenario that unfolded there may not be repeated elsewhere. However, the extreme swings in the EU's handling of banking problems will clearly not assist in the region's economic recovery.

Vicious Cycle of Creating New Bubbles to Paper over Old Ones

The conclusion to be drawn from the above is that the Eurozone has to revise the Maastricht Treaty so that member nations in balance sheet recessions can carry out adequate fiscal stimulus not only for their own sake, but also to minimize the cost and related problems for the ECB and other Eurozone nations. The Treaty in its current form is entirely inadequate for today because it makes no allowance for balance sheet recessions. That places a heavier burden on ECB monetary policy whenever a balance sheet recession occurs somewhere in the Eurozone, even though monetary policy itself is largely ineffective in this type of recession.

Because the ECB's monetary policy applies uniformly throughout the Eurozone, the use of monetary accommodation to rescue Germany after the IT bubble burst created bubbles in southern Europe, and when the ECB then tried to rescue those countries after 2008 with ultralow interest rates, nothing happened because they were in balance sheet recessions. But if monetary policy is kept accommodative for too long, countries like Germany that are not in balance sheet recessions may begin to experience financial excesses and imbalances. This state of affairs is a tragedy for both the ECB and the Eurozone as a whole.

A measure should also be introduced to contain the procyclical and destabilizing capital flows that are unique to the Eurozone and that have taken interest rates to exceptionally low levels in southern Europe before 2007 and in Germany today, creating an environment conducive to the formation of financial imbalances including asset price bubbles. The Eurozone economy will eventually be derailed if the current seesaw-like policy is continued.

EU Election Results the Result of Economic Policy Errors

The two structural defects could even threaten democratic structures in the Eurozone. Support for existing political structures could dry up overnight if people wake up to the fact that they have no control over their own futures.

The DPV sponsored the forum in Frankfurt mentioned earlier in this chapter because German psychoanalysts are worried that the extended recession could have a detrimental effect on people's mental health and undermine their relationship with society. The DPV itself was created after the war to help both the victims and perpetrators of Nazi policies. The only nonpsychoanalyst speakers invited to the forum were myself and the investor and philanthropist George Soros.

Building on the arguments in my speech, Soros warned that the deficit-reducing measures Germany is demanding of periphery countries risks repeating the error of the Allied governments whose harsh economic dictates in the wake of World War I forced Germany into the hands of the Nazis. Those words carried special weight coming from a man who was born in Hungary and was persecuted by the Nazis as a child. As someone who had previously warned that the continuation of Europe's current mis-taken policies could threaten democratic structures in some of the member countries,[7] I found myself in total agreement with the famous investor.

By May 2014, people had become so desperate that anti-EU parties emerged victorious in the European Parliament elections in the United Kingdom, France, and Greece, shocking the political establishment. In Italy, Prime Minister Matteo Renzi's Democratic Party, running on a platform of structural reform, won 40.8 percent of the vote, but the anti-EU 5.Star Movement still managed to win 21.2 percent of the vote to come in second.

The voter turnout of 43 percent was one of the lowest on record, sug-gesting the European Parliament itself is somewhat removed from people's daily lives. Nevertheless, the election results underscore just how many peo-ple are unhappy and distrustful of the direction Europe is headed in.

The gains made by the euroskeptics prompted the media and markets alike to warn about a loss of momentum in the fiscal consolidation and struc-tural reforms considered essential to the region's competitive revival. The problems are said to be particularly pronounced in France. The powers-that-be have labeled the triumphant euroskeptics "populist" (an adjective used by the *Financial Times*) and are desperately trying to paint their policies as being irresponsible.

All of the anti-EU parties that came out on top in the recent elections are indeed populist and irresponsible inasmuch as they are opposed to immigra-tion and blame immigrants for many of their countries' domestic problems. After all, there is no reason why stricter controls on immigration at this point would meaningfully improve the lives of people facing economic difficulties.

On the other hand, the establishment's argument that it believes it has implemented responsible policies deserves to be critically reexamined. Most countries in Europe slipped into severe balance sheet recessions following the collapse of the massive housing bubble, yet not a single government has recognized that and implemented the correct policy response. To make matters worse, establishment policies have centered on fiscal consolidation, which is the one policy a government must *not* implement during a balance sheet recession. That decision has had painful consequences for the people of Europe.

European Policymakers Mistake Balance Sheet Problems for Structural Problems

Moreover, the establishment has made the situation worse by mistaking bal-ance sheet problems for structural problems, repeating Japan's error 15 years

---

[7] Koo, *The Holy Grail of Macroeconomics* (2008), p. 250.

earlier. While every country suffers from a variety of structural problems, the recessions currently unfolding in Europe are due mostly—perhaps about 80 percent?—to balance sheet problems, with structural issues responsible for only the remaining 20 percent or so.

The situation also varies from one country to the next. In Spain and Ireland, which experienced particularly large bubbles, balance sheet problems are responsible for a greater percentage of the ongoing recession, while in Italy, which did not see a major bubble, the problems are probably more structural in nature.

Regardless of national differences, that the Eurozone as a whole is in a balance sheet recession should be clear from the fact that net private-sector savings amounted to 5.25 percent of GDP in 2013 (Figure 5.23) at a time of zero interest rates. At such times the economy will not improve unless the government does the opposite of what the private sector is doing—for example, borrowing and spending the unborrowed savings amounting to 5.25 percent of GDP that the private sector is no longer borrowing and

FIGURE 5.23 Eurozone in Balance Sheet Recession: Private Sector Increases Savings Significantly after Bubble

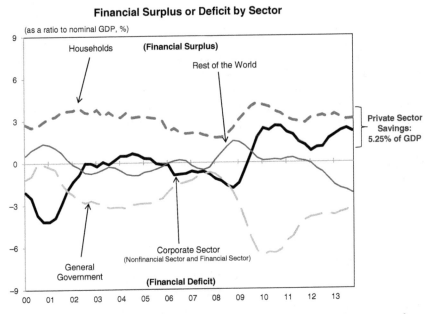

Note: All entries are four-quarter moving averages. The latest figures are four-quarter averages ending in 2013 Q4.

Sources: ECB and Eurostat.

spending. But in Europe neither the EU nor ECB President Mario Draghi seem aware of the extent of private-sector savings. As a result, they continue to argue in favor of fiscal consolidation and structural reform.

There is no reason why Europe's economy should improve when the authorities are implementing such misguided policies. It should therefore come as no surprise that many people forced to live under such policies for the past six years would cast their votes for the euroskeptics, the only parties to come out against austerity.

Policymakers Need to Ask Why Euroskeptics Made Such Gains

The euroskeptics were successful in the May 2014 elections not because they were populist. They were successful *in spite of* their populist leanings because the established parties were unable to break out of their policy orthodoxy. It was their bad policy choices that dragged the economy down and left residents no choice but to vote for the euroskeptics.

If it was the populist aspect of these parties that had attracted voters in the recent election, their historical election performance would have been much better than it actually was. Their much-improved showing in the recent elections can be attributed instead to the fact that, after waiting for six fruitless years, voters realized the situation was not going to improve as long as the established parties remained in power.

Every country has its share of extreme nationalists who blame immigrants and foreigners for society's problems. But the euroskeptics' ability to garner a quarter of all votes and actually emerge victorious in a number of countries despite the region's democratic traditions and high levels of education suggests that ordinary people who traditionally voted for the established parties switched allegiance. That is worrying.

Disappointment with Established Parties Led to Rise of Nazis and World War II

It is worrying because the same phenomenon occurred in Germany in 1933. Chancellor Heinrich Brüning, unaware that Germany was in a severe balance sheet recession, pushed ahead with orthodox austerity policies, just as the EU and the ECB have insisted this time.

His decisions pushed the unemployment rate up to 28 percent, and as the German people experienced extreme poverty and lost faith in the established political parties they began voting for the final alternative—the Nazi party.

It was in the 1933 elections that the Nazis came to power, winning 43.9 percent of the vote. It was not as if nearly half of the German people woke up one morning and suddenly began hating immigrants and Jews. What happened was that they finally lost faith in established parties that remained bound by policy orthodoxy.

For better or for worse, Adolf Hitler quickly implemented the kind of fiscal stimulus needed to overcome a balance sheet recession—public works projects undertaken in the early years of the Nazis that included construction of the autobahn expressway system. By 1938, just five years later, the nation's unemployment rate had fallen to 2 percent.

This was viewed as a great success by people both inside and outside Germany—in contrast, the democracies of the United States, France, and the United Kingdom continued to suffer from high unemployment as policymakers proved unable to move beyond orthodox fiscal consolidation. Germany's economic success made Hitler overconfident and helped lead to the tragedy of World War II. Nothing is worse than a dictator with a bad agenda having a correct economic policy. And the problem was made far worse in the thirties by the inability of democracies to switch to the right policy until the actual opening of hostilities.

Once the war began, the democracies were able to carry out the same sorts of policies that Hitler had implemented six years earlier. The combined productive capacity of the Allies soon overwhelmed that of the Third Reich, but not before millions perished in the hostilities.

Continued Disregard for People's Voice Puts Democracy in Jeopardy

It is said that history repeats itself, and it is ironic that the austerity policies demanded of Brüning's government by the Allies 80 years ago were the same policies that the EU and the German government are now insisting Spain and Ireland implement, as pointed out by George Soros.

The recent election results should prompt the EU and ECB to reconsider their stances. The real problem lies with those people and groups whose only reaction to the election results is concern that they will delay fiscal consolidation and structural reforms. If the EU and ECB disregard the election outcome and continue to demand fiscal retrenchment and structural reforms, some member countries may find their economic crisis accompanied by a crisis in democracy.

U.S. Voters Had Policy Choices, Unlike Their European Counterparts

ECB President Mario Draghi responded to the election results at his press conference on June 5, 2014, by praising the "diversity of views" expressed by voters. However, the choices available to European voters over the past six years have been far more limited than those available to U.S. voters.

In the United States, the Republican Party has called for fiscal consolidation and small government, while the Democrats—along with former Fed Chairman Ben Bernanke—have continually talked about the dangers of the fiscal cliff. U.S. voters have therefore been presented with a clear choice.

There have been a number of tough political battles along the way, including the federal debt ceiling, the government shutdown, and the automatic across-the-board cuts in spending known as sequestration. Nevertheless, the United States managed to keep from falling off the fiscal cliff.

That made it possible for businesses and households to continue repairing their balance sheets, and their financial positions have steadily improved. The May 2014 jobs report, for example, showed that U.S. employment is finally back to pre-Lehman levels.

In Europe, meanwhile, not a single leader has discussed the dangers of the fiscal cliff even though their balance sheet recessions were at least as severe as the U.S. downturn. This underscores the constraints placed on Eurozone leaders by the defective Maastricht Treaty, which makes no allowance for balance sheet recessions.

If businesses and households are saving a combined 9 percent of GDP and the government is only permitted to borrow 3 percent, the remaining 6 percent will drop out of the economy's income stream as unborrowed savings and open up a deflationary gap. For those people whose lives are devastated by the deflationary gap, the first step is to free their countries from this 3 percent constraint imposed by the Treaty—hence the surge in support for anti-EU parties.

Social security programs today are far more extensive than in the 1930s, making modern democracies more resistant to such recessions. Nevertheless, people's mistrust and unhappiness could eventually explode if complacent governments and bureaucrats continue to implement these misguided policies.

It is hoped that the EU, the ECB, and the German government will open their eyes to the reality of balance sheet recessions and take the necessary fiscal measures to address them before it is too late. If they do so, Europeans will resume voting in a direction more conducive to the proper functioning of democracy.

The Euro Can Be Saved with Two Repairs

The euro represents one of humanity's greatest achievements. The structures underpinning the Eurozone were erected over decades by a large group of capable individuals who considered numerous possibilities. It was because of their ceaseless efforts that the actual transition to the euro went so smoothly.

But just as the launch of a new aircraft inevitably reveals numerous problems, the introduction of the euro brought to light two flaws. The first was that the Maastricht Treaty had made no allowance for balance sheet recessions, and the second was the extremely procyclical and destabilizing capital flows brought about by having a plurality of government bond markets within the same currency zone. The lack of understanding of these two problems among the authorities and market participants was what made the euro crisis so severe.

However, the euro would function beautifully as a unified currency—and would be able to look forward to a long future—if only these two defects were remedied.

Encouraging countries in balance sheet recessions to administer fiscal stimulus is essential to saving both those economies and the broader Eurozone from fallacy-of-composition problems. That will also prevent distortions in monetary policy by freeing the ECB from having to take on an excessively broad role in rescuing balance sheet recession countries, a role it is ill-equipped to perform.

The relatively minor regulatory change of attaching different risk weights to holdings of domestic versus foreign government bonds would go a long way toward reducing procyclical and destabilizing capital flows among government bond markets. This modification would not threaten the improvements in private sector productivity or efficiency gains brought about by the adoption of the single currency. And if it succeeds in preserving the tremendous achievement that is the euro, it will have been a very small price to pay.

Countries such as Germany are worried that their costs will increase if the periphery nations fail to undertake deficit-reduction efforts, but those fears are based on ignorance and misunderstandings. All of these countries—with the possible exception of Greece—have massive pools of unborrowed private sector savings that are sufficient to finance their fiscal deficits as long as those savings can be channeled to their own government bond markets. If that can be achieved with differentiated risk weights, government bond yields will come down and the euro crisis will be brought to an end without costing German taxpayers anything.

If Europeans can find someone to lead the EBA and Eurogroup who understands the difference between systemic and ordinary banking crises as summarized at the bottom of Figure 1.20, the revitalization of the Eurozone economy will be just a matter of time.[8]

---

[8] The four types of banking crises indicated at the bottom of Figure 1.20 are fully explained in Koo, *The Holy Grail of Macroeconomics* (2008), pp. 230–233.

Time will probably be needed to achieve the consensus needed for these changes because today's policymakers were never taught about balance sheet recessions at university. But the necessary efforts will have been more than worth it if these two simple changes can put the finishing touches on the tremendous achievement that is the euro.

CHAPTER 6

China's Economic Challenges

China's economy remains strong relative to those of Japan, the United States, or Europe, even if growth has slowed to around 7 percent a year—these nations, after all, have experienced balance sheet recessions and the painful aftermath. The decoupling argument that was so popular in the wake of the Lehman collapse turns out to have been correct in the end.

Readers may wonder why China, with its robust economy and high real estate prices, is being featured in a book about balance sheet recessions. China was actually at risk of falling into its own balance sheet recession in 2008, but it was the first to deal with the situation and did so in a way that was uniquely Chinese.

I used to disagree with the proponents of decoupling, believing that it was exports that had supported China's economy and that a slump in key Western markets would weigh heavily on China as well. Indeed, when the global financial crisis (GFC)-triggered slump in the United States and Europe hit the export industries of China's coastal regions, it was feared that as many as 60 million laborers might be forced to return to their rural homes. Additionally, the authorities were so concerned about the severe shortage of employment opportunities for university graduates that they increased the number of graduate school places in a bid to keep student unrest to a minimum. China also experienced a collapse of its equity and real estate bubbles around 2008, and house prices fell sharply in cities like Shenzhen.

All in all, China was a textbook candidate for a balance sheet recession in the fall of 2008. But the authorities kept that from happening by quickly administering RMB 4 trillion in fiscal stimulus, the most effective medicine for such a recession. This was equivalent to 17 percent of gross domestic product (GDP), or about three times as large as the Obama administration's $787 billion economic package, which amounted to slightly more than 5 percent of GDP over the same two-year period.

The Obama administration was extremely careful about how it spent the money because it was terrified of being criticized in the media for wasting money, as Japan's government had been on so many occasions. Consequently, there was a substantial lag between passage of the spending bill and the actual increase in government expenditures, and this lag allowed the U.S. economy to weaken further, with a huge loss of jobs.

In China, in contrast, the already quick pace of public works spending picked up further, with order after order from the government providing a quick boost to the economy and offsetting the adverse effect of domestic balance sheet problems and a slowdown in exports. Jin Zhongxia, director of the People's Bank of China's Financial Research Institute, said that China carried out 30 years' worth of infrastructure investment in just 10 years (Nikkei, August 28, 2013). The slowdown in GDP was therefore only temporary, and while exports remained soft the economy as a whole headed toward a strong recovery.

The authorities' success in averting a drop in GDP not only bolstered their self-confidence but enhanced their stature in the public's mind, which contributed further to the economic expansion. In the end, China was the first nation to understand the key lesson of Japan's balance sheet recession—the importance of fiscal stimulus—and implemented it with appropriate speed and scale.

As mentioned in Chapter 2, many of China's leading economists read my first book in English, *Balance Sheet Recession* (John Wiley & Sons, 2003), and the second, *The Holy Grail of Macroeconomics* (John Wiley & Sons, 2008), was translated into Chinese and published in November 2008, long before Mr. Bernanke, Mr. Krugman, and other influential figures in the West began to pay attention to it. Moreover, the book was published by a government-affiliated press and received wide distribution.

China's Local Governments Began Borrowing en Masse

In addition to fiscal policy, China fully mobilized its monetary policy arsenal. Chinese banks still follow government directives, and a directive at the end of 2008 to start lending money sparked a rush to lend. Private demand for funds ordinarily falls precipitously during a balance sheet recession, rendering monetary policy impotent, but China had an essentially unlimited supply of borrowers in its local governments.

Senior local government officials seeking promotion had to raise the economic growth rate in their province or region and see that it was recognized by the central authorities. From the outset, therefore, they had an incentive to launch large numbers of new projects in the hope of lifting the growth rate. This incentive structure also forced the central government to place numerous restrictions on bank lending to local governments and on local government borrowing from banks to keep the economy from overheating.

However, the central government responded to the global economic crisis that followed Lehman Brothers' collapse by relaxing constraints on the activities of local governments, which began borrowing and spending aggressively.

Decoupling Would Not Have Been Possible in Ordinary Democracy

Naturally, China still places numerous restrictions on the amount of money that local governments can borrow, but like Japan's "third sector" 20 years earlier, local authorities have used project finance, whereby investment firms called financing platforms are created to borrow money and fund government projects. There was a perfect dovetailing of interests between the banks, which had been told by the central government to lend more, and local governments, which wanted to borrow money via project finance. The result was a massive expansion of money and credit.

China was able to avert a recession sparked by events in the West because it quickly launched a huge fiscal stimulus program—something that would not have been possible in most democracies until economic conditions had deteriorated much further—and pushed ahead with public works programs without the need for endless debate on whether that constituted the most effective use of the money.

Local governments stepped up to borrow money for their numerous shovel-ready projects just as the private sector was suffering from balance sheet problems and a drop in exports. It was because of their efforts that monetary policy—which is generally impotent during a balance sheet recession—remained extremely effective in China. Bank lending expanded sharply along with the money supply.

Some of the public works projects carried out under this accelerated economic stimulus led to the construction of what were later dubbed "ghost towns," but the amount of GDP saved by averting a recession (like the ¥2,000 trillion figure for Japan noted in Chapter 1) was many multiples of the amount spent on such towns.

This decoupling probably would not have happened if China had been an ordinary democracy—it was possible only because the authorities fully utilized the nation's "Chinese" (communist) characteristics. The authorities should be praised for leveraging those characteristics so effectively and so speedily. Their actions helped not only the domestic economy but also the global economy as China increased its nonoil imports by 55 percent by April 2014 over the pre-Lehman peak of July 2008.

In comparison, U.S. nonoil imports had increased just 13.4 percent in March 2014 from the pre-Lehman peak of June 2008. In the Eurozone, non-oil imports were up only 7 percent in March 2014 from the pre-Lehman peak of September 2008, and Japanese nonoil imports had just managed to return to the pre-Lehman peak of May 2007.

In absolute terms, China's monthly nonoil imports increased by nearly US$60 billion, more than double the combined increase for the United States, the Eurozone, and Japan. These numbers underscore the out-sized contribution Chinese policies made to the global economy.

China's Remaining Problems Include Overcapacity and Income Inequality

The success of 2008–2009 also carried the seeds of a number of problems, chief among them inflation and a real estate bubble. Thus the country sits at the opposite end of the spectrum from Japan, the United States, and Europe, which have undergone balance sheet recessions and disinflation.

In 2011 the Chinese authorities began hiking interest rates and raising banks' reserve ratios. At the micro level they raised the required down payment for home purchases from 30 percent to 40 percent, sharply curtailed lending to real estate firms, and used all the policy tools at their disposal to stop the practice of property flipping. Some real estate developers found themselves unable to obtain funding domestically and were forced to borrow overseas. These policies—like the Japanese MOF directive in 1990 that capped real estate lending growth at the rate of overall lending growth—were intended to prick the bubble, but unlike Japan in 1990 China also faced an inflation problem.

Twenty-five years ago Japan was clearly in the midst of a massive real estate bubble, but consumer prices were stable, and the wholesale price index actually continued to fall through early 1989. The Bank of Japan (BOJ) raised short-term interest rates to 8 percent in an attempt to stamp out the bubble at a time when consumer prices were rising by less than 4 percent a year. In 2011, meanwhile, consumer prices in China were climbing at a rate of 6.5 percent a year. In particular, food prices—which have a direct impact on household finances—were rising by 14.8 percent a year. The resulting impact on the general public was far greater than it had been in Japan, where inflation was much lower and income levels much higher.

China Understands Political Ramifications of Inflation

The leaders of the Communist Party of China (CPC) know better than anyone that high inflation often leads to a change of government in China. They themselves have benefited from this in the past.

During the civil war in the latter half of the 1940s, a key reason the CPC was able to triumph over the Kuomintang with its modern weaponry from the United States and imperial Japanese forces was that the Kuomintang government had failed to keep inflation in check and had lost its support among the middle class as well as the wealthy. This experience left a deep impression on both parties. After fleeing to Taiwan, for example, the Kuomintang drew on its bitter mainland experiences and kept the main banks under strict government ownership and control for the next 45 years, right up to the 1990s. The party's greatest concern was losing control over the financial sector and prices.

The CPC is well aware that it could experience the same fate as the Kuomintang if it allows inflation to get out of control and is therefore vigilant against the threat of rising prices. Indeed, inflation was one of the factors that led to the Tiananmen Incident in 1989. The fact that China's current government was not elected democratically and has effectively abandoned communism has also led to constant questions about its legitimacy. The elite are worried that, when the going gets tough, ordinary Chinese may wonder why they should have to follow the dictates of such a government.

A key source of the party's legitimacy is the exceptional economic growth that has occurred under its leadership and produced dramatic improvements in living standards. Over the past 30 years, under CPC leadership, China's economy has posted the strongest growth in the history of mankind.

By 2011, however, the party was confronting the twin problems of inflation and a housing bubble, both of which are major threats that could turn the people against the government. Both problems were triggered by rapid growth in the money supply, a result of the government's directive to banks at the end of 2008—when the GFC had almost forced exporters to lay off tens of millions of workers—to lend as much as possible. Since 2011 the Chinese authorities' primary objective has been to tackle inflation and contain the bubble, and to achieve that they have had to reverse the policies implemented at the end of 2008.

There is a real possibility that these efforts to prick the bubble will tip China's economy into a balance sheet recession, as real estate prices are already falling in some areas. And the more successful the authorities' efforts in this regard, the more NPLs banks and shadow banks will be left with. China's policymakers are well aware of these risks since they know better than anyone the mechanisms of Japan's balance sheet recession. They also know what must be done when a balance sheet recession hits.

They understand that fiscal stimulus is the answer. In an autocratic nation like China, with no opposition parties or independent media to object, it is possible to administer as much fiscal stimulus as needed. Moreover, the stimulus can be delivered with a speed and flexibility that would be unthinkable in a democracy. A highway that would take 10 years to build in a democracy can be constructed in six months. Consequently, China may be the only country in which fiscal stimulus acts more quickly than monetary policy.

China's Shadow Banking Sector: Misunderstandings and Realities

While clamping down on bubbles, the Chinese authorities naturally have to worry about bad loans in the banking sector. Specifically, they want to avoid an outcome like the mountain of bad loans created by Japan's so-called third sector of public-private joint ventures, and to this end have directed banks to carefully monitor the recoverability of project finance loans. Even under project finance arrangements, banks need to maintain appropriate loan-to-value ratios and are prohibited from lending the entire value of the project, with local governments required to put up a certain percentage. In reality, however, this "equity" is often borrowed from another bank, a practice the authorities have now begun to crack down on.

On the subject of bad loans, China's shadow banking sector has recently attracted a great deal of attention, with reports creating the impression of a rogue sector engaged in nearly unlimited credit creation. But such reports are based on a number of misunderstandings.

To begin with, these instruments were created when certain borrowers' desire to borrow money, even at a slightly higher interest rate, coincided with dissatisfied bank depositors receiving low (regulated) yields on their deposits. In that sense, they are similar to the money market mutual funds that sprang up in the United States in the 1970s when Regulation Q kept the bank deposit rate well below the inflation rate. In many cases the bank where the deposits are held serves as the intermediary, which is effectively no different from the Japanese practice of bank depositors shifting their money from low-yielding savings accounts to higher-yielding mutual funds sold by the same institution.

Here the depositors withdraw funds from their savings account to buy the shadow banking product, reducing the bank's deposits and forcing it to scale back lending as well. Hence this shift of deposits only entails a qualitative shift—not a quantitative increase—in lending. In fact, China's leading financial institutions are developing competing products to ensure the emergence of the shadow banking sector does not spark an outflow of deposits. Additionally, much of what is called shadow banking in China is actually carried out by banks under government supervision, and in that sense is very different from the unsupervised shadow banking sectors in the Western economies. The financial authorities are currently instructing banks to put these (off-balance-sheet) transactions on their balance sheets.

Problem: Sharp Growth in Lending to Local Governments Post-Lehman

One thing the authorities are worried about is the financial health of the financing platforms established by local governments. Local governments had borrowed some RMB 10 trillion by 2010, with RMB 5 trillion borrowed in just the two years starting in 2009, when the RMB 4 trillion stimulus package was unveiled. It is estimated that local governments will be able to repay the loans on only two-thirds of these projects, with the remaining one-third requiring assistance from the central government. Many borrowers in the latter category are local governments in relatively poor districts, and while the central government has announced its intention to offer support, a variety of problems may emerge during the implementation.

In particular, many of the projects undertaken as part of the emergency economic stimulus of 2009 were later expanded by local governments after initial approval by the central government, and a careful audit will probably be necessary to separate the piggy-backed portion from what was originally approved. A friend who recently visited China told the story of seeing a massive new sports stadium that had been erected in the middle of nowhere and was capable of seating tens of thousands of spectators and hosting international sporting events—this in a regional city with a population of about 700,000. Upon seeing this, he questioned the city's ability to pay even the annual upkeep costs for the facility.

Many of the loans made to local governments are, in fact, problematic. On the other hand, the shadow banking sector has been responsible for providing funding to private enterprises that were traditionally prevented by financial regulation from obtaining the money they needed. The authorities' directive to banks to bring these loans back on their balance sheets is thought to reflect an acknowledgment of that role.

Additionally, while many pundits both inside and outside the country are criticizing the government for building wasteful, inefficient projects like the ghost towns and the stadium mentioned above, most of these were public works projects designed to preserve the 60 million jobs that would have been lost as a result of the GFC, which originated in the West. While some of those projects may not have been as useful as they could have been, the fact remains that they fulfilled their initial objective of sustaining employment. The economy most likely would have fallen into a destructive recession if the government had decided not to administer fiscal stimulus because of a lack of high-quality projects.

If anything, Japan and other neighboring nations should thank China for erecting those stadiums. Had the Chinese government chosen instead to spend the money on building nuclear submarines or stealth fighters, which could not be criticized since they are invisible, it would have posed a major threat to the security of neighboring nations.

Decoupling of China and Developed Economies to Continue

One reason why I previously disagreed with the concept of decoupling is that annual U.S. consumption of $11 trillion is far greater than the combined consumption of $4 trillion in India and China, which implies it would be difficult for the latter to offset a slump in the former.

But if China's economy continues to grow at an annual rate of 7 percent using "CPC-like" methods and India continues expanding at a similar pace, combined consumption in the two nations will grow by 7 percent of $4 trillion, or $280 billion, a year. Meanwhile, assuming growth of 2 percent a year, annual consumption in the United States will increase by only $220 billion. From the perspective of companies around the world, China and India clearly offer greater promise as a place to invest limited business resources.

Additionally, whereas emerging economies like China and India have the potential to continue growing at high rates for an extended period of time, the developed economies already have saturated markets and are expected to remain hampered by balance sheet problems and related after-effects for at least a few more years. The more companies—whether Chinese or foreign—invest in China, the fewer business resources and money will be earmarked for the developed world, which will suffer as a result.

The disparity in growth rates between China and the developed economies is therefore expected to persist until the private sectors of the West put their balance sheet problems behind them.

Problems Facing China's Economy

Aside from the problem of bubbles and balance sheet recessions, China also faces numerous challenges relating to its communist past and its stage of economic development. These include overcapacity in many industries, income inequality, a dearth of consumption and a surfeit of investment, and rapidly increasing wages.

Iron and steel and numerous other industries are said to suffer from overcapacity, and unsold inventories are also reportedly a major problem at many state-owned enterprises. The Chinese authorities have responded by stressing the importance of cash-flow-based management and by instructing state-owned firms to exit businesses that are not generating cash.

While China's state-owned enterprises are often derided in the West as a symbol of poor governance and the source of various problems, the current view domestically is that the government should be able to run a firm with the same flexibility and governance as any owner-operated firm if it exercises its control as sole owner. They believe this approach offers the potential for better governance than at large Western firms, where large numbers of dispersed shareholders are unable to implement meaningful checks on management. There is something to be said for this view, although it assumes that the monitoring authorities are not corrupt and that the officials in charge of individual companies stay long enough at their jobs to implement meaningful changes.

China also suffers from tremendous income inequality, although senior officials argue that today's inequality is fundamentally different from inequality in the past. Historically, income inequality in China referred to the gap between people who had enough to eat and those who did not. The latter had nothing to lose, and once their discontent reached a critical level it could quickly boil over into major social and political unrest.

Today's income inequality, in contrast, refers to the gap between people who are eating very good food and those who are eating only ordinary food. It is argued by some that China's continued stability in spite of this disparity is attributable to the fact that most ordinary people are far better off today than they were just two or three decades ago. However, even those who espouse this view will start to worry if the current inequality persists into the future.

Some also argue that China's economy is highly unbalanced, with domestic consumption representing just 35 percent of GDP. This lack of domestic consumption is the flip side of an economy driven by investment. Many, including the United States government, have criticized this lack of balance, saying China's excessive savings and inadequate consumption are a major factor behind the trade imbalances between the two nations.

The biggest reason why the Chinese save so much, goes the argument, is that the nation lacks a proper social security system, forcing people to save a great deal of money for their retirement. That, they say, is why the establishment of a social security system is essential to the normalization of China's economy. However, the time needed to establish such a system and earn the public's trust in a developing country with a population of 1.3 billion has created a sense of hopelessness on this issue. Even in the United States, many people distrust the Social Security System despite its having been around since the 1930s. Some also warn that the growing number of wealthy individuals with their low propensity to consume means it will be difficult to expect any improvement in the problem of excess savings.

As for the sharp rise in wages in coastal regions, many firms have been forced to grant large pay hikes to their employees, to the extent that some are asking whether they can afford to remain in China or perhaps need to move their factories to a lower-wage country like Bangladesh.

These wage hikes have also contributed to inflation, the fourth problem noted above. The fear is that inflation will cause workers to demand higher salaries, and as more companies raise their wages inflation will accelerate in a vicious cycle. In particular, some worry that cost-push pressures from rising wages will lift global inflation by causing China to stop exporting deflation and start exporting inflation fueled by surging domestic wages.

There are a variety of other issues facing China's economy, but in most cases they are discussed separately, and the measures proposed to address them are similarly scattered.

China Has Already Passed the Lewis Turning Point

However, most of these problems are actually part of a single, inevitable progression of events that happens in any agrarian country undergoing industrialization. Understanding the essence of this progression will make it obvious what is going to happen and what needs to be done about it.

China recently reached what economists call the Lewis turning point, defined as the point in time where, as a nation's economy becomes increasingly industrialized, urban factories have finally absorbed all the surplus labor in rural areas.

From the standpoint of a capitalist (or business owner, whether domestic or foreign), the world prior to the Lewis turning point is an extremely lucrative one in which it is possible to secure a boundless supply of labor from rural districts simply by paying the going wage. In this world, capitalists need not worry about a shortage of labor and can expand their businesses essentially without limit as long as they have the necessary production facilities and can make products that consumers want. Capitalists able to supply products in demand before the Lewis turning point is reached can earn huge profits, further increasing their incentive to expand.

Figure 6.1 illustrates this from the perspective of labor supply and demand. The labor supply curve is almost horizontal (DHK) until the Lewis turning point (K) is reached because there is an essentially unlimited supply of rural laborers who want to work in the cities. Any number of such laborers can be assembled simply by paying a given wage (DE).

In this graph, capital's share is represented by the area of the triangle formed by the left axis, the labor demand curve, and the labor supply curve, while labor's share is represented by the rectangle below the labor supply curve. At the time of labor demand curve D_1, capital's share is the triangle BDG, and labor's share is the rectangle DEFG. The capital share BDG may be shared by a few persons or families, whereas the labor share DEFG is likely to be shared by millions of workers.

FIGURE 6.1 China Passes the Lewis Turning Point

Industrialization of Chinese (or any Agrarian) Economy

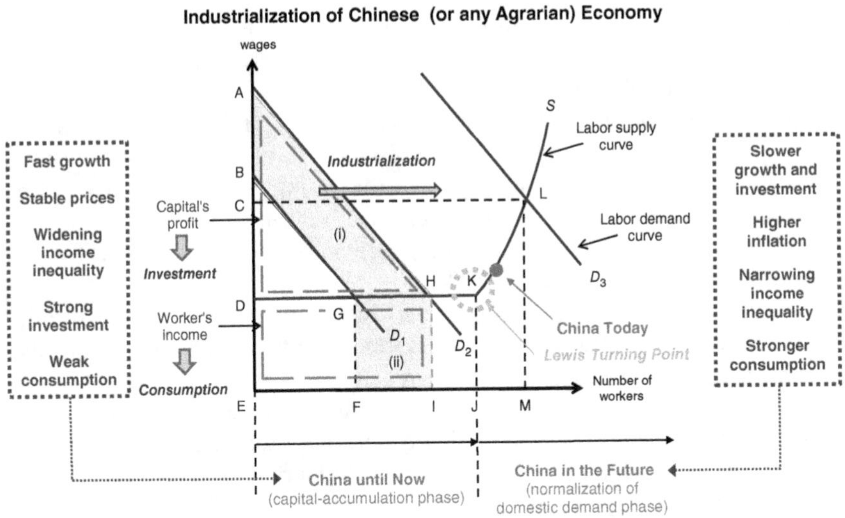

Source: Nomura Research Institute.

Successful capitalists in this setting will continue to invest in an attempt to make even more money. That raises the demand for labor, causing the labor demand curve to shift steadily to the right (from D_1 to D_2) even as the labor supply curve remains flat. As the labor demand curve shifts to the right, total wages received by labor increase from the area of the rectangle DEFG at time D_1 to the area of rectangle DEIH at time D_2 as the length of the rectangle below the labor supply curve grows. However, the growth is linear. The share of capital, meanwhile, increases at far more than a linear rate as the labor demand curve shifts to the right, growing from the area of the triangle BDG at D_1 to the area of the triangle ADH at D_2.

Until the Lewis turning point is reached, GDP growth increases the portion of GDP that accrues to the capitalists, exacerbating inequalities. A key reason why a handful of families and business groups in Europe a century ago and in Japan prior to World War II were able to accumulate such massive wealth is that they faced an essentially flat labor supply curve (wealth accumulation in North America and Oceania was not quite as extreme because these economies were characterized by a shortage of labor).

Rapid Economic Growth Continues until Lewis Turning Point

During this phase, income inequality, symbolized by the gap between rich and poor, widens sharply as capitalists' share of income (the triangle) increases much faster than labor's share (the rectangle). Because capitalists are profiting so handsomely, they will continue to reinvest profits in an attempt to make even more money. Sustained high investment rates mean domestic capital accumulation also proceeds rapidly. This is the take-off period for a nation's economic growth.

Until the economy reaches the Lewis turning point, however, low wages mean most people will still have hard lives, even though things may improve modestly because they are no longer in the countryside. Business owners, in contrast, can accumulate tremendous wealth during this period. What this means is that China's savings are being generated by domestic and foreign businesses, not ordinary households.

Many analysts have argued that the Chinese save so much because the nation lacks a proper social security system, as mentioned earlier. But this is true of any country that has yet to reach the Lewis turning point and is not something that can be resolved by establishing a social security system. Many Western pundits have completely forgotten that their own countries went through an identical phase during their period of industrialization a century or so ago.

Marx and Engels, who lived in Europe before the Lewis turning point was reached, were incensed by the horrendous inequality and miserable working and living conditions of ordinary people and responded by devising the theory of communism, which called for capital to be shared by the laborers. In that sense, the birth of communism may itself have been a historical imperative of sorts.

In Japan, this period of migration to the cities lasted until the early 1960s, when middle and high school graduates from rural areas were collectively seeking employment in the cities.

Ordinary Chinese laborers receive minimal wages and have very little money to save. Their lives are not easy. The rich Chinese tourists that are thronging luxury brands' stores across the West and Japan are capitalists. The living standards of ordinary Chinese are simply not at the point where they can afford such products.

The investment that currently represents the lion's share of GDP is being undertaken by both Chinese and foreign companies. Businesses will continue to reinvest a large portion of their profits as long as those profits persist, regardless of whether the nation has a credible social security system or not.

U.S.-Led Free Trade Regime Enabled the Emergence of Asia

In the pre-1945 world, there was a constraint that slowed this progression down. And that was the lack of demand or lack of market. If the workers constituted the bulk of consumption demand, they could not have provided enough demand for all the goods produced because their share of income was so low. In order to overcome this constraint, Western powers tried to colonize the rest of the world so that they have both the source of raw materials and a captive market to which to sell the produced goods. It was believed in those days that national economies cannot grow without territorial expansions.

That led to constant wars and killings until 1945 when the enlightened and victorious Americans introduced the free trade regime, which allowed anyone with competitive products to sell to anyone else. And the United States took the lead in opening its own market. That allowed not only Japan and Germany, which lost all their colonies, but all countries to prosper without the need to secure captive markets via colonization.

Once Japan discovered the above formula for success in the 1950s, the export oriented growth mode based on free trade spread to Taiwan, South Korea, and eventually to the rest of Asia in the process known as the flying geese pattern of industrialization. The biggest beneficiary of all, of course, was China, which was able to transform one of the poorest agrarian societies of 1.3 billion people to be the second largest economy in the world in just 30 years.

The 30 years following the Deng Xiaoping's opening of the Chinese economy probably qualify as the fastest and greatest economic growth story in history, but it was made possible precisely because the U.S.-led free-trade system allowed Chinese and foreign companies producing in China to sell anywhere in the world. If it were not for the market provided by the free-trade regime, the same growth could have taken many times longer.

Economy Starts to Mature Only after Passing the Lewis Turning Point

As domestic business owners and foreign firms continued to generate profits and increase investment, China eventually reached the Lewis turning point. I estimate this happened around 2011, although there is some disagreement on this issue.[1] Once an economy reaches this point, the labor supply curve (KLS in Figure 6.1) takes on a positive slope as the surplus of rural labor dries up. This is reflected in the steep recent rise in Chinese wages.

Once an economy reaches the Lewis turning point, the total wages of labor—which had grown only linearly until then—start to increase rapidly as the labor supply curve now has a very steep positive slope. For example,

---

[1] Ryoshin Minami, Fumio Makino, and Hao Renping, eds., *Chugoku Keizai no Tenkan-ten (Turning Point for the Chinese Economy)* (Tokyo: Toyo Keizai, 2013).

if labor demand increases just a little, from J to M in Figure 6.1, total wages accruing to labor will rise dramatically, from the area of rectangle DEJK to the area of rectangle CEML. From that point on the economy begins to mature and normalize.

Once the Lewis turning point is reached, labor finally has the bargaining power to demand higher wages, which reduces the profit share of local and foreign business owners. But they will continue to invest in China as long as that share is higher than in other countries, and their investment will lead to further tightness in the labor market.

It is at this point that the inequality problem begins to correct itself. And as labor's share increases, consumption's share of GDP will increase at the expense of investment, and eventually China's economy will normalize.

Marx and Engels' greatest mistake was to assume that the extreme inequality they witnessed (points G and H in Figure 6.1) would continue forever. In reality, it was just one inevitable step on the path toward industrialization.

Local and Global Lewis Turning Points and Inequality

This increase and decrease in inequality before and after the Lewis turning point may also explain at least a part of Thomas Piketty's recent work[2] in which he noted that inequality in the West increased until World War I but subsequently decreased until 1970s. Although Piketty attributes this to the destruction of wealth brought about by two world wars and the introduction of progressive income tax, this was also a period in which urbanization came to an end in most of these countries.

The post-1970 increase in inequality in these countries as noted by Piketty may also be due to the fact that Asian countries starting with Japan started exporting to the West as they were heading toward their own Lewis turning points. For those capitalists in the West who could utilize the resources in Asia, it was a great opportunity to make more money. For those affected manufacturing workers in the West, this was not good news at all. Some of the pain these workers felt was of course offset by the fact that, as consumers, they benefited from cheaper imported products.

This suggests that there are at least two relevant Lewis turning points for a country's development, the country's own turning point and the *global* turning point. For the capitalist in the developed world, the fact that there are developing countries that are still before their Lewis turning points presents

---

[2] Thomas Piketty, *Capital in the Twenty-First Century (Capital au XXIe siècle)* (Cambridge, MA: Belknap Press, 2014).

an opportunity to make money by lowering their production cost. For the workers in the developed world, the same globalized environment represents more competition from the low-wage developing countries.

That in turn will increase inequality in the developed world until everybody in the world is gainfully employed, that is, when all countries in the world have moved beyond their Lewis turning points. The fact that China has already passed that point should come as a big relief for those workers in the developed world, but there are still India and others that can potentially keep downward pressures on wages in the developed world.

China Increasingly Tolerant of RMB Appreciation as Transition to Consumption-Led Economy Proceeds

As China becomes increasingly attractive as a consumer market, it will lose its appeal as a production base. At the very least, it will be difficult for capitalists to expect the same kinds of returns they have enjoyed up to now. However, China has great potential for growth as a consumer market, with the purchasing power of local consumers expected to increase as labor's share rises and the RMB appreciates. Automobile sales in 2013 exceeded 20 million units, making China the largest single market in the world and roughly equal to the markets of the United States and Japan combined.

From the perspective of forex policy, the government's primary focus before reaching the Lewis turning point should be to ensure that all working-age citizens are able to find meaningful work. During that phase of economic development it is essential to foster labor-intensive export industries, which means a strong local currency is not desirable. The government should also avoid protectionist capital-intensive import replacement policies before the economy reaches the Lewis turning point. This is in order to prevent the labor market from becoming segmented, which could create major impediments to subsequent economic development.

If government protects specific industries and their workers before a country reaches the Lewis turning point, the labor market will be split into two groups: a protected group, which enjoys a comparatively good standard of living, and a group that is unable to benefit from industrialization and is left behind in poverty because protected import replacement industries are not growing fast enough to absorb excess workers in rural areas. This leads to severe, long-term disparities of the kind observed in parts of Latin America.

Once the problem of surplus labor is resolved and wages start to experience upward pressure, inflation becomes a problem, and a strong local currency may now be preferred. The implication here is that the Chinese authorities are more likely to tolerate currency appreciation if the pool of surplus rural labor has actually dried up.

Business owners, meanwhile, are likely to object to a stronger currency at a time when rising wages are already undermining their international competitiveness. But these are the same people who took advantage of the surplus of rural labor to earn large profits by paying workers as little as possible. Now life gets a little tougher for them. As China reaches full employment and wages normalize, labor-intensive industries that depend on low wages for their profitability will have to raise labor productivity or leave China.

Almost all of these changes are the inevitable result of the industrialization of an agrarian society. As the surplus labor supply in the countryside dries up, the balance of investment, consumption, and wages will gradually normalize. Some of this process can be accelerated with policy changes, but it should not be forgotten that these changes can take decades, even in the West.

The West Is Conflating Problems of Trade Imbalance and Financial Crisis

Since 2010, Western countries have been trying to shift debate at the G20 and other international forums away from local and global economic recoveries to the correction of external imbalances. But from the perspective of China and other emerging economies that have been driving global economic growth, this is little more than an attempt to pass the buck.

Emerging markets have achieved steady growth by pursuing solid economic management and avoiding U.S.-style financial capitalism. From their perspective, the global economy fell into turmoil because the West created a bubble, attached dubious ratings to highly questionable financial instruments, and then sold these securities around the world. Why should they have to help clean up the resulting mess?

It is difficult to make a convincing case that China's forex policy was responsible for the recent financial crisis—after all, current imbalances would have existed even without the bubble and subprime loan problems, and the financial crisis triggered by the bursting of the bubble and subprime loan problems would probably have occurred even without these imbalances. But that has not stopped the United States from repeatedly urging Chinese currency reforms at the G20, with increasingly negative implications for its global leadership.

In effect, Western countries are trying to resolve two separate and independent problems as if they were one—the traditional problem of global trade imbalances on one hand and the recent financial and economic crisis, which was triggered by subprime lending and the collapse of asset price bubbles, on the other. The end result is that they have been chasing two hares and catching neither.

These two issues need to be addressed separately and in the correct order. Western governments must first fix their own economies, which are suffering from balance sheet recessions, and clean up their financial sectors, which were responsible for selling so many dubious financial instruments. Once they make a certain amount of progress on those fronts, then and only then should they address the preexisting condition of imbalances. By doing so, they will be able to discuss those imbalances without creating the impression they are trying to blame emerging markets for economic problems in the developed world.

At present, unfortunately, Western countries do not appear to be able or willing to change their approach. The resulting rift with the emerging economies has transformed the G20 into what some have dubbed the G0, an international body with no decision-making powers. If the West fixes its problems, which is still far from a certain outcome, China should be more willing to talk about its currency and global imbalances now that the country has passed the Lewis turning point and most of its citizens are gainfully employed.

Liberalized Financial Sector and Capital Flows Could Weaken RMB

As for the liberalization of capital flows, a key element of the RMB reforms, Chinese who have suddenly become rich over the last decade or so are starting to move some of their money overseas for diversification and as a hedge against an eventual correction in the economy or asset prices. Naturally, China's rapidly growing economy still offers far more attractive investment returns than the sluggish economies of the West, so there are built-in limits to any outflows. But in the short term they could weigh on the RMB.

In the first half of the 1980s, when the United States was running a huge trade deficit with Japan, it demanded a liberalization of the Japanese financial sector in order to push the yen higher. Japanese capital flows were in fact liberalized significantly under the so-called Yen-Dollar Committee. The end result, however, was that capital outflows from Japan exceeded inflows and the yen, much to the chagrin of U.S. authorities, fell from around ¥200 to the dollar at the beginning of the talks to nearly ¥280 at one point. The weakness in Japan's currency continued for more than three years and exacerbated trade imbalances, eventually forcing the United States to directly curb the dollar's strength through coordinated intervention by proposing the Plaza Accord in September 1985.

The U.S. government expects the RMB will appreciate if China opens up its financial sector, but it may be making the same mistake it made with Japan 30 years earlier. If Chinese citizens decide to take some of their assets overseas, financial liberalization could easily lower the value of the RMB, just as the yen fell against the dollar three decades ago. The Chinese government would almost certainly welcome such weakness and attribute it to U.S. demands for liberalization.

With overseas capital flowing into the country in search of investment opportunities and export earnings being reinvested domestically, the RMB has yet to come under pressure. However, direct inward investment is likely to slow now that wages are rising and clouds have appeared on the economic horizon, and some of the export earnings that were being reinvested locally may be sent overseas instead. While such changes affect only a portion of the whole, they nonetheless have the potential to change exchange rate trends at the margin.

Further increases in the value of the RMB are quite possible in the long run given China's large trade surpluses. But temporary weakness is also a possibility.

China Could Fall into the "Middle-Income Trap" If It Neglects to Advance Its Industrial Base

Although many of China's current problems will solve themselves now that the economy has passed the Lewis turning point, the business of managing the economy also becomes significantly more difficult. Unless industry becomes more advanced as wages rise, the nation will fall into what economists call the middle income trap. The labor-intensive industries that developed on the back of inexpensive Chinese labor will eventually migrate to countries like Vietnam and Myanmar, and if no new industries spring up to take their place, economic growth will come to a halt.

Prior to the Lewis turning point, the pool of low-wage labor will prompt foreign manufacturers and domestic business owners alike to continue investing in the country, leading to higher growth rates, as long as the government makes necessary investments in education, roads, ports, and other physical infrastructure. And the Chinese government did an excellent job of providing those ingredients. But the situation becomes more complicated once the Lewis turning point is reached.

Japan, Korea, and Taiwan Escaped from Middle-Income Trap

Surprisingly few countries have managed to escape from the middle-income trap. Aside from the developed economies of Europe, Oceania, and North

America, the short list of examples includes Japan in the 1960s and Taiwan and Korea from the 1980s onward. Each of these Asian countries made huge efforts to succeed. In Japan, the authorities decided not to recognize the Kilby patents, a series of essential patents for integrated circuits, to foster the development of the semiconductor industry, and both public and private sectors invested heavily in the sector.

Japan still has a number of well-known camera manufacturers, but in the 1970s these firms grew increasingly nervous about competition from China and other low-wage Asian nations—at the time, they even refused to allow Chinese visitors into their factories. Canon responded to the challenge by boldly incorporating electronics in its products and creating a highly innovative production system, then the first of its kind, that did not require minor but costly adjustments by employees after cameras had rolled off the assembly line. Thus it was able to overcome the negative impact of rising wages on competitiveness.

Taiwan, meanwhile, reinvented itself as a high-tech island. In Hsinchu City, about an hour and a half from Taipei by car, a large block of land was set aside as a science park in the mid-1980s to form the setting for a residential environment and R&D platform not unlike those found in Silicon Valley. Many researchers who left the country during the Kuomintang dictatorship of the previous three decades were invited back with their families to live and work in what was almost an extraterritorial district that ordinary local residents were not allowed to enter. The schools within the science park teach in English with a curriculum comparable to those in the United States. The result was spectacular growth in Taiwan's high-tech industry.

Korea has until quite recently employed extensive protection of the domestic market to facilitate the development of its automobile sector and other key industries. Japan was also extremely protective of its domestic automobile market until around 1970—the phrase *jidousha-sakoku* or "automobile autarky" was even coined to describe it—while Korea was engaged in the same practice until just a few years ago.

Inasmuch as China has worked together with foreign companies to achieve its astonishing economic growth and industrial development, the Japanese and Korean growth strategy of eschewing foreign capital is not a realistic option. Chinese companies, of course, have become much more competitive, and it is easy to envision some local firms growing briskly in the years to come—after all, the nation has the technology needed to build everything from space rockets to nuclear submarines. The question is whether that will be enough to fulfill the aspirations of its 1.3 billion people. If not, popular discontent could spread. Recently even Chinese companies have started moving some of their operations to Southeast Asia, where labor costs are lower.

The issue, therefore, is how to keep foreign and Chinese companies in China and encourage them to continue investing in the country. Rising domestic wages will certainly make China more attractive as a consumer market, and the ability to produce near the center of consumption would provide at least one reason for businesses to stay. On the other hand, problems confronted on a daily basis include not only rapidly climbing wages but also widespread corruption and an underdeveloped legal system. These problems have become so intractable that when a group of Japanese consultants held a seminar in China on "how to get out of China" in early 2014, hundreds of executives showed up. Because of the huge turnout and the sensitivity of the issue, the organizers requested that no business cards be exchanged at the event.[3]

Moreover, the anti-Japan demonstrations in 2012 and the authorities' subsequent response (or lack thereof) has forced Japanese and non-Japanese foreign firms alike to reconsider the political and diplomatic risks involved in doing business there. China's territorial disputes with Japan, the Philippines, Vietnam, and India are also seen by foreign companies as a major source of country risk, given that many firms' supply chains now stretch across the region. The risk of maintaining operations in China would be perceived as very high if the exports and imports of intermediate products between these countries and China could be blocked by the Chinese government for political or diplomatic reasons.

China has achieved tremendous economic development over the past 30 years, but that was partly because the nation had yet to reach the Lewis turning point. Now that it has, the easy part is over and a new kind of growth strategy is needed. China also maintained good relations with its neighbors at least until a few years ago, which made it the favorite destination for companies around the world. Now that positive image is being eroded by the government's numerous diplomatic and territorial disputes.

In academic and policy debates on economic development in China, some have argued that while former President Hu Jintao oversaw strong economic growth and led the country through the GFC with only modest fallout, he made little progress on structural reform, with correspondingly negative implications for the nation's economic future. Some see this as a very pressing issue, even referring to the 10 years of the Hu administration as a "lost decade" from the standpoint of structural reform.

A solid consensus has yet to form, with opinions split on what kinds of reforms are most urgently needed. Nevertheless, there is a strong sense of urgency and a belief that things must not continue along the present path.

---

[3] "Sayonara Dalian, Aitsugu tettai semina" ("Wave of Seminars on How to Get Out of Dailin"), *Nikkei Veritas*, April 20, 2014.

Labor Disputes Increase Sharply after the Lewis Turning Point Is Reached

To make matters worse, countries that have reached the Lewis turning point also tend to experience a sharp increase in labor disputes as workers achieve bargaining power for the first time. The question is how this will play out in a country like China with an autocratic government.

In Japan and Korea, for example, the number of strikes and other labor disputes rose sharply around the time that population inflows to urban centers like Tokyo and Seoul began to slow (Figures 6.2 and 6.3). The high frequency of strikes and demonstrations in Japan in early 1970s was captured in the well-known phrase, "No to price hikes, no to demonstrations, no to everything!" On the political front, a deep and contentious rift opened up between the business-friendly LDP and the labor-friendly Japan Socialist Party (since renamed the Social Democratic Party). It was also around this time that a student movement demanding greater social justice flourished and was the focus of much attention. Korea also experienced numerous

FIGURE 6.2 Labor Demands Skyrocket after Passing Lewis Turning Point: Japan

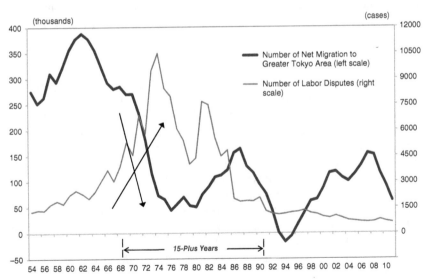

Note: Greater Tokyo Area consists of Tokyo Metroplois, Kanagawa prefecture, Saitama prefecture, and Chiba prefecture.

Sources: Ministry of Internal Affairs and Communications, "Report on Internal Migration in Japan"; and Ministry of Health, Labour and Welfare, "Survey on Labour Disputes."

FIGURE 6.3 Labor Demands Skyrocket after Passing Lewis Turning Point: South Korea

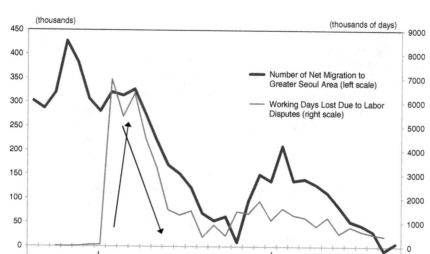

Note: Greater Seoul Area consists of Seoul city, Incheon city, and Gyeonggi-do.

Sources: Statistics Korea, "Internal Migration Statistics," and "Korea Statistical Year Book."

violent labor disputes in the second half of the 1980s as the migration to urban areas neared an end and the nation embraced democracy.

At that time it was feared that these disputes would have serious implications for production and economic growth in Japan and Korea. But in retrospect they were the natural result of long-ignored workers' voices suddenly bursting forth as the economy reached the Lewis turning point and labor achieved bargaining power for the first time.

In other words, the demonstrations, strikes, and fierce parliamentary debates were a way for exploited workers to blow off steam. That period of upheaval paved the way for the establishment of a post-Lewis-turning-point social and political order, a process that took about 15 years in Japan. In effect, the turmoil represented a necessary adjustment in the search for a new social order.

While political turmoil will intensify at the beginning of this adjustment period, economic development will actually facilitate the search for a new order. This is because the problem of inequality, which intensified as the economy moved toward the Lewis turning point, will reverse itself as labor's share of output starts increasing rapidly. In other words, there is an endgame to this process, and the seemingly endless confrontations and disruptions will actually bring people together as they learn what can reasonably be expected from the other side.

The Dilemma of Patriotism with an External Enemy

China, meanwhile, has an autocratic government that is highly intolerant of demonstrations and strikes, which are seen as undermining social stability. Autocratic governments facing widespread discontent tend to create external enemies to divert the public's attention away from domestic problems. Whether the sudden increase in the incidence of border disputes since 2012 has anything to do with China passing through the Lewis turning point remains to be seen. But the temptation must be there, particularly now that the Chinese Communist Party's raison d'etre—communism—is being abandoned, and the government is forced to rely more on economic development and patriotism to justify its legitimacy. And if the economy must slow because of the factors mentioned above, fanning patriotism becomes even more important for the autocratic government. If that is behind China's disputes with Japan, Vietnam, the Philippines, and India over the past two years, both China and the rest of the world may have a serious problem on their hands.

With 30 years of robust economic growth leaving the country confident and militarily strong, a growing number of hawks also want to see a Greater China. Some are even saying China should retake everything it lost starting with the Opium War of 1840. In their view even Vladivostok, which was ceded to Russia in 1860, should revert back to Chinese control.

The willingness among some Chinese leaders to flex the nation's military muscles is said to be so strong that one worried Chinese official described the atmosphere as being similar to that in Japan just before the attempted coup d'état by a group of young army officers on February 26, 1936. Known as the 2.26 Incident, the coup itself was quickly suppressed by the emperor, but the event eventually led to the loss of civilian control over the military.

Such trends in China could threaten the foreign companies that have made such a large contribution to the nation's economic growth. If these firms decide against further investment in China, the country's efforts to develop a more advanced industrial base, a difficult task under the best of circumstances, could be delayed even further. A slide into the middle-income trap and increased frustration among the people could add fuel to the diplomatic and territorial disputes in a vicious cycle.

Working-Age Population Peaked Just as the Lewis Turning Point Was Reached

Complicating matters for China is the fact that it reached the Lewis turning point just as its working-age population topped out as a percentage of the total population. This sort of demographic combination is quite unusual. In Japan, the working-age population did not begin to shrink until more than 20 years after the Lewis turning point was passed. In China—partly because of the one-child policy—these two events occurred almost simultaneously (Figure 6.4).

Moreover, China's working-age population as a percentage of the total population rose sharply for more than 30 years starting in the late 1970s, providing a major boost to the nation's economy in the form of what economists call a population bonus. In the context of Figure 6.1, this means the labor supply curve had been shifting steadily to the right over the last 30 years, and to that extent so did the Lewis turning point. This allowed China's period of high economic growth and capital accumulation to continue much longer than it would have otherwise.

FIGURE 6.4 China May Grow Old before It Grows Rich: Ratio of Working Age Population Has Started to Fall in China

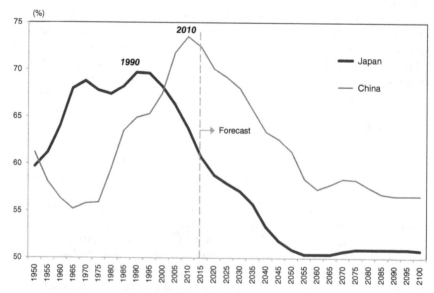

Source: Population Division of the Department of Economic and Social Affairs of the United Nations Secretariat, World Population Prospects.

Will China Grow Old before It Grows Rich?

But if the working-age population shrinks the labor supply curve will have to shift to the left. All other factors being constant, that implies fewer workers and upward pressure on wages, with correspondingly negative implications for economic growth. That demographics will cease to be a positive for China and start to work in the other direction is an issue of great concern to local analysts and economists and has sparked fears that the nation will grow old before it grows rich.

For now, the nation's working-age population as a percentage of the total population has only just begun to shrink—and both are still increasing in absolute terms. The working-age population is expected to peak around 2015 (Figure 6.5), while the total population should top out around 2030 (Figure 6.6). However, when we define the working-age population as the National Bureau of Statistics of China did in 2013—as the 15–59 cohort instead of the standard 15–64—the working-age population actually began to contract in 2012.

FIGURE 6.5 China May Grow Old before It Grows Rich: Working Age Population Is about to Shrink in China

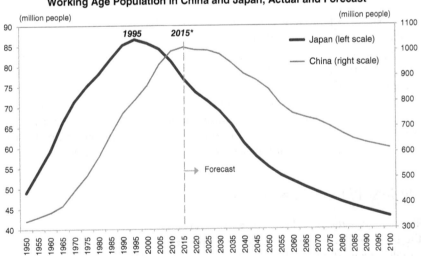

Working Age Population in China and Japan, Actual and Forecast

*The Chinese National Statistical Office indicated that the working-age population actually declined starting in 2012 when the definition of working-age population was revised to ages 15–59 from ages 15–64.

Source: Population Division of the Department of Economic and Social Affairs of the United Nations Secretariat, World Population Prospects.

FIGURE 6.6 China May Only Have 15–20 Years to Escape from Middle-Income Trap

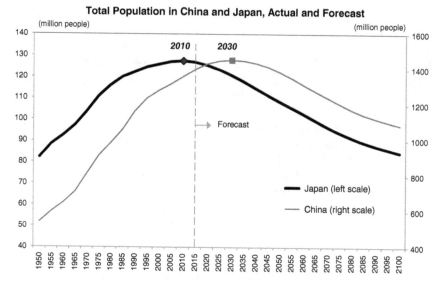

Total Population in China and Japan, Actual and Forecast

Source: Population Division of the Department of Economic and Social Affairs of the United Nations Secretariat, World Population Prospects.

Japan's working-age population peaked in 1995, and its total population peaked in 2010. The fact that these peaks coincided with a slowdown in the Japanese economy is of great interest to Chinese policymakers, even though Japan was also confronting a severe balance sheet recession during this period as discussed in Chapter 4.

The fact that China's population bonus peaked at almost the same time as the country reached the Lewis turning point suggests the economy does not have much time to find a way out of the middle-income trap. It may face severe difficulties if it fails to escape the trap by around 2030.

The Next 15 to 20 Years Are Critical

That suggests the next 15 to 20 years are critical. If successful, China will join the ranks of the developed economies and enjoy a rich "retirement." If not, it will remain stuck in the middle-income trap with a huge and frustrated population.

Some time ago, a popular topic of discussion among pundits was when China would overtake the United States to become the world's largest economy. But it is meaningless to apply the growth rate of a country that has yet to reach the Lewis turning point and also enjoys a massive population bonus to one that has already reached the Lewis turning point and now labors under a negative population bonus.

The Xi government's focus on quality instead of quantity and its reduced emphasis on high growth rates is very appropriate given the realities it faces. Still, it remains to be seen whether China can address its challenges and find a way out of the middle-income trap in the time it has left, particularly since public demands are likely to mount now that the nation has passed the Lewis turning point.

Uncertainty Due to Corruption and Lack of Legal Infrastructure Must Be Removed ...

How can China persuade foreign and Chinese companies to stay and increase their investment? One thing the authorities can do is to minimize the uncertainty stemming from corruption and the lack of a credible legal infrastructure by aiming to become a nation under the rule of law. The elimination of such uncertainty would remove a major headache for companies and might persuade some of them to stay the course in China even if labor is now cheaper elsewhere.

This is the argument Malaysia used when Japanese firms and other foreign companies that had invested in Southeast Asia after the 1985 Plaza Accord began moving factories to China in the 1990s in response to the lure of cheaper labor. The argument was that Malaysia's legal system was similar to that of the United Kingdom, and while wages were higher than in China, the country was a much safer bet in all other respects.

There is something to be said for this argument. Additionally, the Japanese companies that incurred major losses in the anti-Japan demonstrations in 2012 and the foreign companies that saw how the Chinese government treated those firms after the demonstrations are now much more sensitive to this kind of country risk. Investment by Japanese firms in China was already down 30 percent on a year-over-year basis in 2013 H1. China must now try to do what Malaysia did 15 years ago. Without significant progress in this direction, rising wages could prompt a large number of businesses, both foreign and Chinese, to move their operations elsewhere.

President Xi's ongoing campaign to stamp out corruption is running straight into the vested interests that have sprung up over the last 30 years. I have had the opportunity to discuss this topic with people in government think tanks and the local media. It came as something of a shock to find that they were all extremely pessimistic on the outlook for cleaning up the corruption that has become endemic in Chinese society. They believe it will be next to impossible to eliminate the corruption that has penetrated all facets of society. But there is a much greater risk that China will become stuck in the middle-income trap unless society and the economy are built on the rule of law, as otherwise many able individuals and companies will not be given a fair chance.

Appealing to Patriotism without Creating External Enemies

Although the challenges are enormous, there is a way for the Chinese authorities to overcome these vested interests and proceed with reforms by appealing to patriotism without relying on external enemies. This can be achieved by the Xi government declaring that the next 15 to 20 years represent China's *first*—and *last*—opportunity in 200 years to become a first-class nation. President Xi should emphasize that, with so little time available, the government's first policy priority will be to achieve the long-denied dream of the Chinese people to win the world's respect. In effect, the government needs to offer a vision of China that nobody in the country can say "no" to.

In retrospect, China and the Chinese people have faced a long series of tribulations over the last two centuries. The nation was trampled first by Western imperial powers and later by Japan. Not only were historical artifacts destroyed, but millions of Chinese lost their lives, and those who did not were often treated as second-class citizens, or worse. No Chinese person will forget the sign in a park in the British Concession in Shanghai that read, "No dogs and Chinese allowed," in which the dogs came ahead of the Chinese.

Even after the current political system was established following the Chinese Civil War, tens of millions perished in the Great Leap Forward and the Cultural Revolution, which also set the economy back many decades. Conditions during the 1960s were so bad the nation was among the world's poorest.

Deng Xiaoping's reforms and open-door policies were an attempt to regain what had been lost and ultimately led to 30 years of the fastest economic growth in human history. If this momentum can be sustained with appropriate changes to economic and social policies, Chinese society will look very different 15 years from now.

Economic growth of 6 percent for the next 15 years would lift incomes by 140 percent. When the anticipated rise in the value of the RMB is also taken into account, that would not only keep China from falling into the middle-income trap but would also put it within shooting distance of joining the developed world. For example, if the economy grew 6 percent per year and the RMB appreciated 3 percent per year during this period, per capita GDP in China would be more than US$30,000 15 years from now.

Here the key word is "respect." A nation that, like prewar Japan, develops a world-class military and grows increasingly hegemonic while tolerating low living standards for its own people would hardly be deserving of the world's respect. Similarly, pre-war Germany had strong economy and military but still failed to win the world's respect because of the Nazi government's extreme disregard for the welfare of its minorities and neighbors.

On the other hand, if China could follow Deng Xiaoping's directive to "hide capabilities and bide time (*tao guang yong hui*)" for another 15 years and work peacefully with other nations while building a civil and prosperous society at home, the Chinese people *will* win the world's respect. Post-war Germany and Japan grew to become the world's second and third largest economies while winning global respect after they jettisoned their pre-war territorial ambitions. The post-war success of these two countries proved that territorial expansion, once considered crucial to the survival and growth of a nation, is no longer necessary nor sufficient condition for prosperity under the free-trade system. On the contrary, territorial expansion can actually reduce economic growth and damage prosperity if it prompts alarmed countries to close their markets to Chinese products.

China also faces the problems of the Lewis turning point and a shrinking population bonus. While it has the chance to enter the ranks of the world's leading nations for the first time in two centuries, it has only a 15 to 20 years window of opportunity, and the government needs to address these problems with a sense of real urgency.

If the Xi government can project such a vision and a sense of urgency, few vested interests could object to the goal of achieving what has been denied to the Chinese people for the last 200 years. That, in turn, should make it possible for the government to carry out the necessary reforms.

China Could Become a World-Class Nation for the First Time in Two Centuries

Given China's short window of opportunity, policies that might scare away the foreign companies that have contributed so much to the nation's economic growth and industrial advancement are entirely out of the question. Anything that could deny Chinese access to markets around the world is also out of question.

Viewed in this light, the recent diplomatic spats with Japan, the Philippines, India, and Vietnam are trivial affairs that must not be allowed to consume precious time and energy over the next 15 to 20 years and squander this rare opportunity. That would be an unforgivable betrayal of the Chinese nation.

Wiping out corruption will not be easy even with such a vision, but the example of the Kuomintang in Taiwan inspires hope. Past Kuomintang governments were so corrupt that they were ultimately abandoned by both the Chinese people and the United States. But the attitude of civil servants and bureaucrats toward the general public changed dramatically after Taiwan's democratization movement began in 1988. This change was particularly evident after Lee Teng-hui, a native of Taiwan, was elected president. A key reason for the change was that the Taiwanese were able to take pride in building a new nation by sharing a common vision of a democratic society.

Today, Taiwan's success in building a civil society, establishing a democratic political system and the rule of law, and developing an efficient health care system is respected around the world. And that was all achieved within the last 20 years. Taiwan's example suggests that a major shift in awareness is not out of the question if today's Chinese can adopt a common goal of becoming a first-class nation respected around the world. If the Taiwanese can do it, there is no reason why the Chinese cannot.

It should also be noted that some countries, while lacking democratic political structures, have legislation similar to the U.S. Freedom of Information Act that allows citizens to monitor the government policymaking process, and this has played a meaningful role in reducing corruption. Such examples should serve as reference for the Chinese authorities.

Just as nobody 30 years ago foresaw the China of today, it is very difficult to project what the nation will look like 15 years from now. It should also be noted that most of the developed nations established their current social systems, including protections for human and civil rights, only after they passed the Lewis turning point. China stands at the very beginning of that journey, and if the Chinese strive to build an economy and a society based on the vision of a first-class nation that is respected by other countries, the society could be very different 15 years from now.

On the other hand, if the Xi government is unable to present a vision for achieving what has been denied to the Chinese people for the last two centuries, it may have to rely on external enemies to keep itself in power, which would benefit neither China nor its neighbors. Indeed, the worst possible scenario for China is that it ends up following in the footsteps of pre-war Japan, with its civil government losing control of an overambitious military, or of pre-war Germany, with its drive to take back everything it lost as a result of World War I. If China moves in that direction it could also lose access to the markets in the developed world, which was absolutely crucial for its spectacular economic growth during the last 30 years.

Chinese Ambition and Industry Must Be Steered in Right Direction

President Xi's ongoing campaign to stamp out corruption touched the powerful State-Owned Asset Supervisory and Administration Commission

(SASAC), the regulator of China's state-owned enterprises, and even the military, reportedly causing a great deal of trepidation among people at all levels of government and beyond. But a successful anticorruption drive and the creation of solid legal and judicial infrastructure are essential to efforts aimed at increasing investment by both local and foreign businesses.

China has hundreds of millions of ambitious, enterprising, studious, and hard-working people. Although the nation's demographics are not encouraging, the numbers alone do not capture the motivation that simmers beneath the simple head count. And the Chinese drive for success and willingness to work and study hard are still as strong as ever. Hence there is still plenty of room for China's economy to grow if the authorities can establish structures to channel this energy in the right direction. China became the world's largest purchaser of industrial robots in 2013, according to the International Federation of Robotics.[4] This can be seen as a sign of the nation's determination to raise productivity and avoid the middle-income trap.

President Xi Jinping often talks about "the resurgence of the Chinese nation" in his speeches. If by that he means focusing on the reforms needed to bring the country into the ranks of the world's leading nations in the limited time it has, China should be able to avoid the middle-income trap.

---

[4] "Industry Thrives on Rise of the Machines," *Financial Times* (Asian Edition), June 2, 2014, p. 19.

Afterword

I began writing this book in the summer of 2013 after realizing that I would turn 60 in just a few months. My colleagues at Nomura Securities and its clients both inside and outside Japan had been asking me when my next book was coming out, and while there was a great deal I wanted to say, the enormity of the task made me reluctant to get started.

But faced with the impending milestone, I decided I could no longer keep putting it off. The global economy—and particularly the Eurozone—were moving in exactly the direction I had feared, and I felt a warning had to be issued. There were also aspects that needed to be understood regarding Abenomics and the quantitative easing policies of Japan, the United States, and the United Kingdom.

Having made that decision, however, I soon realized that my regular job of informing investors in Japan and elsewhere would leave little time for writing. Daily interaction with these investors, many of whom manage billions of dollars, always kept me focused and honest. But given the time constraints, I chose to write in Japanese instead of English, as originally planned, relying heavily on the assistance offered by Mr. Takeyoshi Matsushita, a senior advisor at publishing house Tokuma Shoten, and Mr. Koichi Chikaraishi, a member of the publisher's editorial committee, to help compile and edit the book. Mr. Chikaraishi and Mr. Yuichi Hashikami made themselves available literally 24 hours a day during the book's preparation.

Initially I had hoped to make this the definitive, unabridged work on balance sheet recession theory and include a theoretical framework, including the economy's yin and yang phases as presented in *The Holy Grail of Macroeconomics* (John Wiley & Sons, 2008). But as I was commenting on various events in the global economy, the book quickly grew to over 300 pages, and I simply ran out of room.

This is a reflection on just how much has happened in the global economy over the past few years. The euro crisis, which was a treasure trove of information on the application of balance sheet recession theory to real economies, was a particularly rich source of thought-provoking events. Even the six-month period between the publication of the Japanese version in

December 2013 and the completion of the English manuscript in June 2014 required many additions and updates.

Interest in balance sheet recessions has finally started to pick up in Europe in the past two years, and I am frequently invited to speak there. I accept these invitations whenever possible in the hope that this new theory, which arose out of Japan's experience, could help hasten the recoveries in Western economies facing the same problems that have occurred in Japan. Unfortunately that has left very little time to write.

As a result, this book was written on planes, at hotels, and during holidays and late evenings at home. I must express my deepest thanks to my wife, Chyen-Mei, for her understanding and support. And I will never be able to express fully my gratitude to my two assistants—Ms. Yuko Terado, who takes better care of my health and schedule than I do, and Mr. Masaya Sasaki, who helped compile the data used in this book, and particularly the hard-to-find flow-of-funds data for various countries. And I must thank Mr. Chris Green, who did an absolutely wonderful job in translating the original Japanese into English. It was his repeat performance after *Holy Grail*, and I feel so fortunate that I was able to work with someone with such a strong commitment to producing a readable text on economics. Any remaining mistakes are of course mine and mine alone.

I would also like to express my gratitude to Nomura Securities, Nomura Research Institute, and all their employees for keeping me around for so long. I have made many policy proposals in my 31 years with the organization. Many of them—including a postponement of the cap on deposit insurance, capital injections with minimal conditions to troubled banks, sustained fiscal stimulus, and market-opening measures designed to prevent an appreciation of the yen—were less than popular among policymakers and the media. Yet never once was I asked to refrain from making such proposals.

I have since discovered that policymakers did put pressure on my employer, but the Nomura directors kept it to themselves. And they offered their full support throughout my three decades here, including the time I was developing balance sheet recession theory, which represents a new departure for economics. For that reason as well, I would like to take this occasion to thank everyone at Nomura Securities and Nomura Research Institute.

Richard C. Koo
June 2014

Bibliography

Banca d' Italia. "Financial Accounts."

Banco de España. "Financial Accounts of the Spanish Economy."

Banco de Portugal. "Financial Accounts."

Bank for International Settlements. "84th Annual Report," 2014. www.bis. org/publ/arpdf/ar2014e.htm.

———. "Residential Property Price Statistics."

Bank of England. "M4 and M4 Lending Excluding Intermediate OFCs."

———. "Notes and Coin and Reserves Balances."

Bank of Greece. "Financial Accounts."

———. "Monetary Aggregates."

Bank of Japan. "Sousai Teirei Kisha-Kaiken Youshi, 2014 Nen 4 Gatsu 8 ka" (Summary of the Governor's Press Conference), April 8, 2014. www. boj.or.jp/announcements/press/kaiken_2014/kk1404a.pdf.

Bank of Japan. "Deposits, Vault Cash, and Loans and Bills Discounted."

———. "Flow of Funds."

———. "Loans and Bills Discounted by Sector."

———. "Monetary Base."

———. "Monetary Survey."

———. "Money Stock."

———. "Reserves."

———. "Tankan."

Bernanke, Ben S. "What the Fed Did and Why: Supporting the Recovery and Sustaining Price Stability." *Washington Post*, November 4, 2010. www.washingtonpost.com/wp-dyn/content/article/2010/11/03/AR2010110307372.html.

———. "Monetary Policy since the Onset of the Crisis." Speech at the Federal Reserve Bank of Kansas City Economic Symposium, Jackson Hole, Wyoming, August 31, 2012. www.federalreserve.gov/newsevents/speech/bernanke20120831a.htm.

———. "Communication and Monetary Policy." Speech at the National Economists Club Annual Dinner, Herbert Stein Memorial Lecture, Washington, D.C., November 19, 2013. www.federalreserve.gov/newsevents/speech/bernanke20131119a.htm.

Board of Governors of the Federal Reserve System. *Banking and Monetary Statistics, 1914–1970*, 2 vols. Washington, D.C., 1976.

———. "Transcript of Chairman Bernanke's Press Conference, April 25, 2012," 7–8. www.federalreserve.gov/mediacenter/files/FOMCpresconf 20120425.pdf.

———. "Transcript of Chairman Bernanke's Press Conference, September 18, 2013," 23. www.federalreserve.gov/mediacenter/files/FOMCpresconf 20130918.pdf.

———. "Aggregate Reserves of Depository Institutions and the Monetary Base."

———. "Assets and Liabilities of Commercial Banks in the United States."

———. "Financial Accounts of the United States."

———. "Industrial Production and Capacity Utilization."

———. "Money Stock Measures."

Cabinet Office, Japan. "Annual Report on National Accounts."

———. "Quarterly Estimates of GDP."

Central Bank of Ireland. "Quarterly Financial Accounts."

Central Statistics Office, Ireland. "Quarterly National Accounts."

Deutsche Bundesbank. "Financial Account."

———. "Monetary Aggregates."

———. "Trade in Goods with Nonresidents."

Dudley, William C. "The Economic Outlook and Implications for Monetary Policy." Remarks before the New York Association for Business Economics, New York City, 2014. www.newyorkfed.org/newsevents/speeches/2014/dud140520.html.

The Economist. "The Global Housing Boom: In Come the Waves," June 16, 2005. www.economist.com/node/4079027.

Eggertsson, Gauti B., and Paul Krugman. "Debt, Deleveraging, and the Liquidity Trap: A Fisher-Minsky-Koo Approach." *The Quarterly Journal of Economics* 127, no. 3 (2012): 1469–1513.

European Central Bank. Mario Draghi's Interview with *Le Monde.* July 21, 2012. www.ecb.europa.eu/press/inter/date/2012/html/sp120721.en.html.

———. "Euro Area Accounts."

———. "Long-Term Interest Rate Statistics for EU Member States."

———. "Minimum Reserves and Liquidity."

———. "Monetary Developments in the Euro Area."

———. "Unit Labour Costs."

Eurostat. "Provision of Deficit and Debt Data for 2013—First Notification," April 23, 2014. epp.eurostat.ec.europa.eu/cache/ITY_PUBLIC/2-23042014-AP/EN/2-23042014-AP-EN.PDF.

———. "Government Revenue, Expenditure, and Main Aggregates."

———. "Harmonised Indices of Consumer Prices."

————. "Production in Industry."

————. "Quarterly National Accounts."

————. "The Structure of Government Debt."

————. "Unemployment Rate by Sex and Age Groups."

Financial Times. "Bundesbank Shows Signs of Yielding," May 9, 2012. www.ft.com/intl/cms/s/0/5a40a056-99fb-11e1-accb-00144feabdc0.html#axzz36xR8eEDr.

International Monetary Fund. "Global Financial Stability Report: Old Risks, New Challenges," April 2013.

————. "Unconventional Monetary Policies—Recent Experience and Prospects" 27, 2013. www.imf.org/external/np/pp/eng/2013/041813a.pdf.

————. "Unconventional Monetary Policies—Recent Experience and Prospects—Background Paper," 2013. www.imf.org/external/np/pp/eng/2013/041813.pdf.

Italian National Institute of Statistics. "Quarterly National Accounts."

Japan Real Estate Institute. "Urban Land Price Index."

Koo, Richard. *Balance Sheet Recession: Japan's Struggle with Uncharted Economics and Its Global Implications*. Singapore: John Wiley & Sons, 2003.

————. *"In" to "Yo" no Keizai-Gaku* (The Economics of Yin and Yang: Bubbles and Balance Sheet Recessions). Tokyo: Toyo Keizai, 2007.

————. *The Holy Grail of Macro Economics: Lessons from Japan's Great Recession*. Singapore: John Wiley & Sons, 2008.

Koo, Richard, and Shigeru Fujita. "Zaisei-saiken no Jiki wa Shijo ni Kike: Zaisei-saiken ka Keiki-kaifuku ka" (Listen to the Bond Market for the Timing of Fiscal Reform). *Shukan Toyo Keizai*, February 8, 1997, 52–59.

Krugman, Paul. "It's Baaack: Japan's Slump and the Return of the Liquidity Trap." *Brookings Papers on Economic Activities* 2 (1998): 137–205.

Minami, Ryoshin, Fumio Makino, and Hao Renping, eds. *Chugoku Keizai no Tenkan-ten* (Turning Point for the Chinese Economy). Tokyo: Toyo Keizai, 2013.

Ministry of Finance, Japan. "Budget."

Ministry of Health, Labour and Welfare, Japan. "Survey on Labour Disputes."

Ministry of Internal Affairs and Communications, Japan. "Consumer Price Index."

————. "Report on Internal Migration in Japan."

Motani, Kosuke. *The True Face of Deflation*, Kadokawa Shinsho, 2010.

National Statistics Institute, Spain. "Quarterly Spanish National Accounts."

Nikkei Sangyo Shimbun. "Nikkei Golf Kaiin-Ken Shisu" (Golf Course Membership Price Index).

Nikkei Veritas. "Sayonara Dalian, aitsugu tettai semina" (Wave of seminars on how to get out of Dailin). April 20, 2014.

Nihon Keizai Shimbun. "Kensho Kiki wa Sattaka: Ri-man shokku 5 nen (14) Oshu ni Seiji no Fusakui, Ginko Kyusai, Kokka Shizumeru" (Did the Financial Crisis Really Blow Over? It Is Five Years Since Lehman Shock (14): Politicians' Omissions and Bail-Out of Banks Brought about European Debt Crisis). December 1, 2013, 11.

Obata, Seki. "Subete no Keizai wa Baburu ni Tsujiru. Kobunsha" (All Roads in Economy Load to a Bubble). Tokyo, 2008.

Office for National Statistics, U.K. "Consumer Price Inflation."

———. "Index of Production."

———. "United Kingdom Economic Accounts."

Real Estate Economic Institute, Japan. "Kinki-Ken no Manshon Hanbai Doko" (Report on the Sales of the Condominiums in Kansai Area), Japanese only.

———. "Shuto-Ken no Manshon Hanbai Doko" (Report on the Sales of the Condominiums in Tokyo Metropolitan Area), Japanese only.

RealtyTrac. "All-Cash Share of U.S. Residential Sales Reaches New High in First Quarter Even as Institutional Investor Share of Sales Drops to Lowest Level Since Q1 2012," May 5, 2014. www.realtytrac.com/content/foreclosure-market-report/q1-2014-us-institutional-investor-and-cash-sales-report-8052.

Reuters. "Highlights–Fed Chief Yellen's Testimony to Congressional Committee," May 7, 2014. www.reuters.com/article/2014/05/07/usa-fed-highlights-idUSL2N0NS1L020140507.

———. "Could Take 5–8 Years to Shrink Fed Portfolio: Yellen," May 8, 2014. www.reuters.com/article/2014/05/08/us-usa-fed-yellen-idUSBREA470QE20140508.

Rogoff, Kenneth, and Carmen Reinhart. *This Time Is Different: Eight Centuries of Financial Folly.* New Jersey: Princeton University Press, 2011.

Romer, Christina D. "What Ended the Great Depression." NBER Working Paper 3829 (1991).

S&P Dow Jones Indices. "S&P/Case-Shiller Home Price Indices."

Statistics Korea. "Internal Migration Statistics."

———. "Korea Statistical Yearbook." Seoul.

Statistics Portugal. "Portuguese National Accounts ESA1995."

Tokyo Stock Exchange. "TOPIX."

U.S. Department of Commerce. "Gross Domestic Product (GDP)."

———. "Personal Income and Outlays."

U.S. Department of Labor. "Employment Situation."

United Nations Secretariat, Population Division of the Department Economic and Social Affairs. "World Population Prospects: The 2012 Revision."

Williams, John C. "A Defense of Moderation in Monetary Policy." *Journal of Macroeconomics* 38 (2013): 137–150.

Index